# ROARING TIGERS
## THE HISTORY OF SOUTHERN COLUMBIA FOOTBALL

## MERRILL SHAFFER

SUNBURY PRESS

Mechanicsburg, PA USA

Published by Sunbury Press, Inc.
Mechanicsburg, PA USA

www.sunburypress.com

For information about special discounts for bulk purchases, please contact Sunbury Press Orders Dept. at (855) 338-8359 or orders@sunburypress.com.

To request one of our authors for speaking engagements or book signings, please contact Sunbury Press Publicity Dept. at publicity@sunburypress.com.

FIRST SUNBURY PRESS EDITION: September 2021

Set in Adobe Garamond | Interior design by Crystal Devine | Cover by Lawrence Knorr | Cover photo by Dave Fegley | Edited by Lawrence Knorr.

Publisher's Cataloging-in-Publication Data
Names: Shaffer, Merrill, author.
Title: Roaring tigers : the history of Southern Columbia football / Merrill Shaffer.
Description: First trade paperback edition. | Mechanicsburg, PA : Sunbury Press, 2021.
Summary : From their humble beginnings in 1962, the Southern Columbia Tigers have become the most dominant and successful high school football program in Pennsylvania history. The Tigers have overcome the growing pains of a new team, endured a 26-game losing streak that almost saw the end of the program, and developed into a national high school football power.
Identifiers: ISBN : 978-1-62006-884-7 (softcover).
Subjects: SPORTS & RECREATION / Football | SPORTS & RECREATION / History | HISTORY / United States / State & Local / Middle Atlantic (DC, DE, MD, NJ, NY, PA).

Product of the United States of America
0 1 1 2 3 5 8 13 21 34 55

*Continue the Enlightenment!*

Karen and Lilly: I love you more than anything.

Thank you, Linda Waller, for the inspiration to undertake this project. Your support means the world to me.

Special thanks to Jim Doyle, Dave Fegley, Kurt Ritzman, Jim Roth, Curt Stellfox, and Andy Ulicny. This book would not be possible without your assistance and guidance.

We remember Eric Barnes, Tarik Leghlid, Brian Racker, Terry Sharrow, Keegan Shultz, Tim Snyder, Don Traugh, and every Tiger we have lost. You are forever in our hearts.

This book is dedicated to every player, coach, staff member, parent, family member, volunteer, and fan of the Southern Columbia Tigers, past, present, and future.

# CONTENTS

# CHAPTER 1

# A LITTLE SCHOOL IN CATAWISSA

High school football has been played in Pennsylvania since the late-1800s. For more than a century, the tradition, pageantry, and fanfare of high school football have become engrained into the fabric of communities throughout the Commonwealth. The rich history of scholastic football in Pennsylvania has produced countless championship teams, legendary players and coaches, memorable games, and magical moments that will be relived, retold, and handed down through the generations. Football has become such a part of the culture of schools and towns across Pennsylvania, and it is hard to imagine a Friday night in the fall without the sights, sounds, and colors of a high school game. Legends such as Johnny Unitas, Joe Montana, Joe Namath, Dan Marino, Jim Kelly, Jack Ham, Andre Reed, Jason Taylor, Curtis Martin, Fred Biletnikoff, Herb Adderley, Randy White, Lenny Moore, Marvin Harrison, Tony Dorsett, Mike Ditka, Mike Munchak, Bill Cowher, George Blanda, Bert Bell, Chris Doleman, Lamar Hunt, Stan Jones, Leroy Kelly, Charley Trippi, Joe Schmidt, Russ Grimm, Emlen Tunnell, Art Rooney, Dan Rooney, Chuck Bednarik, Bill George, Jimbo Covert and Ty Law all started their Hall of Fame careers on the scholastic gridirons of the Keystone State.

Pennsylvania has undoubtedly produced many legendary high school players and coaches, powerhouse teams, and historical games and rivalries. However, tucked away in the rich farm land of central Pennsylvania, in the small town of Catawissa, is a story that needs to be told. Just up the road, on Route 487, from the famous Knoebels Amusement Resort, sits a small school that surprisingly few people have heard of or recognize. However, to the people of Catawissa, Elysburg, Ralpho Township, Roaring Creek Township, and the surrounding communities, they know very well the story of perhaps the most dominant team in the history of Pennsylvania high school football. On Friday nights in the fall, throngs of fans pack Tiger Stadium to watch a team that has won eleven Pennsylvania Interscholastic Athletic Association State Football Championships, more than any other program in Pennsylvania high school history. A team named the best small-school football team in the country three times, has played in 19 PIAA state football championship games, has claimed 19 PIAA Eastern Championships, has earned two Eastern Conference Championships, and has won 28 District IV football championships. A program that has won a state-record 88 consecutive regular-season games, set the state record for the most points scored in a single season, produced an NFL running back and Super Bowl champion. A receiver who set state records for most career receiving yards and touchdowns. A running back who holds the state record for the most rushing and total touchdowns scored in a high school career. A placekicker who set the state record for the most successful point-after attempts in a single season and who outscored every team they played that year just by kicking extra points. A legendary coach who set the Pennsylvania state record for the most career victories. This is the story of the Southern Columbia Tigers.

The Southern Columbia Area School District was formed as the result of a merger of the schools from Catawissa, Ralpho Township, and Roaring Creek Valley. The schools merged before the 1962-1963 academic year. The District encompasses 108 square miles and comprises Catawissa Borough, Catawissa Township, Cleveland Township, Franklin Township, Roaring Creek Township and Locust Township in Columbia County, and Ralpho Township in Northumberland County. Southern Columbia is composed of an elementary school (grades K-4), a middle school (grades 5-8), and a high school (grades 9-12), with a total enrollment of approximately 1,430 students. Southern Columbia's students have excelled in the areas of music, technology, and athletics. The District has maintained a 95% graduation rate, and 80% of graduates have moved on to institutions of higher education. Southern Columbia is ranked in the top five percent of all schools in Pennsylvania in academic performance.

Southern Columbia athletics have enjoyed great success in team and individual competitions. The Tigers compete in 13 varsity and eight junior high sports. Dating back to the 1960s, Southern athletes and teams have won numerous league, conference, sectional, district, and state championships in baseball, field hockey, softball, track and field, soccer, wrestling, and basketball. However, the Tigers' football team has been the pinnacle of success for Southern Columbia athletics.

# CHAPTER 2

# THE 1960s
## (THE BEGINNING)

The story of Southern Columbia Tigers Football began in 1962. At the time of the merger, soccer was the sport of primary interest and popularity in the area. However, high school teachers Charles Nesbitt and Patrick Mondock and Catawissa High School Alum Jim "Stecky" Williams believed that football had a place at Southern Columbia. They gathered community support for the sport to be implemented at the new school and convinced the administration to approve the first football team at Southern Columbia in 1962.

Charles Nesbitt was named the school's first Athletic Director, a position he would hold until 1984. Upon his graduation from Kingston High School, Nesbitt enlisted in the United States Air Force and later enrolled at East Stroudsburg State College, earning a BS in Health and Physical Education. He had an athletic background and went on to be the captain of the wrestling team at East Stroudsburg. Nesbitt would earn a Master of Education and Guidance from Bucknell University. He began his teaching career at Catawissa High School in 1950, where he coached basketball, baseball, and soccer. With his selection as Southern Columbia's Athletic Director, Nesbitt's influence in the early years of Southern Columbia athletics cannot be understated. He held office in the Columbia County League, was the first district representative with the District IV Committee, was named the first president of the District IV Athletic Directors Association, served on Pennsylvania State Athletic Directors Executive Counsel, and was a member of the Eastern Conference Steering Committee. Nesbitt was a PIAA official for wrestling, basketball, baseball, and an NCAA Intercollegiate soccer official. The gymnasium at Southern Columbia High School was named in his honor.

Patrick Mondock was born and raised in Honesdale, Pennsylvania, and was a four-year starter on the Honesdale High School football team. He would attend Lock Haven University, where he was named to the Associated Press Little All-American Football Team. He earned his undergraduate degree from Lock Haven and a Masters of Health and Physical Education from the University of West Virginia. Mondock was named the first head football coach at Southern Columbia and was tasked with finding players and coaches to field a team. Coach Mondock began recruiting players by going door-to-door to students' homes and eventually got enough commitments to field an exhibition team that would play a junior varsity schedule in the fall of 1962. Science and history teacher Roy Sanders joined Mondock as an assistant coach for Southern Columbia's first foray into scholastic football.

The Tigers played their first junior varsity football game at home against Northumberland, losing 19-12. Southern would lose the first four games of their exhibition schedule before winning their first junior varsity game, with a home shutout victory against Tri-Valley. They would earn a tie the following week versus Mahanoy before dropping their final game to finish their inaugural junior varsity season 1-6-1. Although they only managed one win in 1962, the Tigers' junior varsity team put forth a solid effort and paved the way for the future of high school football at Southern Columbia.

## 1962 JUNIOR VARSITY SEASON

| Opponent | Location | W/L | Score |
|---|---|---|---|
| Northumberland | Home | L | 12-19 |
| Nescopeck | Home | L | 6-24 |
| Central Columbia | Home | L | 6-13 |
| Danville | Away | L | 13-39 |
| Tr-Valley | Home | W | 7-0 |
| Mahanoy | Home | T | 13-13 |
| Mount Carmel | Away | L | 0-33 |
| Muncy | Away | L | 0-20 |

COACHING STAFF: Patrick Mondock, Head Coach; Roy Sanders, Assistant Coach

ATHLETIC DIRECTOR: Charles Nesbitt

ROSTER: Doyle Breech, Dan Bridy, Jack Cox, Max Creasy, Ralph Dexter, John Eveland, Ted Fetterman, David Forney, Dale Hauntzleman, David Helwig, Bill Hoffner, Bob Hughes, Charles Leisenring, Alvin Levan, Heister Linn, Lee Linn, Bob Litwhiler, Richard Long, Jerry Manhart, J.ohn Merrill, Gary Mowery, Lee Pensyl, Ted Pensyl, Dale Rarig, Ken Rarig, Dennis Romanoski, Jim Shaeffer, Bob Starr, Gary Swank, Edwin Walters, Stan Wasilewski, Don Whitenight, Tom Whitenight

1
9
6
3

The Southern Columbia Tigers played their first varsity football season in 1963. Athletic director James Nesbitt joined head coach Patrick Mondock and assistant Roy Sanders to complete the coaching staff for the Tigers' inaugural season. Southern Columbia played its first-ever varsity football game on the road against South Williamsport on September 6, 1963. Ray Griffith would score the first touchdown in school history on a 67-yard pass from Mick Fleming. The Tigers would drop their opening game to the Mounties, 40-13. Southern traveled to Northwest Luzerne for their second road game to open the season. In a hard-fought contest, the Southern Columbia Tigers earned their first victory in school history, defeating the Rangers by a score of 13-6 on September 13, 1963. Alvin Levan blocked two punts in the game, one setting up the winning touchdown. More than 500 fans attended the Tigers' first home game in program history in week three against Tri-Valley on September 21, 1963. Dave Forney scored two touchdowns on an 85-yard kickoff return in the first quarter and a 3-yard run late in the fourth against the Bulldogs. The game would end stalemated in a 14-14 tie. Southern would alternate wins and losses the rest of the season, including victories over North Penn, Nescopeck, and Frackville. Quarterback Mick Fleming threw for seven touchdown passes on the year. Forney would finish with four touchdowns, and Ray Griffith would tally three touchdown catches. The Tigers finished their inaugural varsity season a respectable 4-4-1. Coach Mondock's team played

## 1963 SEASON

| Opponent | Location | W/L | Score |
|----------|----------|-----|-------|
| South Williamsport | Away | L | 13-40 |
| Northwest Luzerne | Away | W | 13-6 |
| Tri-Valley | Home | T | 14-14 |
| Central Columbia | Away | L | 12-32 |
| North Penn | Away | W | 13-6 |
| Jersey Shore | Away | L | 0-33 |
| Nescopeck | Away | W | 24-19 |
| Penns Valley | Away | L | 21-42 |
| Frackville | Home | W | 19-15 |

COACHING STAFF: Patrick Mondock, Head Coach; Charles Nesbitt, Assistant Coach; Roy Sanders, Assistant Coach

ATHLETIC DIRECTOR: Charles Nesbitt

ROSTER: Dale Breech, Doyle Breech, Tom Breech, Dan Bridy, Tom Brokenshire, Warren Carl, Jack Cox, Max Creasy, Glenn Fetterman, Ted Fetterman, Mick Fleming, David Forney, Ray Griffith, Dale Hauntzleman, David Helwig, Bill Hoffner, Howard Kerstetter, Charles Leisenring, Alvin Levan, Heister Linn, Bob Litwhiler, Ed Long, Jerry Manhart, Dennis Mensch, John Merrill, Gary Mowery, Dale Rarig, Ken Rarig, Robin Shoup, Morgan Snyder, Bob Starr, Gary Swank, Edwin Walters, Don Whitenight, Ed Whitenight, Mike Yeager with grit and determination, and they laid the groundwork for a program that would become one of the greatest teams in Pennsylvania state history over the next six decades.

**1964** The Southern Columbia Tigers made great strides in 1964. In Coach Mondock's final season at the helm, Southern would open the year with a 37-0 blowout of Northwest Luzerne. In that game, quarterback Mick Fleming would pass for 226 yards, averaging 25.1 yards per completion. Receiver Gary Mowery torched the Rangers for 125 yards and three touchdowns. For the second straight year, the Tigers would play to a tie against Tri-Valley. The Southern defense put forth a magnificent effort, registering two safeties in a 10-7 victory over Central Columbia. The Tigers would put together their first-ever winning streak, with three mid-season victories, including shutout wins over North Penn and Nescopeck. The Tigers would close the season with back-to-back victories against Penns Valley and Frackville. Fleming would finish the year with five touchdown passes. Southern Columbia would conclude their second season an impressive 6-2-1. Coach Mondock would complete his tenure at Southern Columbia with an overall record of 10-6-2.

## 1964 SEASON

| Opponent | Location | W/L | Score |
|---|---|---|---|
| Northwest Luzerne | Away | W | 37-0 |
| Tri-Valley | Away | T | 13-13 |
| Shamokin Catholic | Home | L | 0-26 |
| Central Columbia | Away | W | 10-7 |
| North Penn | Home | W | 20-0 |
| Nescopeck | Away | W | 37-0 |
| Jersey Shore | Away | L | 7-14 |
| Penns Valley | Home | W | 20-6 |
| Frackville | Away | W | 7-6 |

COACHING STAFF: Patrick Mondock, Head Coach; Charles Nesbitt, Assistant Coach; Roy Sanders, Assistant Coach

ATHLETIC DIRECTOR: Charles Nesbitt

ROSTER: Dale Breech, Doyle Breech, Tom Breech, John Brokenshire, Tom Brokenshire, Al Bucconear, Dennis Burkett, Jack Cox, Don Dressler, Glenn Fetterman, Mick Fleming, Chris Grimes, Bill Hoffner, Bob Keller, Howard Kerstetter, Gary Linn, Heister Linn, Bob Litwhiler, Ed Long, Fred Long, Bob Lunger, Nick Mattucci, Dennis Mensch, Len Miller, Gary Mowery, Dale Rarig, Al Retallack, William Rider, Rich Roberts, Dennis Romanoski, Larry Rumbel, Barry Seidel, Jim Shaeffer, Robin Shoup, Charles Shultz, Morgan Snyder, Rodney Snyder, Bob Starr, Gary Swank, Randy Swartz, Edwin Walters, Ted Williams, Mike Yeager, Ted Yeager

After the 1964 season, Patrick Mondock accepted the head football coach position at Ridgway High School in Western Pennsylvania. He coached at Ridgway until 1970 and was then hired as an assistant coach at NCAA Division III Washington and Jefferson College, south of Pittsburgh, in 1971. Mondock became the head football coach at Washington and Jefferson in 1972. He would lead the Presidents' program from 1972 to 1982. Later, he would work for the National Football League scouting organization, BLESTO (Bears, Lions, Eagles, Steelers Talent Organization). Mondock conducted talent evaluations for prospective college football prospects. His time at BLESTO led to a position in the scouting department with the Indianapolis Colts, where he worked for eight years. In 1994, Mondock was hired by the Seattle Seahawks as Eastern Scouting Supervisor, where he remained until 1997. He was named Seattle's College Scouting Director in 1998 and worked as an area scout in 1999. In 2000, Mondock was hired as a Regional Scouting Supervisor, evaluating college players in the eastern region of the United States by the New Orleans Saints. He remained in this position with the Saints until his retirement in 2004. Patrick Mondock devoted his life to high school, college, and professional football. Although he would have great success at the game's highest levels, the foundation that he built at Southern Columbia would form the cornerstone of the great dynasty to come.

**1965** Before the 1965 season, Jon Vastine was named the second head football coach at Southern Columbia. Vastine was a graduate of Danville High School, a four-year starter on the football team, earning All-Susquehanna Valley Conference and All-State Honorable Mention honors. He attended Presbyterian College in South Carolina on a football scholarship. Vastine was a four-time letter winner at Presbyterian and was named an Associated Press Little All-American as a punter. He played in the 1960 Tangerine Bowl. Vastine began his coaching career as an assistant at Plymouth High School, becoming head coach the following season. Vastine would spend one season as an assistant coach at his alma mater in Danville before accepting the position at Southern Columbia.

Richard Johns joined the staff as an assistant coach in 1965. The Tigers struggled on both sides of the ball throughout the season. Offensively, they failed to score more than 13 points in any game, and the defense gave up an average of 32.5 points per game. Southern was unable to win a game in Coach Vastine's first season, going 0-9, suffering blowout losses to Central Columbia, Danville, Shikellamy, Shamokin, Selinsgrove, Berwick, and Milton.

## 1965 SEASON

| Opponent | Location | W/L | Score |
|----------|----------|-----|-------|
| Bloomsburg | Away | L | 8-12 |
| Central Columbia | Away | L | 13-40 |
| Lourdes Regional | Away | L | 6-12 |
| Danville | Away | L | 6-53 |
| Shikellamy | Home | L | 6-39 |
| Shamokin | Away | L | 0-30 |
| Selinsgrove | Home | L | 6-33 |
| Berwick | Home | L | 13-34 |
| Milton | Away | L | 12-40 |

COACHING STAFF: Jon Vastine, Head Coach; Richard Johns, Assistant Coach; Roy Sanders, Assistant Coach

ATHLETIC DIRECTOR: Charles Nesbitt

ROSTER: Tim Bittner, Doyle Breech, Tom Breech, John Brokenshire, Tom Brokenshire, Dennis Burkett, Bill Cox, Don Dressler, Chris Grimes, Dan Grodzinski, Terry Hartman, Fred Hess, George Krick, John Levan, Gary Linn, Ed Long, Bob Lunger, Byron Madara, David Marquette, Nick Mattucci, Len Miller, Gary Mowery, Donald Reese, Al Retallack, William Rider, Rich Roberts, Larry Rumbel, Barry Seidel, Charles Shultz, Morgan Snyder, Rodney Snyder, Bob Starr, James Tingley, Mike Yeager, Ted Yeager

**1966**  Coach Vastine's Tigers rebounded from the program's first winless season to finish with a winning record in 1966. Playing their first ten-game season, Southern Columbia would start 1966 with a three-game winning streak. In a mid-season victory over Danville, quarterback Rich Roberts connected with Barry Seidel for an 88-yard touchdown pass, one of three touchdowns on the day for Seidel. In the season's final game, Ted Yeager returned a punt 90 yards for a touchdown in a win over Milton. Roberts would pass for eight touchdowns on the season. Mike Yeager had three touchdown receptions for the year. The Tigers would finish 5-4-1 in Coach Vastine's final season, and he would finish his coaching career at Southern with a record of 5-13-1. The 1966 Southern Columbia Tigers hold a special place in the program's history as they won the Susquehanna Valley Conference Championship, the school's first football title.

**1967**  Jon Vastine would return to Danville High School as head football coach while remaining an American history teacher at Southern Columbia. He will always hold a special place in Tiger history as the first head coach to win a football championship.

Joe Sarra graduated from Belle Vernon High School in western Pennsylvania in 1955 and attended California University of Pennsylvania. He was an

## 1966 SEASON

| Opponent | Location | W/L | Score |
|---|---|---|---|
| Bloomsburg | Home | W | 14-6 |
| Central Columbia | Home | W | 25-19 |
| Lourdes Regional | Home | W | 20-6 |
| Hughesville | Away | L | 6-20 |
| Danville | Home | W | 19-6 |
| Shikellamy | Away | L | 12-32 |
| Jersey Shore | Away | L | 0-7 |
| Selinsgrove | Away | T | 13-13 |
| Juniata | Away | L | 2-18 |
| Milton | Home | W | 19-7 |

COACHING STAFF: Jon Vastine, Head Coach; Richard Johns, Assistant Coach; Roy Sanders, Assistant Coach

ATHLETIC DIRECTOR: Charles Nesbitt

ROSTER: Dave Bissett, Tim Bittner, Tom Breech, John Brokenshire, Tom Brokenshire, Dennis Burkett, Bill Cox, Chris Grimes, Dan Grodzinski, Thomas Heath, Robert Herring, John Higgins, Ned Hoffner, Paul Jankowski, Bob Keller, David Kichman, Gary Linn, Ed Long, Bob Lunger, David Marquette, Nick Mattucci, Len Miller, Donald Reese, Al Retallack, William Rider, Dale Roadarmel, Rich Roberts, Larry Rumbel, John Schrader, Barry Seidel, Charles Shultz, Morgan Snyder, Rodney Snyder, Donald Traugh, Mike Yeager, Ted Yeager, Tom Yeager

outstanding fullback and linebacker at California, helping to lead the Vulcans to an undefeated season in 1958 and a Pennsylvania State Athletic Conference Championship. Sarra was also a catcher and outfielder on the California baseball team. He received a BS in Education and Guidance from California and later earned a Master of Secondary School Education from the University of West Virginia. In 1961, Sarra was named head football and basketball coach at East Washington (PA) High School. Between 1962 and 1966, he was an assistant football coach at Hempfield and Belle Vernon High Schools. Sarra was named Southern Columbia's third head coach in 1967.

Albert Glennon and Dick Staber joined the coaching staff in 1967. The Tigers would alternate wins and losses throughout the season to finish at 5-5. However, Southern would earn three shutout victories in their five wins, including a 50-0 shellacking of Central Columbia, a 26-0 win over Hughesville, and 35-0 drubbing of Northwest Luzerne. In the season-ending win over Milton, Ted Yeager rushed for four touchdowns in the Tigers' 40-26 victory. Jere Miller had four touchdown catches for the year. Coach Sarra's offense showed some firepower, averaging 34.2 points per game in their five victories.

## 1967 SEASON

| Opponent | Location | W/L | Score |
|---|---|---|---|
| Bloomsburg | Away | L | 12-21 |
| Central Columbia | Away | W | 50-0 |
| Lourdes Regional | Away | L | 6-14 |
| Hughesville | Home | W | 26-0 |
| Danville | Away | L | 13-21 |
| Northwest Luzerne | Home | W | 35-0 |
| Jersey Shore | Home | L | 14-34 |
| Selinsgrove | Home | W | 20-14 |
| Juniata | Home | L | 0-19 |
| Milton | Away | W | 40-26 |

COACHING STAFF: Joe Sarra, Head Coach; Albert Glennon, Assistant Coach; Charles Nesbitt, Assistant Coach; Dick Staber, Assistant Coach

ATHLETIC DIRECTOR: Charles Nesbitt

ROSTER: Scott Adams, Dave Appel, Richard Bartlow, Jack Breech, John Brokenshire, Dennis Burkett, Bill Cox, Jack Eveland, Thomas Eveland, Lanny Fetterman, Chris Grimes, Randy Herring, John Higgins, Blake Hoffman, Ned Hoffner, Paul Jankowski, David Kichman, Rick Krum, Donald Leffler, Bob Lunger, Philip Lyons, Edward Maciejewski, Dennis Marquette, Robert Martin, Nick Mattucci, Jere Miller, Len Miller, David Raker, Randy Reese, William Rider, Rich Roberts, Mike Sabo, John Schrader, Joe Scovak, Barry Seidel, Charles Shultz, John Smith, Rodney Snyder, Terry Snyder, Vic Thompson, Donald Traugh, Wayne Traugh, Charles Verdekal, Frank Wagner, Vic Webb, Eugene Weller, Ted Yeager, Randy Yocum

**1968**   Southern Columbia dropped the opening game of the 1968 season before running off three straight victories and winning five of their first seven games. However, back-to-back losses to Selinsgrove and Juniata late in the year derailed a promising season. A final game win over Milton gave Coach Sarra's Tigers a 6-4 record. Southern's defense pitched shutouts against Lourdes Regional and Crestwood and gave up only 38 points in their six wins. In their victory over Milton, Wayne Traugh and Robert Herring each had two interceptions. Kicker Paul Jankowski connected on a 43-yard field goal against Hughesville. Herring had five touchdown receptions on the year, and Jankowski converted three field goals. Donald Ickes served as a new assistant coach in 1968.

**1969**   In 1969, Southern Columbia would go through an up and down season that saw them finish the year at .500. Several high notes were certainly blowout wins against Hughesville, Northwest Luzerne, and a shutout victory over Milton. However, the highlight of the season was undoubtedly the Tigers' 76-0 massacre of Crestwood. Southern's 76 points were the most scored in a game in their short history. The Tigers scored 11 touchdowns in the game, including four scoring passes, three from quarterback Randy

## 1968 SEASON

| Opponent | Location | W/L | Score |
|---|---|---|---|
| Bloomsburg | Home | L | 7-24 |
| Central Columbia | Home | W | 14-13 |
| Lourdes Regional | Home | W | 7-0 |
| Hughesville | Away | W | 23-12 |
| Danville | Home | L | 7-14 |
| Northwest Luzerne | Away | W | 22-6 |
| Crestwood | Away | W | 30-0 |
| Selinsgrove | Away | L | 0-33 |
| Juniata | Away | L | 38-7 |
| Milton | Home | W | 23-7 |

COACHING STAFF: Joe Sarra, Head Coach; Donald Ickes, Assistant Coach; Charles Nesbitt, Assistant Coach; Dick Staber, Assistant Coach

ATHLETIC DIRECTOR: Charles Nesbitt

ROSTER: John Adams, Scott Adams, Jack Breech, Robert Bunge, Marvin Dreisbauch, Thomas Eveland, Robert Farnsworth, Lanny Fetterman, Dan Grodzinski, Robert Herring, Blake Hoffman, Ned Hoffner, Paul Jankowski, David Kichman, Dale Klawitter, Donald Leffler, Stanley Lesevick, Doug Litwhiler, Charles Long, Philip Lyons, Bob Maciejewski, Dennis Marquette, Andrew Melich, David Raker, Fred Rhodes, Mike Sabo, John Schrader, Jeffery Seidel, Richard Snyder, Terry Snyder, Steven Styer, Mark Talarovich, Donald Traugh, Wayne Traugh, Frank Wagner, Eugene Weller, Randy Yocum

Yocum to Dennis Marquette. Tom Eveland scored four touchdowns on runs of 75 and 15 yards, a kick return of 78 yards, and a punt return of 70 yards. Bob Maciejewski scored two touchdowns on a 2-yard run and a pass from Brian Raker. Mike Sabo contributed a 21-yard run. Jeff Seidel kicked ten extra points during the game. Marquette would total four touchdown receptions on the season, and Seidel kicked 16 extra points. Terry Sharrow was added to the coaching staff. Southern would finish the 1969 season, the last in the tenure of Coach Sarra, with a 5-5 record. Joe Sarra's overall record at Southern Columbia stood at 16-14.

In 1970, Joe Sarra accepted the head coach position at Miami of Ohio University, coaching the freshman football team. In 1971, Sarra was hired as an assistant football coach at Lafayette College. He spent the next twelve seasons at Lafayette, serving as both offensive and defensive coordinator. Sarra joined Head Coach Joe Paterno's staff at Penn State in 1984. Over the next 16 years, Sarra would serve as the Nittany Lions' linebackers and defensive line coach. He coached in 15 bowl games, including the 1987 Fiesta Bowl, where Penn State defeated the Miami Hurricanes to win College Football's National

## 1969 SEASON

| Opponent | Location | W/L | Score |
|----------|----------|-----|-------|
| Bloomsburg | Away | L | 6-22 |
| Central Columbia | Away | W | 14-6 |
| Lourdes Regional | Away | L | 6-30 |
| Hughesville | Home | W | 34-6 |
| Danville | Away | L | 26-39 |
| Northwest Luzerne | Home | W | 35-8 |
| Crestwood | Home | W | 76-0 |
| Selinsgrove | Home | L | 7-33 |
| Juniata | Home | L | 12-22 |
| Milton | Away | W | 6-0 |

COACHING STAFF: Joe Sarra, Head Coach; Albert Glennon, Assistant Coach; Terry Sharrow, Assistant Coach; Dick Staber, Assistant Coach

ATHLETIC DIRECTOR: Charles Nesbitt

ROSTER: Don Abraczinskas, James Adams, Mike Adams, Dale Bisset, Jack Breech, Ralph Domanski, Thomas Eveland, Ed Gosciminski, Blake Hoffman, Dale Klawitter, George Leffler, Stanley Lesevick, Philip Lyons, Bob Maciejewski, Dennis Marquette, Andrew Melich, Brian Raker, David Raker, Fred Rhodes, Robin Rhodes, Mike Sabo, Dennis Schmidt, Bruce Schrader, Jeffery Seidel, Richard Snyder, Steven Styer, Mark Talarovich, Robert Traugh, Wayne Traugh, Frank Wagner, Randy Yocum

Championship. In 2000, Sarra became an Administrative Assistant for Joe Paterno. After Penn State player Adam Taliaferro suffered a significant spinal cord injury in a game against Ohio State in 2000, Coach Paterno appointed Sarra as the team's liaison with the Taliaferro family. Sarra was actively involved in Taliaferro's rehabilitation and recovery from his injury. He retired from Penn State in 2005. Sarra was a registered PIAA official in football, basketball, and baseball. He officiated for one season in the American Football League. Sarra received the Michael Duda Award for Athletic Achievement from the California University of Pennsylvania, was selected for the All-American Football Foundation's Lifetime Achievement Award for Assistant Coaches Who Make A Difference, was inducted into the Pennsylvania Sports Hall of Fame, elected to Mid-Mon Valley All Sports Hall of Fame, selected for the Belle Vernon Area Football Hall of Fame, elected to the California University of Pennsylvania Athletic Hall of Fame and received the Joseph D. Sarra Community Service Award from the National Football Foundation College Hall of Fame. Sadly, Joe Sarra passed away at the age of 75 on July 19, 2012.

# CHAPTER 3

# THE 1970s
## (A NEW DECADE)

Bob Gutshall attended Altoona High School, where he starred as a halfback on the football team and, after his senior season, was named to the Pennsylvania All-Star Team for the 1960 Big 33 Classic. Gutshall was recruited by the University of Pittsburgh and played his freshman year for the Panthers. He transferred to Lock Haven University and twice led the Bald Eagles in rushing, becoming a triple threat on the gridiron, excelling in passing and punting. Gutshall was named an All-American and was selected to the All-Pennsylvania State Athletic Conference West Team in 1964. He would play one season of professional football as a running back for the Atlantic City Senators of the Atlantic Coast Football League in 1966. Gutshall served as an assistant coach at Bloomsburg University for one season before accepting the head football coach position at Southern Columbia in 1970.

The Southern Columbia Tigers struggled at the start of the 1970 season, losing their first three games, including back-to-back shutout losses to Central Columbia and Lourdes Regional. Coach Gutshall's offense managed only 42 points in their seven losses, with the Tigers being shutout four times. Season highlights included Jim Adams returning a fumble 87 yards for a touchdown, Bob Maciejewski returning a blocked punt for a score against Scranton Prep, and Maciejewski's two kickoff returns for touchdowns on the year. The Tigers finished the campaign at 3-7. Assistant coaches Bill Moyer and Mike Sall joined staff, and former coach Roy Sanders returned for the 1970 season.

## 1970 SEASON

| Opponent | Location | W/L | Score |
|---|---|---|---|
| Bloomsburg | Home | L | 6-22 |
| Central Columbia | Home | L | 0-35 |
| Lourdes Regional | Home | L | 0-30 |
| Hughesville | Away | W | 3-0 |
| Danville | Home | L | 0-13 |
| Northwest Luzerne | Away | L | 18-19 |
| Scranton Prep | Away | W | 18-0 |
| Selinsgrove | Away | L | 0-47 |
| Weatherly | Away | W | 36-14 |
| Milton | Home | L | 18-19 |

COACHING STAFF: Bob Gutshall, Head Coach; Bill Moyer, Assistant Coach; Mike Sall, Assistant Coach; Roy Sanders, Assistant Coach; Jon Vastine, Assistant Coach

ATHLETIC DIRECTOR: Charles Nesbitt

ROSTER: Don Abraczinskas, James Adams, Mike Adams, Dale Bisset, Bob Colosimo, Ralph Domanski, Doug Dyer, Ed Gosciminski, Dennis Haladay, Ed Horne, George Leffler, Bob Maciejewski, Andrew Melich, Steve Miller, Andy Molick, Tom Nesbitt, Mike Palachick, Brian Raker, Robin Rhodes, Doug Roadarmel, Bruce Schrader, Jeffery Seidel, Richard Snyder, Roger Steffen, Steven Styer, Mark Talarovich

**1971** Assistant Coach Dennis Burkett joined the Southern Columbia staff for head coach Gutshall's final season in 1971. The Tigers would suffer a dismal season, losing their first five games by a combined score of 160-20, before managing a mid-season tie versus Northwest Luzerne. Southern struggled on both sides of the scrimmage line, as they were shutout six times and gave up an average of 24.6 points per game. The Tigers' lone victory was a 31-6 win over Weatherly. They would finish the 1971 season 1-8-1, and Coach Gutshall would finish his career at Southern Columbia with an overall record of 4-15-1.

**1972** After leaving Southern Columbia in 1971, Bob Gutshall would rejoin the coaching staff at Bloomsburg University and serve as an assistant coach at Milton High School. Gutshall was inducted into the Lock Haven University Football Hall of Fame in 2014.

Frank Miriello was hired as the head football coach at Southern Columbia for the 1972 season. He was born and raised in Kulpmont, Pennsylvania. He attended Mount Carmel High School, where he was a standout football player. Miriello spent one semester at Ferrum College in Virginia before transferring to East Stroudsburg University. At East Stroudsburg, Miriello was named a First Team All-Pennsylvania State Athletic Conference linebacker and was selected as a Scholar-Athlete by the National Football Foundation. He was

## 1971 SEASON

| Opponent | Location | W/L | Score |
|---|---|---|---|
| Bloomsburg | Away | L | 0-30 |
| Central Columbia | Away | L | 6-27 |
| Lourdes Regional | Away | L | 0-32 |
| Hughesville | Home | L | 0-35 |
| Danville | Away | L | 14-36 |
| Northwest Luzerne | Home | T | 14-14 |
| Mid-Valley | Home | L | 0-22 |
| Selinsgrove | Home | L | 0-20 |
| Weatherly | Home | W | 31-6 |
| Milton | Away | L | 0-42 |

COACHING STAFF: Bob Gutshall, Head Coach; Dennis Burkett, Assistant Coach; Bill Moyer, Assistant Coach; Roy Sanders, Assistant Coach

ATHLETIC DIRECTOR: Charles Nesbitt

ROSTER: Dan Abraczinskas, Mike Adams, Bob Colosimo, Richard Dexter, John Domanski, Ralph Domanski, Doug Dyer, Ed Gosciminski, Dennis Haladay, Gary Latshaw, George Leffler, Don Maurer, Greg Miller, Steve Miller, Tom Nesbitt, Brian Raker, Wayne Raker, Robin Rhodes, Bruce Schrader, Dennis Shell, John Sheptock, Carl Smith, Jim Starr, Roger Steffen, Dave Stellfox

a significant contributor and a co-captain for East Stroudsburg's PSAC Championship teams in 1964 and 1965. Upon his graduation, Miriello served as an assistant football coach at East Stroudsburg. Before being named head coach at Southern Columbia, Miriello held assistant positions with the Shamokin and Williamsport School Districts.

Tragedy struck the Southern Columbia community on June 23, 1972. Former quarterback Brian Raker drowned while taking part in a rescue effort to help a family trapped in their cabin due to rising flood waters from Hurricane Agnes along Mugser Run near Knoebels Amusement Resort. Racker was a 1972 graduate of Southern Columbia High School and intended to attend Manlius Prep School in Syracuse, New York, that fall. A plaque at the base of the flagpole in the east end of Tiger Stadium was dedicated in Racker's honor in the fall of 1972. The plaque read, "In fond memory of Brian C. Raker '72 quarterback, Southern Tigers, 1969, 1970, 1971 whose life was lost during courageous rescue efforts in the flood of June 1972. Dedicated Homecoming, October 7, 1972, by his teammates of the 1971 squad. Also dedicated to the memory of all Southern students and alumni whom God has seen fit to call home."

Southern Columbia lost the first five games of the 1972 season, including three straight shutout losses to Central Columbia, Lourdes Regional, and Hughesville. After a mid-season win against Northwest Luzerne, the Tigers dropped three of their final four games, managing a 45-0 victory over

## 1972 SEASON

| Opponent | Location | W/L | Score |
|---|---|---|---|
| Bloomsburg | Home | L | 21-34 |
| Central Columbia | Home | L | 0-44 |
| Lourdes Regional | Home | L | 0-44 |
| Hughesville | Away | L | 0-14 |
| Danville | Home | L | 14-32 |
| Northwest Luzerne | Away | W | 21-13 |
| Columbia Montour Vo-Tech | Away | L | 22-28 |
| Selinsgrove | Away | L | 0-35 |
| Weatherly | Away | W | 45-0 |
| Milton | Home | L | 7-12 |

COACHING STAFF: Frank Miriello, Head Coach; Bill Derr, Assistant Coach; Bill Hoffner, Assistant Coach; Kevin Karrs, Assistant Coach

ATHLETIC DIRECTOR: Charles Nesbitt

ROSTER: Ken Bittner, Bob Colosimo, Daveler, Daryl Dillard, Doug Dyer, Dennis Haladay, Jim Haladay, Rich Kovalewski, Gary Latshaw, Bob Leffler, Jim Linn, Dave Mackey, Don Maurer, Greg Miller, Steve Miller, Blyler Nahodil, Tom Nesbitt, Brad Rarig, Mike Sanders, John Sheptock, Frank Snyder, Dave Stellfox

Weatherly. Steve Miller had a tremendous performance in this game, contributing six touchdowns, including four rushing scores. Miller would also return two interceptions for touchdowns on the season. Rich Kovalewski rushed for 524 yards on the year. Dennis Haladay kicked two field goals, converted 16 extra points, and led the Tigers in scoring with 22 points. Southern went 2-8 in Coach Miriello's first campaign, being outscored 256-130. Assistant coaches Bill Derr, Bill Hoffner, and Kevin Karrs joined the Tigers staff in 1972.

1
9
7
3
Southern Columbia improved their record in 1973. Coach Miriello's Tigers lost their opening game to Bloomsburg before back-to-back victories over Central Columbia and a shutout win against Freeland. Punter Dave Stellfox would connect on a 64-yard boot versus Freeland, and the defense would return two interceptions for touchdowns. The Tigers' defense also had a stellar effort in a 45-0 win over Columbia Montour Vo-Tech, sacking the opposing quarterback nine times. However, Southern suffered three straight losses before splitting their final four games. Southern Columbia was shutout in five of their six losses, including blowouts by Danville, Selinsgrove, and Milton. The Tigers would finish 1973 with a record of 4-6. Standout star Dennis Haladay, who had five fumble recoveries and kicked two field goals in 1973, was named to the All-State Honorable Mention Team. Rich Kovalewski rushed the ball 165 times for 674 yards. Doug Richie had ten pass receptions for 157 yards and three touchdowns.

## 1973 SEASON

| Opponent | Location | W/L | Score |
|---|---|---|---|
| Bloomsburg | Away | L | 0-14 |
| Central Columbia | Away | W | 16-14 |
| Freeland | Away | W | 28-0 |
| Hughesville | Home | L | 3-13 |
| Danville | Away | L | 0-47 |
| Northwest Luzerne | Home | L | 0-10 |
| Columbia Montour Vo-Tech | Home | W | 45-0 |
| Selinsgrove | Home | L | 0-32 |
| Weatherly | Home | W | 28-14 |
| Milton | Away | L | 0-32 |

COACHING STAFF: Frank Miriello, Head Coach; Bill Derr, Assistant Coach; Bill Hoffner

ATHLETIC DIRECTOR: Charles Nesbitt

ROSTER: Peter Abraczinskas, Dave Adams, Jeff Bell, Ken Bittner, John Candelora, Mike Daveler, Don Dent, Greg Gutekunst, Dennis Haladay, Jim Haladay, Keith Hoffman, Randy Johnson, Jim Kessler, Rich Kovalewski, Brad Kreisher, Jim Linn, Dave Mackey, Don Maurer, Randy Milbrand, Blyler Nahodil, Joe Petro, Jim Pratt, Doug Richie, Kevin Sabotchick, Mike Sanders, John Sheptock, Rick Steele, Dave Stellfox, Karl Weikel

**1974** 1974 would be Coach Miriello's last season as Southern Columbia's head coach. The Tigers would respond with their first winning record in eight years. Southern would start the season with three straight wins. However, they failed to score a point in the next three games, including a grueling 0-0 tie against Northwest Luzerne. Southern would split the final four games, featuring a 33-0 shutout of Columbia Montour Vo-Tech, to finish the season at 5-4-1. Quarterback Mike Daveler would end the year with 138 pass attempts for 538 yards. Doug Richie had 17 pass receptions for 219 yards and averaged 16.1 yards per punt return. Joe Geiger and Charlie Troxell joined the coaching staff. Coach Miriello would finish his career at Southern Columbia with an 11-18-1 overall record.

**1975** After leaving Southern Columbia, Frank Miriello would become the head football coach at Warrior Run High School. 1n 1978, Miriello joined the first-ever coaching staff at Washington and Lee University in Lexington, Virginia. He was the offensive line coach at Washington and Lee until 1981. Miriello spent one year as an assistant coach at Hampton-Sydney College and three seasons at the Virginia Military Institute. In 1985, Miriello was the head coach at Steelton-Highspire High School before being named head football and lacrosse coach at Mercersburg Academy from 1986-1989. He returned to Washington and Lee as an assistant football and lacrosse coach in 1990. Miriello was the Generals' defensive coordinator in 1991 before being

## 1974 SEASON

| Opponent | Location | W/L | Score |
|---|---|---|---|
| Bloomsburg | Home | W | 7-0 |
| Central Columbia | Home | W | 8-7 |
| Freeland | Home | W | 35-12 |
| Hughesville | Away | L | 0-13 |
| Danville | Home | L | 0-18 |
| Northwest Luzerne | Away | T | 0-0 |
| Columbia Montour Vo-Tech | Home | W | 33-0 |
| Selinsgrove | Away | L | 7-26 |
| Weatherly | Home | W | 27-6 |
| Milton | Home | L | 16-25 |

COACHING STAFF: Frank Miriello, Head Coach; Bill Derr, Assistant Coach; Joe Geiger, Assistant Coach; Bill Hoffner, Assistant Coach; Charlie Troxell, Assistant Coach

ATHLETIC DIRECTOR: Charles Nesbitt

ROSTER: Greg Abraczinskas, Peter Abraczinskas, Mike Achy, Dave Adams, Jeff Bell, Steve Britch, Jerry Brokenshire, Rod Campbell, Mike Daveler, Don Dent, Mike Fedder, Mark Gardner, Paul Gilbert, Greg Gutekunst, Jim Haladay, John Hoy, Randy Johnson, Joe Keefer, Joe Kovalewski, Rich Kovalewski, Ken Latshaw, Bob Leffler, Jim Linn, Terry Long, Dave Mackey, Randy Milbrand, Blyler Nahodil, Glenn Pensyl, Jim Pratt, Larry Quinton, Doug Richie, Mike Sanders, Frank Snyder, Rick Sober, Mike Stine, Karl Weikel

named Washington and Lee's interim head coach in 1995. He was hired as head football coach in 1996. Miriello would lead Washington and Lee's football program until his retirement in 2012, becoming the school's all-time leader in victories and posting .500 or better records in 12 of his 17 seasons as head coach. He would lead the Generals to two Old Dominion Athletic Conference Championships and a pair of NCAA tournament berths. Miriello was named ODAC Coach of the Year in 1996, 2001, 2004, 2006, and 2010. In 2006, Miriello was awarded the American Football Coaches Association South Region Coach of the Year and SportExe Division III Coach of the Year.

Al Cihocki was hired as head football and baseball coach at Southern Columbia in 1975. He was born in Nanticoke, Pennsylvania, and was a three-sport star at John S. Fine High School. Cihocki attended Ithaca College in Ithaca, New York, where he earned three letters in football and led the team in tackles as a junior and senior. He was also a member of the Bombers' baseball team. He earned a bachelor's degree in Physical Education and later received a master's degree from Wilkes College. Before his position at Southern Columbia, Cihocki was an assistant football coach at Ithaca College and later an assistant baseball coach at his father's program at Luzerne County Community College. He also served as head football coach at Cambridge High School in Cambridge, New York.

## 1975 SEASON

| Opponent | Location | W/L | Score |
| --- | --- | --- | --- |
| Bloomsburg | Away | L | 0-36 |
| Central Columbia | Away | L | 0-25 |
| Freeland | Away | W | 26-6 |
| Hughesville | Home | L | 0-8 |
| Danville | Home | L | 0-34 |
| Northwest Luzerne | Home | L | 0-12 |
| Columbia Montour Vo-Tech | Home | W | 22-6 |
| Selinsgrove | Home | L | 16-50 |
| Weatherly | Home | L | 14-21 |
| Milton | Away | L | 12-15 |

COACHING STAFF: Al Cihocki, Head Coach; Joe Geiger, Assistant Coach; Bill Hoffner, Assistant Coach; Charlie Troxell, Assistant Coach

ATHLETIC DIRECTOR: Charles Nesbitt

ROSTER: Greg Abraczinskas, Peter Abraczinskas, Dale Adams, Dave Adams, Jeff Bell, Jerry Brokenshire, Rod Campbell, Don Dent, Gary Fetterman, Paul Gilbert, John Hoy, Randy Johnson, Jim Kessler, Dan Knoebel, Joe Kovalewski, Terry Long, Bill Marquette, Randy Milbrand, Glenn Pensyl, Jim Pratt, Larry Quinton, Doug Richie, Tony Russo, Kevin Sabotchick, Jeff Skjoldal, Rick Sober, Rick Wilson, Mike Wondoloski, Kent Woodruff, Ron Yeager, Jon Zeigler

The 1975 Tigers struggled out of the gate, losing five of its first six games, being shutout in each by Bloomsburg, Central Columbia, Hughesville, Danville, and Northwest Luzerne. The Southern defense forced nine turnovers in a victory over Columbia Montour Vo-Tech. The Tigers would drop their final three games of the season. However, they received workmanlike efforts from quarterback Jim Kessler, who had 30 pass attempts against Selinsgrove and running back Jim Pratt, who carried the ball 39 times versus Milton. Kessler would finish the season with five touchdown passes. Southern Columbia would finish 2-8 in Coach Cihocki's first season.

1
9
7
6

Southern Columbia played their first eleven-game season in 1976. The Bicentennial was not kind to the Tigers. Coach Cihocki's team would lose the first nine games, including blowout losses to Muncy, Bloomsburg, Danville, Northwest Luzerne, Selinsgrove, and Milton. Southern managed a week ten victory over Weatherly. The Tigers gave up a staggering 378 points, averaging 34.3 per game. They finished the season at 1-10. John Boyer, Jay McGinley, Al Retallack, and Dick Roberts joined the coaching staff in 1976.

## 1976 SEASON

| Opponent | Location | W/L | Score |
| --- | --- | --- | --- |
| Muncy | Away | L | 0-38 |
| Bloomsburg | Home | L | 6-49 |
| Central Columbia | Home | L | 8-13 |
| Freeland | Home | L | 12-31 |
| Hughesville | Away | L | 14-35 |
| Danville | Home | L | 14-40 |
| Northwest Luzerne | Away | L | 0-42 |
| Columbia Montour Vo-Tech | Away | L | 8-18 |
| Selinsgrove | Away | L | 6-53 |
| Weatherly | Away | W | 30-6 |
| Milton | Home | L | 12-53 |

COACHING STAFF: Al Cihocki, Head Coach; John Boyer, Assistant Coach; Joe Geiger, Assistant Coach; Jay McGinley, Assistant Coach; Al Retallack, Assistant Coach; Dick Roberts, Assistant Coach; Roy Sanders, Assistant Coach

ATHLETIC DIRECTOR: Charles Nesbitt

ROSTER: Greg Abraczinskas, Dave Adams, Peter Adamski, Stu Appel, Brett Barnes, Fred Billman, Bill Breech, Steve Britch, Jerry Brokenshire, Rod Campbell, Jeff Cox, John Creasy, Joe Danilowicz, Andre Decates, Fred Ehret, Gary Farnsworth, Gary Fetterman, Bill Hendricks, John Hoy, Curt Jones, Joe Keefer, Dan Kessler, Joe Kovalewski, Dan Laubach, Peter MacMahon, Jim McCarthy, Greg Miller, Jeff Miller, Bill Paisley, Glenn Pensyl, Tom Poploski, Rudy Rhodes, Doug Richie, Tony Russo, Scott Schiel, Bill Sevison, Tim Shultz, Brian Snyder, Rick Sober, Mike Stine, Steve Taylor, Jeff Updegrove, Don Vought, Mike Wondoloski, Kent Woodruff

**1977** The Tigers opened the 1977 season with consecutive losses before posting back-to-back wins, including a tough 6-0 shutout of Freeland. John Creasy would have two fumble recoveries in the win over Freeland. Southern would alternate wins and losses for the rest of the year. The week six matchup with Danville featured the first game pitting two Southern Columbia coaches against one another, as former coach Jon Vastine was now heading the Ironmen. In an emotional game, the Tigers pulled out a 27-14 victory. Brian Snyder led the team in scoring, contributing 20 points. Bob Chesney was added to the coaching staff. Southern finished 1977 at 5-6.

**1978** The 1978 season began with consecutive losses to Muncy and Bloomsburg. A week three home game against Central Columbia was played in a dense fog. The coaches, fans, and radio announcers could not see the action on the field. The Tigers earned a hard-fought 10-6 victory, with Rick Swank's 61-yard touchdown being the deciding score. Southern would win their next game against Freeland before suffering back-to-back losses at mid-season. Against Danville, the defense would recover four Ironmen

## 1977 SEASON

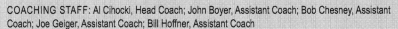

| Opponent | Location | W/L | Score |
|---|---|---|---|
| Muncy | Home | L | 9-19 |
| Bloomsburg | Away | L | 6-20 |
| Central Columbia | Away | W | 10-7 |
| Freeland | Away | W | 6-0 |
| Hughesville | Home | L | 14-20 |
| Danville | Away | W | 27-14 |
| Northwest Luzerne | Home | L | 0-42 |
| Columbia Montour Vo-Tech | Home | W | 33-0 |
| Selinsgrove | Home | L | 3-36 |
| Weatherly | Home | W | 25-6 |
| Milton | Away | L | 7-35 |

COACHING STAFF: Al Cihocki, Head Coach; John Boyer, Assistant Coach; Bob Chesney, Assistant Coach; Joe Geiger, Assistant Coach; Bill Hoffner, Assistant Coach

ATHLETIC DIRECTOR: Charles Nesbitt

ROSTER: Don Adamski, Stu Appel, Brett Barnes, Bill Breech, Jerry Brokenshire, Rod Campbell, John Creasy, Joe Danilowicz, Carl Drumheller, Fred Drumheller, Fred Ehret, Joe Eisenhooth, John Hoy, Curt Jones, Dan Kessler, Joe Kovalewski, Dan Laubach, Jeff Miller, Blaine Opie, Rudy Rhodes, Tony Russo, Roark Sampsell, Robert Sampsell, Brian Snyder, Rick Sober, Steve Taylor, Don Vought

fumbles; however, the Tigers would lose five fumbles of their own and drop the game, 6-0. In a win over Northwest Luzerne, Brett Barnes returned a punt 90 yards for a touchdown. Southern would lose three of their last four games to finish 4-7. Jeff Swank had a stellar season, with 33 pass receptions for 655 yards and six touchdowns. He also returned two interceptions and a punt for scores. Brian Snyder kicked five field goals and made 14 extra points, scoring 29 points for the year. 1978 was the last season for Al Cihocki as the Tigers' head coach. He would finish his career with Southern Columbia with an overall record of 12-31.

1
9
7
9
After leaving Southern Columbia, Al Cihocki served as an assistant football coach at Central Columbia High School for one season and Bloomsburg University for two years. He would return to Southern Columbia as an assistant coach in 1982, where he has remained ever since. Cihocki has been a valuable and respected member of the Tigers' staff and has helped the team win eleven PIAA State Football Championships. In addition to his football coaching duties, Cihocki has led the Southern Columbia girls' softball team for decades. He has guided the team to numerous Mid Penn League championships and District IV playoff appearances. Al Cihocki has had a lasting and meaningful impact on athletics at Southern Columbia.

## 1978 SEASON

| Opponent | Location | W/L | Score |
|---|---|---|---|
| Muncy | Away | L | 7-14 |
| Bloomsburg | Home | L | 0-28 |
| Central Columbia | Home | W | 10-6 |
| Freeland | Home | W | 42-14 |
| Hughesville | Away | L | 14-27 |
| Danville | Home | L | 0-6 |
| Northwest Luzerne | Away | W | 23-20 |
| Columbia Montour Vo-Tech | Away | L | 17-20 |
| Jim Thorpe | Away | L | 0-17 |
| Weatherly | Away | W | 24-8 |
| Cardinal Brennan | Home | L | 20-48 |

COACHING STAFF: Al Cihocki, Head Coach; Joe Geiger, Assistant Coach; Bill Hoffner, Assistant Coach; Charlie Troxell, Assistant Coach

ATHLETIC DIRECTOR: Charles Nesbitt

ROSTER: Don Adamski, Stu Appel, Brett Barnes, Bill Breech, Randy Campbell, Mike Chamberis, John Creasy, Joe Danilowicz, Carl Drumheller, Ned Drumheller, Fred Ehret, John Eisenhooth, Stan Eisenhooth, Kurt Harder, George Henry, Curt Jones, Dan Kessler, Tom Leffler, Peter MacMahon, Jeff Miller, Bill Paisley, Tony Russo, Tom Shultz, Brian Snyder, Jeff Swank, Rick Swank, Dennis Toczylousky, Don Vought, Don Zeigler

Former Tiger player Mike Yeager assumed the head coaching duties at Southern Columbia in 1979. Yeager was a star player for the Tigers, earning three letters in football at Southern. He went on to play football for East Stroudsburg University and was a two-year letter winner for the Warriors. Before taking the reins at Southern Columbia, Yeager served one year on the staff at Clairton High School. He then spent one season as a graduate assistant at his alma mater East Stroudsburg and was named the offensive coordinator at the University of Bridgeport in Connecticut. Yeager worked as a secondary coach at Virginia Tech University for three seasons.

In head coach Mike Yeager's only season with the Tigers, the team struggled through a winless season. Southern was shutout in their first three games and five times during the year. The Tigers scored only 52 points, averaging 4.7 points per game for the season. The defense played admirably, averaging only 17.9 points against per game, suffering close losses to Muncy, Central Columbia, Hughesville, Danville, Columbia Montour Vo-Tech, and Weatherly. The game versus Danville was memorable in that it featured brother against brother, as Southern Columbia coach Mike Yeager and Danville coach Ted Yeager faced each other. The game was played in a driving rainstorm and turned into a defensive struggle, ultimately won by the Ironmen, 7-0. Andy Mills and Andy

# 1979 SEASON

| Opponent | Location | W/L | Score |
|---|---|---|---|
| Muncy | Home | L | 0-12 |
| Bloomsburg | Away | L | 0-26 |
| Central Columbia | Away | L | 0-3 |
| Freeland | Away | L | 7-22 |
| Hughesville | Home | L | 6-14 |
| Danville | Away | L | 0-7 |
| Northwest Luzerne | Home | L | 7-30 |
| Columbia Montour Vo-Tech | Home | L | 12-14 |
| Jim Thorpe | Home | L | 0-28 |
| Weatherly | Home | L | 6-14 |
| Cardinal Brennan | Away | L | 14-27 |

COACHING STAFF: Mike Yeager, Head Coach; John Boyer, Assistant Coach; Bill Hoffner, Assistant Coach; Andy Mills, Assistant Coach; Charlie Troxell, Assistant Coach; Andy Ulicny, Assistant Coach

ATHLETIC DIRECTOR: Charles Nesbitt

ROSTER: Greg Breech, Randy Campbell, Jim Dargan, Carl Drumheller, Ned Drumheller, Bob Drunkenmiller, Greg Franceschini, Kurt Harder, Ron Hartman, Bob Henry, George Henry, John Krankowski, Tom Leffler, Chris Long, Dave Lunger, Dave McDonald, Mark McGlynn, Jeff Miller, Joe Miller, Chet Miskiel, Bryan Mull, Mike Patterson, Drew Pensyl, Jack Ramsey, Jim Rosenberger, Gordon Shellenburger, Tom Shultz, Rick Swank, Mark Tappe, Bob Williams, Fran Young

Ulicny joined the coaching staff, and John Boyer returned. Unfortunately, Coach Yeager finished with an 0-11 record at Southern Columbia.

———

After his tenure as head coach at Southern Columbia, Mike Yeager spent one year as an assistant coach at Central Columbia High School before serving one season as head football coach at Milton Hershey High School. Yeager would become a member of the Board of Education at Southern Columbia Area High School, where he served as President.

# CHAPTER 4

# THE 1980s
## (THE TRANSITION)

Andy Ulicny would become the first assistant to be named head football coach at Southern Columbia in 1980. A native of Shenandoah, Pennsylvania, Ulicny was a scholar-athlete at Shenandoah Valley High School. He led the Blue Devils' football team in rushing yards and scoring as a senior in 1975. Ulicny was elected to the Shenandoah Valley High School Wall of Fame in 2000. He attended the University of Pennsylvania, majoring in English and Anthropology. He earned bachelor's degrees in both majors in just three years and graduated Summa Cum Laude with a Master of Education in 1979. Ulicny accepted a position as an English teacher at Southern Columbia High School that fall. Upon joining the teaching staff at Southern Columbia, Ulicny was named an assistant football coach.

After the 1979 season, the administration at Southern Columbia seriously considered dropping the football program. At the time, the Tigers' overall varsity football record stood at 58-108-5, and the team was in the midst of a 12-game losing streak. Before the 1980 season, there were only nine players signed up to play football. Andy Ulicny approached the Southern Columbia administrators and made the case that scholastic football was an essential part of the high school experience and argued that it was an important and meaningful tool for teamwork, sportsmanship, work ethic, and community pride. Although he only had one year of coaching experience as an assistant, Ulicny said he would take over the head coaching duties to keep the program viable. The administration agreed to support football at Southern Columbia and tasked Ulicny with doing whatever was necessary to keep the program afloat. As the decade of the 1980s

## 1980 SEASON

| Opponent | Location | W/L | Score |
|---|---|---|---|
| Muncy | Away | L | 0-37 |
| Bloomsburg | Home | L | 0-33 |
| Central Columbia | Home | L | 12-42 |
| Freeland | Home | L | 26-30 |
| Hughesville | Away | L | 6-7 |
| Danville | Home | L | 6-26 |
| Northwest Luzerne | Home | L | 12-34 |
| Columbia Montour Vo-Tech | Away | L | 12-13 |
| Montgomery | Home | L | 0-19 |
| Weatherly | Away | L | 14-40 |

COACHING STAFF: Andy Ulicny, Head Coach; Alan Lonoconus, Assistant Coach; Andy Mills, Assistant Coach; Jim Roth, Assistant Coach

ATHLETIC DIRECTOR: Charles Nesbit

ROSTER: Ron Bickert, Greg Breech, Sankey Brumley, Randy Campbell, Don Cook, Don Craig, Matt Crowl, Jim Dargan, Jay Drumheller, Ned Drumheller, Bob Drunkenmiller, Greg Franceschini, Bill Freeman, John Fulmer, Stan Harder, Buddy Hartman, George Henry, Scott Hoffman, Ed Jankowski, Dave Kovalewski, John Krankowski, Tom Leffler, Chris Long, Gary Lunger, Mike MacMahon, Mark McGlynn, Aaron Menapace, Joe Miller, Jack Ramsey, Rob Reber, Tom Reich, Joe Rose, Tom Shultz, Chris Steinroch, Mark Tappe, Bob Williams, Mike Williams, Ed Yeick, Fran Young

began, Tiger football was essentially starting over. Ulicny literally began calling potential freshmen players on the telephone, asking them if they were willing to join the football team. He was able to recruit enough players to field a team in 1980. Knowing things were likely to get worse before getting better, Ulicny knew that the future of Southern Columbia football rested on the shoulders of the underclassmen.

Unfortunately, the Tigers struggled through a second consecutive winless season in head coach Andy Ulicny's first year at the helm in 1980. Southern would lose all ten games, suffering shutout losses to Muncy, Bloomsburg, and Montgomery. Southern Columbia's losing streak would reach 22 games. However, the Tigers played competitive games against Freeland, Hughesville, and Columbia Montour Vo-Tech, losing by an average of just two points. In the game versus Freeland, misfortune seemed to conspire against Southern. The Tigers outrushed Freeland 294 to 13 but gave up touchdowns on two hook and lateral pass plays. At the end of the first quarter, the scoreboard clock malfunctioned and was not operational for the rest of the game. An official on the field kept the game time. On what was believed to be the game's final play, the Tigers defense dropped a potential game-ending interception. As Southern began to celebrate their victory, the officials ruled that the game clock had not expired and granted Freeland one final play. Freeland ran a screen pass from the Southern Columbia 14 yard line, which was ruled a game-winning touchdown, despite protests from the Tigers' defense, who claimed that the receiver was out of bounds two yards short of the goal line. Highlights from the season included quarterback Randy Campbell's eleven pass completions against Central Columbia and running back Matt McGlynn's two 100-yard rushing games. Alan Lonoconus and Jim Roth were added to the coaching staff.

1
9
8
1

1981 saw the Tigers open the season with four straight shutout losses, and their losing streak reached 26 games. A week five game against Hughesville was scheduled for Thursday night, October 1st. In previous years, the Southern Columbia School District had been closed on the Friday during the week of the Bloomsburg Fair. However, the administration had decided that the district would hold classes on that Friday in 1981. As the teams prepared for their Thursday night matchup, torrential thunderstorms delayed the start of the game about a half-hour. Coach Ulicny used the time to give an emotional pregame speech to his players, and the Tigers took the field with great resolve to end their losing streak. The Southern defense played a sensational game, holding Hughesville to zero rushing yards and only 73

## 1981 SEASON

| Opponent | Location | W/L | Score |
|---|---|---|---|
| Muncy | Home | L | 0-31 |
| Bloomsburg | Away | L | 0-33 |
| Central Columbia | Away | L | 0-13 |
| Tri-Valley | Away | L | 0-14 |
| Hughesville | Home | W | 21-0 |
| Danville | Away | L | 6-41 |
| Northwest Luzerne | Home | T | 8-8 |
| Columbia Montour Vo-Tech | Home | W | 33-7 |
| Montgomery | Away | W | 24-0 |
| Weatherly | Home | W | 41-0 |

COACHING STAFF: Andy Ulicny, Head Coach; Alan Lonoconus, Assistant Coach; Andy Mills, Assistant Coach, Jim Roth, Assistant Coach

ATHLETIC DIRECTOR: Charles Nesbitt

ROSTER: Greg Breech, Chris Britch, Brian Brumley, Ed Colodonato, Matt Crowl, Jim Dargan, Jay Drumheller, Keith Erdman, Greg Franceschini, Bill Freeman, John Fulmer, Scott Gattshall, Greg Haladay, Buddy Hartman, Mike Hoffman, Ed Jankowski, Dave Kovalewski, Steve Llewellyn, Chris Long, Dave Lunger, Gary Lunger, Wayne Lutz, Mike MacMahon, Wade Mays, Aaron Menapace, Andy Miller, Rob Reber, Tom Reich, Matt Reiprich, Jim Rosenberger, Ken Schetroma, Brad Sharrow, Mark Tappe, Gene Welkom, Bob Williams, Todd Wilson, Fran Young through the air. Jay Drumheller scored on a one-yard run in the first quarter for a 7-0 lead. Greg Franceschini had a 5-yard touchdown run in the second, and Southern led 14-0 at halftime. Dave Lunger caught a two-yard touchdown pass from Tom Reich in the fourth quarter as the Tigers finally put their losing streak to rest with a convincing 21-0 victory. The Southern Columbia administration reversed their decision and canceled classes the next day to celebrate the team's monumental win. The victory over Hughesville seemed to inspire the Tigers, as they finished the rest of the season 3-1-1, including back-to-back shutout wins against Montgomery and Weatherly to end the year. Southern would finish 1981 with a record of 4-5-1. Running back Greg Franceschini had a terrific season, rushing for 782 yards on 140 carries. He would have four 100-yard rushing games on the year, including 225 yards against Montgomery and an 87-yard touchdown run versus Columbia Montour Vo-Tech. Jim Dargan kicked two field goals against Danville. He scored 23 points on the season, with three field goals and 14 extra points.

1
9
8
2
Southern Columbia had a huge turnaround in 1982. The Tigers opened the season with a victory over Jim Thorpe before suffering back-to-back losses to Bloomsburg and Central Columbia. They would win two of their next three games and earn victories in their final five to finish the season at 8-3, earning the Mid Penn League Division Championship. Southern was rewarded with their first-ever playoff appearance, with a berth in the Mid Penn Conference Championship Game against East Juniata. The defenses would dominate the game, and it ended regulation in a scoreless tie. The contest remained scoreless late in the overtime period when Jay Drumheller's interception set up terrific field position. Nearing the end of overtime, Buddy Hartman threw a crushing block on a trap play to spring Wayne Lutz for the winning touchdown as the scoreboard clock reached zero. Southern Columbia would win their first playoff game in grand fashion with a thrilling 6-0 victory over the Tigers. Coach Ulicny's team would finish 1982 with an overall record of 9-3. Jay Drumheller had, perhaps, the greatest individual season of any Tiger player up to that point. He had the first 1,000 yard rushing season in the program's history. Drumheller would finish with 212 carries for 1,237 yards, including five 100-yard rushing games, and averaged 5.8 yards per carry. He rushed for 259 yards against Montgomery and 207 yards versus Tri-Valley. Drumheller had touchdown runs of 98 yards against Freeland, 97 yards versus Tri-Valley, and 88 yards against Hughesville. Greg Haladay chipped in with 498 yards on 114 carries, and Wayne Lutz had two 100-yard rushing games on the

## 1982 SEASON

| Opponent | Location | W/L | Score |
|---|---|---|---|
| Jim Thorpe | Away | W | 34-6 |
| Bloomsburg | Home | L | 0-29 |
| Central Columbia | Home | L | 7-12 |
| Tri-Valley | Home | W | 18-7 |
| Hughesville | Away | W | 20-17 |
| Danville | Home | L | 9-10 |
| Northwest Luzerne | Away | W | 21-7 |
| Columbia Montour Vo-Tech | Away | W | 28-6 |
| Montgomery | Home | W | 45-6 |
| Weatherly | Away | W | Forfeit |
| Freeland | Away | W | 42-16 |
| **Mid Penn Conference Championship Game** | | | |
| East Juniata | Away | W | 6-0 |

COACHING STAFF: Andy Ulicny, Head Coach; Al Cihocki, Assistant Coach; Alan Lonoconus, Assistant Coach; Andy Mills, Assistant Coach; Jim Roth, Assistant Coach

ATHLETIC DIRECTOR: Charles Nesbitt

ROSTER: Jim Becker, Brian Brumley, Vince Butaitis, Jeff Crowl, Matt Crowl, Rob Deeter, Ron Deeter, Jay Drumheller, Jeff Edmunds, Bill Freeman, John Fulmer, Scott Gattshall, Jeff Gutekunst, Greg Haladay, Bob Haney, Buddy Hartman, Ed Jankowski, Dave Kovalewski, John Kreiger, Steve Llewellyn, Dave Lunger, Wayne Lutz, Mike MacMahon, John Marks, Aaron Menapace, Andy Miller, Bruce Petro, Rob Reber, Tom Reich, Matt Reiprich, Ken Schetroma, Brad Sharrow, Tim Sharrow, Tom Sharrow, Mark Tappe, Steve Tehansky, Dewey Townsend, Gene Welkom, Todd Wilson

season. As the team's placekicker, Lutz scored 22 points with one field goal and 19 extra points. Quarterback Tom Reich had 92 pass attempts, 41 completions, and 668 yards. Receiver Dave Lunger contributed 18 pass receptions for 313 yards and, defensively, had three interceptions against Danville. Former head coach Al Cihocki returned to the coaching staff as an assistant, and Jim Dietz was added to the staff.

1983 would be Andy Ulicny's last year as head coach at Southern Columbia. It would be the most successful season in the program's 21-year varsity history. After splitting the first two games, the Tigers won their remaining nine games, including consecutive shutout victories over Hughesville, Danville, Northwest Luzerne, and Columbia Montour Vo-Tech. Southern had six shutouts in eleven games and outscored their opponents 292-40 on the season. The Tigers' defense was utterly dominant, intercepting 27 passes, returning four for touchdowns, and blocking eight punts. Matt Crowl intercepted six passes against Hughesville, returning two for scores. Bill Freeman recorded 97 tackles (72 solo). Greg Haladay blocked four punts on the year. Vince Butaitis

## 1983 SEASON

| Opponent | Location | W/L | Score |
|---|---|---|---|
| Jim Thorpe | Home | W | 33-8 |
| Bloomsburg | Away | L | 6-13 |
| Central Columbia | Away | W | 6-0 |
| Freeland | Home | W | 32-7 |
| Hughesville | Home | W | 33-0 |
| Danville | Away | W | 15-0 |
| Northwest Luzerne | Home | W | 32-0 |
| Columbia Montour Vo-Tech | Home | W | 42-0 |
| Montgomery | Away | W | 30-6 |
| West Hazelton | Away | W | 28-0 |
| North Penn | Home | W | 35-6 |
| **Eastern Conference Division Championship Game** | | | |
| Bishop O'Hara | Away | W | 36-16 |
| **Eastern Conference Championship Game** | | | |
| Mahanoy Area | Away | W | 10-0 |

COACHING STAFF: Andy Ulicny, Head Coach; Al Cihocki, Assistant Coach; Jim Dietz, Assistant Coach; Alan Lonoconus, Assistant Coach; Andy Mills, Assistant Coach; Jim Roth, Assistant Coach

ATHLETIC DIRECTOR: Charles Nesbitt

ROSTER: Jim Becker, Mike Bennett, Brian Brumley, Vince Butaitis, John Cecco, Jeff Crowl, Matt Crowl, Rob Deeter, Ron Deeter, Jay Drumheller, Jeff Edmunds, Harry Fenwick, Bill Freeman, John Fulmer, Jeff Gutekunst, Greg Haladay, Ed Jankowski, Scott Kerstetter, Brian Knopp, Dave Kovalewski, John Kreiger, Steve Llewellyn, Craig Long, Chet Lutz, Wayne Lutz, Mike MacMahon, John Marks, Aaron Menapace, Andy Miller, Bruce Petro, Tom Reich, Brad Sharrow, Tim Sharrow, Tom Sharrow, Tim Simons, Barry Sudol, Steve Tehansky, Dewey Townsend, Gene Welkom, Todd Wilson

returned a blocked punt 15 yards for a touchdown versus Central Columbia. John Marks also returned a blocked punt for a score during the year. The Tigers' had a stellar offensive season. Jay Drumheller had 293 carries, gaining 1,965 yards, averaging 6.7 yards per carry. He had eleven 100-yard games, including 212 yards against Montgomery. Tom Reich would pass for 490 yards and four touchdowns on 33 completions. Aaron Menapace scored 34 points, with three field goals and 25 extra points. The Tigers finished the season at 10-1 and would win the Mid Penn League Division Championship. Southern would face Bishop O'Hara for the Eastern Conference Division Championship. Jay Drumheller rushed for 206 yards, and Vince Butaitis blocked two punts to lead the Tigers to a 36-16 victory to set up a championship game showdown with Mahanoy Area. A snow storm hit Mahanoy City the day before the title game, which melted and turned the playing field to mud. The defense turned in one final outstanding performance, holding the Golden Bears scoreless. Jay Drumheller scored on a touchdown run, and the Tigers added a field goal for a 10-0 victory and the

1983 Eastern Conference Championship. Matt Crowl, Jay Drumheller, John Fulmer, Bill Freeman, and Ed Jankowski were named to the All-State Honorable Mention Team. Drumheller was selected as the *Reading Eagle* newspaper Running Back of the Year, and Andy Ulicny was named Coach of the Year. Jay Drumheller finished his high school career at Southern Columbia with 669 carries for 4,111 yards and 42 touchdowns. Andy Ulicny would finish his head coaching career at Southern Columbia with an overall record of 25-19-1.

———

Andy Ulicny's contributions to Southern Columbia Football cannot be overstated. With the program on the verge of being disbanded, Ulicny not only saved and kept the football team viable and operational, but the Tigers flourished under his leadership. Taking over a team amid a 26-game losing streak, Southern Columbia was the Eastern Conference Champions within four years. In Coach Ulicny's tenure, the Tigers went from a winless season to ending the losing streak, then Mid Penn Conference Champions, to winning the Eastern Conference. Ulicny changed the football team's culture, from a losing program with the belief that they could not win, by instilling confidence, a winning attitude, and a focus on the team's future. Ulicny gave his heart and every ounce of energy to turn the program around, and he deserves much credit for helping form the dynasty that the Tigers would become. Ulicny would step down as head coach after the 1983 season. He would remain a popular English teacher at Southern Columbia High School until his retirement in 2016, also coaching the girls' softball team during his career. Ulicny would work many years announcing for WHLM radio broadcasting high school and Bloomsburg University football games, serving as a color analyst.

1
9
8
4

Jim Roth was named head football coach at Southern Columbia in 1984. Roth attended Shikellamy High School, where he played football and baseball and was a member of the wrestling team. He attended Lock Haven University, earning a bachelor's degree in Health and Physical Education in 1979. Roth was a defensive back on the Bald Eagles football team. Upon graduation, Roth was a frequent substitute physical education teacher with the Line Mountain School District and coached with the Eagles' junior high wrestling team. Roth accepted a teaching position with the Southern Columbia School District in 1980 and joined the Tigers' football coaching staff. Having been an assistant on the Tigers' staff, Roth had seen the highs and lows of the football program. During a winless season, he had suffered with the team through the majority of Southern's 26-game losing streak and saw the program nearly dropped by the administration. Roth had also been a part of the Tigers' resurrection and saw them grow from a losing team to Eastern Conference Champions. All the while, Roth was helping to turn the Tigers into a dominant defensive unit and planting the seeds for Southern's transition to a new offense that would pave the way for the dynasty in the decades to come. After four years of running a standard one-back offense, Roth explored the idea of implementing the Wing-T formation at Southern. He met with Susquehanna University head football coach Rocky Rees, who had been highly successful with the Wing-T offense, advancing to the NCAA Division III Quarterfinals in 1986. Armed with a new offensive scheme, an emphasis on speed, strength, conditioning, and athleticism, and a focus on the continuity of the coaching staff and the football program, Roth would take Southern Columbia to heights never before seen in Pennsylvania high school history.

Roy Sanders attended Coal Township High School, where he was a three-sport athlete and a three-year starter at quarterback for the Purple Demons. He attended Bloomsburg and Bucknell Universities, earning a Master of Education. Sanders enlisted in the United States Army after college and served honorably in the Korean War. He was awarded the Korean Service, United Nations, Good Conduct, and National Defense Service Medals. After his honorable discharge, Sanders accepted a teaching position with the Ralpho Township Schools and joined the staff at the newly formed Southern Columbia School District with the merger in 1962. He served as an assistant football coach under Pat Mondock, Jon Vastine, and Al Cihocki. He would become Southern Columbia's second athletic director in 1984, a position he would hold until 1988. In addition to football, Sanders would also coach the girls' basketball, baseball, and soccer teams. Sanders became a PIAA official for six decades. He officiated football, softball, baseball, and basketball games. Sanders was a member of the Shamokin Area Chapter of PIAA Officials and was inducted into the Pennsylvania Sports Hall of Fame. Sadly, Roy Sanders passed away in 2012.

Jim Roth began his head coaching career at Southern Columbia in 1984. The Tigers would continue their winning ways in Coach Roth's first season. His first coaching victory came in an opening night game in Jim Thorpe, a 20-0 shutout of the Olympians. After dropping their next two games, the Tigers would run the table and win their final eight regular-season contests, including lopsided victories over Freeland, St. Clair, Danville, Columbia Montour Vo-Tech, Line Mountain Tri-Valley, and Weatherly. Freshman running back Jerry Marks would have a tremendous season. He would rush for 1,769 yards on

## 1984 SEASON

| Opponent | Location | W/L | Score |
|---|---|---|---|
| Jim Thorpe | Away | W | 20-0 |
| Bloomsburg | Home | L | 6-48 |
| Central Columbia | Home | L | 12-24 |
| Freeland | Away | W | 33-12 |
| St. Clair | Away | W | 53-12 |
| Danville | Home | W | 40-15 |
| Columbia Montour Vo-Tech | Away | W | 35-0 |
| Line Mountain | Away | W | 41-26 |
| Tri-Valley | Home | W | 42-20 |
| Weatherly | Home | W | 31-14 |
| Lourdes Regional | Away | W | 20-14 |
| **Mid Penn Conference Championship Game** | | | |
| Bucktail | Away | W | 47-8 |

COACHING STAFF: Jim Roth, Head Coach; Al Cihocki, Assistant Coach; Alan Lonoconus, Assistant Coach; Andy Mills, Assistant Coach; Gary Wilson, Assistant Coach

ATHLETIC DIRECTOR: Roy Sanders

ROSTER: Todd Anoia, Jim Becker, Mike Bennett, Scott Bittner, Brian Brumley, Vince Butaitis, John Cecco, Jeff Crowl, Rob Deeter, Ron Deeter, George Derr, John Eveland, Todd Feese, Shawn Freeman, Jeff Gutekunst, Greg Haladay, Tim Johnson, Scott Kerstetter, Brian Knopp, Wayne Laskoski, Dave Lichtel, Todd Linn, Craig Long, Chet Lutz, Jerry Marks, John Marks, Andy Miller, Bruce Petro, Steve Schu, Brad Sharrow, Tim Sharrow, Tom Sharrow, Tim Simons, Barry Sudol, Steve Tehansky, Dewey Townsend, Tim Vought, Scott Weaver, Gene Welkom, Shawn Weller, Rob Whitenight, Walt Williams, Jim Yeick, Steve Young

211 carries, averaging 8.3 yards per rushing attempt. Marks scored 26 rushing touchdowns and had four scoring receptions. He also had 374 return yards on kickoffs. Marks had ten 100-yard rushing games, including 292 yards against Line Mountain and 238 yards versus Tri-Valley. He also returned a kickoff 86 yards for a touchdown against St. Clair. Tim Sharrow topped the century mark three times, and Brad Sharrow had a 100-yard game. Quarterback Dewey Townsend completed 48 of 93 passes for 871 yards and eight touchdowns. Jim Yeick had 13 pass receptions for 296 yards and averaged 28.3 yards per kickoff return. John Cecco kicked 20 extra points for the season. Defensively, the Tigers received outstanding performances from Steve Tehansky, who had 79 tackles (51 solo), and Vince Butaitis, who contributed 66 tackles. The Tigers would finish the regular season at 9-2 and win the Mid Penn League Division Championship. Southern would face Bucktail in the Mid Penn League Championship Game. The Tigers would blowout the Bucks, 47-8, to win the Conference Championship and finish the season with an overall record of 10-2. Vince Butaitis, Greg Haladay, and Jerry Marks were named to the All-State Honorable Mention Team. Gary Wilson was added to the coaching staff.

1
9
8
5

1985 was another terrific season for Southern Columbia. Coach Jim Roth's Tigers won their first eight games on the year, including blowouts of Bloomsburg, Freeland, St. Clair, and Columbia Montour Vo-Tech. Southern dropped two of their last three games to finish the regular season at 9-2 but won the Mid Penn League Division Championship again. Running Back Jerry Marks would have a phenomenal sophomore season. He rushed for 1,509 yards. Marks carried the ball 277 times and had 195 receiving yards. He had nine 100-yard rushing games, with 212 yards versus Shenandoah and 251 yards against Lourdes Regional. Tim Sharrow rushed for 685 yards and averaged 7.5 yards per carry. Quarterback Scott Kerstetter had 43 completions on 89 pass attempts for 734 yards and four touchdowns. Receiver Jim Yeick caught 14 passes for 415 yards and had four touchdown receptions. He averaged 23 yards per catch. John Cecco kicked 17 extra points on the season. The Tigers had a staggering 525 yards of total offense in the game against Freeland. Jeff Crowl recovered five opponents' fumbles for the year. Vince Butaitis

## 1985 SEASON

| Opponent | Location | W/L | Score |
|---|---|---|---|
| Jim Thorpe | Home | W | 13-12 |
| Bloomsburg | Away | W | 40-20 |
| Central Columbia | Away | W | 6-3 |
| Freeland | Home | W | 34-8 |
| St. Clair | Home | W | 28-7 |
| Danville | Away | W | 34-21 |
| Columbia Montour Vo-Tech | Home | W | 40-21 |
| Shenandoah | Home | W | 20-11 |
| Tri-Valley | Away | L | 15-20 |
| Weatherly | Away | W | Forfeit |
| Lourdes Regional | Home | L | 19-20 |
| **Eastern Conference Division Championship Game** | | | |
| Lackawanna Trail | Away | W | 14-13 |
| **Eastern Conference Championship Game** | | | |
| Tri-Valley | Away | L | 16-27 |

COACHING STAFF: Jim Roth, Head Coach; Al Cihocki, Assistant Coach; Alan Lonoconus, Assistant Coach; Forest McLintock, Assistant Coach; Aaron Menapace, Assistant Coach; Andy Mills, Assistant Coach; Gary Wilson, Assistant Coach

ATHLETIC DIRECTOR: Roy Sanders

ROSTER: Jim Becker, Scott Bittner, Joe Broscious, Vince Butaitis, John Cecco, Jeff Crowl, Rob Deeter, Ron Deeter, Jeff Edmunds, John Eveland, Todd Feese, Shawn Freeman, Jeff Gutekunst, Todd Heath, Paul Hilliard, Joel Hornberger, Mike Johnston, Scott Kerstetter, Brian Knopp, Wayne Laskoski, Dave Lichtel, Todd Linn, Chet Lutz, Jerry Mack, Jerry Marks, Bruce Petro, Chris Rarig, Joe Raup, Mick Reiprich, Steve Schu, Tim Sharrow, Tom Sharrow, Steve Tehansky, Dave Trathen, Dave Travis, Tim Vought, Scott Weaver, Shawn Weller, Rob Whitenight, Jim Yeick, Steve Young recorded 101 tackles (66 solo). Steve Tehansky contributed 77 total tackles (57 solo). The Tigers braved treacherous conditions to travel for a Saturday playoff game against Lackawanna Trail, only to have the game postponed due to freezing rain. The game was rescheduled for the following Monday afternoon while classes were still in session. The Southern Columbia faculty and students listened to the broadcast of the game on the radio, which turned into a thriller. With the Tigers leading Lackawanna Trail 14-7 late in the game, the Lions scored a touchdown to pull within a point. Lackawanna Trail lined up for a two-point conversion rather than kick the extra point to tie the game and send it to overtime. Southern's defense broke up the conversion pass to preserve a thrilling 14-13 victory in the Eastern Conference Division Championship Game. Unfortunately, the Tigers' season ended with a disappointing 27-16 loss to Tri-Valley in the Eastern Conference Championship Game. Southern Columbia would finish the 1985 season with a 10-3 overall record. Vince Butaitis, Jerry Marks, and Steve Tehansky were selected for All-State Honorable Mention honors. Forest McLintock and Aaron Menapace joined the coaching staff.

1
9
8
6

1986 would be an up and down season for the Tigers. After winning their first two games versus Jim Thorpe and Bloomsburg, they would drop back-to-back contests to Central Columbia and Freeland. Southern would alternate wins and losses before posting two victories and a tie to finish the year. Highlights included lopsided wins over Columbia Montour Vo-Tech and Tri-Valley and a shutout victory against Cardinal Brennan. Running Back Jerry Marks had a remarkable junior year, rushing for 2,028 yards, becoming the first Tigers' player to rush for 2,000 yards in a season. He carried the ball 316 times, averaging 6.4 yards per rushing attempt. Marks had eight 100-yard rushing games. He had 250 yards versus Jim Thorpe, 270 yards against Bloomsburg, 322 yards versus Freeland, 200 yards against Danville, 286 yards versus Tr-Valley, and 250 yards against Cardinal Brennan. Marks also had eight pass receptions for 146 yards on the year. The Tigers would rush for 486 yards and seven touchdowns in the game versus Tr-Valley. Mark Meloy would contribute two 100-yard rushing games in 1986. Southern had a solid defensive year. The team recorded two safeties and had 42 quarterback sacks on the season. Steve Young had 72 tackles (42 solo). Southern would finish the regular season 6-4-1 and qualify for the District IV Playoffs but lost their opening contest 22-0 to South Williamsport. Jerry Marks was selected to the *Reading Eagle* newspaper Running Back of the Year. Southern Columbia would finish Coach Roth's second season with an overall record of 6-5-1.

## 1986 SEASON

| Opponent | Location | W/L | Score |
|---|---|---|---|
| Jim Thorpe | Away | W 2 | 6-7 |
| Bloomsburg | Home | W | 15-13 |
| Central Columbia | Home | L | 7-9 |
| Freeland | Away | L | 24-43 |
| Northwest Luzerne | Away | W | 27-6 |
| Danville | Home | L | 6-10 |
| Columbia Montour Vo-Tech | Away | W | 34-12 |
| Shenandoah | Away | L | 0-16 |
| Tri-Valley | Home | W | 52-34 |
| Cardinal Brennan | Home | W | 32-0 |
| Lourdes Regional | Away | T | 6-6 |

**Division IV Class A Semifinal Game**

South WilliamsportAwayL 0-22

COACHING STAFF: Jim Roth, Head Coach; Al Cihocki, Assistant Coach; Alan Lonoconus, Assistant Coach; Forest McLintock, Assistant Coach; Aaron Menapace, Assistant Coach; Andy Mills, Assistant Coach; Gary Wilson, Assistant Coach

ATHLETIC DIRECTOR: Roy Sanders

ROSTER: Shawn Amershek, Mike Becker, Scott Bittner, Rick Bobkoskie, Kenyon Brenish, Joe Broscious, Scott Cecco, Mark Crowl, Kenny Davenport, Merrill DeGreen, Dan Diehl, John Dyer, Todd Feese, Shawn Freeman, Todd Heath, Troy Heath, Clint Herr, Paul Hilliard, Mike Johnston, Nick Kent, Kollyn Kerstetter, Dave Krieger, Wayne Laskoski, Ed Levan, Dave Lichtel, Todd Linn, Rob Lorrey, Jerry Marks, Shawn McClintock, Mark Meloy, Sean Patrick, Dave Porzi, Chad Rarig, Chris Rarig, Joe Raup, Steve Schu, John Shultz, Dave Trathen, Dave Travis, Scott Weaver, Rob Whitenight, Steve Young

1
9
8
7

1987 would be another successful campaign for Coach Roth and the Tigers. Southern opened the year with back-to-back victories against Jim Thorpe and Bloomsburg. After a week three loss to Central Columbia, the Tigers won five consecutive games, including blowout victories over Freeland, Northwest Luzerne, Bishop Hafey, and Columbia Montour Vo-Tech. After dropping a game to Tri-Valley, Southern finished with lopsided wins against Cardinal Brennan and Lourdes Regional. The Tigers would finish the regular season at 9-2. Running Back Jerry Marks would finish his senior season with 1,769 rushing yards on 267 carries, averaging 6.6 yards per rushing attempt. He had ten 100-yard rushing games, including 318 yards, versus Danville. Mark Meloy would also have a 100-yard rushing game. Quarterback John Dyer threw for 435 yards and four touchdowns. Dave Trathen contributed eight pass receptions. The defensive unit received several dominant performances. Joe Raup had 109 tackles (79 solo) and four fumble recoveries. Dave Travis contributed 99 tackles (68 solo). Ed Levan had 70 tackles (44 solo). The Tigers clinched the Mid Penn League Division Championship. Southern would face

## 1987 SEASON

| Opponent | Location | W/L | Score |
|---|---|---|---|
| Jim Thorpe | Home | W | 38-6 |
| Bloomsburg | Away | W | 8-0 |
| Central Columbia | Away | L | 0-20 |
| Freeland | Home | W | 32-8 |
| Northwest Luzerne | Home | W | 32-8 |
| Danville | Away | W | 34-29 |
| Bishop Hafey | Home | W | 22-8 |
| Columbia Montour Vo-Tech | Home | W | 31-8 |
| Tri-Valley | Away | L | 0-33 |
| Cardinal Brennan | Away | W | 36-0 |
| Lourdes Regional | Home | W | 40-6 |
| **Eastern Conference Division Championship Game** | | | |
| Williams Valley | Away | W | 14-12 |
| **Eastern Conference Championship Game** | | | |
| Mahanoy Area | Away | L | 6-18 |

COACHING STAFF: Jim Roth, Head Coach; Al Cihocki, Assistant Coach; Alan Lonoconus, Assistant Coach; Forest McLintock, Assistant Coach; Aaron Menapace, Assistant Coach; Andy Mills, Assistant Coach; Gary Wilson, Assistant Coach

ATHLETIC DIRECTOR: Roy Sanders

ROSTER: Shawn Amershek, Mike Becker, Kenyon Brenish, Scott Cecco, Jay Clossen, Mark Crowl, Kenny Davenport, Merrill DeGreen, Russ Dunkleberger, John Dyer, Jason Feese, Todd Fleming, Mark Freeman, Troy Heath, Clint Herr, Paul Hilliard, Mike Johnston, Bret Keller, Kollyn Kerstetter, Mike Kerstetter, Dave Krieger, John Laubach, Ed Levan, Jerry Marks, Mike Matukaitus, Shawn McClintock, Mark Meloy, Greg Miller, Randy Payeskie, Dave Porzi, Steve Price, Chad Rarig, Joe Raup, Dave Trathen, Dave Travis

Williams Valley for the Eastern Conference Division Championship. The game would be played in extreme cold, with windchill temperatures near -40 degrees. Dave Trathen would score a 61-yard touchdown to tie the game. John Dyer's keeper for a two-point conversion would seal a hard-fought 14-12 victory and a berth in the Eastern Conference Championship Game. The Tigers would face Mahanoy Area and suffer a disappointing 18-6 loss in the Eastern Conference Final. Southern Columbia would finish 1987 with a 10-3 overall record. Jerry Marks earned the *Reading Eagle* newspaper Running Back of the Year and an All-State First Team selection.

1
9
8
8
When Jerry Marks finished his football career at Southern Columbia, he was the all-time leading rusher in Pennsylvania high school football history. Marks rushed for 7,075 yards on 1,071 carries, averaging 6.6 yards per attempt. He scored 93 rushing touchdowns. Marks had 37 100-yard rushing games, 23 150-yard games, eleven 200 yard games, and two

300-yard rushing games. He had 16 pass receptions for 574 yards and scored seven receiving touchdowns. Marks returned 21 kickoffs for 490 yards and had 27 punt returns for 347 yards. Marks converted eleven two-point conversions and scored 645 points in his high school career. In addition to his outstanding football career at Southern Columbia, Marks was a two-time PIAA State Wrestling Champion. He would attend Bloomsburg University, where he was a four-year player for the Huskies' football team and a member of the Bloomsburg wrestling program. Marks still holds Bloomsburg University records for rushing attempts in a single game (59), also a Pennsylvania State Athletic Conference record, and net yards gained in a game (300). After spending several years as an assistant at Berwick High School, Jerry Marks returned to his alma mater to become the Tigers' head wrestling coach. He guided Southern wrestlers to numerous PIAA State medals, including two champions, a team championship at the PIAA Individual Wrestling Tournament and three silver medals in the PIAA Team Wrestling Championships. Marks has been named PIAA, *PA Wrestling,* and District IV Coach of the Year. Marks' number 21 was retired by the Southern Columbia Tigers.

1988 would be an outstanding season for Southern Columbia. The Tigers started the year with blowout wins against Jim Thorpe and Bloomsburg. After a close loss to Central Columbia in week three, Southern would win seven of their final eight games, including shutout victories over Northwest Luzerne, Bishop Hafey, and Lourdes Regional. Quarterback John Dyer would throw for four touchdown passes versus Columbia Montour Vo-Tech. He had 39 completions on 88 attempts for 772 passing yards. Dyer would average 19.7 yards per completion on the season. The Tigers had a three-headed monster in the running game. Mark Crowl had 147 carries and rushed 711 yards, with two 100-yard rushing games. He also chipped in with 13 receptions for 221 receiving yards. Mark Meloy carried the ball 115 times for 674 rushing yards, averaging 5.9 yards per attempt. Meloy returned a kickoff 85 yards for a touchdown against Bishop Hafey. Chad Rarig rushed for 663 yards, averaging 7.3 yards per carry, and had a 100-yard rushing game. The Tigers offense posted an impressive 475 yards rushing in a victory over Cardinal Brennan. Kenyon Brenish had nine receptions for 205 yards on the year. Jason Sudol scored 44 points on three field goals and 35 extra points. Southern had an impressive defensive unit led by Ed Levan's eleven quarterback sacks and three forced fumbles and Troy Heath's 105 tackles (78 solo). The Tigers' defense forced six fumbles in a lopsided win over Freeland. Coach Roth's team would finish the regular season at 9-2 and won the Mid Penn League Division Championship

## 1988 SEASON

| Opponent | Location | W/L | Score |
|---|---|---|---|
| Jim Thorpe | Away | W | 51-7 |
| Bloomsburg | Home | W | 34-12 |
| Central Columbia | Home | L | 6-14 |
| Freeland | Away | W | 38-7 |
| Northwest Luzerne | Away | W | 50-0 |
| Danville | Home | L | 6-16 |
| Bishop Hafey | Away | W | 30-0 |
| Columbia Montour Vo-Tech | Away | W | 35-12 |
| Tri-Valley | Home | W | 21-8 |
| Cardinal Brennan | Home | W | 34-6 |
| Lourdes Regional | Away | W | 23-0 |
| **Eastern Conference Division Championship Game** | | | |
| Old Forge | Away | W | 10-0 |
| **Eastern Conference Championship Game** | | | |
| Tri-Valley | Away | W | 34-7 |

COACHING STAFF: Jim Roth, Head Coach; Al Cihocki, Assistant Coach; Alan Lonoconus, Assistant Coach; Forest McLintock, Assistant Coach; Aaron Menapace, Assistant Coach; Andy Mills, Assistant Coach; Gary Wilson, Assistant Coach

ATHLETIC DIRECTOR: Roy Sanders

ROSTER: Mike Becker, Matt Bloom. Kenyon Brenish, Rick Cecco, Scott Cecco, Jay Clossen, Mark Crowl, Matt Crowl, Kenny Davenport, Merrill DeGreen, Russ Dunkleberger, John Dyer, Brad Feese, Jason Feese, Todd Fleming, Marc Freeman, Troy Heath, Clint Herr, Bret Keller, Rick Kent, Mike Kerstetter, John Laubach, Ed Levan, Rob Lorrey, Leroy Lunger, Shawn McClintock, Mark Meloy, Greg Miller, Rob Oliva, Randy Payeskie, Allen Pickering, Dave Porzi, Chad Rarig, Shane Reamer, Rob Shoup, Harry Slotterback, Jason Sudol, Bill Swank

again. In the Eastern Conference Division Championship Game, the Tigers faced Old Forge. Southern held the Blue Devils scoreless in a 10-0 victory to earn a championship game rematch with Tri-Valley in a dominant defensive performance. The defense again flexed their muscles and held the Bulldogs to a single score, and the offense steamrolled Tri-Valley for a lopsided 34-7 win and the 1988 Eastern Conference Championship. Ed Levan and Troy Heath were named to the All-State Second Team, and Scott Cecco earned All-State Honorable Mention honors.

1
9
8
9
Terry Sharrow became Southern Columbia's third athletic director in 1989. A native of Catawissa, Sharrow was a member of the first graduating class at the newly formed Southern Columbia School District in 1963. He was elected class president and actively unified a segmented student body from three former high schools. Sharrow was one of two students to select a class ring proclaiming Southern Columbia as his new school. He played

basketball and baseball for the Tigers and scored the first points in basketball on Southern Columbia's home floor. He was also the Most Valuable Player of the baseball team. Sharrow was selected as the president of the Varsity Club, played clarinet in the high school band, served on the yearbook and school newspaper staffs, was a member of the drama club, and was elected the school's first prom king. He attended Bloomsburg University, earning a B.S. in Business Education in 1967 and a Master of Education in 1970. He was a member of the Huskies' State Championship baseball team while at Bloomsburg. Sharrow began his teaching career at Manheim Central High School in 1967. He returned to his alma mater in 1969, where he would remain for 44 years. During his time at Southern Columbia, he would serve as an assistant football coach and coach baseball and basketball. Sharrow was a PIAA official in baseball and basketball. He would serve as Southern's Athletic Director for 25 years. Sharrow was a registered Athletic Administrator, a member of the Pennsylvania Athletic Directors Association and the National Interscholastic Athletic Administration Association. He was inducted into the Pennsylvania Sports Hall of Fame. Sharrow served as Chairman of the Business Education Department at Southern Columbia and helped establish the school's FBLA Club and cooperative education program. Always active in the community, Sharrow coached midget football and Little League baseball, served as a Scoutmaster for the Cub Scouts and Boy Scouts, and was treasurer for the Borough of Catawissa. Sadly, Terry Sharrow passed away on January 4, 2021

Coach Jim Roth's Tigers would post a one-loss regular season in 1989. After winning two of their first three contests, Southern would win their remaining eight regular-season games to finish the year at 10-1 and claim the Mid Penn League Division Championship. The Tigers posted blowout victories over Jim Thorpe, Bloomsburg, Northwest Luzerne, Danville, Bishop Hafey, Columbia Montour Vo-Tech, and Lourdes Regional. Southern's offense featured a devastating running attack. Chad Rarig rushed for 1,092 yards on 183 carries, and he had five 100-yards rushing games on the season. Brad Feese carried the ball 113 times for 695 yards and had one 100-yard game. Marc Freeman posted 565 yards on 116 carries. Dave Michaels contributed a 100-yard rushing game. Shane Reamer had 41 pass completions for 799 yards, and ten touchdown passes. Greg Miller caught 17 passes for 315 yards and four touchdowns, including six receptions in the victory over Northwest Luzerne. Jason Sudol scored 47 points on two field goals and 41 extra points. The Tigers' defense posted 19 fumble recoveries and returned four interceptions for touchdowns on the season, including two pick-sixes versus Bloomsburg. Greg Miller had seven

## 1989 SEASON

| Opponent | Location | W/L | Score |
|---|---|---|---|
| Jim Thorpe | Home | W | 27-0 |
| Bloomsburg | Away | W | 46-16 |
| Central Columbia | Away | L | 7-23 |
| Freeland | Home | W | 34-20 |
| Northwest Luzerne | Home | W | 41-18 |
| Danville | Away | W | 42-20 |
| Bishop Hafey | Home | W | 49-6 |
| Columbia Montour Vo-Tech | Home | W | 38-0 |
| Tri-Valley | Away | W | 25-13 |
| Cardinal Brennan | Away | W | 17-6 |
| Lourdes Regional | Away | W | 29-6 |
| **PIAA Class A Eastern Conference Semifinal Game** | | | |
| Pottsville Nativity | Away | L | 20-26 (Overtime-Shootout) |

COACHING STAFF: Jim Roth, Head Coach; Al Cihocki, Assistant Coach; Alan Lonoconus, Assistant Coach; Andy Mills, Assistant Coach; Curt Stellfox, Assistant Coach; Gary Wilson, Assistant Coach

ATHLETIC DIRECTOR: Terry Sharrow

ROSTER: Tim Amershek, Tom Amershek, James Anoia, Matt Bloom, Jason Brokenshire, Rick Cecco, Jay Clossen, Matt Crowl, Keith Danilowicz, Russ Dunkleberger, Brad Feese, Jason Feese, Marc Freeman, Matt Girardi, Bret Keller, Mike Kerstetter, Brian Knoebel, Sean Linn, Jamie Mack, Dave Michaels, Greg Michaels, Rob Oliva, Randy Payeskie, Allen Pickering, Chad Rarig, Rick Raup, Shane Reamer, Rob Shoup, Stan Strzempek, Jason Sudol, Bill Swank, Jeremy Tomaschik, Derek White

interceptions on the year. Brad Feese picked off six passes and returned two for touchdowns. Jeremy Tomaschik returned an interception 82 yards for a touchdown against Bloomsburg. Jason Feese forced three fumbles on the season. Curt Stellfox joined the coaching staff. The Tigers were heavy favorites entering their playoff game against Pottsville Nativity. Southern ran 100 offensive plays in the game and rushed for a staggering 442 yards. However, Pottstown Nativity would return a kickoff 91 yards for a touchdown and return two punts 74 and 76 yards for scores. The game would end tied at 20-20. The teams would then play a scoreless overtime period and move to a tie-breaking shootout, where each team would take possession at the opposition's 10-yard line. The Tigers were held scoreless on their first series. Pottsville Nativity would score from the one-yard line on the final play of their first possession to upset Southern Columbia 26-20 in the Eastern Conference Semifinal Game. Southern would finish 1989 with an overall record of 10-2.

# CHAPTER 5

# THE 1990s
## (ENTERING THE GOLDEN ERA)

In 1990, the Tigers would post their first-ever undefeated regular season. The only close game Southern would play was a 21-20 victory over Central Columbia. The Tigers outscored their opponents 395-116, averaging 35.9 points scored per game. Southern's offense rushed for 46 touchdowns on the season. Brad Feese rushed for 1,118 yards on 172 carries and had five 100-yard rushing games. He also had 12 receptions for 176 yards. Shane Reamer had 46 completions on 121 attempts for 703, and 10 touchdown passes. Greg Miller caught 17 passes for 310 yards and five touchdown receptions. Bill Swank contributed ten receptions and had three receiving touchdowns. Jason Sudol scored 54 points, kicking four field goals and converting 42 extra points. He kicked two field goals in the win over Central Columbia. Southern's stout defense gave up an average of only 10.5 points per contest. The team had 23 interceptions and returned four fumbles for touchdowns during the season. Matt Bloom had 86 tackles (51 solo), including 19 stops (11 solo) in the victory over Bloomsburg. Bill Swank returned two interceptions for touchdowns on the year. Keith Danilowicz returned two fumbles for touchdowns against Columbia Montour Vo-Tech. Rick Cecco returned a blocked punt for a score versus Northwest Luzerne. Greg Miller would finish his career at Southern Columbia with 15 interceptions, and Ed Levan would record 17 career sacks. Southern earned another Mid Penn League Division Championship, finishing the regular season at 11-0. The Tigers' squared off against Muncy in the District IV Semifinal Game. Southern pounded the Indians in a 41-19 victory to move on to the District IV Final. The Tigers faced Canton, but the offense struggled against the Warriors,

## 1990 SEASON

| Opponent | Location | W/L | Score |
|---|---|---|---|
| Jim Thorpe | Away | W | 42-0 |
| Bloomsburg | Home | W | 44-8 |
| Central Columbia | Home | W | 21-20 |
| Freeland | Away | W | 35-14 |
| Northwest Luzerne | Away | W | 47-6 |
| Danville | Home | W | 27-8 |
| Bishop Hafey | Away | W | 42-14 |
| Columbia Montour Vo-Tech | Away | W | 41-12 |
| Tri-Valley | Home | W | 30-20 |
| Cardinal Brennan | Home | W | 40-8 |
| Lourdes Regional | Away | W | 26-6 |
| **District IV Class A Semifinal Game** | | | |
| Muncy | Home | W | 41-19 |
| **District IV Class A Championship Game** | | | |
| Canton | Away | L | 6-14 |

COACHING STAFF: Jim Roth, Head Coach; Al Cihocki, Assistant Coach; Alan Lonoconus, Assistant Coach; Andy Mills, Assistant Coach; Curt Stellfox, Assistant Coach; Gary Wilson, Assistant Coach

ATHLETIC DIRECTOR: Terry Sharrow

ROSTER: Tim Amershek, Tom Amershek, James Anoia, Ryan Billig, Mike Blass, Matt Bloom, Jason Brokenshire, Lewis Carl, Rick Cecco, Matt Crowl, Keith Danilowicz, Brad Feese, Matt Girardi, Jason Hauck, Jeff Jeffrey, Brian Knoebel, Sean Linn, Tom Litwin, Jamie Mack, Dave Michaels, Greg Miller, Ryan Patrick, Layne Rarig, Rick Raup, Shane Reamer, Jason Roadarmel, Chris Schock, Rob Shoup, Dan Shroyer, Dave Strzempek, Stan Strzempek, Jason Sudol, Corey Surak, Bill Swank, Jeremy Tomaschick, Derek White, Dan Yost, Scott Zeigler

managing only six points. The defense played admirably, but Southern fell to Canton 14-6, bringing the 1990 season to a disappointing end. The Tigers would finish with an overall record of 12-1. James Anoia and Dave Michaels were All-State selections. Head Coach Jim Roth would be named *Reading Eagle* newspaper Coach of the Year.

1
9
9
1
The 1991 Southern Columbia Tigers would extend their regular-season winning streak to 16 games. The only blemish in the 1991 regular season campaign was a 14-14 tie versus Danville in week six. The Tigers posted lopsided wins over Jim Thorpe, Bloomsburg, Freeland, Northwest Luzerne, Bishop Hafey, Columbia Montour Vo-Tech, and Lourdes Regional. Southern's offense relied heavily on their stout running game. The Tigers rushed for 3,736 yards, averaging 6.3 yards per carry and scoring 46 rushing touchdowns. Southern had 4,825 yards of total offense and scored 384 points, and converted 18 two-point conversions. The team scored a total of

67 touchdowns and 456 points. The Tigers averaged 12.6 yards per rushing attempt versus Bloomsburg and 11.1 yards per offensive play against Northwest Luzerne. The offense featured a multi-running back attack. Jason Brokenshire ran for 1,031 yards on 154 carries and had four 100-yard games. He also caught eight passes for 151 yards. Dave Michaels rushed for 1,006 yards on 153 carries and had four 100-yard rushing games. He had 14 receptions for 172 yards. Michaels returned a punt for a touchdown and converted four two-point conversions on the year. Mike Zimmerman chipped in with a 100-yard rushing game. Jeremy Tomaschick completed 60 passes on 127 attempts for 1,035 yards and 16 touchdowns. He completed 90 percent of his passes in the win over Columbia Montour Vo-Tech. Ryan Patrick had 21 receptions for 469 yards and seven touchdowns. He had three scoring catches against Northwest Luzerne. David Noll kicked 18 extra points for the season. Matt Bloom had 74 tackles

## 1991 SEASON

| Opponent | Location | W/L | Score |
|---|---|---|---|
| Jim Thorpe | Home | W | 33-12 |
| Bloomsburg | Away | W | 45-6 |
| Central Columbia | Away | W | 30-23 |
| Freeland | Home | W | 46-14 |
| Northwest Luzerne | Home | W | 43-0 |
| Danville | Away | T | 14-14 |
| Bishop Hafey | Home | W | 60-13 |
| Columbia Montour Vo-Tech | Home | W | 32-6 |
| Tri-Valley | Away | W | 22-11 |
| Cardinal Brennan | Away | W | 20-7 |
| Lourdes Regional | Home | W | 37-6 |
| **District IV Class A Semifinal Game** | | | |
| Sayre | Home | W | 34-18 |
| **District IV Class A Championship Game** | | | |
| Canton | Away | W | 32-14 |
| **PIAA Class A Eastern Championship Game** | | | |
| Schuylkill Haven | Neutral | L | 8-29 |

COACHING STAFF: Jim Roth, Head Coach; Al Cihocki, Assistant Coach; Alan Lonoconus, Assistant Coach; Andy Mills, Assistant Coach; Curt Stellfox, Assistant Coach; Gary Wilson, Assistant Coach

ATHLETIC DIRECTOR: Director: Terry Sharrow

ROSTER: Tim Amershek, Tom Amershek, James Anoia, Ryan Billig, Matt Bloom, Joe Bobkoskie, Chris Bressi, Patrick Bressi, Jason Brokenshire, Lewis Carl, Jeff Compton, Matt Crowl, Jason DeGreen, Jon Fetterman, Harvey Fetterolf, Matt Girardi, Tony Helwig, Rick Hornberger, Jeff Jeffrey, Bobby Jones, Tom Keefer, Rob Kingston, Jason Kleman, Jeremy Linn, Jamie Mack, John Mayernick, Dave Michaels, David Noll, Ryan Patrick, Layne Rarig, Butch Romanoski, Chris Schock, Paul Scisly, Dan Shroyer, Shawn Snyder, Stan Strzempek, Corey Surak, John Todd, Jeremy Tomaschick, Randy Toth, Dave Wojtowicz, Dan Yost, Scott Zeigler, Mike Zimmerman

(46 solo) and would end his career at Southern Columbia with 230 stops (153 solo). Matt Girardi would end his high school career with 17 quarterback sacks. The Tigers would finish the regular season at 10-0-1. The Tigers faced Sayre in the District IV Playoffs. Southern dominated the Redskins and won their opening-round game 34-18. In the District IV Final, the Tigers earned a rematch from the previous postseason against Canton. This time, the result was different. Southern rushed for 199 yards, and Dave Michaels scored four two-point conversions. The Tigers' defense dominated the Warriors, holding them to 21 rushing yards on 20 carries. Southern Columbia would win the game 32-14 to earn their first District IV Championship and advance to their first PIAA State Playoff Game. In the PIAA Class A Eastern Championship Game, Southern faced Schuylkill Haven. The Tigers offense only managed eight points against the Hurricanes and their season came to a disappointing end with a 29-8 loss to the eventual state champions. Southern Columbia finished 1991 with a 12-1-1. James Anoia and Dave Michaels were All-State selections.

1  1992 would be another successful season for Coach Roth's Tigers. They
9  opened the year with easy victories over Wyalusing and Bloomsburg.
9  However, a week three home loss to Central Columbia was the first time
2  the Tigers were shutout since 1987. After the stunning loss to the Blue
Jays, Southern would rebound to run the table and win their remaining eight games, including lopsided victories over Danville, Muncy, Loyalsock, North Penn, South Williamsport, and Hughesville. In the win over Loyalsock, quarterback Jeremy Tomaschik set team records for completions (16) and passing yards (365) in a game. Bobby Jones had two touchdown receptions on the same night, breaking the team record for scoring catches (9) in a season. The offense racked up 599 yards of total offense in the blowout of the Lancers. Southern won the Mid Penn Conference Championship and qualified for the District IV Playoffs with their win over Hughesville in the regular-season finale. In the District IV Class A Semifinal Game, the Tigers again hosted South Williamsport in a rematch from week ten. However, this time the game was much more competitive. The contest was a defensive struggle that remained scoreless after the first quarter. Dave Michaels scored on a 10-yard run to open the scoring in the second, but South Williamsport led 7-6 at the half after their 14-yard scoring run. Jeremy Tomaschik rushed for a 2-yard touchdown, and Michaels ran for a two-point conversion in the third quarter to give the Tigers a 14-7 lead. The Southern defense got key plays on a Dave Wojtowiscz interception, a sack from Lewis Carl, and a timely tackle for a loss by Harvey Fetterolf to stop

a Mountaineer threat to make the lead hold up, and the Tigers earned a hard-fought 14-7 victory in their playoff opener. The Tigers traveled to Canton for the District IV Class A Championship Game. For the second consecutive week, Southern found themselves in a defensive dogfight. The Tigers' defense put in a monumental effort, holding the Warriors to 64 total yards and only four first downs for the game. They got interceptions from Corey Surak and Rick Hornberger. Mike Zimmerman scored on a 20-yard touchdown run in the second quarter, and Southern led 6-0 at halftime. Canton recovered a Tiger fumble at the Southern 3-yard line and scored to take a 7-6 lead in the third. On the game's final drive, trailing by one, the Tiger offense got themselves in field goal range. Coach Roth sent kicker Justin Barnes onto the field with three seconds remaining in the game. The snap was high, but holder Jon Fetterman fielded it, got the ball in position, and Barnes' kick split the uprights with no time

## 1992 SEASON

| Opponent | Location | W/L | Score |
|---|---|---|---|
| Wyalusing | Away | W | 31-12 |
| Bloomsburg | Home | W | 53-24 |
| Central Columbia | Home | L | 0-14 |
| Montgomery | Away | W | 43-34 |
| Bucktail | Away | W | 39-27 |
| Danville | Home | W | 29-0 |
| Muncy | Away | W | 41-12 |
| Loyalsock | Away | W | 66-23 |
| North Penn | Home | W | 49-13 |
| South Williamsport | Home | W | 44-6 |
| Hughesville | Away | W | 39-13 |
| **District IV Class A Semifinal Game** | | | |
| South Williamsport | Home | W | 14-7 |
| **District IV Class A Championship Game** | | | |
| Canton | Away | W | 9-7 |
| **PIAA Class A Semifinal Game** | | | |
| Scotland | Neutral | L | 8-22 |

COACHING STAFF: Jim Roth Head Coach; Al Cihocki, Assistant Coach; Alan Lonoconus, Assistant Coach; Andy Mills, Assistant Coach; Curt Stellfox, Assistant Coach; Gary Wilson, Assistant Coach

ATHLETIC DIRECTOR: Terry Sharrow

ROSTER: Eric Adams, Justin Barnes, Matt Bell, Ryan Billig, Brett Bloom, Joe Bobkoskie, Steve Bubnis, Lewis Carl, Jeff Compton, Jon Fetterman, Harvey Fetterolf, Tony Helwig, Jeremy Hoagland, Rick Hornberger, Bobby Jones, Jason Kleman, Jon Leisenring, Adam Levan, Jeremy Linn, John Mayernick, Dave Michaels, Jared Miller, Mike Moncavage, Todd Nolan, Layne Rarig, Randy Rarig, Rob Reese, Nate Roadarmel, Butch Romanoski, Todd Rusn, Chris Schock, Paul Scisly, Shawn Snyder, Steve Snyder, Carl Sokoloski, Jason Stanchock, Corey Surak, John Todd, Jeremy Tomaschik, Randy Toth, Tom Weaver, Gary Wilson, Dave Wojtowicz, Charlie Yost, Scott Zeigler, Mike Zimmerman remaining for a thrilling 9-6 playoff victory. The Tigers' season would come to a disappointing end in the PIAA Class A Semifinal Game versus Scotland. The defense had an interception, fumble recovery, and a forced intentional grounding in the endzone for a safety, but Scotland capitalized on several Tiger mistakes and advanced with a 22-8 win. Mike Zimmerman rushed for 1,005 yards and scored 12 touchdowns. Dave Michaels had 915 yards rushing and totaled 14 scores. Michaels also passed 2,000 career rushing yards during the season. Nate Roadarmel chipped in with eight touchdowns on the year. Jeremy Tomaschik passed for more than 1,000 yards. Bobby Jones had 626 receiving yards, and a team-record 11 touchdown catches. The 1992 Tigers finished the season with an overall record of 12-2.

1
9
9
3
Although 1993 would see the Tigers continue their success, it would result in one of the most frustrating and disappointing endings in recent memory. Southern would reel off nine consecutive victories, winning each convincingly. The Tigers would again rely on their potent ground attack, as they rushed for more than 300 yards as a team in four games. Butch Romanoski would total six 100-yard rushing games on the year, and Nate Roadarmel (twice) and Mike Zimmerman would also top the century mark during the season. Jon Fetterman would provide steady leadership at quarterback, contributing to the offense on the ground and through the air. The defense pitched two shutouts and gave up seven or fewer points in seven games. The Tigers defensive unit had a terrific game in a shutout win versus Montgomery. They had six sacks (two by Layne Rarig), an interception, and two fumble recoveries. The week seven victory over Muncy would prove to be memorable, as it was the 100th career win for head coach Jim Roth. During the week nine victory over North Penn, two school records were broken. Mike Zimmerman broke Jerry Marks' record for career punt return yardage with 562, and Harvey Fetterolf set a new record with his 231st career tackle. However, a loss in week ten to South Williamsport would alter the Tigers' playoff future. Losing a hard-fought 17-14 game, a controversial unsportsmanlike conduct penalty late in the fourth quarter allowed the Mounties to maintain possession and run down the clock. Because District IV could only have one representative in the PIAA State Playoffs, South Williamsport held an advantage over the Tigers with their victory. Because there were two routes to the PIAA tournament, by either the District IV or Eastern Conference Playoffs, Southern now had to hope for a Mountaineers loss in the Eastern Conference Tournament.

The Tigers began postseason play in the District IV Class A Semifinal game at home versus Loyalsock. Butch Romanoski opened the scoring with a one-yard touchdown run in the first quarter. Second-quarter touchdown runs by Nate Roadarmel, and Romanoski pushed the Tigers' lead to 21-0 at halftime. Romanoski would score his third touchdown of the game on a 4-yard run in the third quarter, and Southern would win their playoff opener 27-6 over the Lancers. The Tigers would face Bloomsburg at Tiger Stadium in the District IV Class A Championship Game. Quarterback Jon Fetterman would miss the game due to a shoulder injury, but backup Brad Osevala stepped in, and the Southern offense didn't miss a beat. Nate Roadarmel scored a pair of first-quarter touchdowns on an 18-yard run and a 34-yard pass from Osevala for a quick lead. Butch Romanoski and Mike Zimmerman each had scoring runs in the second to make the score 27-0. However, Bloomsburg connected on two scoring passes and cut the lead to 27-14 at the half. The defense recorded two interceptions

## 1993 SEASON

| Opponent | Location | W/L | Score |
|---|---|---|---|
| Warrior Run | Away | W 4 | 0-13 |
| Bloomsburg | Away | W | 35-13 |
| Central Columbia | Away | W | 33-3 |
| Montgomery | Home | W | 40-0 |
| Bucktail | Home | W | 33-7 |
| Danville | Away | W | 34-7 |
| Muncy | Home | W | 45-7 |
| Loyalsock | Home | W | 28-0 |
| North Penn | Away | W | 47-20 |
| South Williamsport | Away | L | 14-17 |
| Hughesville | Home | W | 36-17 |
| **District IV Class A Semifinal Game** | | | |
| Loyalsock | Home | W | 27-6 |
| **District IV Class A Championship Game** | | | |
| Bloomsburg | Home | W | 42-14 |

COACHING STAFF: Jim Roth, Head Coach; Vince Butaitis, Assistant Coach; Al Cihocki, Assistant Coach; Jerry Marks, Assistant Coach; Aaron Menapace, Assistant Coach; Andy Mills, Assistant Coach; Curt Stellfox, Assistant Coach; Gary Wilson, Assistant Coach

ATHLETIC DIRECTOR: Terry Sharrow

ROSTER: Eric Adams, Justin Barnes, Matt Baylor, Matt Bell, Joe Bobkoskie, Larry Boyer, Brett Bloom, Dave Danilowicz, Jon Fetterman, Mike Fetterman, Harvey Fetterolf, Chris Grassley, Andy Helwig, Tony Helwig, Gary Hine, Jeremy Hoagland, Rick Hornberger, Rod Kingston, Jason Kleman, Jon Leisenring, Ben Martin, Tim Martin, Mike Mattivi, John Mayernick, Steve Mayernick, Bill Miller, Jared Miller, Mike Moncavage, Todd Nolan, Brad Osevala, Layne Rarig, Randy Rarig, Rob Reese, Nate Roadarmel, Butch Romanoski, Todd Rush, Mark Scisly, Paul Scisly, Todd Sharrow, Matt Shingara, Shawn Snyder, Adam Strzempek, John Todd, Randy Toth, Rob Visnosky, Pat Wiehe, Dave Wojtowicz, Charlie Yost, Mike Zimmerman and shut down the Panthers the rest of the way. Southern got two scoring runs from Zimmerman in the second half and earned another District IV Title with a 42-14 victory. However, the Tigers had to wait until the next day, when South Williamsport played in the Eastern Conference Championship Game, to learn their playoff fate. When South Williamsport won their championship game, Southern's season came to an abrupt and frustrating end. Most disappointing was that the Tigers did not have a chance for a rematch with South Williamsport, as the Tigers had given them in 1992, to determine the District IV representative in the PIAA playoffs. Butch Romanoski would top 1,000 yards for the season. He rushed for 1,038 yards and scored 17 touchdowns. Nate Roadarmel had 881 rushing yards and scored 17 touchdowns. He was the team's leading receiver with 423 yards and four touchdown receptions. Mike Zimmerman contributed 698 yards on the ground and scored 13 touchdowns. Jon Fetterman threw for 847 yards and seven scores. Rick Hornberger, Randy Toth, and Dave Wojtowicz led the team with three interceptions. Toth was the team leader in fumble recoveries with two. Harvey Fetterolf had 100 tackles (59 solo). His 267 career tackles were a school record. Layne Rarig registered 5.5 sacks. Rarig and Justin Barnes were All-State selections. The Tigers finished 1993 at 12-1, but the season certainly had a feeling of what might have been.

1
9
9
4

Since they began playing high school football in the early 1960s, the Southern Columbia Tigers had experienced their share of disappointment and heartbreak. From a 26-game losing streak and having the program nearly dropped by the administration to the missed opportunities in recent seasons, the 1994 Tigers were about to embark on a remarkable journey that would exorcize their demons and see them reach the promised land. The season would start with a week one contest at Line Mountain. The pre-season football camps featuring 7-on-7 drills were about to pay dividends for the Tigers' defense as they faced Line Mountain's no-huddle offense. By using five and six receivers in spread formations, the Eagles looked to test the Southern secondary. The young Tigers were more than ready as they kept the Line Mountain offense in check for most of the game. Nate Roadarmel scored the first points of the season on a 2-yard touchdown run in the opening period. Butch Romanoski pushed the lead to 14-0 on a 3-yard run in the second quarter. Line Mountain cut the lead on a 26-yard touchdown pass before the half, and Southern led 14-6 at the break. Roadarmel and Todd Sharrow scored on touchdown runs of 6 and 30 yards to put the game out of reach for the Eagles. Roadarmel and Joe Murphy each scored on 2-yard runs in the fourth.

Line Mountain added two late scoring passes to make the final score 42-19. Southern rushed for 402 yards for the game. Romanoski ran for 194 yards and a touchdown. Roadarmel had 88 yards and three scoring runs. Ricco Rosini chipped in with 49 rushing yards. Sharrow had 31 yards on the ground and a touchdown, and Murphy contributed 22 yards and a score.

Week two was the home opener at Tiger Stadium versus the Bloomsburg Panthers. Receiver Ardie Kissinger, playing for the Tigers after transferring from Bloomsburg, would immediately haunt his former teammates. On the first play of the game, Kissinger hauled in a 52-yard pass from Brad Osevala, taking the ball to the Panthers' 7-yard line, setting up Butch Romanoski's 2-yard touchdown plunge. Kissinger would torment his former team again later in the game, forcing a Bloomsburg fumble in the third quarter. The Tigers would score on their first four possessions, getting additional touchdowns on a one-yard run from Ricco Rosini, a 46-yard scamper from Nate Roadarmel, and a 26-yard run from Romanoski to take a 28-0 lead in the first quarter. Todd Sharrow scored on runs of 6 and 33 yards in the second, and Southern led 42-0 at halftime. Dave Danilowicz scored on a 17-yard run in the third quarter. Bloomsburg got a touchdown early in the fourth, and Joe Murphy tacked on a 70-yard scoring run to make the final 54-8. Southern rushed for 351 yards and had 470 yards of total offense. Murphy led the way with 96 rushing yards and a touchdown. Sharrow had 81 yards on the ground and a score. Roadarmel had 77 yards and two scores, while Romanoski tacked on 48 yards and a touchdown. Danilowicz rushed for 28 yards and a score. The defense held Bloomsburg to 68 yards rushing and only 62 through the air. The unit had an interception and a fumble recovery.

The offense continued to roll in a home game against Troy. Nate Roadarmel scored two first-quarter touchdowns on a 61-yard run and a 42-yard pass from Brad Osevala. Osevala connected with Ardie Kissinger on an 11-yard scoring pass, and Butch Romanoski had a six-yard touchdown run to put the game away by halftime. Troy scored on a fumble recovery in the third. Ricco Rosini scored on a 28-yard run, and Troy got a late touchdown run the make the final score 40-12. Southern rushed for 395 yards as a team. Roadarmel led the way with 75 yards rushing and a score. He also had 42 yards receiving and a touchdown reception. Rosini had 111 yards and a score. Romanoski chipped in 71 yards rushing and a touchdown. Osevala threw for 69 yards and two scores, and Kissinger had 30 yards receiving and a touchdown catch.

Southern traveled to Lewisburg for a matchup with the Green Dragons. The Tigers would dominate on both sides of the ball in a 46-6 blowout victory.

Southern ran for 334 yards and had 124 more through the air. The defense had three interceptions and bottled up the Green Dragon offense. Nate Roadarmel and Butch Romanoski each had touchdown runs of 5 and 2 yards in the first quarter. Romanoski tacked on scoring runs of 4 and 8 yards in the second. The Tigers led 26-6 at the break. Southern got a 51-yard touchdown run from Roadarmel, a 25-yard scoring pass from Brad Osevala to Ardie Kissinger, and Joe Murphy's 10-yard touchdown burst to blow the game open in the third quarter. Romanoski rushed for 93 yards and had three touchdowns. Roadarmel had 71 yards on the ground and two scores. Osevala passed for 124 yards and a touchdown, and Kissinger had 80 receiving yards and a touchdown catch.

Southern got off to an uncharacteristically slow start in a home game against Warrior Run. The game was scoreless after a quarter. Butch Romanoski scored on a 12-yard run in the second for a 7-0 halftime lead. However, Warrior Run ran the second-half kickoff back for a touchdown to cut the lead to 7-6. After that, the Tigers' offense began to roll. Romanoski scored on a 4-yard run. Justin Barnes' interception set up Brad Osevala's 14-yard keeper, and Romanoski scored again on a one-yard plunge to push the lead to 27-6. Joe Murphy added a fourth-quarter touchdown run to make the final 34-6. Southern continued to rack up 300-yard rushing games with 342 against Warrior Run. Romanoski had a big night with 139 yards and three scores. Murphy added 64 yards rushing and a touchdown.

A week six trip to Hughesville almost spilled ink on the masterpiece, as Southern found themselves in a dogfight with the upstart Spartans. Hughesville matched the Tigers blow for blow in a game that would go down to the final seconds. The Spartans scored first on an 11-yard run, and for the first time in 1994, the Tigers trailed in a game. Todd Sharrow had a one-yard touchdown run, and Southern converted a two-point conversion to lead 8-7 after the first. Sharrow scored again in the second on a 3-yard run, but Hughesville tied the game at 14-14 on a 20-yard pass play. After a scoreless third, Brad Osevala scored on a one-yard plunge to put Southern ahead 20-14. However, Hughesville went on a 92-yard drive, scoring on a 10-yard run to take a 21-20 lead with 5:25 left to play. With the ball on the Spartans' 40-yard line and 1:32 left on the clock, Romanoski took a pitch, stopped, and fired a pass down the sideline. With a defender draped all over him, Ardie Kissinger made a spectacular catch and was forced out of bounds at the Hughesville 6-yard line. Romanoski finished off the drive with a 2-yard touchdown run with 38 seconds left to play to put the Tigers up 26-21. Justin Barnes intercepted a fourth-down pass to seal the Tigers' thrilling come-from-behind victory on Hughesville's final drive.

Sharrow had a game-high 146 yards rushing and two touchdowns. Romanoski ran for 97 yards and a score. Kissinger had 56 yards receiving, including his clutch 34-yard catch to set up the winning score.

A trip to Minersville got the Tigers back on track. The offense rolled with 321 yards on the ground and 151 through the air. Butch Romanoski opened the scoring on a 5-yard run in the first. Brad Osevala hit Ardie Kissinger with a 28-yard scoring pass to make it 14-0. Nate Roadarmel tacked on a second-quarter 5-yard touchdown to push the lead to 21-0 at the half. Romanoski scored again in the third, and Andy Helwig returned an interception 34 yards for a pick six in the fourth quarter to make the final score 34-0. Romanoski rumbled for 157 yards and two touchdowns. Roadarmel chipped in with 65 rushing yards and a score. Osevala threw for 151 yards and a touchdown. Kissinger had 90 receiving yards and a touchdown grab.

Loyalsock gave the Tigers' fans heart failure for the second time in three weeks in a week eight road game. The Lancers gave Southern everything they could handle in a nail-biter that went down to the wire. Ardie Kissinger and Brad Osevala hooked up on a 27-yard touchdown pass to open the scoring in the first quarter. Ricco Rosini and Todd Sharrow scored on runs of 11 and 2 yards, and it appeared that Southern was in for an easy night's work. When Kissinger scored on receptions of 5 and 38 yards, the Tigers took a 34-6 lead into halftime. Coach Roth removed his starters from the game; however, Loyalsock kept their first string on the field against the Southern backups. The Lancers mounted a second-half comeback, pulling to within 34-28, forcing the Tigers to put their starters back in the game. Late in the fourth quarter, the Lancers moved the ball to the Tigers' 4-yard line, setting up a first and goal with 47 seconds remaining in the game. During a timeout, Coach Roth implored his defense to make a final stand. On first down, the Lancers moved the ball to the Southern one-yard line. Southern's Steve Snyder stopped the ball carrier for a loss on second down. A third-down bootleg was stopped by Chris Grassley for a two-yard loss, setting up fourth and goal. On Loyalsock's last play, Jason Stanchock and Justin Barnes stuffed a run to the right, preserving the Tigers' 34-28 victory. Southern relied heavily on their passing game as Osevala threw for 125 yards and three scores. Kissinger had 76 yards receiving and three touchdown receptions. Sharrow and Rosini each had scoring runs.

A rivalry game against Central Columbia awaited Southern the following week at Tiger Stadium. Andy Helwig's interception on the Blue Jays' opening drive set up Butch Romanoski's 4-yard scoring run. However, Central had a 64-yard touchdown run, and the Blue Jays had a 7-6 lead after one. Nate

Roadarmel's one-yard touchdown run gave Southern a 12-7 lead at the intermission. Central connected on a 27-yard field goal to cut the lead to 12-10 after three. In the fourth quarter, Brad Osevala scored on a one-yard keeper to push the lead to 19-10. Justin Barnes' interception late in the fourth allowed the Tigers to run out the clock and win the game. Roadarmel rushed for 82 yards and a touchdown. Romanoski had 80 yards on the ground and a score. With their victory, the Tigers won the Central Susquehanna Conference Division II Championship.

Southern faced the Danville Ironmen in the regular-season finale at Tiger Stadium. In another close game, the Tigers would pull out another victory. Nate Roadarmel scored early on a one-yard run, only to see Danville take a 7-6 lead on a 73-yard scoring pass in the first quarter. Butch Romanoski gave the Tigers a 12-7 halftime lead with a 5-yard touchdown run. After a scoreless third quarter, Romanoski scored again on a 24-yard run early in the fourth. Danville closed the gap on a 28-yard pass play. Roadarmel put the game out of reach with a 2-yard scoring plunge. Danville scored on the last play of the game to bring the final score to 26-20. Southern continued their rushing barrage with 342 yards. Romanoski had 159 yards and two scores. Roadarmel ran for 104 yards and two touchdowns. The Tigers entered the District IV playoffs as the top seed.

The Tigers opened the postseason in the District IV Class A Semifinal Game against Lourdes Regional at Tiger Stadium. In the first quarter, Steve Snyder's sack forced a fumble that Mike Moncavage recovered at the Red Raiders' 10-yard line. The play set up Butch Romanoski's 10-yard touchdown run to open the scoring. Todd Sharrow would tack on a 10-yard scoring run to give the Tigers a 14-0 first-quarter lead. Romanoski scored early in the second on a one-yard run to make it 21-0. Ardie Kissinger then scored a record-setting touchdown. Brad Osevala connected with Kissinger on a 91-yard touchdown pass that broke the Tigers' record for the longest scoring play set by Gary Murry and Mick Fleming in 1964. The Tigers led 28-0 at halftime. Ricco Rosini scored on a 9-yard run in the third. Joe Murphy scored from one yard out and rumbled 48 yards for a touchdown in the fourth quarter. Lourdes got two late touchdowns to make the final 48-14. Romanoski ran for 109 yards and two touchdowns. Murphy added 63 yards and two scores. Rosini rushed for 43 yards and a touchdown. Sharrow pitched in with 11 yards and a scoring run. Osevala threw for 165 yards and a touchdown. Kissinger hauled in 116 receiving yards and his record-setting touchdown catch.

The Tigers faced South Williamsport in the District IV A Class Championship Game at Tiger Stadium. The Mounties' vaunted defense came into the game having given up only 34 points all season and looked to challenge the Tigers' high-powered rushing attack. Southern took to the air on their opening touchdown, a 45-yard scoring pass from Brad Osevala to Nate Roadarmel in the first quarter. Butch Romanoski plowed in for a one-yard scoring run early in the second. The Mounties cut into the lead with a 43-yard scoring run. Romanoski raced 57-yards for a touchdown and added a 2-yard scoring run for a 27-7 lead at the break. Romanoski scored again on a 10-yard run in the third. South Williamsport had a 71-yard scoring run in the fourth quarter before Romanoski scored his fifth touchdown of the game on a 4-yard dive. The Tigers earned a convincing 41-15 victory over the Mounties, winning the District IV Class A Championship. The Tigers bludgeoned South Williamsport for 331 yards rushing, 169 through the air, and 500 yards of total offense, scoring more points against the Mounties than they had given up all year. Romanoski had a huge game with 172 yards rushing and five touchdowns. Nate Roadarmel added another 93 yards on the ground. Osevala had 169 yards passing and a touchdown.

Southern advanced to the PIAA Class A Eastern Semifinal Game versus Delone Catholic in Carlisle. It would prove to be a big night for Ardie Kissinger. During the game, Kissinger would break the school record for receptions in a season (37), breaking Bobby Jones' mark of 34. Butch Romanoski scored a first-quarter touchdown on a seven-yard run. Delone had a 27-yard touchdown run to cut the lead to 8-6. Southern's running game took over in the second quarter. Brad Osevala plowed in on a one-yard keeper, and Nate Roadarmel scored on runs of 6 and 67 yards to give the Tigers a 31-6 halftime lead. Ricco Rosini had a 37-yard touchdown run in the third, and Delone scored a late touchdown in the final period. The 38-13 victory gave the Tigers their first-ever state playoff win. The offense manhandled the Squires, rushing for 329 yards and rolling for 436 yards of total offense. Roadarmel rumbled for 127 yards and two touchdowns. Romanoski had 98 yards rushing and a score, and Rosini added 56 yards and a rushing touchdown. The Tigers were now headed to the second round of the state playoffs for the first time.

The Tigers faced Susquehanna Community in the PIAA Class A Eastern Final Game in Shamokin. The two teams would alternate touchdowns in the first quarter. Southern struck first on a 56-yard scoring pass from Brad Osevala to Ardie Kissinger. The Sabers then returned the ensuing kickoff 82 yards for the tying score. Kissinger and Osevala hooked up again on a 29- yard touchdown pass only to see Susquehanna tie the game again with a 15-yard scoring pass of their own. The teams were deadlocked at 12-12 after one. Butch Romanoski gave the Tigers an 18-12 halftime lead with an 18-yard touchdown burst in the second. Romanoski scored again in the third quarter with a 22-yard run to push the lead to 26-12. Ricco Rosini and Nate Roadarmel sealed the deal with scoring runs of 7 and 5 yards in the fourth. The Sabers scored a late touchdown to make the final score 40-20. Romanoski had a huge game with 175 yards and two touchdowns. Rosini had 77 yards and a scoring run. Roadarmel contributed 55 rushing yards and a touchdown Osevala threw for 85 yards, all to Kissinger, and the two combined for two touchdown passes. Southern Columbia advanced to their first-ever state championship game.

Enthusiasm and excitement were everywhere as Tiger Fever swept the Southern Columbia community. The rain and cold did not deter the throngs of fans, including three charter buses full of boosters, who made the trek to Mansion Park in Altoona to see Southern take on Western Beaver in the PIAA Class A Championship Game. The Tiger faithful gave the team a thunderous ovation as they took the field. If nerves were a factor, they seemed to strike Western Beaver first, as they fumbled the opening kickoff, which Mike Mattivi recovered at the 27-yard line. Ricco Rosini rumbled 28 yards for the opening touchdown less than a minute into the game. Butch Romanoski scored on a 6-yard run, and Nate Roadarmel added a one-yard plunge to give the Tigers a 22-0 lead after the first quarter. Western Beaver scored a second-quarter touchdown on a 62-yard pass to pull within striking distance. However, Ardie Kissinger broke the Golden Beavers' back with a 69-yard punt return for a touchdown to make the score 29-6 at the half. Kissinger's play set the record for the longest punt return in a PIAA Championship Game. The Tigers' offense poured it on in the third quarter. Brad Osevala hit Kissinger for an 85-yard scoring pass, Rosini ran 17 yards for a touchdown, and Roadarmel capped the scoring with a one-yard scoring run. Kissinger's touchdown set the PIAA Championship Game record for the longest touchdown reception. The defense took over and controlled Western Beaver with an interception and fumble recovery, holding them to 73 yards passing for the game. As the time ticked off the clock, the reality of the moment began to hit the Tigers and their fans. Emotions ran high as the Southern Columbia Tigers were crowned the 1994 PIAA Class A Champions with a dominant 49-6 victory. Jim Roth earned a state championship in his eleventh year as head coach. Romanoski rushed for 105 yards and a touchdown. Roadarmel ran for 66 yards and two scores. Rosini added 47 yards on the ground and two touchdowns. Osevala threw for 199 yards and a touchdown. Kissinger had 166 receiving yards and a touchdown catch and returned a punt for a score. His 166 receiving yards set a PIAA Class A Championship Game record.

Justin Barnes set a PIAA Championship Game record by kicking five extra points. The 1994 Southern Columbia Tigers finished the season with a 15-0 record. Southern scored 579 points, averaging 38.6 per game. The Tigers had two 1,000-yard rushers on the season. Butch Romanoski, who would continue his football career at the University of Delaware, ran for 1,710 yards and scored 26 touchdowns. Nate Roadarmel, who missed three games due to a shoulder injury, rushed for 1,020 yards and scored 18 touchdowns. Ricco Rosini would contribute 667 rushing yards and seven scores. Todd Sharrow scored seven touchdowns, and Joe Murphy added five scores. Brad Osevala threw for 1,397 yards and 12 touchdowns. Ardie Kissinger, who would continue his football

## 1994 SEASON

| Opponent | Location | W/L | Score |
|---|---|---|---|
| Line Mountain | Away | W | 42-19 |
| Bloomsburg | Home | W | 54-8 |
| Troy | Home | W | 40-12 |
| Lewisburg | Away | W | 46-6 |
| Warrior Run | Home | W | 34-6 |
| Hughesville | Away | W | 26-21 |
| Minersville | Away | W | 34-0 |
| Loyalsock | Away | W | 34-28 |
| Central Columbia | Home | W | 19-10 |
| Danville | Home | W | 26-20 |
| **District IV Class A Semifinal Game** | | | |
| Lourdes Regional | Home | W | 48-14 |
| **District IV Class A Championship Game** | | | |
| South Williamsport | Home | W | 41-15 |
| **PIAA Class A Eastern Semifinal Game** | | | |
| Delone Catholic | Neutral | W | 38-13 |
| **PIAA Class A Eastern Final Game** | | | |
| Susquehanna Community | Neutral | W | 40-20 |
| **PIAA Class A Championship Game** | | | |
| Western Beaver | Neutral | W | 49-6 |

COACHING STAFF: Jim Roth, Head Coach; Jim Becker, Assistant Coach; Al Cihocki, Assistant Coach; Greg Haladay, Assistant Coach; Bob Handerahan, Assistant Coach; John Marks, Assistant Coach; Andy Mills, Assistant Coach; Curt Stellfox, Assistant Coach

ATHLETIC DIRECTOR: Terry Sharrow

ROSTER: Antenor Alverez, Justin Barnes, Matt Baylor, Matt Bell, Cory Billig, Brett Bloom, Larry Boyer, Jason Crawford, Donald Cryder, Dave Danilowicz, Mike Fetterman, Chris Grassley, Shane Hart, Andy Helwig, Jeremy Hoagland, Rodney Kingston, Ardie Kissinger, Jon Leisenring, Mark Madara, Mike Mattivi, Steve Mayernick, Bill Miller, Mike Moncavage, Joe Murphy, Todd Nolan, Brad Osevala, Rob Reese, Nate Roadarmel, Butch Romanoski, Nick Rosini, Ricco Rosini, Todd Rush, Mark Scisly, Todd Sharrow, Matt Shingara, Steve Snyder, Jason Stanchock, Gary Stine, Adam Strzempek, Bob Visnosky, Rob Yancoskie, Pat Wiehe, Charlie Yost career at Bucknell University, set school records with 42 receptions for 1,042 yards and 11 touchdowns. Justin Barnes kicked 42 extra points and one field goal. He led the team with 11 interceptions. Steve Snyder had 102 tackles (64 solo) and Matt Bell 101 tackles 56 solo) led the team. Jon Leisenring registered 6.5 sacks. Kissinger, Romanoski, Barnes, and Mark Scisly were All-State selections.

1
9
9
5

Southern Columbia began the 1995 season as the defending PIAA Class A Champions. With a talented roster of returning players, the Tigers looked poised for another deep playoff run and had a realistic shot at defending their title. Southern opened the year at home at Tiger Stadium against Line Mountain. The season got off to an ominous start as Line Mountain ran the opening kickoff back for a 86-tard touchdown. However, the Tigers rushed for 348 yards and passed for 207 more in a 42-36 opening-game victory. Ricco Rosini ran for 169 yards, and Southern got two rushing touchdowns from Todd Sharrow and one each from Rosini, Joe Murphy, and Scott Bloom. Brad Osevala threw a touchdown pass to Andy Helwig, who had 131 receiving yards.

In week two, the Tigers traveled to Bloomsburg. Scoring on nine of their first ten possessions, Southern crushed the Panthers, 62-16. For the second week in a row, Todd Sharrow scored two touchdowns on the ground. The Tigers got rushing scores from Joe Murphy, Scott Bloom, and Nate Danilowicz. Southern rolled with 387 rushing yards. Brad Osevala threw three touchdown passes, one to Chris Grassley and two to Andy Helwig. The defense controlled Bloomsburg with four interceptions and a fumble recovery.

The following week at Troy, Andy Helwig started the game with a bang, returning the opening kickoff for an 85-yard touchdown. Ricco Rosini had his second 100-yard game of the season, rushing for 104 yards and two scores. The Tigers offense also got rushing touchdowns from Joe Murphy, Todd Sharrow, and Scott Bloom. Brad Osevala connected with Andy Helwig for two scoring throws. The Tigers' defense had three interceptions and a fumble recovery in Southern's 37-14 victory.

The Tigers easily beat Lewisburg 45-15 in a week four contest at Tiger Stadium. Southern's offense rumbled for 328 yards rushing and 484 total yards of offense. Scott Bloom and Joe Murphy each scored three touchdowns, and Brian Shroyer added a scoring run. Brad Osevala threw for 156 yards and a touchdown. The defense intercepted three Lewisburg passes.

The Tigers had another blowout win at Warrior Run. Ricco Rosini and Joe Murphy rushed for 100 yards and scored two touchdowns in a 47-14 rout. Southern ground out 356 rushing yards. Brad Osevala threw for 197 yards and three scores, all to Andy Helwig.

The Tigers cruised to a 41-14 home win over Hughesville. Ricco Rosini ran for 141 yards and two touchdowns. Scott Bloom chipped in with two scoring runs. Brad Osevala threw for a touchdown to Andy Helwig and ran for another, as the Tigers rushed for 307 yards and had 115 through the air.

A week seven matchup pitted the Tigers, the top-ranked Class A team in the state, against fifth-ranked Minersville. After leading by only seven at the break, the Tigers took control in the second half and rolled to a 43-20 victory. Ricco Rosini rushed for 157 yards and two scores. Joe Murphy scored three touchdowns, and Scott Bloom added a scoring run. Brad Osevala threw for a touchdown and rushed for a score.

A week eight home game against Loyalsock proved to be a struggle. Bob Visnosky intercepted the Lancers' first pass to set up Todd Sharrow's first-quarter touchdown run. However, Loyalsock would trade touchdowns with the Tigers and take a 14-13 halftime lead. Brad Osevala would have a big third quarter, running for one score and throwing a touchdown pass to Andy Helwig. Southern would hold on for a hard-fought 29-27 win.

The Tigers had an easy shutout victory on the road at Central Columbia. Joe Murphy and Brad Osevala had first-quarter touchdown runs, and Ricco Rosini scored in the second for a 20-0 halftime lead. Osevala and Murphy rounded out the scoring in the third stanza and sealed a 32-0 blowout. Rosini and Murphy combined for 119 yards on the ground and two touchdowns. Osevala threw for 74 yards and a touchdown and rushed for two scores. The Tigers rushed for 323 yards as a team. Southern clinched the Central Susquehanna Conference Division II Championship.

The Tigers finished a second straight undefeated season with a 35-7 win at Danville. The defense dominated with five sacks in the first quarter, finishing with an interception and a fumble recovery. Ricco Rosini opened the scoring with a 69-yard run in the first. Andy Helwig pulled in a 35-yard scoring pass from Brad Osevala for a 14-0 lead. Joe Murphy scored on a 2-yard run to push the lead to 21-7 at the half. Todd Sharrow and Murphy had scoring runs in the second half to close out the Ironmen. Rosini ran for 117 yards and a touchdown. Murphy added 44 yards rushing and two scores. Sharrow chipped in with 43 yards on the ground and a touchdown. Osevala had 134 passing yards and fired a touchdown to Helwig.

Southern opened the postseason at home in the District IV Class A Semifinal Game versus Lourdes Regional. After Andy Helwig's 47-yard touchdown catch from Brad Osevala, the Tigers' defense took over. Bob Visnosky recovered a Red Raider fumble to set up Osevala's one-yard scoring dive. Osevala would tack on a 51-yard touchdown run before Pat Wiehe sacked the Red Raiders' quarterback in the endzone for a safety. Osevala would then hit Joe Murphy with a 9-yard scoring pass to give the Tigers a 29-0 lead after the first quarter. Ricco Rosini's 3-yard touchdown run in the second made it 36-8 at the half. Murphy and Dave Danilowicz had second-half touchdown runs to make the final 48-22. Southern had 351 rushing yards. Rosini ran for 89 yards and a score. Murphy had 64 yards on the ground and scored a rushing and receiving touchdown. Osevala threw for 94 yards and two scores. He also added two rushing touchdowns. Helwig had 85 receiving yards and a scoring catch. The Tigers' defense registered two interceptions and recovered two Red Raider fumbles.

Southern faced Loyalsock at Tiger Stadium in the District IV Class A Championship Game. The Tiger defense completely dominated the game, holding Loyalsock to -2 yards passing, recording an interception and fumble recovery in a 33-0 blowout of the Lancers. Todd Sharrow scored twice in the second quarter to give the Tigers a 14-0 lead at the break. Scott Bloom, Joe Murphy, and Dave Danilowicz had scoring runs in the fourth quarter as Southern won the District IV Title. Ricco Rosini led the rushing attack with 96 yards. Sharrow (two), Bloom, Murphy, and Danilowicz all contributed touchdown runs.

The Tigers advanced to the PIAA Class A Eastern Semifinal Game against Columbia at Mount Carmel. After falling behind 6-0 after the first quarter, Chris Grassley picked off a Columbia pass and returned it 29 yards for a touchdown to give the Tigers an 8-6 lead. Ricco Rosini added a 34-yard scoring run only to have Columbia return the ensuing kickoff for a touchdown. Southern led 16-12 at the half. Rosini had a 3-yard scoring run in the third to push the lead to 24-12. Todd Sharrow and Joe Murphy closed out the Crimson Tide with fourth-quarter touchdown runs to make the final 36-18. Rosini led the Tigers with 167 rushing yards and two touchdowns, and Sharrow and Murphy chipped in with scoring runs. Southern rushed for 392 yards.

Southern played Pius X in the PIAA Class A Eastern Final Game in Brodheadsville. The Tigers jumped out to a quick lead on Joe Murphy's 68-yard touchdown run and Brad Osevala's 38-yard scoring pass to Andy Helwig in the first quarter. Osevala scored on a 15-yard run, but the Royals scored two touchdowns in the second to close the gap to 24-14 at halftime. In the third, Nick Rosini's interception set up Osevala's 3-yard touchdown run to increase the Tigers' lead to 30-14. Helwig and Osevala hooked up a second time on an 8-yard scoring pass to give Southern a 38-20 victory. Murphy rushed for 134 yards and a touchdown. Osevala had a big game, throwing for 133 yards and two touchdowns to go along with two scoring runs. Helwig contributed 110 receiving yards and two scoring receptions. Southern rushed for 378 yards. The defense held Pius X to 10 passing yards. The Tigers advanced to their second straight PIAA Class A Championship Game with their 32nd consecutive victory.

Southern faced Farrell for the state championship at Mansion Park in Altoona. The game would turn into a monumental defensive struggle. Neither

## 1995 SEASON

| Opponent | Location | W/L | Score |
|---|---|---|---|
| Line Mountain | Home | W | 42-36 |
| Bloomsburg | Away | W | 62-16 |
| Troy | Away | W | 37-14 |
| Lewisburg | Home | W | 45-15 |
| Warrior Run | Away | W | 47-14 |
| Hughesville | Home | W | 41-14 |
| Minersville | Home | W | 43-20 |
| Loyalsock | Home | W | 29-27 |
| Central Columbia | Away | W | 32-0 |
| Danville | Away | W | 35-7 |
| **District IV Class A Semifinal Game** | | | |
| Lourdes Regional | Home | W | 48-22 |
| **District IV Class A Championship Game** | | | |
| Loyalsock | Home | W | 33-0 |
| **PIAA Class A Eastern Semifinal Game** | | | |
| Columbia | Neutral | W | 36-18 |
| **PIAA Class A Eastern Final Game** | | | |
| Pius X | Neutral | W | 38-20 |
| **PIAA Class A Championship Game** | | | |
| Farrell | Neutral | L | 0-6 |

COACHING STAFF: Jim Roth, Head Coach; Jim Becker, Assistant Coach; Al Cihocki, Assistant Coach; Harvey Fetterolf, Assistant Coach; Mike Johnston, Assistant Coach; John Marks, Assistant Coach; Andy Mills, Assistant Coach; Tim Snyder, Assistant Coach; Curt Stellfox, Assistant Coach

ATHLETIC DIRECTOR: Terry Sharrow

ROSTER: Shawn Adams, Cory Billig, Scott Bloom, Duane Breech, Matt Bubnis, Jason Crawford, Dave Danilowicz, Nate Danilowicz, Justin DeGreen, Brad Deitterick, Mike Fedash, Mike Fetterman, Chad Francis, Chris Grassley, Andy Helwig, Jeremy Hoagland, Nate Kevick, Rodney Kingston, Eric King, Zak Knorr, Chuck Kowalchick, Jason Maciejewski, Mark Madara, Mike Mattivi, Steve Mayernick, Bill Miller, Mike Moncavage, Joe Murphy, Brad Osevala, Nick Podgurski, Dave Reeves, Nick Rosini, Ricco Rosini, Manuel Sanchez, Mark Scisly, Todd Sharrow, Matt Shingara, Brian Shroyer, Gary Stine, Adam Strzempek, Bob Visnosky, Rob Walters, Pat Wiehe, Rob Yancoskie offense was able to find any sustained success. The pivotal play of the game occurred in the first quarter when Brad Osevala attempted to pitch the ball to Todd Sharrow. The ball wound up on the ground and was recovered by the Steelers. Farrell would convert the turnover into a 26-yard touchdown run for a 6-0 lead. The Tigers defense played an exceptional game, keeping Farrell off the scoreboard for the rest of the game. After Southern stopped the Steelers on a fourth and goal in the second quarter, Farrell never got deeper than the Tigers' 31-yard line the rest of the game. However, the Tigers were never able to find any offensive success, and Farrell won the PIAA Class A Championship by a score of 6-0.

The disappointing ending to the season could not overshadow the success of the 1995 Tigers. A second consecutive undefeated regular season and a second straight appearance in the Class A title game proved that Southern Columbia had arrived as a Pennsylvania high school football power. The Tigers had fantastic performances throughout the 1995 season. Ricco Rosini would rush for 1,523 yards and 14 touchdowns. Joe Murphy ran for 979 yards and scored 19 touchdowns. Scott Bloom had 711 rushing yards and eight scoring runs. Todd Sharrow contributed with nine touchdowns on the year. Brad Osevala, who would continue his football career at Bloomsburg University, threw for 1,771 yards and 18 touchdowns. Andy Helwig had 38 receptions for 1,077 yards and 13 scoring catches. Helwig also led the team with seven interceptions. Rosini had 88 tackles (52 solo). Bill Miller registered 8.5 sacks. Helwig, Steve Mayemick, and Mark Scisly were All-State selections. The Tigers posted a 14-1 record in 1995.

**1996** After the disappointing end to the previous season, the 1996 Southern Columbia Tigers set a goal of reaching the PIAA Class A Championship Game for a third consecutive year. Although they would be starting the season with a new quarterback, Southern looked to lean heavily on their returning trio of powerful running backs. Ricco Rosini started the season with a bang, running back the opening kickoff for an 89-yard touchdown in a 40-14 road victory over Line Mountain. In the first quarter, Joe Murphy added an 11-yard scoring run before Rosini ran 52 and 2 yards for touchdowns in the second to give the Tigers a 27-7 halftime lead. Rosini scored again on an 89-yard scoring run, and Matt Bloom closed out the Eagles with a one-yard touchdown plunge. Rosini finished with 203 yards and three scoring runs, in addition to his kickoff return for a touchdown. Bloom added 77 rushing yards and a touchdown. Murphy had 61 yards on the ground and a score. Southern rushed for 481 yards as a team.

The Tigers rolled to a 47-8 blowout of Bloomsburg in their home opener. Southern got first-half touchdowns on a 32-yard run by Joe Murphy, a 5-yard quarterback keeper from Nick Slater, a 10-yard burst by Scott Bloom, a one-yard dive from Ricco Rosini, and a 36-yard scoring pass from Slater to Bloom to take a 34-0 lead at the break. Shaun Gaul and Brian Shroyer added third-quarter touchdown runs to close out the scoring. Murphy led the way with 59 rushing yards and a touchdown. Gaul had 52 yards and a scoring run. Rosini added 36 yards rushing and a touchdown. Bloom contributed 24 yards on the ground and added a scoring run and touchdown reception. Southern ran for 306 yards. Slater threw for 154 yards and a score and ran for a touchdown. The victory gave the Tigers their 30th consecutive regular-season win.

The week three matchup against Mount Carmel at Tiger Stadium was a clash of state powers. 6,500 fans attended the game to see Southern, one of the top-ranked teams in Pennsylvania in Class A, take on the Red Tornadoes, the number one team in Class AA. Unfortunately, the wheels came off for the Tigers, and Mount Carmel rolled to a 41-12 rout. The Red Tornadoes scored four times in the first half, as the Tigers could only muster a 58-yard scoring run from Ricco Rosini. Mount Carmel led 27-6 at halftime. Mark Yurkiewicz scored on a 41-yard run in the second half, but Mount Carmel scored twice to close out the Tigers. The Red Tornadoes capitalized on four Southern turnovers and held the Tigers to only 19 passing yards. Rosini rushed for 89 yards and a score. Yurkiewicz added 52 yards on the ground and a touchdown

Southern got back on track with a 33-0 shutout in a road game against Lewisburg. Ricco Rosini scored on runs of 24, 9, and one yard, and Scott Bloom added a 2-yard touchdown plunge to push the lead to 27-0 at the break. Shaun Gaul closed out the scoring with a 58-yard touchdown run in the fourth. Southern rushed for 476 yards and had 538 yards of total offense. Rosini ran for 142 yards and two touchdowns. Bloom added 140 yards and a scoring run. Gaul rushed for 61 yards and a touchdown. The defense held the Green Dragons to 104 total yards.

The following week, Southern beat Warrior Run 27-13 in a home game at Tiger Stadium. After giving up an early touchdown run, the Tigers held the Defenders in check, controlling the game with an interception and fumble recovery, including Nick Rosini's pick six to give Southern the lead. Scott Bloom and Joe Murphy scored on first-half runs of 24 and 17 yards, and Bloom finished off the Defenders with a 57-yard touchdown jaunt in the third. Bloom rushed for 151 yards and two scores. Ricco Rosini added 114 yards on the ground. Murphy ran for 60 yards and a touchdown.

In a road game at Hughesville, the Tigers built a 35-6 halftime lead on Scott Bloom's one-yard plunge, Ricco Rosini's 30-yard run, Jason Maciejewski's 34-yard fumble return, Nick Slater's 24-yard scoring strike to Bloom, and Cory Billig's 32-yard interception return. Bloom and Mark Yurkiewicz added scoring runs of 9 and 32 yards in the second half to close out the Spartans. Rosini ran for 72 yards and a touchdown. Bloom rushed for 53 yards and a score and had a touchdown reception. Yurkiewicz added 64 yards on the ground and a touchdown. Slater passed for 114 yards and a score. The Tigers' defense contributed twelve points to the scoring.

It was a record-setting night for the Tigers in a 55-21 thrashing of Minersville. Southern rushed for 621 yards and set a school record with 635 yards of total offense. Matt Bloom and Ricco Rosini combined for 500 yards on the ground and eight touchdowns. Bloom scored twice in the first on runs of 75 and 23 yards. He added a 70-yard touchdown scamper in the second quarter to make the score 21-14 at the half. In the third, Rosini scored on runs of 43, 46, and 51 yards, and Bloom rumbled 19 and 56 yards for touchdowns to cap the scoring. Bloom rushed for 294 yards and five touchdowns. Rosini added 206 yards and three scores. The Southern defense had four interceptions and a fumble recovery in the victory.

A pounding rain storm that turned the field to mud did little to slow the Tigers' rushing attack in a 41-7 win at Selinsgrove. Southern ground out 382 rushing yards in the blowout of the Seals. Scott Bloom scored on runs of 21, 42, and 8 yards in the first half, and Ricco Rosini and Joe Murphy added touchdown runs of 77 and 5 yards to put the game out of reach at halftime, 28-7. Bloom scored again on an 8-yard run, and Eric Steffen added a 3-yard touchdown dive in the second half to finish off the Seals. Rosini ran for 120 yards and a score. Bloom scored three touchdowns and had 96 yards on the ground. Murphy rushed for 94 yards and a score. Steffen added 30 yards rushing and a touchdown. Southern rumbled for 382 rushing yards in the win.

The homecoming game in week nine against Central Columbia turned into a nightmare, as the Tigers suffered their second defeat of the season with a 48-27 loss. The lone highlight for Southern was Ricco Rosini, who had touchdown runs of 27 and 79 yards and returned a kickoff 84 yards for a score. He would finish with 176 rushing yards. However, the Blue Jays' passing attack racked up five touchdowns, and the Tigers had no answers for the Central offense.

The Tigers ended the regular season with a hard-fought 29-21 victory over the Danville Ironmen at Tiger Stadium. Danville took an early lead with a 12-yard pass play, but Ricco Rosini answered with a 33-yard touchdown run to tie the score at 7-7 after one. Rosini and Matt Bloom had scoring runs of 14 and one yard, and the Tigers led 21-14 at halftime. Danville tied the game at 21-21 in the third. Bloom scored the winning touchdown on a one-yard dive to close out the Ironmen late in the final period. Rosini and Bloom combined for 262 yards on the ground and four scores. Southern rushed for 314 yards.

The Tigers began the 1996 postseason with the District IV Class A Semifinal Game against Bristol at Tiger Stadium. The defense got off to a fast start as Mike Myers returned a first-quarter interception 27 yards for the opening score. Joe Murphy added a one-yard plunge to put Southern up 14-0 after one. Ricco Rosini and Scott Bloom ran for touchdowns of 11 and 5 yards to make it 28-6 at halftime. Rosini, Eric Steffen, and Mark Yurkiewicz scored rushing touchdowns in the second half to close out Bristol, 48-14. Rosini ran for 115 yards and two touchdowns. Steffen rushed for 43 yards and a score. Bloom added 43 yards and a touchdown. Murphy chipped in with 31 yards on the ground and a score. Yurkiewicz contributed 28 yards and a rushing touchdown.

Southern advanced to host the District IV Class A Championship Game versus Muncy. Once again, the defense flexed their muscles. The Tigers had three interceptions, one of which was returned by Scott Bloom for a touchdown, recovered two Muncy fumbles, and Steve Mayernick tackled an Indian ballcarrier in the endzone for a first-quarter safety. Ricco Rosini scored on a four-yard run, Nick Slater scampered 9 yards for a touchdown, Rosini plowed in from one yard out, and Joe Murphy had a 17-yard touchdown run in the first to give the Tigers a 30-0 lead. Rosini and Murphy pushed the Southern lead to 44-0 at halftime with touchdown runs of 6 and 14 yards. In the second half, Bloom returned an interception for a pick six, Shaun Gaul raced 42 yards for a touchdown, and Brian Shroyer scored on a 3-yard keeper to give the Tigers a 63-22 blowout win. Southern rushed for 344 yards. Rosini had three touchdown runs and 53 yards rushing. Murphy ran for 56 yards and two scores. Gaul added 62 yards on the ground and a touchdown. Shroyer rushed for 31 yards and a score. Yurkiewicz had 29 yards and a scoring run. Southern earned their sixth consecutive District IV Class A Championship.

The Tigers entered the state playoffs in the PIAA Class A Eastern Semifinal Game against Camp Hill in Middletown. After Ricco Rosini's 12-yard touchdown run early in the first, Joe Murphy and Nick Slater hooked up on scoring passes of 58 and 34 yards for a 19-0 lead after one. Murphy and Slater connected again on a 29-yard touchdown pass in the second. Scott Bloom added a 20-yard scoring run followed by Murphy's 15-yard scamper to push the lead to 40-0 at the break. Mark Yurkiewicz finished off the Lions with a 4-yard touchdown run in the third quarter, and the Tigers defeated Camp Hill, 46-22. Southern had 363 yards rushing. Rosini ran for 71 yards and a touchdown. Bloom added 57 yards and a scoring run. Murphy tacked on 57 yards and had a rushing touchdown and three scoring receptions. Yurkiewicz rushed for 124 yards and a touchdown. Slater threw for 144 yards and three scores.

Southern advanced to the PIAA Class A Eastern Final Game versus Shenandoah Valley in Sunbury. The Tigers jumped to an early 7-0 lead on Ricco Rosini's 6-yard run early in the first. However, the Blue Devils took the lead in the second with two scoring runs. Rosini put the Tigers back on top with a 5-yard scamper to give Southern a 13-12 lead at halftime. Rosini would

## 1996 SEASON

| Opponent | Location | W/L | Score |
|---|---|---|---|
| Line Mountain | Away | W | 40-14 |
| Bloomsburg | Home | W | 47-8 |
| Mount Carmel | Home | L | 12-41 |
| Lewisburg | Away | W | 33-0 |
| Warrior Run | Home | W | 27-13 |
| Hughesville | Away | W | 49-20 |
| Minersville | Away | W | 55-21 |
| Selinsgrove | Away | W | 41-7 |
| Central Columbia | Home | L | 27-48 |
| Danville | Home | W | 29-21 |
| **District IV Class A Semifinal Game** | | | |
| Bristol | Home | W | 48-14 |
| **District IV Class A Championship Game** | | | |
| Muncy | Home | W | 63-22 |
| **PIAA Class A Eastern Semifinal Game** | | | |
| Camp Hill | Neutral | W | 46-22 |
| **PIAA Class A Eastern Final Game** | | | |
| Shenandoah Valley | Neutral | W | 19-12 |
| **PIAA Class A Championship Game** | | | |
| Farrell | Neutral | L | 12-14 |

COACHING STAFF: Jim Roth, Head Coach; Justin Barnes, Assistant Coach; Al Cihocki, Assistant Coach; Mike Johnston, Assistant Coach; John Marks, Assistant Coach; Andy Mills, Assistant Coach; Tim Snyder, Assistant Coach; Richard Steele, Assistant Coach; Curt Stellfox, Assistant Coach

ATHLETIC DIRECTOR: Terry Sharrow

ROSTER: Shawn Adams, Jay Andress, Mike Apichell, Cory Billig, Scott Bloom, Ryan Breach, Matt Bubnis, Jason Crawford, Justin DeGreen, Mike Fedash, Shaun Gaul, Zac Getkin, Nate Kevick, Zak Knorr, Chuck Kowalchick, Jason Maciejewski, Mark Madara, Steve Mayernick, Marty McCormick, Ben Meiser, Joe Murphy, Mike Myers, Marc Osevala, Nick Podgurski, Dave Reeves, Nick Rosini, Ricco Rosini, Ken Ruckle, Roy Schlesinger, Mark Scisly, Brian Shroyer, Nick Slater, Eric Steffen, Gary Stine, Ron Walters, Matt Yancoskie, Rob Yancoskie, Mark Yurkiewicz give the Tigers some breathing room with a one-yard plunge in the third. The Southern defense made the lead stand, shutting down Shenandoah Valley the rest of the way, registering two key interceptions. When the final gun sounded, the Tigers had a hard-fought 19-12 victory and advanced to their third consecutive PIAA state final game. Rosini rushed for 198 yards and scored three touchdowns. However, he hobbled off the field with an apparent leg injury but appeared hopeful to play in the state championship game.

For the second time in as many years, the Tigers faced Farrell in the PIAA Class A Championship Game at Mansion Park in Altoona. Fate dealt the Tigers a cruel blow in their highly anticipated rematch against the Steelers, as leading rusher Ricco Rosini learned that he had fractured his leg in the Eastern Final. He was on crutches on the sideline as the Tigers looked to avenge their loss to Farrell the previous year. The Steelers scored first and took a 6-0 lead after one. Southern tied the game at 6-6 in the second when Nick Slater hit Matt Yancoskie for a 25-yard touchdown pass. Just as in 1995, the game turned into a defensive struggle. Both defenses dominated the line of scrimmage, keeping the opposing offenses in check. However, Farrell broke through with a 9-yard touchdown in the third, converted a two-point conversion, and took a 14-6 lead. The Tigers' defense came up with a huge play as Steve Mayernick recovered a Farrell fumble to set up Scott Bloom's 5-yard touchdown run with 8:13 left in the fourth quarter. The Tigers attempted to tie the game on a two-point conversion. However, Mark Yurkiewicz was stopped short of the goal line, and the Tigers trailed 14-12. Farrell was able to control the rest of the quarter, and Southern was, once again, on the short end of a hard-fought title game, losing a heartbreaker, 14-12.

A disappointing loss did not diminish the Tigers' accomplishments in 1996. Coach Roth established Southern Columbia as a legitimate state football power, leading the Tigers to three straight PIAA championship games. Ricco Rosini rushed for 1,720 yards and scored 27 touchdowns. Scott Bloom totaled 1,342 rushing yards and scored 22 total touchdowns. Joe Murphy ran for 872 yards and seven scores. He would finish his career at Southern Columbia with 2,300 yards rushing and 34 touchdowns. Mark Yurkiewicz scored four touchdowns. Brian Shroyer, Shaun Gaul, and Eric Steffen totaled six rushing touchdowns, each scoring a pair. Nick Slater threw for 953 yards and five touchdowns. Mike Myers had three interceptions. Nick Rosini registered 8.5 sacks. Scott Bloom with 108 (63 solo), Ricco Rosini with 105 (71 solo) and Nick Rosini with 104 (69 solo) led the team in tackles. Steve Mayemick and Mark Scisly were All-State selections. The Tigers finished 1996 with a 12-3 overall record.

1
9
9
7

After two consecutive heartbreaking state championship games losses, Southern hoped for another deep run in the PIAA playoffs in 1997. The Tigers opened the regular season at home against Line Mountain. Ricco Rosini would run for four touchdowns, Mark Yurkiewicz added three scoring runs, and Eric Steffen and Nick Slater would each score on a touchdown run as Southern earned a 61-22 opening-night victory. Southern rushed for a whopping 511 yards, including 216 by Rosini and 131 from Yurkiewicz. The Tigers' defense controlled the Eagles with two interceptions and a pair of fumble recoveries.

Southern traveled to Bloomsburg for a matchup with the Panthers. The Tigers rumbled for 487 rushing yards. Ricco Rosini had three scoring runs, and Southern had rushing touchdowns from Scott Bloom, Shaun Gaul, Mark Yurkiewicz, and Brian Shroyer as the Tigers dismantled the Panthers, 47-0. Rosini ran for 141 yards, and the defense held Bloomsburg to 69 total yards, and just three first downs, while registering three interceptions.

A week three road game with Mount Carmel was a highly anticipated matchup with the defending Class AA state champions. All of the scoring occurred in the second quarter in a tremendous defensive battle. Ricco Rosini scored on runs of 3 and 57 yards for a 13-6 lead. Mount Carmel would drive to the Tigers' 37-yard line with 3:32 left in the game. Eric Steffen's fourth-down sack preserved the Tigers' victory. The win ended Mount Carmel's 20-game winning streak. Rosini ran for 174 yards. The defense recovered three fumbles in a solid effort.

A home game with Lewisburg would be a special night for Coach Jim Roth. Ricco Rosini and Mark Yurkiewicz scored a pair of rushing touchdowns, and the Tigers had scoring runs from Eric Steffen and Paul Nazarchyk in a 41-16 drubbing of the Green Dragons. The Tigers rushed for 436 yards. Rosini rumbled for 231 yards on the night. The victory was the 150th career win for Coach Roth.

The offense continued to roll in a 48-15 beat down at Warrior Run. The Tigers rushed for 337 yards and had a staggering 600 yards of total offense. Nick Slater fired touchdown passes to Ricco Rosini, Matt Bubnis, and Ryan Breach. Rosini rushed for two touchdowns, and the Tigers had scoring runs from Scott Bloom and Marty McCormick in the blowout win. Slater threw for 263 yards, and Rosini had 114 on the ground.

Ricco Rosini and Scott Bloom totaled 397 rushing yards and four touchdowns in a 37-7 home victory over Hughesville. Rosini had a whopping 338 yards on the ground in the lopsided win. Brian Shroyer added a scoring run, and Southern totaled 498 rushing yards.

The Tigers rushing attack continued to roll in a week seven home game against Minersville. Southern rushed for 345 yards, including 131 from Ricco Rosini. Rosini had four rushing touchdowns, and Paul Nazarchyk added a scoring run. Nick Slater threw for 90 yards and a touchdown to Scott Bloom.

Next, the Selinsgrove Seals visited Tiger Stadium. Ricco Rosini ran for 142 yards and three scores, Brian Shroyer rushed for 105 yards and a touchdown, and Scott Bloom added 41 yards on the ground and a scoring run as the Tigers rumbled for 354 rushing yards in a 41-20 victory. Nick Slater threw for 130 yards and a touchdown to Ryan Breach. Shroyer and Zak Knorr had interceptions, and Ben Meiser recovered a fumble in a solid defensive effort.

The rushing barrage continued in a road contest versus Central Columbia. The Tigers rushed for 412 yards. Ricco Rosini ran for 190 yards and four touchdowns, and Mark Yurkiewicz had 101 rushing yards and a scoring run. Jason Maciejewski had three interceptions to lead the defense as Southern pummeled the Blue Jays, 33-6.

The Tigers' hopes for an undefeated regular season ended in the season finale at Danville. The Ironmen took advantage of four Southern turnovers for a 40-13 victory. Ricco Rosini ran for 113 yards and a touchdown, and Scott Bloom had a scoring run in the loss.

The Tigers opened the postseason at home in the District IV Class A Semifinal Game versus Jenkintown. Southern got back on track with a solid 41-19 win over the Drakes. Southern rushed for 317 yards. Ricco Rosini ran for 148 yards and two scores. Scott Bloom rushed for 45 yards and a touchdown. Mark Yurkiewicz had 59 yards and a scoring run. Nick Slater threw for 65 yards and two touchdowns to Bloom.

The Tigers hosted the District IV Class A Championship game against Canton. It would be a memorable night for senior running back Ricco Rosini. He would break Jerry Marks' team records for touchdowns in a season (33), points scored in a season (204), and rushing yards in a season (2,089). Rosini ran for 129 yards and two touchdowns. Scott Bloom added 102 rushing yards. Mark Yurkiewicz rushed for 34 yards and a score. Nick Slater threw for 113 yards and fired three touchdown passes to Rosini, Yurkiewicz, and Ryan Breach. The Tigers defeated the Warriors, 40-14. The Southern defense held Canton to -2 yards rushing, and Jason Maciejewski registered two interceptions. The Tigers won their seventh consecutive District IV Class A Championship.

Southern advanced to the PIAA Class A Eastern Semifinal Game against Steelton-Highspire at Shamokin. The Tigers amassed 433 total yards of offense in a 42-22 victory over the Rollers. Ricco Rosini ran for 224 yards and four touchdowns, and Brian Shroyer rushed for 54 yards and a score. Nick Slater passed for 112 yards and a touchdown to Ryan Breach. Jason Maciejewski and Zak Knorr each had an interception against the Rollers.

Southern faced the Riverside Vikings, the top-ranked Class A team in the state, in the PIAA Eastern Final Game in Wilkes-Barre. Ricco Rosini and Scott Bloom scored on first-half touchdown runs, and the Tigers led 13-6 at the half. Rosini ran for a touchdown in the third, and Southern took a 21-14 lead into the fourth. However, Riverside would score 21 points in the fourth quarter,

## 1997 SEASON

| Opponent | Location | W/L | Score |
|---|---|---|---|
| Line Mountain | Home | W | 61-22 |
| Bloomsburg | Away | W | 47-0 |
| Mount Carmel | Away | W | 13-6 |
| Lewisburg | Home | W | 41-16 |
| Warrior Run | Away | W | 48-15 |
| Hughesville | Home | W | 37-7 |
| Minersville | Home | W | 42-14 |
| Selinsgrove | Away | W | 41-20 |
| Central Columbia | Away | W | 33-6 |
| Danville | Away | L | 13-40 |
| **District IV Class A Semifinal Game** | | | |
| Jenkintown | Home | W | 41-19 |
| **District IV Class A Championship Game** | | | |
| Canton | Home | W | 40-24 |
| **PIAA Class A Eastern Semifinal Game** | | | |
| Steelton-Highspire | Neutral | W | 42-22 |
| **PIAA Class A Eastern Final Game** | | | |
| Riverside | Neutral | L | 28-35 |

COACHING STAFF: Jim Roth, Head Coach; Justin Barnes, Assistant Coach; Al Cihocki, Assistant Coach; Mike Johnston, Assistant Coach; John Marks, Assistant Coach; Andy Mills, Assistant Coach; Nate Roadarmel, Assistant Coach; Tim Snyder, Assistant Coach; Richard Steele, Assistant Coach; Curt Stellfox, Assistant Coach

ATHLETIC DIRECTOR: Terry Sharrow

ROSTER: Jay Andress, Mike Apichell, Adam Auman, Garrett Bembenek, Scott Bloom, Ryan Breach, Matt Bubnis, Justin DeGreen, Mike Fedash, Shaun Gaul, Zac Getkin, Rob Gittler, Andy Hornberger, Nate Kevik, Roy Kingston, Eric Kirby, Zak Knorr, Chuck Kowalchick, Mark Kreisher, Wes Lindemuth, Jeff Lowry, Jason Maciejewski, Marty McCormick, Ben Meiser, Brett Meyers, Paul Nazarchyk, Marc Osevala, Nick Podgurski, Dave Reeves, Ricco Rosini, Ken Ruckle, P.J. Sargent, Brian Shroyer, Nick Slater, Jason Sock, Greg Sones, Eric Steffen, Eric Tressler, Pete Trometter, Tyler Weaver, Matt Yancoskie, Mark Yurkiewicz including a back-breaking 57-yard punt return, and the Vikings would advance with a 35-28 victory.

The Tigers had many great performances in 1997. Ricco Rosini would have one of the finest seasons in Tigers' history. He finished the year with 2,481 yards rushing and 38 touchdowns. He was named 1997 Small School Player of the Year. Rosini, who would play football for Bucknell University, would finish his career at Southern with 6,413 rushing yards and 86 touchdowns. Mark Yurkiewicz ran for 655 yards and nine scores. In an injury-shortened season, Scott Bloom rushed for 627 yards and scored 11 touchdowns. He was an All-State Second Team selection. Brian Shroyer, Shaun Gaul, and Eric Steffen combined for seven rushing touchdowns. Nick Slater threw for 1,161 yards and 12 scoring passes. Ryan Breach chipped in with four touchdown receptions. Jason Maciewicz had seven interceptions, and Zak Knorr picked off six passes to lead the team. Eric Steffen registered 4.5 sacks. Scott Bloom had 93 tackles (60 solo) to lead the Tigers.

1
9
9
8

The Tigers sought to return to a championship level in 1998. Southern opened the season on the road against Pius X. The defense scored the first points of the year as Marc Osevala recovered a Royal fumble in the endzone for a 7-0 lead. However, Pius X scored twice early in the second quarter to lead 14-7. Eric Steffen ran for a 2-yard touchdown only to see the Royals rush for another score. Nick Slater dove into the endzone on a one-yard keeper to give the Tigers a 21-20 halftime lead. Shaun Gaul added a 13-yard touchdown run in the third to push the lead to 28-20. Mark Yurkiewicz and Slater scored on runs of 16 and 28 yards to finally put the feisty Royals away, 42-28. Southern rushed for 422 yards. Gaul led the way with 146 yards and a touchdown. Yurkiewicz added 120 yards rushing and a score. Steffen rushed for 62 yards and a touchdown. Slater threw for 38 yards and ran for two scores.

The Tigers hosted Bloomsburg in week two. Shaun Gaul opened the scoring with a 46-yard scoring run in the first quarter. Mark Yurkiewicz scored twice in the second for a 21-3 Southern lead at the intermission. Yurkiewicz scored again early in the third. Nick Slater hit Matt Bubnis for a 25-yard touchdown pass, and Jeff Lowry scored on a 6-yard run to push the lead to 41-3 after three. Bloomsburg scored a late touchdown to make the final score 41-9. The Tigers' defense held the Panthers to 48 yards rushing and 83 yards through the air. Southern's ground game pounded out 315 yards. Gaul rushed for 134 yards and a score. Yurkiewicz ran for 65 yards and two touchdowns. He also had a scoring reception. Lowry added a rushing touchdown. Slater threw for 128 yards and two scores. Bubnis had 102 receiving yards and a touchdown.

The week three home game versus Mount Carmel proved to be a disaster for the Tigers. Southern's offense never got in gear, and their vaunted rushing attack was held to 27 yards on 27 carries. The Red Tornadoes scored four rushing touchdowns, and the Tigers suffered a rare shutout loss, 26-0. Shaun Gaul led the Tigers with a minuscule 23 yads rushing. Nick Slater threw for 214 yards in the game.

Southern found themselves in a battle in a road game against Lewisburg that would go down to the wire. After a touchdown run and a field goal, Lewisburg led 10-0 at the half. Mark Yurkiewicz got the Tigers on the board with a 15-yard touchdown run in the third to cut the Green Dragon lead to 10-6. Nick Slater's quarterback sneak from one yard out gave the Tigers their first lead in the fourth. Lewisburg got the ball on their 13-yard line with 2:04 remaining in the game and no timeouts. The Dragons drove to the Southern 20-yard line with seven seconds left. Lewisburg sent their kicker on to try a 37-yard field goal to tie the game. The kick was up and had plenty of distance; however, the ball drifted to the left, barely missing the upright as time expired to give the Tigers a hard-fought 13-10 victory. Shaun Gaul rushed for 103 yards. Yurkiewicz had 32 yards on the ground and a score. Slater ran for a touchdown and had 39 passing yards.

The Tigers were in another battle with Warrior Run at Tiger Stadium in week five. The Defenders scored first on a 57-yard pass play. Nick Slater piled in from one yard out to tie the score at 7-7 after the opening quarter. Warrior Run scored early in the second, but P.J. Sargent returned the ensuing kickoff for an 85-yard touchdown to tie the game again at 14-14. The Defenders scored again before the half to lead 20-14 at the break. After a scoreless third, the Tigers finally took control in the fourth quarter. Shaun Gaul ran for a 5-yard score, and Mark Yurkiewicz put the final nails in the coffin with touchdown runs of 45 and 17 yards. Southern earned a 35-20 win. The Southern defense got interceptions from Eric Steffen and Matt Bubnis, and the unit recovered two fumbles. The Tigers rumbled for 305 yards on the ground. Gaul rushed for 146 yards and a touchdown. Yurkiewicz added 90 yards rushing and two scores. Slater chipped in with a rushing touchdown.

The week six game at Hughesville marked the fourth straight contest where the Tigers' opponent scored first. The Spartans led 7-0 after one. In the second quarter, P.J. Sargent ran for a 6-yard touchdown, and the Tigers' converted a two-point conversion to lead 8-7 at halftime. Hughesville scored early in the third to retake the lead. Shaun Gaul had a 16-yard scoring run, and another successful conversion gave Southern a 16-13 lead after three. Mark Yurkiewicz and Gaul put the game out of reach with touchdown runs of 5 and 53 yards in the fourth quarter to give the Tigers a 30-13 victory. Gaul ran for 117 yards and two touchdowns. Sargent ran for 86 yards and a score. Yurkiewicz added 15 yards and a rushing touchdown.

Next for the Tigers was a road contest against Marian Catholic. Nick Slater kicked a 24-yard field goal for a 3-0 lead. The Colts scored on a 73-yard run to take a 7-3 lead after one. Southern's defense turned up the heat on Marian Catholic in the second half. Ben Meiser sacked the Colts' quarterback in the endzone for a safety, and Andy Hornberger returned a fumble 16 yards for a touchdown to give the Tigers the lead, 13-7. Eric Steffen added a 3-yard scoring run in the fourth to make the final 20-7. Steffen rushed for 36 yards and a score. Shaun Gaul ran for 160 yards.

The Tigers suffered their second loss of the season in a road game at Selinsgrove. The Seals scored three times before Mark Yurkiewicz's 5-yard touchdown run in the second. Selinsgrove led 21-6 at the break. The Seals scored again early in the third. Eric Steffen cut the lead to 28-12 with a 7-yard scoring run. Yurkiewicz ran for a 3-yard touchdown in the fourth, but the Tigers could get no closer and dropped the game 28-18 to the Seals. Shaun Gaul led with 101 rushing yards. Yurkiewicz scored twice and had 47 yards on the ground.

Southern got back on track with a week nine home game versus Central Columbia. Mark Yurkiewicz scored on an 11-yard run, Nick Slater fired a 15-yard pass to Matt Yancoskie, P.J. Sargent scored on a 12-yard scamper, Slater added a 28-yard field goal, and the Tigers' defense pitched a shutout in a 24-0 win over the Blue Jays. Shaun Gaul rushed for 113 yards. Yurkiewicz added 78 yards on the ground and a score. Sargent chipped in with 89 rushing yards and a touchdown. Slater passed for 89 yards and a score. Yancosckie had 15 receiving yards and a score. With the victory, the Tigers won the Central Susquehanna Conference Division II Championship.

Southern wrapped up the regular season against Danville at Tiger Stadium. Following a Danville touchdown, P.J. Sargent scored on a 74-yard run to tie the game at 7-7 after one. A Southern touchdown and Nick Slater's 21-yard field goal pushed the Tigers' lead to 17-7 at halftime. After a scoreless third, Shaun Gaul scored on a 5-yard burst early in the fourth quarter. The Ironmen scored twice to cut the lead to 24-19. Late in the fourth, deep in Southern territory, Danville appeared to score a go-ahead touchdown on a pass into the endzone. However, the play was called back on a penalty for an illegal receiver downfield. Southern held off the Ironmen for a season-ending 24-19 victory. The Tigers rushed for 313 yards. Sargent ran for 106 yards and a score. Gaul rushed for 94 yards and a touchdown.

The Tigers started the postseason in the District IV Class A Semifinal Game versus Lourdes Regional at Tiger Stadium. Southern got first-quarter touchdown runs from Eric Steffen (3 yards), Shaun Gaul (3 yards), and Mark Yurkiewicz (10 yards) to build a 20-0 lead. Gaul scored twice in the second on a 13-yard run and a 23-yard pass from Nick Slater, and P.J. Sargent added a 7-yard rushing touchdown to increase the lead to 41-10 at the half. Matt Kaskie finished the scoring with a 14-yard touchdown run in the third to make the final 47-10. Southern pounded the Red Raiders with 357 yards rushing. Yurkiewicz led the way with 102 yards on the ground and a touchdown. Gaul had 61 rushing yards and two scoring runs. He also had a touchdown reception. Kaskie added 48 rushing yards and a score. Steffen ran for 38 yards and a touchdown. Sargent chipped in with 18 rushing yards and a touchdown. Slater threw for 58 yards and a score.

Southern moved on to the District IV Class A Championship Game at home against Montgomery. The Red Raiders opened the scoring in the second, but the Tigers got touchdown runs from Eric Steffen (7 yards) and Mark Yurkiewicz (2 yards) to take a 14-6 lead into the break. Nick Slater scored on an 11-yard keeper to run the score to 21-6 in the third. Yurkiewicz scored on a 13-yard pass from Slater, and Shaun Gaul rumbled for a 13-yard touchdown run to make the final score 34-19. Gaul ran for 117 rushing yards and a score. Yurkiewicz rushed for 45 yards and a touchdown and had a scoring reception. Steffen had 31 yards on the ground and a touchdown. Slater passed for 84 yards and a touchdown. The Tigers won their eighth consecutive District IV Class A Championship.

The Tigers took on the Scotland Cadets in the PIAA Class A Eastern Semifinal Game in Harrisburg. P.J. Sargent had two first-quarter touchdowns on a 55-yard run and an 80-yard punt return, and Mark Yurkiewicz ran for a 26-yard score to give Southern a 20-0 lead. Nick Slater hit Shaun Gaul for a 6-yard touchdown pass, and Southern led 27-7 at halftime. Scotland scored twice in the third to cut the lead to 27-20, but Gaul and Sargent put the Cadets away in the fourth with touchdown runs of 3 and 68 yards. The Tigers advanced to the Eastern Final with a 41-28 victory. Southern had three running backs rush for 100 yards in the game (Sargent, 124 and two touchdowns; Gaul, 107 and a score; Mark Yurkiewicz, 105). Slater had a touchdown pass. The defense controlled Scotland with three interceptions (two by Sargent) and two fumble recoveries.

The Tigers took on the Schuylkill Haven Hurricanes in the PIAA Class A Eastern Final Game in Sunbury. Southern jumped to a 21-0 first-quarter lead on Mark Yurkiewicz's five-yard run, Shaun Gaul's 57-yard burst, and Nick Slater's nine-yard keeper. The Hurricanes responded with two scores in the second, and Southern led 21-14 at the break. Schuylkill Haven tied the game with a touchdown early in the third quarter, but P.J. Sargent put the Tigers back in front with a 71-yard scoring run. Southern led 27-21 after three. Gaul opened the fourth with a one-yard scoring plunge, only to see the Hurricanes pull within a score with a touchdown run. Late in the fourth quarter, Yurkiewicz appeared to finally put Schuylkill Haven away with a 3-yard touchdown run to make the score 42-28. However, the feisty Hurricanes would not go down without a fight. They returned the ensuing kickoff 91 yards for a touchdown to cut the

## 1998 SEASON

| Opponent | Location | W/L | Score |
|---|---|---|---|
| Pius X | Away | W | 42-28 |
| Bloomsburg | Home | W | 41-9 |
| Mount Carmel | Home | L | 0-26 |
| Lewisburg | Away | W | 13-10 |
| Warrior Run | Home | W | 35-20 |
| Hughesville | Away | W | 30-13 |
| Marian Catholic | Away | W | 20-7 |
| Selinsgrove | Away | L | 18-28 |
| Central Columbia | Home | W | 24-0 |
| Danville | Home | W | 24-19 |
| **District IV Class A Semifinal Game** | | | |
| Lourdes Regional | Home | W | 47-10 |
| **District IV Class A Championship Game** | | | |
| Montgomery | Home | W | 34-19 |
| **PIAA Class A Eastern Semifinal Game** | | | |
| Scotland | Neutral | W | 41-28 |
| **PIAA Class A Eastern Final Game** | | | |
| Schuylkill Haven | Neutral | W | 42-35 |
| **PIAA Class A Championship Game** | | | |
| Rochester | Neutral | L | 0-18 |

COACHING STAFF: Jim Roth, Head Coach; Al Cihocki, Assistant Coach; Jason Crawford, Assistant Coach; Mike Johnston, Assistant Coach; John Marks, Assistant Coach; Andy Mills, Assistant Coach; Pete Saylor, Assistant Coach; Tim Snyder, Assistant Coach; Richard Steele, Assistant Coach; Curt Stellfox, Assistant Coach

ATHLETIC DIRECTOR: Terry Sharrow

ROSTER: Jay Andress, Garrett Bembenek, Ryan Breach, Matt Bubnis, Shawn Connaghan, Chase Delancey, Nick Fisher, Mike Fox, Shaun Gaul, Zac Getkin, Eric Gilroy, Rob Gittler, Chris Grayson, Andy Hornberger, Matt Kaskie, Roy Kingston, Steve Kowalchick, Mark Kreisher, Wes Lindemuth, Jeff Lowry, Shane Martz, Jon Mattivi, Ben Meiser, Brett Meyers, Paul Nazarchyk, Marc Osevala, Matt Porter, Nate Richard, Chadd Roadarmel, Kyle Romig, Ken Ruckle, P.J. Sargent, Paul Shingara, Mike Shoffler, Nick Slater, Tom Smeltzer, Greg Sones, D.J. Spotts, Eric Steffen, Pete Trometter, Tyler Weaver, Matt Yancoskie, Mark Yurkiewicz lead to 42-35 with less than two minutes to play. The entire stadium knew what was coming next, as the Hurricanes lined up for an onside kick which had been successful earlier in the quarter. However, Eric Steffen successfully fielded the kick, and the Tigers were able to run out the final 1:49 to earn a well-deserved 42-35 victory over a very game Schuylkill Haven team. Sargent led with 141 yards rushing and a touchdown. Gaul contributed 76 yards and a score. He also had a touchdown reception. Yurkiewicz had 69 yards on the ground and two scores. Slater threw for 72 yards, passed for a touchdown, and ran for a score. The Tigers secured their spot in the PIAA Class A Championship Game for the third time in five years.

Southern Columbia advanced to the PIAA Class A Championship Game against the Rochester Rams at Hersheypark Stadium. As with their last two championship games, it would be a defensive battle with Rochester. The Rams scored a first-quarter touchdown, and the game would remain 7-0 at halftime. The Tigers' defense held their own against the Rams, but the offense struggled to put together sustained drives. Rochester scored again in the third and put the game away with a touchdown in the final period to win the championship, 18-0. The Tigers rushing game was led by Shaun Gaul, who could only amass 33 yards. Nick Slater threw for 99 yards, but the Tigers were shutout for the second time in a championship game.

Although the season ended disappointingly, the Tigers had several outstanding performances. Shaun Gaul rushed for 1,531 yards and scored 12 touchdowns. Mark Yurkiewicz had 881 yards rushing and scored 16 touchdowns. He would finish his career with the Tigers with 2,181 yards and 28 scores. P.J. Sargent contributed 587 yards on the ground and scored seven touchdowns. Eric Steffen pitched in with 490 rushing yards and five scores. Nick Slater threw for 1,037 yards and seven touchdowns. Steffen had 147 tackles (97 solo) and would finish as Southern's all-time leader with 320. Sargent registered five interceptions. Jay Andress recorded 5.5 sacks. Steffen and Marc Osevala were All-State selections. The 1998 Tigers would finish the season with an overall record of 12-3.

1
9
9
9
For the 1999 season, Coach Roth looked to retool the backfield to continue the Tigers' dominant ground attack. A new quarterback would be taking over the reins of the offense, but there was optimism about the prospects of another deep run in the state playoffs. Southern began the year with a home game versus Pius X. Perhaps more so than in the past, Coach Roth readily used his kicking game, and Wes Lindemuth scored the first points of the season with a 27-yard field goal. Andy Hornberger added a

25-yard touchdown reception from quarterback Matt Kaskie, and the Tigers led 10-0 after the first quarter. Shaun Gaul rumbled into the endzone from one yard out, and Lindemuth connected on a 29-yard field goal in the second to push the lead to 20-0 at the break. The Royals scored twice in the third quarter to pull within 20-14. In the fourth quarter, Nate Richard finished off the Royals with a one-yard plunge to make the final 26-14. Richard led the Tigers' ground attack with 83 yards and a touchdown. Gaul added another 78 yards rushing and a score. Kaskie threw for 154 yards and his first career touchdown to Hornberger in his first start at quarterback.

The Tigers traveled to Bloomsburg for a road matchup with the Panthers. Matt Kaskie hit Sean Connaghan for a 14-yard touchdown pass early in the first. Sean Gaul then scored on runs of 3 and 2 yards to make it 20-0 after the opening quarter. In the second, Kaskie connected with Paul Nazarchyk on a 56-yard scoring pass and fired a 41-yard touchdown strike to Gaul to give the Tigers a 33-0 halftime lead. Gaul scored his fourth touchdown of the game on a 14-yard run in the third. Bloomsburg scored a late touchdown to make the final 40-7. Gaul led the way with 125 rushing yards and three touchdowns. He also added a scoring reception. Kaskie passed for 141 yards and three touchdowns. Nazarchyk hauled in a 25-yard touchdown catch. The defense got interceptions from Garrett Bembenek and Andy Hornberger and registered three for the game.

Southern, the top-ranked Class A team in the state, traveled to Mount Carmel to take on the number one Class AA and defending state champion Red Tornadoes in front of an overflow crowd. Mount Carmel scored first to lead 7-0 after the opening quarter. Matt Kaskie found Andy Hornberger for a 62-yard touchdown pass to cut the lead to 7-6 at the half. The Red Tornadoes pushed the lead to 14-6 in the third. Although Kaskie hooked up with Paul Nazarchyk on a 71-yard touchdown throw, Mount Carmel scored twice in the fourth quarter to win the game, 27-12. Kaskie threw for 187 passing yards and two touchdowns to Hornberger and Nazarchyk. However, the Mount Carmel defense effectively contained the Tigers' potent running game, with Shaun Gaul leading the team with a dismal 33 yards.

Southern looked to rebound in a home game against Lewisburg at Tiger Stadium. The Tigers built a 10-0 lead on a Wes Lindemuth 23-yard field goal and a one-yard touchdown run by Nate Richard. The Green Dragons scored a touchdown just before the half to make the score 10-7 at the intermission. The teams traded scores in the third quarter, with Shaun Gaul scoring on a 25-yard burst. The Green Dragons got a touchdown run to take the lead, 19-13. Southern reclaimed the lead, 23-19, on a 30-yard scamper by Gaul. But Lewisburg got a late touchdown pass to go in front 25-23 with 42 seconds left to play. The Tigers drove the ball into field goal range, and Coach Roth sent Lindemuth on for a 35-yard attempt. However, the kick was low and was not close, and in a reversal of fortune from the previous year, Lewisburg won the game, 25-23. It was the first time Southern had lost back-to-back games since 1986. The Tigers' offense put up good numbers, rushing for 320 yards. Gaul had a tremendous effort, rushing for 200 yards and two touchdowns. Richard ran for 110 yards and a score. Matt Kaskie threw for 129 yards for the game.

A week five road game at Warrior Run turned into another nail-biter. After a scoreless first quarter, Shaun Gaul scored on a one-yard plunge. However, the Defenders scored before the half and led 7-6 at the break. Nate Richard gave the Tigers a 14-7 lead in the third on a 3-yard touchdown run. This set up a wild fourth quarter. Warrior Run got a touchdown pass to tie the game at 14-14. Richard ripped off a 5-yard scoring run to put the Tigers back in front, 20-14. But the pesky Defenders retook the lead, 21-20, on a 66-yard pass play. Late in the final quarter, Matt Kaskie plowed in from one yard out with 14 seconds remaining, and Gaul converted a two-point conversion to give Southern a dramatic 28-21 victory. The Tigers rumbled for 351 yards on the ground. Gaul led the way with 184 yards rushing and a touchdown. Richard added 91 rushing yards and two scores. Kaskie added a rushing touchdown.

The Tigers returned home to face the Hughesville Spartans. Hughesville scored in the first quarter to take a 6-0 lead. Matt Kaskie connected with Shaun Gaul for a 4-yard touchdown pass to tie the game. The Spartans got a scoring pass to retake the lead, 13-6. Kaskie hit Jeff Lowry for an 11-yard score to cut the lead to 13-12 at halftime. Gaul plowed in from one yard out, and Kaskie scampered for a 27-yard touchdown in the fourth quarter to pull out a 26-13 victory. Gaul ran for 117 yards and a touchdown. He also had a scoring reception. Kaskie passed for 69 yards and two touchdowns and ran for the winning score.

Marian Catholic visited Tiger Stadium for a week seven matchup. Nate Richard got the Tigers on the board in the first on a 7-yard run. Southern got two scores in the second on a Matt Kaskie one-yard quarterback sneak and a 5-yard touchdown pass from Kaskie to Richard. Southern led 21-0 at the break. Paul Nazarchyk pushed the score to 28-0 with a one-yard touchdown dive. The Colts scored two late touchdowns in the fourth to make the final score 28-12. Shaun Gaul ran for 125 yards. Nazarchyk had 80 yards on the ground, had a touchdown run, and hauled in a scoring reception. Kaskie threw for 163 yards and a touchdown and had a scoring run.

The Tigers hosted the Selinsgrove Seals at Tiger Stadium. Southern got first-half scoring runs from Nate Richard (3 yards) and Shaun Gaul (4 yards) to lead 14-0 at the break. Andy Hornberger scored twice in the third on a one-yard run and a 48-yard interception return, and Gaul added a one-yard touchdown burst, and the route was on. Steve Kowalchick capped the scoring in the fourth with a 2-yard touchdown run to make the final 40-0. The Tigers' defense held the Seals to 89 total yards of offense and had three interceptions and a fumble recovery. Gaul ran for 84 yards and a touchdown. Richard rushed for 40 yards and a score. Hornberger and Kowalchick each added touchdown runs. Matt Kaskie threw for 151 yards.

Southern traveled to Central Columbia for a week nine road game. Nate Richard scored on a 3-yard run early in the first. The Blue Jays tied the game at 7-7 after the opening quarter. Richard and Shaun Gaul scored on runs of 14 and 9 yards, and Central got a 47-yard pass play to make the score 21-14 at halftime. After a scoreless third, Paul Nazarchyk ended the scoring with a 3-yard run in the fourth quarter to give the Tigers a 28-14 win. Southern rushed for 340 yards. Gaul ran for 148 yards and a touchdown. Richard added 67 yards and two scores. Nazarchyk chipped in with 25 yards on the ground and a touchdown.

The Tigers visited the Danville Ironmen in the regular-season finale. Danville opened the scoring with a 62-yard pass play. The Tigers grabbed a 13-7 lead in the first on a 72-yard touchdown burst from Andy Hornberger and a 7-yard run by Matt Kaskie. The Ironmen scored a touchdown and connected on a field goal in the second to lead 17-13 at the intermission. Hornberger gave Southern the lead back on a 26-yard touchdown run. Shaun Gaul scored on a 6-yard run early in the fourth to push the Tigers' lead to 27-17. However, Danville got a 6-yard touchdown pass to cut the lead to 27-24. The Ironmen recovered a fumble and returned it 32 yards for the winning score to make the final, 31-27. It was the first time the Tigers had lost three games in the regular season since 1986. Hornberger rushed for 135 yards and two scores. Gaul ran for 54 yards and a touchdown.

The Tigers again qualified for the District IV Class A Playoffs and hosted the Loyalsock Lancers in the Semifinal Game. Steve Kowalchick rumbled for a 3-yard touchdown, and Matt Kaskie hit Chris Grayson for a 48-yard scoring pass to give Southern a 14-0 lead after the first. After a Lancer touchdown, the offense rolled. Kaskie found Jeff Lowry for a 17-yard touchdown pass and connected with Sean Connaghan on a 14-yard scoring throw, and Wes Lindemuth added a 27-yard field goal to give the Tigers a commanding 31-6 halftime lead.

Lowry and Kaskie hooked up again on a 41-yard touchdown pass, and Jason Brobst returned a punt 65 yards for a score for a 45-6 lead after three. Brobst tacked on a 25-yard touchdown run in the fourth quarter to make the final 52-13. Kaskie had a huge day, throwing for 243 yards and four touchdowns. Lowry had had 87 yards receiving and two scores. Connaghan and Grayson added touchdown receptions. Brobst and Kowalchick each had scoring runs.

The Tigers hosted the Montgomery Red Raiders in the District IV Class A Championship Game. The Tigers' defense came up with a big play to set up the opening score. Wes Lindemuth recovered a fumbled lateral and returned it to the Montgomery one-yard line. Shaun Gaul plowed in for a 7-0 lead in the first. Paul Nazarchyk and Gaul sandwiched scoring runs around a Red Raider touchdown to give Southern a 21-6 lead at the intermission. Matt Kaskie hit Andy Hornberger for a 45-yard scoring pass and a 27-6 lead after three. Jason Brobst capped the scoring in the fourth with a 19-yard touchdown run. The Tigers advanced to the PIAA Playoffs with a 34-6 victory. Gaul ran for 139 yards and two touchdowns. Nazarchyk had 43 yards rushing and a score. Brobst added 28 yards on the ground and a touchdown. Kaskie threw for 104 yards and hit Hornberger for a scoring pass. The defense had two interceptions and recovered two Montgomery fumbles.

The Tigers faced the Steelton-Highspire Rollers in the PIAA Easter Semifinal Game in Sunbury. The game would be a thriller that went down to the wire. The Rollers took a 7-0 lead after the first quarter. Tom Smeltzer came up with a huge defensive play, recovering a Steel High fumble to set up Andy Hornberger's 64-yard touchdown run to tie the game. Wes Lindemuth connected on a 31-yard field goal, and Matt Kaskie hit Jeff Lowry for a 16-yard touchdown pass in the second. The Rollers scored on a 70-yard pass, and Southern led 17-13 at the half. Shaun Gaul had two 16-yard scoring runs in the third quarter, Steel High had a touchdown run, and the Tigers led 32-19 after three. Steel High scored on a 45-yard run in the fourth to pull within 32-25. In the game's final two minutes, the Rollers drove from their 16-yard line to the Tigers' 8-yard line. Needing a touchdown to tie the game, the Rollers quarterback fired a pass in the flat. Southern's Sean Connaghan came up with a game-saving interception at the goal line to preserve the Tigers' 32-25 victory. Hornberger ran for 135 yards and a touchdown. Gaul had 119 rushing yards and two scores. Kaskie passed for 76 yards and a touchdown to Lowry.

Southern would play another thrilling game against Tri-Valley in the PIAA Class A Eastern Final Game at Fountain Springs. After a Tri-Valley touchdown, Shaun Gaul tied the game with a one-yard plunge in the first. The Bulldogs and Gaul traded touchdowns again, on another one-yard run, to make the score 15-15 at the half. Tri-Valley scored on a 2-yard run to take a 22-15 lead. Matt Kaskie snuck in from 2 yards out, but the Tigers trailed 22-21 after three. In the fourth quarter, Tri-Valley drove inside the Tigers' 10-yard line. For the second week in a row, Sean Connaghan came up with a huge defensive play on a goal-line stand. The Bulldogs' quarterback threw a pass into the endzone, but Connaghan wrestled the ball away from the intended receiver and returned it 56 yards to the Tri-Valley 44. That set up Kaskie's one-yard keeper to give the Tigers a 29-22 lead. However, the game was not over, and the rugged Bulldogs

## 1999 SEASON

| Opponent | Location | W/L | Score |
|----------|----------|-----|-------|
| Pius X | Home | W | 26-14 |
| Bloomsburg | Away | W | 40-7 |
| Mount Carmel | Away | L | 12-27 |
| Lewisburg | Home | L | 23-25 |
| Warrior Run | Away | W | 28-21 |
| Hughesville | Home | W | 26-13 |
| Marian Catholic | Home | W | 28-12 |
| Selinsgrove | Home | W | 40-0 |
| Central Columbia | Away | W | 28-14 |
| Danville | Away | L | 27-31 |
| **District IV Class A Semifinal Game** | | | |
| Loyalsock | Home | W | 52-13 |
| **District IV Class A Championship Game** | | | |
| Montgomery | Home | W | 34-6 |
| **PIAA Class A Eastern Semifinal Game** | | | |
| Steelton-Highspire | Neutral | W | 32-25 |
| **PIAA Class A Eastern Final Game** | | | |
| Tri-Valley | Neutral | W | 29-22 |
| **PIAA Class A Championship Game** | | | |
| South Side | Neutral | L | 21-27 |

COACHING STAFF: Jim Roth, Head Coach; Al Cihocki, Assistant Coach; Jason Crawford, Assistant Coach; Andy Helwig, Assistant Coach; Mike Johnston, Assistant Coach; Chuck Kowalchick, Assistant Coach; John Marks, Assistant Coach; Andy Mills, Assistant Coach; Pete Saylor, Assistant Coach; Tim Snyder, Assistant Coach; Richard Steele, Assistant Coach; Curt Stellfox, Assistant Coach

ATHLETIC DIRECTOR: Terry Sharrow

ROSTER: Garrett Bembenek, Lucas Boyer, Jason Brobst, Jared Brokenshire, Al Cihocki, Sean Connaghan, Chase Delancey, Mitch Fetterman, Joe Fisher, Nick Fisher, Mike Fox, Shaun Gaul, Chris Grayson, Chuck Gundrum, Travis Hoopengardner, Matt Kaskie, Roy Kingston, Joel Knoebel, Steve Kowalchick, Mark Kreisher, Eric Levan, Wes Lindemuth, Jeff Lowry, Shane Martz, Jon Mattivi, Ryan McGeary, Brett Meyers, Jason Mills, Mike Motyka, Shawn Mummey, Paul Nazarchyk, Marc Osevala, Matt Porter, Nate Richard, Chadd Roadarmel, Chase Roadarmel, Kyle Romig, Casey Rosini, Mike Shoffler, Rob Shoop, Tom Smeltzer, Brad Sones, Greg Sones, D.J. Spotts, Justin St. Clair, Greg Swartzlander, Eric Trometter, Pete Trometter drove to the Southern 4-yard line. The Tigers' defense came up with another goal-line stand and turned Tri-Valley away on a fourth and goal run to preserve a hard-fought 29-22 win. Gaul ran for 137 yards and two scores. Kaskie ran for a pair of touchdowns. The Tigers advanced to their second straight PIAA Class A Championship Game.

Southern faced the South Side Rams in an epic PIAA Class A Championship Game at Hersheypark Stadium. South Side scored on a 6-yard run to take a 6-0 lead after one. The Rams scored again early in the second on a 5-yard pass play for a 12-0 lead. Matt Kaskie got the Tigers on the board with a 17-yard run to cut the lead to 12-7. South Side added a field goal and led 15-7 at the half. The Rams scored on a 2-yard run in the third to take a 21-7 lead. Andy Hornberger pulled the Tigers to within 21-14 at the end of the third with a 2-yard touchdown run. In the fourth, Jeff Lowry hauled in a 22-yard pass from Kaskie to tie the game at 21-21. Late in the game, Kaskie threw a seam pass to what appeared to be an open Lowry, but the Rams' defensive back made a diving interception to give South Side a chance to take the lead. The Rams scored on a 3-yard run with nine seconds left in the game, and South Side claimed the PIAA Class A Championship. It was another heartbreaking loss in a championship game for the Tigers. Kaskie threw for 196 yards and a touchdown pass to Lowry. He also added a scoring run. Hornberger had a touchdown run for the Tigers.

The stinging championship game loss did not diminish the individual achievements of the 1999 Tigers. Shaun Gaul rushed for 1,642 yards and scored 20 touchdowns. Nate Richard ran for 630 yards and had nine scores. Andy Hornberger added 521 yards on the ground and scored eight touchdowns. Paul Nazarchyk ran for 266 yards and had five scores. Steve Kowalchick and Jason Brobst each scored two touchdowns. Matt Kaskie threw for 1,884 yards and 16 touchdowns. He also rushed for six scores. Jeff Lowry had 622 receiving yards and five touchdowns. Sean Connaghan hauled in two touchdown receptions and had 449 receiving yards. Connaghan and Greg Sones led the team with six sacks. Tom Smeltzer registered 89 tackles (58 solo). Brett Myers had five interceptions. Gaul and Marc Osevala were All-State selections. The 1999 Southern Columbia Tigers had a record of 11-4.

# CHAPTER 6

# THE 2000s
## (THE CHAMPIONSHIP YEARS)

Coach Roth's Tigers entered the 2000 season with the same Wing-T offense, but with an experienced quarterback and more emphasis on the passing game. Although the ground game would still be Southern's bread and butter, quarterback Matt Kaskie would have one of the finest seasons of any Tigers signal-caller. Running back Nate Schiccatano would transfer from Shamokin and pay immediate dividends. The Tigers opened the season on the road at Loyalsock. It wouldn't take Schiccatano to impress his new teammates. He scored the first touchdown of the year on a 2-yard run. Southern scored first-quarter touchdowns on a 68-yard scoring pass from Kaskie to Sean Connaghan, and Nate Richard's 8-yard run to take a 20-0 lead after one. In the second, Richard scored on a 5-yard touchdown run, and Schiccatano would score on a 75-yard gallop and a 75-yard punt return. Steve Kowalchick would return an interception 23 yards for a pick six to cap the scoring before the half. The Tigers defeated the Lancers, 48-0. In his Southern debut, Schiccatano rushed for 126 yards and a touchdown. He also returned a punt for a score. Richard ran for 67 yards and two touchdowns. Kaskie threw for 133 yards and a touchdown. Connaghan had 81 receiving yards and a score. The defense held the Lancers scoreless with two interceptions and a fumble recovery.

The first home game of the season was against the Bloomsburg Panthers. Nate Richard got the Tigers off to a quick start by returning the opening kickoff 80 yards for a touchdown. After Nate Schiccatano's one-yard scoring plunge, Richard scored again with a 7-yard run. In the second, Schiccatano had a 37-yard touchdown run, and Matt Kaskie hit Chris Grayson with a 16-yard scoring pass to give the Tigers a 35-0 lead at the half. Schiccatano scored his third touchdown of the game in the third quarter on a 29-yard burst, and Bloomsburg scored a late touchdown in the fourth to make the final 42-6. Schiccatano led the way with 152 rushing yards and three touchdowns. Richard ran for 46 yards and a score. Kaskie passed for 140 yards and a touchdown to Grayson.

The Tigers once again had a showdown with Mount Carmel in a week three road contest with the Red Tornadoes. After Mount Carmel got an early touchdown, Matt Kaskie scored on a 40-yard keeper, and the Tornadoes led 7-6 after one. Mount Carmel scored again in the second for a 13-6 lead at the break. The Tornadoes put the game out of reach with a touchdown run in the fourth. Kaskie hit Nate Richard for a late 69-yard scoring pass. Mount Carmel won the highly-anticipated matchup, 19-12. Kaskie led the Tigers' offense with 131 yards passing and a touchdown. He also rushed for 73 yards and a score. Richard had a touchdown reception.

Southern's offense got back on track in a big way in a 64-20 blowout at Lewisburg. The Tigers rushed for 421 yards and had 578 total yards of offense. Nate Schiccatano ran for 119 yards and three scores. He also added a touchdown reception. Richard rushed for 95 yards and two touchdowns. Jason Brobst and Casey Rosini each contributed a rushing score. Matt Kaskie threw for 157 yards and two touchdowns. He also had a scoring run. Sean Connaghan hauled in 66 receiving yards and a touchdown.

The Tigers' offense continued to roll against Warrior Run at Tiger Stadium. Matt Kaskie fired touchdown passes of 55 and 34 yards to Sean Connaghan, and Southern led 14-7 after one. In the second, Eric Trometter scored on a 5-yard run, Kaskie ran for a 30-yard touchdown, and Kaskie found Matt Porter for a 41-yard touchdown pass to push the lead to 35-7 at the intermission. Kaskie and Connaghan hooked up for their third touchdown on a 20-yard pass, and Jason Brobst rumbled for a 13-yard scoring run for a 49-7 third-quarter lead. Steve Kowalchick and Casey Rosini scored on runs of 2 and 12 yards for a 63-7 victory. Kaskie threw for 247 yards and four touchdowns and added a rushing score. Connaghan had 156 receiving yards and three touchdowns. Porter added 41 receiving yards and a scoring grab. Kowalchick, Trometter, Rosini, and Brobst each scored rushing touchdowns.

Southern continued their high-flying offense at Hughesville. Eric Trometter opened the scoring on a one-yard plunge, but Hughesville answered to tie the game at 7-7 in the first. Nate Schiccatano scored on a 58-yard jaunt for a 14-7 halftime lead. Schiccatano then scored three third-quarter touchdowns on a 28-yard pass from Matt Kaskie and runs of 56 and 10 yards to put the game out of reach. Jason Andress and Casey Rosini added scoring runs of 10 and 7 yards in the fourth to close out the Spartans, 48-7. Schiccatano rushed for 123 yards and three scores and had a touchdown reception. Nate Richard ran for 126 yards. The Tigers rumbled for 403 rushing yards. Trometter added 46 rushing yards and a score. Andress and Rosini contributed touchdown runs. Kaskie passed for 81 yards and a score.

A week seven road trip against the South Williamsport Mountaineers continued the offensive onslaught. After spotting the Mountaineers an early touchdown, the defense stepped up. Nate Schiccatano returned an interception 97 yards for a score to tie the game. Matt Kaskie gave Southern the lead on a 60-yard keeper, and Schiccatano gave the Tigers a 21-7 first-quarter lead on a 16-yard touchdown run. Southern put the game away in the second quarter. Jason Brobst returned a punt for a 54-yard score, Kaskie hit Nate Richard on a 12-yard scoring pass, Schiccatano ran for a 27-yard touchdown, and Kaskie rumbled for a 63-yard score, and the Tigers built a 49-7 lead at the half. South Williamsport got a touchdown in the third, and Brobst capped the scoring with a 13-yard run in the fourth quarter. Southern earned a lopsided 54-14 victory. The Tigers rushed for 345 yards. Schiccatano ran for 43 yards and two touchdowns. Richards had 67 rushing yards and had a touchdown reception. Brobst added 13 yards on the ground and a score. Kaskie threw for 40 yards and a touchdown. He also ran for 127 yards and two scores.

The Tigers hit a bump in the road at Selinsgrove. The Seals scored two early touchdowns before Nate Schiccatano got Southern on the board with a 64-yard run. Selinsgrove led 14-7 after one. Schiccatano tied the game early in the second with a 5-yard touchdown run. However, Selinsgrove broke the game open with two touchdowns and a field goal to take a 31-14 lead into the break. Matt Kaskie found Sean Connaghan for a 13-yard scoring pass to cut the lead to 31-21 in the third. The Seals scored on a touchdown run, and Kasie ran into the endzone from 3 yards in the fourth, and the Seals earned a 37-27 victory. Schiccatano had 86 yards on the ground and two touchdowns. Kaskie passed for 96 yards and a score. He also ran for a touchdown. Connaghan had 40 yards receiving and a scoring reception.

The Tigers righted the ship versus Central Columbia at Tiger Stadium. A Nate Richard 9-yard touchdown run and Jason Brobst's 33-yard field goal gave the Tigers a 10-0 first-quarter lead. Nate Schiccatano's 48-yard scoring jaunt pushed the lead to 17-0 at halftime. After a scoreless third, Matt Kaskie spotted Sean Connaghan for a 27-yard touchdown pass, and Steve Kowalchick scored on a 7-yard run for a 31-0 shutout win over the Blue Jays. Kowalchick ran for 118 yards and a touchdown. Schiccatano rushed for 102 yards and a score. Kaskie threw for 139 yards and a touchdown. Connaghan had 27 receiving yards and a score. The defense had a stellar game with an interception by Matt Murdoch and two fumble recoveries. With the victory, the Tigers won the Central Susquehanna Conference Division II Championship.

Southern finished the regular season at home against the Danville Ironmen. Nate Schiccatano started things with a bang with a 91-yard touchdown run in the opening quarter. Matt Kaskie hit Schiccatano for a 27-yard scoring pass, Schiccatano ran for a 13-yard touchdown, Kaskie scored on a 62-yard keeper, and Chris Grayson caught a 17-yard scoring pass from Kaskie for a 34-0 halftime lead. Danville had a scoring pass, and Nate Richard ran for a 24-yard touchdown, and the Tigers led 41-6 after three. Danville got a second touchdown, and Southern had scoring runs of 34 and 6 yards from Jason Brobst and Bryan Berns to make the final 55-12. Southern rushed for 385 yards and had 522 total yards of offense. Schiccatano ran for 114 yards and two touchdowns and had a scoring catch. Berns rushed for 45 yards and a score. Brobst chipped in with 34 yards on the ground and a touchdown. Richard had 31 rushing yards and a score. Kaskie threw for 137 yards and a touchdown and ran for a score. Grayson had 48 receiving yards and a touchdown.

The Tigers hosted Line Mountain in the District IV Class A Semifinal Game. Eric Trometter opened the scoring with a one-yard touchdown plunge. Matt Kaskie followed with a 35-yard keeper to give Southern a 14-0 lead after one. Kaskie found Nate Richard for a 35-yard touchdown pass, Richard pounded in from one yard out, Kaskie scored on a 37-yard scamper, and Matt Porter hauled in a 21-yard touchdown pass from Kaskie, and the Tigers led 42-7 at the break. Line Mountain scored three times in the second half, and Richard had a 26-yard touchdown run as Southern advanced with a 48-28 victory. The Tigers had three players rush for more than 100 yards (Kaskie 130, Richard 114, Schiccatano 110). They rushed for 519 yards as a team and had 626 yards of total offense. Southern got rushing touchdowns from Kaskie, Richard, and Trometter. Kaskie threw for 107 yards and two scores. Richard and Connaghan each had touchdown receptions.

Southern faced the Montgomery Red Raiders at Tiger Stadium for the District IV Class A Championship. Nate Richard got the Tigers on the board with a 13-yard touchdown run. Brad Sones recovered a Montgomery fumble in the endzone for a 13-0 first-quarter lead. Southern put the game out of reach in the second. Richard had an 11-yard scoring run, Matt Kaskie hit Sean

Connaghan on a 21-yard touchdown pass, Eric Trometter scored from 2 yards out, Nate Schiccatano ran for an 8-yard score, and Trometter added a 13-yard touchdown run as Southern led 48-0 at the intermission. Montgomery scored twice in the second half. Joe Fisher returned a Red Raider fumble 10 yards for a fourth-quarter touchdown to make the final score 54-14. Schiccatano ran for 90 yards and a touchdown. Richard rushed for 63 yards and a score and had a touchdown reception. Trometter had 33 rushing yards and two touchdowns. Kaskie passed for 146 yards and two scores. Connaghan had 41 receiving yards and a touchdown. The Tigers won their tenth consecutive District IV Class A Championship.

Southern began the state playoffs in the PIAA Class A Semifinal Game versus Steelton-Highspire in Harrisburg. The Rollers scored first with a touchdown run, but Nate Schiccatano and Eric Trometter scored on runs of 5 and one yard to give the Tigers a 14-6 lead after one. Steel High cut the lead to 14-13 with a touchdown pass. Schiccatano caught a 70-yard scoring pass from Matt Kaskie, and Nate Richard scored from one yard out to push the lead to 28-13. The Rollers scored again before the half, and Southern led 28-20 at the break. After a scoreless third, Steel High pulled within two points with a touchdown pass in the fourth. Kaskie put the Rollers away with a 4-yard touchdown run to make the final 35-26. It was a special night for Kaskie and Sean Connaghan. Kaskie broke Brad Osevala's school records for career passing yards and touchdown passes. Connaghan broke Jeff Lowry's record for career receptions. Kaskie threw for 197 yards and a touchdown and ran for 95 yards and a score. Schiccatano rushed for 47 yards and a touchdown and had a scoring reception. Trometter had 49 rushing yards and a touchdown. Richard finished with 33 rushing yards and a score.

The Tigers faced Lackawanna Trail in the PIAA Class A Eastern Final Game in Sunbury. Nate Richard and Nate Schiccatano got Southern off to a quick start with touchdown runs of 16 and 19 yards for a 14-0 first-quarter lead. The game was essentially over by halftime. Matt Kaskie hit Sean Connaghan on a 63-yard touchdown pass, Richard rumbled 21-yards for a touchdown, and Schiccatano scampered 8 yards for a score and a 35-0 lead. Eric Trometter and Jason Brobst scored on runs of 12 and 19 yards in the third to up the lead to 49-0. After a Lion touchdown, Eric Levan capped the scoring with a 12-yard run to give Southern a 56-7 blowout of Lackawanna Trail. The Tigers rushed for 422 yards and had 650 total yards of offense. Richard ran for 147 yards and two touchdowns. Schiccatano rushed for 66 yards and two scores. Trometter added 57 rushing yards and a touchdown. Brobst chipped in with 22 yards on the ground and a score. Levan contributed 18 rushing yards and a touchdown. Kaskie threw for 220 yards and a score. Connaghan had 112 receiving yards and a touchdown. The Tigers advanced to their sixth PIAA Class A Championship Game in the last seven years.

The Tigers faced a familiar foe in the Rochester Rams in the PIAA Class A Championship Game at Hersheypark Stadium. Rochester scored first, but Nate Richard answered with a 2-yard touchdown run for a 7-6 Southern lead after one. The Rams scored again in the second, and Rochester would take a 12-7

## 2000 SEASON

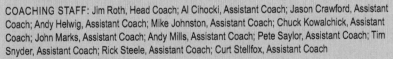

| Opponent | Location | W/L | Score |
|---|---|---|---|
| Loyalsock | Away | W | 48-0 |
| Bloomsburg | Home | W | 42-6 |
| Mount Carmel | Home | L | 12-19 |
| Lewisburg | Away | W | 64-20 |
| Warrior Run | Home | W | 63-7 |
| Hughesville | Away | W | 48-7 |
| South Williamsport | Away | W | 56-14 |
| Selinsgrove | Away | L | 27-37 |
| Central Columbia | Home | W | 31-0 |
| Danville | Home | W | 55-12 |
| **District IV Class A Semifinal Game** | | | |
| Line Mountain | Home | W | 48-28 |
| **District IV Class A Championship Game** | | | |
| Montgomery | Home | W | 54-14 |
| **PIAA Class A Eastern Semifinal Game** | | | |
| Steelton-Highspire | Neutral | W | 35-26 |
| **PIAA Class A Eastern Final Game** | | | |
| Lackawanna Trail | Neutral | W | 56-7 |
| **PIAA Class A Championship Game** | | | |
| Rochester | Neutral | L | 14-22 |

COACHING STAFF: Jim Roth, Head Coach; Al Cihocki, Assistant Coach; Jason Crawford, Assistant Coach; Andy Helwig, Assistant Coach; Mike Johnston, Assistant Coach; Chuck Kowalchick, Assistant Coach; John Marks, Assistant Coach; Andy Mills, Assistant Coach; Pete Saylor, Assistant Coach; Tim Snyder, Assistant Coach; Rick Steele, Assistant Coach; Curt Stellfox, Assistant Coach

ATHLETIC DIRECTOR: Terry Sharrow

ROSTER: Jason Andress, Austin Appel, A.J. Baylor, Bryan Berns, Josh Bixler, Kirby Blass, Jason Brobst, Matt Brobst, Jared Brookenshire, Sean Connaghan, Ben Diehl, Chase Delancy, Mitch Fetterman, Joe Fisher, Nick Fisher, Mike Fox, Ryan Fox, Chris Grayson, Chuck Gundrum, Drew Hampton, Nick Hampton, Travis Hoopergardner, Matt Kaskie, Rob Kerris, Joel Knoebel, Steve Kowalchick, Brian Leffler, Justin Leffler, Eric Levan, Josh Maciejewski, Shane Martz, Will Martz, Jon Mattivi, Kasey McBride, Ryan McGeary, Jason Mills, Mike Motyka, Shawn Mummey, Matt Murdock, Ben Palachick, Matt Porter, Matt Ragot, Nate Richard, Chase Roadarmel, Chad Romig, Kyle Romig, Casey Rosini, Erik Santor, Nate Schiccatano, Justin Schiel, Cody Schnaufer, Mike Shoffler, Rob Shoop, Tom Smeltzer, Chadd Sober, Brad Sones, D.J. Spotts, Justin St. Clair, Greg Swartzlander, Eric Trometter, Mark Wojtowicz lead at the half. Rochester got a touchdown run in the third to push the Rams' lead to 19-7. However, the Tigers would not go down without a fight, and Matt Kaskie scored on a 24-yard keeper to cut the lead to 19-14 going into the fourth quarter. The Tigers fought hard, but the Rams tacked on a 27-yard field goal in the fourth, and Rochester won the state championship, 22-14. Kaskie threw for 162 yards and ran for a touchdown. Richard rushed for 60 yards and a score. Sean Connaghan had 101 receiving yards.

Another disappointing end in a state championship game did not discount the many outstanding achievements in the 2000 season. Nate Schiccatano ran for 1,258 yards and scored 27 touchdowns. Nate Richard rushed for 960 yards and had 18 touchdowns. The Tigers got rushing scores from Matt Kaskie (11), Eric Trometter (7), Jason Brobst (6), Casey Rosini (3), and one each from Jason Andress, Bryan Berns, Steve Kowalchick, and Eric Levan. Matt Kaskie threw for 2,133 yards and 20 touchdowns. Sean Connaghan had 850 receiving yards and nine touchdowns. He was an All-State selection. Chris Grayson and Matt Porter each had two scoring receptions. Matt Brobst kicked 69 extra points and one field goal on the year. Tom Smeltzer registered 100 tackles (59 solo) to lead the team. Brad Sones recorded 10.5 sacks. Shawn Mummey had four interceptions. The Tigers finished the 2000 season with a 12-3 record.

———

Before the 2001 season, assistant coach Tim Snyder was involved in a devastating car accident that left him with debilitating injuries that would remain with him for many years. Tragically, Snyder passed away on September 24, 2011, at the age of 48.

**2001** In 2001, the Southern Columbia Tigers relied on the familiar offensive schemes that had brought the program so much success. However, Coach Jim Roth decided to throw a new wrinkle into the Southern Wing-T; rotating quarterbacks. With the graduation of Matt Kaskie, the Tigers looked to replace their signal-caller with a pair of newcomers. The experiment proved to be a great success. Southern opened the 2001 season at home against the Loyalsock Lancers. Eric Trometter scored the first points of the year with a 4-yard touchdown run. Jason Brobst scored on a 21-yard scamper, and the Tigers led 14-0 after one. Nate Schiccatano added a 21-yard touchdown run to push the lead to 20-0. Loyalsock blocked a punt out of the endzone for a safety, and Southern led 20-2 at the break. The Lancers returned an interception for a score, and Loyalsock cut the lead to 20-8. Jason Brobst raced 84 yards for a third-quarter touchdown and a 27-8 Tiger lead. Trometter added a touchdown run in the fourth to make the final 33-8. Brobst rushed for 196 yards and two touchdowns. Trometter had 64 yards rushing and two scores. Schiccatano ran for 21 yards and a touchdown. Chase Roadarmel threw for 43 yards, while Mark Wojtowicz passed for 14 yards. The Southern defense held Loyalsock to 25 yards rushing on 25 carries.

The Tigers ran for 325 yards and totaled 508 yards of offense in a road game against Bloomsburg. Nate Schiccatano ran for a 3-yard touchdown and caught a 27-yard scoring pass from Mark Wojtowicz for a 14-0 first-quarter lead. Schiccatano scored again early in the second on a 59-yard touchdown run. Wojtowicz hit Matt Murdock for a 63-yard touchdown pass to increase the lead to 21-0. Chase Roadarmel connected with Jason Brobst for a 20-yard scoring pass, and Brobst ran for a 26-yard touchdown as Southern led 41-0 at halftime. Ryan Slater and Bryan Berns added touchdown runs of 7 and 4 yards, and the Tigers defeated Bloomsburg, 54-0. Schiccatano ran for 108 yards and two touchdowns and added a scoring catch. Slater had 71 yards rushing and a touchdown. Brobst rushed for 25 yards and a score and added a scoring reception. Berns had 4 yards and a rushing touchdown. Roadarmel threw for 93 yards and a score. Wojtowicz added 90 yards through the air and two touchdowns. Murdock had 63 yards receiving and a touchdown. The defense pitched a shutout and held the Panthers to one passing yard. The unit registered four interceptions and recovered two fumbles.

Southern faced their nemesis, Mount Carmel, in a week three road game. The game was a defensive battle that remained scoreless at halftime. Nate Schiccatano finally broke the stalemate with a 2-yard scoring run in the third. Jason Brobst scored from 2 yards out to give the Tigers a 15-0 lead. Brobst finished off Mount Carmel with a 40-yard touchdown reception from Mark Wojtowicz, and the Tigers earned a satisfying 22-0 victory. The defense put forth a magnificent effort, holding the Red Tornadoes to 75 yards rushing. Shawn Mummey and Matt Murdoch had an interception, and Rob Shoop registered an interception and a sack. Schiccatano ran for 59 yards and a touchdown. Brobst contributed 56 rushing yards and a score and had a touchdown reception. Wojtowicz threw for 92 yards and a touchdown.

The offense continued to roll, and the defense once again shined a home game against Lewisburg. Southern jumped to a 28-0 first-quarter lead on Chase Roadarmel's one-yard keeper, Roadarmel's 9-yard pass to Matt Murdock, Eric Trometter's 11-yard scamper, and Mark Wojtowicz's 20-yard scoring throw to Brad Soles. The Tigers kept their foot on the gas in the second. Trometter,

Schiccatano, and Brandon Traugh scored on runs of 22, 20, and 47 yards, and Rob Shoop returned an interception 47 yards for a pick six. Southern led 50-0 at the intermission. Jason Andress added a 29-yard touchdown run in the third as Southern defeated the Green Dragons, 63-0. Traugh led the way with 67 yards rushing and a touchdown. Schiccatano rushed for 60 yards and a score. Andress added 29 yards on the ground and a touchdown. Trometter ran for 26 yards and two scores. Roadarmel passed for 53 yards and a touchdown and had a scoring run. Wojtowicz threw for 47 yards and a touchdown. Sones hauled in 34 receiving yards and a score. Murdock had nine yards receiving and a touchdown. The defense had a stellar night, holding Lewisburg to -18 yards rushing and only 36 through the air. Southern had three interceptions and recovered two fumbles.

Another week, another shutout for the Tigers' defense in a 53-0 blowout at Warrior Run. The Defenders unsuccessfully attempted an onside kick to start the game, and Southern immediately took advantage. Nate Schiccatano scored on the first play from scrimmage with a 57-yard touchdown reception from Chase Roadarmel. Schiccatano scored on a 21-yard run, Jason Brobst added a 26-yard touchdown burst, Mark Wojtowicz hit Matt Murdock for a 45-yard touchdown strike, and the Tigers built a 27-0 lead after one. Brobst and Ryan Slater scored on runs of 4 and 3 yards, and Southern led 40-0 at the break. In the fourth quarter, Slater recovered a fumble and returned it 26 yards for a touchdown, and Jason Andress scored on a 53-yard run to put away the Defenders. The defense held Warrior Run to -13 rushing yards. Southern had 447 yards of offense. Andress led the charge with 88 yards on the ground and a touchdown. Slater had 37 yards rushing and a score. Brobst chipped in with 31 rushing yards and two touchdowns. Schiccatano ran for 29 yards and a score. Roadarmel passed for 108 yards and a touchdown, while Wojtowicz threw for 66 yards and a score. Murdock added 75 receiving yards and a touchdown.

The Tigers took on the Hughesville Spartans at Tiger Stadium. Jason Brobst got Southern on the board with a 48-yard run for a 6-0 first-quarter lead. Nate Schiccatano plowed in from 2 yards out, Brobst added a 2-yard touchdown run, and Chase Roadarmel hooked up with Schiccatano for a 33-yard touchdown pass, and the Tigers took a 27-0 lead into the break. Schiccatano had a 2-yard touchdown run in the third for a 34-0 lead. Hughesville scored the first points of the season against the Tigers' defense with a touchdown pass in the fourth to make the final score 34-7. Southern's defense had two interceptions and two fumble recoveries. The Tigers rushed for 311 yards. Eric Trometter led the team with 85 yards on the ground. Brobst ran for 79 yards and two scores.

Schiccatano had 71 yards rushing and two touchdowns and added a scoring grab. Roadarmel threw for 65 yards and a touchdown.

It was a historic and memorable night for Coach Jim Roth in a week seven home game at Tiger Stadium. Coach Roth would capture his 200th career victory in the Tigers' 63-0 win over South Williamsport. Eric Levan opened the scoring with a 3-yard touchdown run, and Southern led 7-0 after the opening quarter. Jason Brobst scored from one yard out, Eric Trometter had a 2-yard touchdown run, Levan returned a punt 61 yards for a score, and Mark Wojtowicz hit Nate Schiccatano for a 12-yard touchdown pass, and the Tigers took a 35-0 lead into the intermission. Southern put the game away in the third quarter. Schiccatano rumbled for a 23-yard touchdown, Matt Murdock returned an interception 35 yards for a pick six, Josh Maciejewski returned an interception 43 yards for a score, and Brandon Traugh added a 23-yard touchdown run, and the Tigers rolled over the Mountaineers. It was another incredible game for the defense. They held South Williamsport to just 29 yards on the ground and 37 passing yards. Southern defenders intercepted three passes. Brobst ran for 66 yards and a score. Schiccatano rushed for 55 yards and a touchdown and added a scoring reception. Traugh chipped in with 30 yards on the ground and a touchdown. Trometter had 20 rushing yards and a scoring run. Levan added 12 rushing yards and a touchdown. Wojtowicz passed for 12 yards and a touchdown.

The Selinsgrove Seals visited Tiger Stadium in a week eight matchup. Selinsgrove scored first on a 65-yard touchdown. Eric Trometter tied the game with a 3-yard scoring run, and the game was deadlocked at 7-7 after the first. Jason Brobst scored on runs of 34 and 51 yards, and Southern led 21-7 at the half. Trometter and Brandon Traugh had touchdown runs of 4 and 53 yards in the fourth as the Tigers beat the Seals, 35-7. Southern rushed for 370 yards. Brobst had 162 yards and two scores. Trometter rushed for 97 yards and two touchdowns. Traugh added 53 yards rushing and a touchdown. Nate Schiccatano chipped in with 69 yards on the ground.

A road game at Central Columbia was up next for the Tigers. After a scoreless first quarter, Jason Brobst rumbled for a 2-yard touchdown to open the scoring. The Blue Jays scored on a touchdown pass, and Southern led 7-6 at halftime. Brobst scored again on a 7-yard run, and Mike Fox recovered a blocked punt in the endzone to give the Tigers a 20-6 third-quarter lead. Eric Trometter capped the scoring in the fourth with a 3-yard touchdown run. Southern defeated Central Columbia, 27-6. The Tigers' defense dominated the Blue Jays. They held Central to -12 yards rushing and just 27 passing yards. In addition to his recovery for a touchdown, Fox recovered a fumble and had an interception. Brad Sones recorded two sacks and blocked a punt. Jason Mills forced a Blue Jay fumble. Brobst rushed for 91 yards and two touchdowns. Trometter had 58 yards rushing and a scoring run. With the victory, the Tigers won the Central Susquehanna Conference Division II Championship.

Southern wrapped up the regular season with a road trip to Danville. In the first, Jason Brobst scored on a 45-yard run, and Mark Wojtowicz found Nate Schiccatano for a 14-yard touchdown pass, and the Tigers led 14-0 after one. Wojtowicz and Schiccatano hooked up again on a 35-yard scoring pass for a 21-0 halftime lead. Schiccatano ran for a 31-yard touchdown, Wojtowicz plowed in on a one-yard keeper, and Southern built a 35-0 lead after three. Brandon Traugh had a 30-yard scoring run in the fourth. Danville added a late touchdown, and Southern beat the Ironmen, 41-7. The defense had another strong effort, holding Danville to 9 rushing yards and had an interception and two fumble recoveries. Brobst rushed for 88 yards and a touchdown. Schiccatano added 47 rushing yards and a scoring run. He also had two touchdown receptions. Traugh ran for 33 yards and a score. Wojtowicz threw for 167 yards and two touchdowns and added a scoring run. Southern completed their fifth undefeated regular season under Coach Jim Roth.

The Tigers opened the postseason in the District IV Class A Semifinal Game against the Montgomery Red Raiders at Tiger Stadium. Chase Road-armel scored on a 29-yard keeper for a 7-0 first-quarter lead. Montgomery tied the game on a 54-yard scoring pass. Jason Brobst gave the Tigers a 13-7 halftime lead with a 3-yard run. Brobst increased the lead to 20-7 on a 2-yard touchdown plunge in the third. Eric Trometter had a 4-yard scoring run, and Ryan Hall returned an interception 51 yards for a touchdown as Southern eliminated Montgomery, 40-14. The Tigers' defense continued to roll, recording six sacks and limiting the Red Raiders to one rushing yard. Hall and Josh Maciejewski recorded interceptions. Brobst had 150 yards on the ground and two touchdowns. Trometter rushed for 74 yards and a score. Roadarmel added a rushing touchdown.

Southern faced the Muncy Indians at home in the District IV Class A Championship Game. Nate Schiccatano scored twice on runs of 8 and 90 yards, and Eric Trometter pounded it in from 4 yards out for a 21-0 lead after the opening period. Wojtowicz found Schiccatano for a 57-yard touchdown pass, but Muncy scored twice to cut the lead to 27-14 at the break. After a scoreless third, the Tigers closed the deal in the fourth quarter. Chase Roadarmel, Trometter, and Eric Levan scored on runs of 10, one and 6 yards. The Indians added a late touchdown to make the final score 48-21. Southern rushed for 406 yards. Schiccatano ran for 149 yards and two touchdowns and added a scoring reception. Trometter rushed for 65 yards and a touchdown. Levan added 11 yards on the ground and a score. Wojtowicz passed for 57 yards and a score, and Roadarmel ran for a touchdown. The defense had two fumble recoveries and Shawn Mummey recorded an interception. The Tigers won their eleventh consecutive District IV Class A Championship.

The Tigers began the state playoffs in the PIAA Class A Quarterfinal Game against the Camp Hill Lions in Sunbury. Mark Wojtowicz fired a 39-yard touchdown pass to Matt Murdock for a 7-0 first-quarter lead. Eric Trometter piled in from one yard out in the second, Camp Hill scored on a touchdown pass, and Southern led 14-7 at the half. The Lions tied the game at 14-14 in the third. That set up a wild fourth quarter. Camp Hill connected on a 31-yard field goal to take a 17-14 lead. The Tigers pulled within one point at 17-15 when the Camp Hill quarterback slipped down in the endzone for a safety. Late in the fourth, Southern drove deep into Camp Hill territory. Jason Brobst scored the go-ahead touchdown with 37 seconds left in the game and converted a two-point conversion on a pass from Chase Roadarmel to take a 24-17 lead. The defense held off one final Camp Hill series to win a thriller. The Tigers held Camp Hill to -5 yards rushing and registered two interceptions. Brobst ran for 84 tards and a touchdown. Trometter added 44 rushing yards and a score. Nate Schiccatano chipped in with 94 yards on the ground. Wojtowicz threw for 34 yards and a touchdown. Murdock had 63 receiving yards and a scoring catch.

Southern faced Pius X in the PIAA Class A Semifinal Game in Orefield. Eric Trometter opened the scoring with a one-yard touchdown dive, and the Tigers led 7-0 after one. Jason Brobst scored on an 18-yard run and a 58-yard reverse for a 21-0 lead. The Royals scored a touchdown before the half to cut the lead to 21-8. That was as close as Pius X would get. In the fourth, Chase Roadarmel hit Brad Sones for a 7-yard touchdown pass, and Mark Wojtowicz snuck in from one yard out as the Tigers earned a 35-8 victory. Southern rushed for 422 yards. Brobst had a big game with 184 yards and two touchdowns, Trometter ran for 28 yards and a score. Roadarmel passed for 28 yards and a touchdown. Sones had 19 receiving yards and a touchdown reception. Defensively, Rob Shoop had an interception and Sones registered a sack.

The Tigers advanced to the PIAA Class A Championship Game at Hersheypark Stadium for the seventh time. They would again face the Rochester Rams in the final for the third time in four years. As with their previous meetings, the game would be a defensive battle. In the first quarter, Rochester made a huge play on defense, returning an interception 50 yards for a touchdown. The score would remain 6-0 at the half. Although the Tigers outgained Rochester 123-58 in the first half, they could not penetrate deep into Rams territory. The Rams opened the second half with a six-minute drive resulting in a 23-yard field goal and a 9-0 lead. Southern could not sustain any offensive success, and Rochester put the game away with an 11-yard scoring pass in the fourth. The Rams won another state championship with a 16-0 victory. The defense put up a valiant effort. Eric Levan had an interception and Brad Sones recovered

## 2001 SEASON

| Opponent | Location | W/L | Score |
|---|---|---|---|
| Loyalsock | Home | W | 33-8 |
| Bloomsburg | Away | W | 54-0 |
| Mount Carmel | Away | W | 22-0 |
| Lewisburg | Home | W | 63-0 |
| Warrior Run | Away | W | 53-0 |
| Hughesville | Home | W | 34-7 |
| South Williamsport | Home | W | 63-0 |
| Selinsgrove | Home | W | 35-7 |
| Central Columbia | Away | W | 27-6 |
| Danville | Away | W | 41-7 |
| **District IV Class A Semifinal Game** | | | |
| Montgomery | Home | W | 40-14 |
| **District IV Class A Championship Game** | | | |
| Muncy | Home | W | 48-21 |
| **PIAA Class A Quarterfinal Game** | | | |
| Camp Hill | Neutral | W | 24-17 |
| **PIAA Class A Semifinal Game** | | | |
| Pius X | Neutral | W | 35-8 |
| **PIAA Class A Championship Game** | | | |
| Rochester | Neutral | L | 0-16 |

COACHING STAFF: Jim Roth, Head Coach; Al Cihocki, Assistant Coach; Jason Crawford, Assistant Coach; Troy Heath, Assistant Coach; Andy Helwig, Assistant Coach; Mike Johnston, Assistant Coach; John Marks, Assistant Coach; Andy Mills, Assistant Coach; Rick Steele, Assistant Coach; Curt Stellfox, Assistant Coach; Don Traugh, Assistant Coach

ATHLETIC DIRECTOR: Terry Sharrow

ROSTER: Jon Adams, Jason Andress, Austin Appel, Adam Baylor, Bryan Berns, Josh Bixler, Nicholas Brassard, Mike Breskiewicz, Jason Brobst, Matthew Brobst, Ben Diehl, Jeremy Evans, Matthew Fahringer, Jeremy Fowler, Mike Fox, Ryan Fox, Alex Gehron, Gary Gilligbauer, Chuck Gundrum, Marcus Gundrum, Ryan Hall, Drew Hampton, Nick Hampton, Andy Hassinger, Josh Hoagland, Rob Kerris, Joel Knoebel, Brian Leffler, Justin Leffler, Eric Levan, Josh Maciejewski, Blaine Madara, Will Martz, Kasey McBride, Jason Mills, Shawn Mummey, Matt Murdock, Ben Palachick, Kirk Peiffer, Chase Roadarmel, Chad Romig, Casey Rosini, Kale Roth, Erik Santor, Nathan Schiccatano, Wes Servose, Rob Shoop, Ryan Slater, Chadd Sober, Brad Sones, Justin St. Clair, Ken Thomas, Brandon Traugh, Eric Trometter, Ryan Weaver, Mark Wojtowicz, Doug Woodruff, Mike Wydra a Rams fumble. Nate Schiccatano led the Tigers with 54 rushing yards. Mark Wojtowicz and Chase Roadarmel combined for 79 yards passing. Matt Murdock had 24 receiving yards.

The Tigers had a tremendous season in 2001. Jason Brobst rushed for 1,351 yards and 19 touchdowns. Nate Schiccatano, who would continue his football career at the University of Notre Dame and Temple University, ran for 957 yards and 12 scores. He would finish his career at Southern Columbia with 2,242 yards and 34 touchdowns. Eric Trometter had 724 rushing yards and scored 13 touchdowns. The Tigers got rushing touchdowns from Brandon Traugh (4), Ryan Slater (3), Chase Roadarmel (3), Jason Andress (2), Eric Levan (2), and one each from Bryan Berns and Mark Wojtowicz. Wojtowicz threw for 701 yards and seven touchdowns. Roadarmel passed for 673 yards and five scores. Matt Murdock had 394 receiving yards and four touchdowns. Brad Sones had 242 receiving yards and two touchdowns. Southern got receiving touchdowns from Schiccatano (6) and Brobst (2). Matthew Brobst converted 68 extra points. Casey Rosini registered 105 tackles (66 solo). Shawn Mummey had two interceptions. Brad Sones recorded 12.5 sacks. Sones, Mike Fox, and Chad Romig were All-State selections. The Tigers finished with a 14-1 record in 2001.

2
0
0
2

In 2002, the Southern Columbia Tigers would use a suffocating defense and a potent mix of their bruising ground attack and an opportunistic passing game to return the program to championship glory. The season opened on the road with a barn burner against the Loyalsock Lancers.

Loyalsock had the only score in the first quarter and led 6-0. Mark Wojtowicz hit Matt Murdock for a 13-yard touchdown pass and a 7-6 lead early in the second. However, the Lancers scored again on a pass play and took a 13-7 lead into the break. Ryan Slater tied the game 13-13 with an 8-yard scoring run in the third to set up a wild fourth quarter. Loyalsock took a ten-point lead with a field goal and a touchdown run. Murdock and Wojtowicz hooked up again on a 30-yard scoring pass to cut the lead to 23-20. Late in the game, Wojtowicz found Bryan Berns for a 52-yard touchdown pass to give the Tigers the lead. The defense held off the Lancers, and Southern earned a hard-fought 27-23 opening-game victory. Wojtowicz threw for 205 yards and three touchdowns. Murdock hauled in two scoring passes and registered 53 receiving yards. Berns rushed for 59 yards and had a touchdown reception. Slater ran for 37 yards and a score. Brandon Traugh led the Tigers with 67 rushing yards.

The Tigers' first home game was a week two slate against Bloomsburg. Southern's offense got off to a slow start, but the defense held the Panthers in check, and the teams played a scoreless first quarter. Brandon Traugh rumbled in from 3 yards out, and Southern took a 6-0 lead at halftime. Bryan Berns scored on runs of 2 and 14 yards, and the Tigers led 21-0 after three. Dan Latorre and Jason Andress traded touchdown runs of 32 and 30 yards with Bloomsburg's two scores in the fourth to win the game, 34-12. The defense shut down the Panthers' running game, holding them to 65 yards. Matt Murdock registered an interception. Berns led the offense with 110 yards on the ground and two touchdowns. Traugh had 59 rushing yards and a score. Latorre ran for 48 yards and a touchdown. Andress chipped in with 31 rushing yards and a scoring run.

Nemesis Mount Carmel visited Tiger Stadium in another District IV power matchup. Southern's offense was never able to find success, and the Tigers were no match for the Red Tornadoes in a blowout loss. Mount Carmel returned a punt 67 yards in the opening period and scored on five offensive series over the final three quarters, while their defense pitched a shutout in a 42-0 blowout. Mark Wojtowicz was limited to 11 passing yards, and Brandon Traugh led the Tigers with only 33 rushing yards in a losing effort.

A road trip to Lewisburg was the right medicine for the Tigers in week four. Brandon Traugh got Southern on the board with a 9-yard touchdown run in the first quarter. The Tigers blew the game open in the second. Bryan Berns scored on a 9-yard run, Traugh had touchdown runs of 49 and 8 yards, Mark Wojtowicz hit Kale Roth for a one-yard scoring pass, and Southern led 34-0 at the intermission. Traugh added a fourth touchdown run on a 30-yard scamper in the third, and Dan Latorre capped the scoring with a 48-yard run in the fourth as Southern shutout the Green Dragons, 48-0. The Tigers running game rolled for 390 yards. Traugh had four scoring runs and ran for 131 yards. Latorre rushed for 43 yards and a touchdown. Berns added 31 rushing yards and a score. Wojtowicz threw for 55 tards and a touchdown to Roth.

The Tigers had another dominant performance versus Warrior Run at Tiger Stadium. After a slow start, Southern got second-quarter touchdown runs of 9 and 3 yards by Matt Murdock and a scoring pass from Mark Wojtowicz to Brandon Traugh. The Tigers led 21-0 at the half. Traugh increased the lead to 28-0 in the third with 2-yard touchdown dive. Murdock scored a third touchdown early in the fourth quarter on a 4-yard run. Warrior Run scored on a touchdown pass, and Ray Snarski finished off the Defenders with a 57-yard scoring run. Southern blew out Warrior Run, 41-8. The Tigers rumbled for

306 yards rushing. Murdock led with 81 yards on the ground and three touchdowns. Snarski ran for 57 yards and a score. Traugh added 13 rushing yards and a touchdown and had a scoring reception. Wojtowicz threw for 63 yards and a touchdown. The Tigers' defense dominated the Defenders, limiting them to 34 yards rushing and recording two interceptions.

Southern continued to roll in a road game at Hughesville. Mark Wojtowicz found Ryan Hall for a 30-yard touchdown pass to get the Tigers on the board in the first. Brandon Traugh added a 5-yard scoring run, and Southern led 14-0 after the first stanza. Hughesville cut the lead in half with a touchdown run early in the second, but Southern put the game away in a scoring frenzy before the half. Matt Murdock scored on a one-yard plunge, Traugh piled in from one yard out, and Matt Brobst connected on a 22-yard field goal to push the lead to 31-7 at the break. The Spartans recovered a fumble in the endzone in the third. Traugh and Jon Adams scored on runs of 43 and 3 yards in the final period to make the final score 45-14. Traugh ran for 104 yards and two touchdowns. Murdock rushed for 57 yards and a score. He also registered 72 receiving yards. Adams added 29 rushing yards and a touchdown. Wojtowicz passed for 129 yards and a score. Hall had 76 receiving yards and a touchdown. The defense turned in another solid effort, holding Hughesville to zero yards rushing and 98 through the air. The unit had two fumble recoveries and an interception.

A week seven game at South Williamsport was played in a driving rainstorm resulting in standing water on the playing field. Jon Adams rumbled for an 11-yard touchdown and a 7-0 lead after one. Mark Wojtowicz scored on a 5-yard keeper and fired a 19-yard touchdown pass to Brandon Traugh to push the lead to 21-0 at halftime. Traugh added a one-yard touchdown plunge in the fourth. The Mountaineers had a late scoring pass to make the final 27-7. Traugh ran for 95 yards and a touchdown and had a scoring reception. Adams rushed for 62 yards and a touchdown. Matt Murdock ran for 42 yards and had 79 receiving yards. Wojtowicz threw for 177 yards and a touchdown and ran for a score. The defense had an interception and fumble recovery and held South Williamsport to 66 yards rushing.

Things went awry for the Tigers in a road game at Selinsgrove. After a scoreless first half, the Seals converted a 42-yard field goal and had a scoring pass for a 10-0 lead in the third. Selinsgrove returned a fumble for a touchdown and added a scoring run for a 24-0 lead in the fourth. Brandon Traugh helped Southern avoid a shutout with a late 6-yard touchdown reception from Mark Wojtowicz. The Seals defeated the Tigers 24-7. Wojtowicz had 96 yards passing and a touchdown. Traugh ran for 39 yards and had a touchdown catch.

Southern righted the ship in a home game against Central Columbia. Matt Murdock scored from one yard out, but the Blue Jays pulled within a point on a scoring pass, and the Tigers led 7-6 after the opening period. Brandon Traugh had a 39-yard touchdown run, and Matt Brobst made a 32-yard field goal to push the lead to 17-6 at the half. Mark Wojtowicz hit Murdock for a 23-yard scoring pass in the third. Central scored on a pass play before the end of the quarter, and Southern led 25-13 heading into the final period. Jon Adams closed out the Blue Jays with a one-yard touchdown dive as the Tigers earned a 32-13 victory. Traugh led with 114 rushing yards and a touchdown. Adams ran for 99 yards and a score. Murdock added 15 yards on the ground and a touchdown and had a scoring reception. Wojtowicz threw for 142 yards and a touchdown. The Southern defense limited Central to 61 yards on the ground and 65 through the air.

The Tigers closed the regular season at Tiger Stadium against Danville. Matt Murdock and Brandon Traugh gave Southern a 14-0 first-quarter lead on runs on one and 16 yards. Ryan Slater scored from 13 yards out, Mark Wojtowicz spotted Justin Leffler for a 5-yard touchdown pass, and the Tigers led 28-0 at halftime. Traugh and Slater scored on runs of 13 and 3 yards in the third. Danville scored two late touchdowns in mop-up time as Southern closed the season with a 42-13 victory. Traugh ran for 85 yards and two scores. Slater rushed for 68 yards and two touchdowns. Murdock added 18 rushing yards and a touchdown. Wojtowicz passed for 145 yards and a score. Leffler had 30 receiving yards and a touchdown. The defense finished the regular season strong, holding the Ironmen to 5 yards passing, registering two interceptions, and recovering a fumble.

The Tigers dominated Lourdes Regional in the postseason opener at Tiger Stadium. Playing in the District IV Class A Semifinal Game, Southern pounded the Red Raiders on both sides of the ball. Matt Murdock opened the scoring with a 46-yard touchdown run. Brandon Traugh added a 21-yard scoring run for a 14-0 lead. Lourdes had a 21-yard field goal, and Mark Wojtowicz connected with Murdock on a 53-yard touchdown pass as the Tigers led 21-3 after one. Southern ended any hope for the Red Raiders in the second. Ryan Slater ran for a 24-yard touchdown, Traugh scored on a 55-yard scamper, Slater pounded in from 4 yards out, and Traugh added a 20-yard touchdown run to push the lead to 48-7 at the break. Lourdes scored a late touchdown in the fourth, and Southern advanced with a 48-9 win. The defense had two interceptions (one by Murdock), three fumble recoveries, and held the Red Raiders to 22 rushing yards. Traugh rushed for 126 yards and three touchdowns. Murdock chipped in with 47 rushing yards and a score and had 52 receiving yards and a touchdown reception. Slater ran for 36 yards and two touchdowns. Wojtowicz threw for 62 yards and a score.

Southern hosted Muncy in the District IV Class A Championship Game. The game was never in doubt as the Tigers got first-quarter touchdowns from Matt Murdock (10-yard run), Brandon Traugh (11-yard run), Ryan Slater (2-yard run), and Jon Adams (26-yard run) as Southern led 26-0 after one. Kale Roth caught a 10-yard touchdown pass from Mark Wojtowicz, and Murdock tacked on a 36-yard scoring run for a 40-0 halftime lead. Slater added a 3-yard touchdown dive in the third. Muncy scored two late touchdowns in the fourth, and Southern crushed the Indians, 47-13. Adams ran for 75 yards and a touchdown. Murdock had 64 rushing yards and two scores. He also had 25 yards receiving. In the game, Murdock tied the school record for career receptions. Traugh added 63 yards on the ground and a touchdown. Slater contributed 49 rushing yards and two scores. Wojtowicz passed for 70 yards and a touchdown throw to Roth. The Tigers won their twelfth straight District IV Class A Championship.

The Tigers played the Camp Hill Lions in the PIAA Class A Quarterfinal Game in Harrisburg. Jon Adams scored on a one-yard plunge, and Southern led 7-0 after the first quarter. Camp Hill pulled within one with a touchdown run early in the second. Mark Wojtowicz hit Kale Roth on a 37-yard touchdown pass, and Adams scored from one yard out as the Tigers took a 21-6 lead into the intermission. Ryan Slater plowed in for a one-yard touchdown run, and Matt Murdock returned an interception 39 yards for a pick six to put the game out of reach for the Lions. Brandon Traugh scored from one yard out before Camp Hill capped the scoring with a touchdown run in the fourth, and the Tigers defeated the Lions, 42-14. Traugh ran for 91 yards and a touchdown. Slater had 39 rushing yards and a score. Adams rushed for two touchdowns. Wojtowicz threw for 103 yards and a touchdown. Roth had 37 receiving yards and a scoring grab. It was a special night for Matt Murdock. He had 46 yards on the ground and 43 receiving yards. During the game, Murdock caught his 57th pass, breaking the record for career receptions set by Sean Connaghan. He finished the game with 59 receptions.

Southern traveled to Selinsgrove to take on Schuylkill Haven in the PIAA Class A Semifinal Game. Brandon Traugh got the Tigers on the board with a one-yard scoring run and a 7-0 first-quarter lead. Jon Adams recovered a Southern fumble in the endzone to increase the lead to 14-0. Mark Wojtowicz hit Traugh for a 13-yard touchdown pass, and Southern led 22-0 at the break.

Ryan Slater put the final nail in the Hurricanes' coffin with an 18-yard touchdown run. As the time ticked away, the Tigers and their fans celebrated a 28-0 shutout victory and a return trip to the state championship game. The Tigers' defense completely controlled the game. The unit limited the Hurricanes to -13 yards passing and only 90 on the ground. They registered an astonishing 17 tackles for loss and recorded five sacks, including three by outside linebackers Kasey McBride (2) and Doug Woodruff (1). Traugh rushed for 55 yards and a touchdown and had a scoring reception. Slater added 18 rushing yards and a touchdown. Wojtowicz passed for 134 yards and a score. It was another big night for Matt Murdock. He caught six passes in the game, breaking the team's single-season record for receptions previously held by Ardie Kissinger. The only negative from the game was the status of quarterback Mark Wojtowicz, who was taken by ambulance to a local hospital with an apparent neck injury.

The Tigers advanced to the PIAA Class A Championship Game at Hersheypark Stadium for the eighth time. They would again play the Rochester Rams, the team who had defeated them each of the last two years and three times overall. With the word that quarterback Mark Wojtowicz was healthy and would play in the title game, the Tigers and their fans felt that things would be different this year. The teams settled in for their usual defensive struggle, and things appeared to be headed in that direction with a scoreless first quarter. Ryan Slater finally broke the deadlock on a one-yard touchdown run in the second. Southern kept their foot on the gas, and instead of relying as heavily on their potent ground game, Coach Jim Roth loosened the reins on his passing attack. Mark Wojtowicz fired a 49-yard touchdown pass to Matt Murdock for a 14-0 lead. The defense then came up with a game-changing play. Kasey McBride sacked the Rams' quarterback and forced a fumble. Austin Appel recovered the ball at the 50-yard line. Wojtowicz then executed a perfect two-minute drill and found Kale Roth in the endzone for a 15-yard scoring pass and a 21-0 lead at the half. Rochester came out of the break and cut the lead to 21-6 with a touchdown pass in the third. Matt Brobst added a 22-yard field goal to push the lead to 24-6 after three. In the fourth, Wojtowicz scored on a 17-yard keeper. Defensive Coordinator Andy Mills turned his defense loose, and the Tigers overwhelmed the Rams down the stretch. As the time ticked off the clock, the Southern Columbia Tigers had finally slayed the Rochester Rams and won the 2002 PIAA Class A Football Championship, 31-6. It was the Tigers' second state championship in school history and the second for head coach Jim Roth, who watched with pride as his team celebrated with the Southern faithful in the stands. The victory was a complete team effort. The Tigers' defense was magnificent, holding Rochester to 57 yards rushing. They had two interceptions (by Murdock and Chadd Sober), a fumble recovery (by Appel), and got sacks from McBride (2) and Slater. Wojtowicz, returning from a neck injury, had a huge game. He threw for 182 yards and two touchdowns and ran for a score. Murdock had 10 yards rushing, 88 yards receiving, and a scoring reception. Roth added 15 receiving yards and a touchdown. Slater ran for 13 yards and a score. Brandon Traugh led the team with 29 rushing yards.

## 2002 SEASON

| Opponent | Location | W/L | Score |
|---|---|---|---|
| Loyalsock | Away | W | 27-23 |
| Bloomsburg | Home | W | 34-12 |
| Mount Camel | Home | L | 0-42 |
| Lewisburg | Away | W | 48-0 |
| Warrior Run | Home | W | 41-8 |
| Hughesville | Away | W | 45-14 |
| South Williamsport | Away | W | 27-7 |
| Selinsgrove | Away | L | 7-24 |
| Central Columbia | Home | W | 32-13 |
| Danville | Home | W | 42-13 |
| **District IV Class A Semifinal Game** | | | |
| Lourdes Regional | Home | W | 48-9 |
| **District IV Class A Championship Game** | | | |
| Muncy | Home | W | 47-13 |
| **PIAA Class A Quarterfinal Game** | | | |
| Camp Hill | Neutral | W | 42-14 |
| **PIAA Class A Semifinal Game** | | | |
| Schuylkill Haven | Neutral | W | 28-0 |
| **PIAA Class A Championship Game** | | | |
| Rochester | Neutral | W | 31-6 |

COACHING STAFF: Jim Roth, Head Coach; Al Cihocki, Assistant Coach; Jason Crawford, Assistant Coach; Troy Heath, Assistant Coach; Andy Helwig, Assistant Coach; Mike Johnston, Assistant Coach; John Marks, Assistant Coach; Andy Mills, Assistant Coach; Pete Saylor, Assistant Coach; Rick Steele, Assistant Coach; Curt Stellfox, Assistant Coach; Don Traugh, Assistant Coach

ATHLETIC DIRECTOR: Terry Sharrow

ROSTER: Jon Adams, Bob Admire, Zach Allen, Austin Appel, A.J. Baylor, Kevin Beishline, Bryan Berns, Mike Breskiewicz, Steve Breskiewicz, Matt Brobst, Dan Crowl, Derek Crowl, Ben Diehl, Jeremy Evans, Jeremy Fowler, Ryan Fox, Alex Gehron, Gary Gilligbauer, Josh Gratti, Ryan Hall, Drew Hampton, Nick Hampton, Andy Hassinger, Dusty Hendricks, Josh Hoagland, Rob Kerris, Matt Koziol, Dan Kreisher, Daren Kremser, Dan Latorre, Justin Leffler, Josh Maciejewski, Blaine Madara, Will Martz, Kasey McBride, Geoff Michalesko, Jeremy Miller, Matt Murdock, Ben Palachick, Kirk Peiffer, Adam Phillips, Eric Raup, Chad Romig, Kale Roth, Erik Santor, Wes Servose, Dan Shoop, Ryan Slater, Ray Snarski, Chadd Sober, Brenton Suruk, Ken Thomas, Brandon Traugh, Ryan Weaver, Kurt Wimble, Mark Wojtowicz, Doug Woodruff, Jon Woodruff, Mike Wydra

Southern had many great performances in 2002. Brandon Traugh rushed for 1,104 yards and 18 touchdowns. Matt Murdock ran for 510 yards and nine scores. He also had 676 receiving yards and five touchdown receptions. Ryan Slater had 334 rushing yards and ten touchdowns. The Tigers also received touchdown runs from Jon Adams (5), Bryan Berns (3), Dan Latorre (2), Mark Wojtowicz (2), Jason Andess (1), and Ray Snarski (1). Mark Wojtowicz threw for 1,636 yards and 16 touchdowns. Southern had touchdown receptions from Kale Roth (4), Brandon Traugh (4), Bryan Berns (1), Ryan Hall (1), and Justin Leffler (1). Bob Admire had 92 tackles (56 solo). Kasey McBride recorded 12 sacks. Matt Murdock registered nine interceptions. Murdock, Matt Brobst, Josh Hoagland, and Chad Romig were All-State selections. The 2002 Southern Columbia Tigers finished the season with a 13-2 record and the PIAA Class A Football Championship.

**2003** In 2003, Coach Jim Roth would again rely on a proven ground game and a stout defense to aid in developing a new quarterback. The Tigers would embark on another magical season and reach the top of the summit for a second consecutive year. The season opener against Loyalsock at Tiger Stadium got off to a dubious start. The Lancers scored two first-quarter touchdowns to take a 14-0 lead. However, Southern bounced back in the second with touchdown runs of 2 and 16 yards by Jon Adams and Dan Latorre and a 50-yard scoring pass from Latorre to Brandon Traugh as the Tigers carried a 21-14 lead into halftime. The game was delayed for an hour and 25 minutes due to heavy rains in the third quarter. Latorre scored again on an 11-yard run, and Loyalsock added a field goal for a 28-17 Southern lead after three. Latorre connected with Kale Roth for a 27-yard touchdown throw to finish off the Lancers, 36-17. The game ended nearly four hours after the opening kickoff. Latorre threw for 124 yards and two touchdowns and added two rushing scores. Roth had 39 receiving yards and a touchdown. Brandon Traugh Rushed for 35 yards and had a touchdown reception. Henry Hynoski led the Southern ground game with 78 yards rushing.

The Tigers traveled to Bloomsburg for a week two matchup with the Panthers. Jon Adams again opened the scoring for Southern with a one-yard touchdown plunge and a 7-0 lead after one. Brandon Traugh added scoring runs of 10 and one yard, and the Tigers led 20-0 at the break. After a scoreless third quarter, Traugh added a 5-yard touchdown run, and after Bloomsburg had a scoring run, Kyle Connaghan finished the scoring with a 61-yard touchdown jaunt. The Tigers earned a 33-6 victory over the Panthers. Connaghan ran for

61 yards and a score. Traugh had 54 yards and three touchdowns. Adams added 50 yards on the ground and a score. The defense held Bloomsburg to just 69 yards rushing and registered an interception and two fumble recoveries.

Southern traveled to Mount Carmel for another highly anticipated game against the defending Class AA State Champion Red Tornadoes. For the third straight week, Jon Adams scored the Tigers' opening touchdown on a one-yard run. Southern led 7-0 after the opening period. Mount Carmel tied the game in the second on a 25-yard pass play. Southern regained the lead when Adams recovered a fumble in the endzone for a 14-7 halftime lead. The Red Tornadoes sandwiched touchdowns around Brandon Traugh's 18-yard scoring run, and the game was squared at 21-21 after three. Traugh scored from one yard out late in the fourth quarter to put Southern back on top, 28-21. The Tigers' defense tried to hold off the Red Tornadoes, but Mount Carmel drove inside the Southern 10-yard line and tied the game with a 9-yard touchdown pass with 59.5 seconds left in regulation. The contest would go to overtime. Mount Carmel came up with a timely interception on Southern's first drive in the extra period and converted the turnover into a game-winning 4-yard touchdown run to give the Red Tornadoes a 34-28 victory. Traugh ran for 83 yards and scored two touchdowns. Adams added 27 rushing yards and a score. Henry Hynoski chipped in with 89 yards on the ground.

The Tigers looked to right the ship when they hosted Lewisburg. Southern essentially put the game out of reach in the first quarter. Brandon Traugh scored on a 20-yard run, Jon Adams had a 12-yard touchdown scamper, Henry Hynoski plowed in from one yard out, and Dan Latorre scored on a 26-yard keeper for a 26-0 lead after one. Traugh ran for a 5-yard touchdown, Hynoski added an 18-yard scoring run and Ryan Slater rumbled 79 yards for a touchdown, and Southern had a commanding 47-0 lead at the half. Lewisburg got on the board with a touchdown run in the third quarter, and Jeremy Sargent capped the scoring with a 10-yard touchdown run in the fourth to make the final score 53-7. The Tigers rushed for 383 yards. Slater led the ground attack with 99 yards and a touchdown. Hynoski rushed for 56 yards and two scores. Traugh had 54 rushing yards and two touchdowns. Sargent chipped with 54 yards and a scoring run. Adams ran for 33 yards and a touchdown. Latorre threw for 91 yards and had a rushing touchdown.

Southern dominated on both sides of the ball in a road game against Warrior Run. Dan Latorre fired a 10-yard touchdown pass to Kale Roth to put the Tigers in front. Doug Woodruff intercepted a Defenders' pass and returned it 33 yards for a score, and Roth and Latorre hooked up again on a 29-yard scoring pass as the Tigers led 21-0 at the end of the first quarter. Latorre rumbled 34-yards on a quarterback keeper, and Brandon Traugh scored on a 43-yard run for a 35-0 lead at the intermission. Henry Hynoski pushed the lead to 42-0 with a 2-yard touchdown plunge in the third. Victor Northern and Derek Crowl added scoring runs of 10 and 30 yards in the final period for a 55-0 shutout victory. Traugh ran for 90 yards and a touchdown. Hynoski had 45 rushing yards and a score. Northern rushed for 32 yards and a touchdown. Crowl added 31 yards on the ground and a scoring run. Latorre passed for 127 yards and two touchdowns and contributed a rushing score. Roth had 54 yards receiving and two touchdowns. The Tigers' defense held Warrior Run to 36 yards on the ground and 21 yards passing yards.

The Tigers continued their dominance against Hughesville at Tiger Stadium. Brandon Traugh struck first for Southern with a 5-yard scoring run, and Henry Hynoski added rushing touchdowns of 3 and 44 yards as the Tigers took a 21-0 lead after one. Hynoski scored again on a 4-yard pass from Dan Latorre, and Ryan Slater added a 2-yard touchdown dive to push the lead to 35-0 at the break. Slater tacked on a 14-yard touchdown scamper to finish off the Spartans, 41-0. Slater led the way with 66 yards rushing and two touchdowns. Hynoski had 55 yards on the ground and three scores and added a touchdown reception. Traugh ran for 34 yards and a score. Latorre threw for 105 yards and a touchdown. With all the offensive fireworks, the real stars of the game were the entire defensive unit. Incredibly, the Tigers' defense held Hughesville without a first down for the game. The Spartans only managed 13 yards rushing and did not gain a yard through the air.

Tigers next hosted South Williamsport. Although the Mountaineers scored first, Jon Adams recovered a fumble and returned it 16 yards to tie the score at 7-7 after the first. Doug Woodruff hauled in a 50-yard bomb from Dan Latorre to give Southern a 14-7 lead at halftime. Brandon Traugh barreled in from 3 yards out in the third quarter, and Wes Servose returned a punt 54 yards for a touchdown to push the lead to 27-7. Traugh added a 3-yard scoring run, and the Mountaineers capped the scoring with a late touchdown in the fourth quarter. Southern earned a 34-14 win over South Williamsport. Latorre threw for 201 yards and a touchdown. Woodruff had 128 receiving yards and a scoring catch. Traugh ran for 83 yards and two touchdowns. The Tigers clinched another Central Susquehanna Conference Division II Championship.

The Crestwood Comets visited Tiger Stadium in a week eight contest. For the second straight week, Southern gave up an opening touchdown. However, the Tigers quickly tied the game and took the lead on a 67-yard touchdown pass from Dan Latorre to Ryan Hall and Henry Hynoski's 3-yard scoring run. The Tigers led 14-7 after the opening stanza. The teams traded touchdowns in the second on Ryan Slater's 16-yard touchdown run and a Comet scoring pass. Southern led 21-14 at the intermission. Southern put the game away in the third quarter. Hynoski rumbled for a 29-yard touchdown, and Slater put the dagger in the Comets with a 39-yard bolt for a 35-14 lead. Southern added fourth-quarter touchdowns on Brandon Traugh's 18-yard run, Ray Snarski's 13-yard scamper, and Derek Crowl's 31-yard burst to make the final 55-14. Southern rushed for 335 yards. Hynoski ran for 94 yards and two touchdowns. Traugh added 68 rushing yards and a score. Slater tacked on 63 yards on the ground and two touchdowns. Crowl chipped in with 42 rushing yards and a score. Snarski ran for 14 yards and a scoring run. Latorre threw for 84 yards and a touchdown. Hall had 74 yards receiving and a touchdown reception. The defense held Crestwood to -61 yards rushing, and registered two interceptions, and recovered two fumbles.

Southern scored another dominant victory on the road against Central Columbia. Brandon Traugh got things started with a 6-yard scoring run, and Dan Latorre found Ryan Hall for a 19-yard touchdown pass and a 14-0 lead in the first quarter. Latorre scored on a 21-yard keeper, and he fired a 9-yard touchdown pass to Traugh to make it 28-0 at the half. Ray Snarski rushed for a 2-yard touchdown in the third, and Derek Crowl ended the scoring with a 4-yard run in the fourth for a 42-0 Tiger victory. Traugh ran for 101 yards and a touchdown and had a scoring reception. Crowl added 65 rushing yards and a score. Snarski rushed for 12 yards and a touchdown. Latorre passed for 178 yards and two scores. Hall had 91 receiving yards and a touchdown catch. The Southern defense held the Blue Jays to 2 yards rushing and 49 passing yards.

The Tigers finished the regular season on the road against Danville. Dan Latorre hooked up with Jon Adams for a 10-yard touchdown pass and a 7-0 first-quarter lead. Ray Snarski barreled 63 yards for a score, and Brandon Traugh added a 2-yard touchdown plunge for a 21-0 lead at halftime. Ryan Hall caught a 50-yard touchdown strike from Latorre. They teamed up again on a 24-yard scoring pass, and Traugh tacked on a 2-yard touchdown run to push the lead to 41-0 after three. In the fourth, Derek Crowl ran for a 23-yard touchdown, and the Tigers shutout the Ironmen, 48-0. Traugh rushed for 83 yards and two scores. Snarski ran for 65 yards and a touchdown. Crowl added 42 rushing yards and a scoring run. Latorre passed for 155 yards and three touchdowns. Hall had 123 receiving yards and a scoring grab. Adams contributed a touchdown reception. The defense put in yet another solid performance with two interceptions and a fumble recovery. They held Danville to -2 rushing yards.

Southern played host to the Bristol Warriors in the District IV Class A Semifinal Game. Henry Hynoski opened the scoring with a one-yard touchdown run and a 6-0 first-quarter lead. Brandon Traugh scored on runs of 2 and 13 yards in the second, and the Tigers led 20-0 at the break. Traugh added a 20-yard touchdown jaunt, and Ryan Slater scored from 13 yards out to push the lead to 32-0 after three. Bristol did not cross midfield until the fourth quarter, when they had a touchdown run. Kyle Connaghan rumbled 63 yards for a score, and the Warriors scored a late touchdown to make the final 38-14. Southern rushed for 429 yards. Traugh led the Tigers with 86 yards on the ground and three touchdowns. Hynoski ran for 80 yards and a score. Slater rushed for 62 yards and had a scoring run. Connaghan added 52 yards and a touchdown.

Bloomsburg traveled to Tiger Stadium for the District IV Class A Championship Game. The Panthers scored first on a 57-yard touchdown pass and led 8-0 after one. Dan Latorre pounded in from 4 yards out to tie the game at 8-8 at the half. The teams played a scoreless third quarter before Southern put the game away in the final period. Brandon Traugh scored on a 35-yard reverse, Ryan Slater scampered 10 yards for a touchdown, and Henry Hynoski took it in from 8 yards out to finish off the Panthers, 29-8. Traugh ran for 112 yards and a touchdown. Hynoski rushed for 51 yards and a score. Slater pitched in with 28 rushing yards and a touchdown run. Latorre threw for 67 yards and had a rushing touchdown. The Tigers clinched their 13th straight District Football Championship.

The Tigers faced a familiar foe in the Steelton-Highspire Rollers in the PIAA Class A Quarterfinal Game in Sunbury. Steel High would give Southern all they could handle in a back and forth affair. The Rollers stunned the Tigers with an 85-yard touchdown pass early in the first quarter. Dan Latorre found Doug Woodruff for a 4-yard scoring throw to tie the game at 7-7 after one. Steel High dominated the second quarter. They scored on 14 and 18 yard passes to take a 19-7 lead at the intermission. The Southern special teams got them back in the game in the third quarter. Kale Roth returned a punt 52 yards for a touchdown. Moments later, Wes Servose took another punt 93 yards to the house to tie the game at 19-19. Servose then came up with a huge play on defense. He intercepted a Roller pass at the Tigers' 9-yard line and returned it to the 35 to set up Jon Adams's 21-yard go-ahead touchdown run, and Southern took their first lead, 25-19 after three. Early in the fourth, Latorre fired a 60-yard touchdown strike to Brandon Traugh. Steel High answered with an 11-yard scoring pass of their own. However, Traugh's one-yard plunge and Henry Hynoski's 21-yard touchdown run put the final nails in the coffin, and the Tigers earned a hard-fought 45-25 victory.

Southern faced Lackawanna Trail in the PIAA Class A Semifinal Game in Scranton. Brandon Traugh scored on runs of 2 and 6 yards to give the Tigers a 14-0 first-quarter lead. After Henry Hynoski plowed in from 4 yards out, Traugh scored his third touchdown of the half on a one-yard dive. Southern led 28-0 at the break. Jon Adams added a 19-yard touchdown scamper in the third, and Traugh scored for a fourth time on a 3-yard run to push the lead to 42-0. The Lions scored a late touchdown in mop-up time, and the Tigers advanced to their sixth consecutive state championship game with a convincing 42-8 win. Southern rushed for 305 yards. Traugh had a great game with 127 yards rushing and four touchdowns. Hynoski ran for 75 yards and a score. Adams added 42 yards on the ground and a touchdown run. The defense limited Lackawanna Trail to 60 yards rushing and had interceptions from Blaine Madara and Doug Woodruff.

The Tigers looked to defend their PIAA Class A Championship versus Bishop Carroll at Hersheypark Stadium. The game was played in a snowstorm, but it did not keep the huge contingent of Southern faithful from cheering on their Tigers to back-to-back state titles. The Huskies got out of the gate quickly with a 3-yard scoring run. However, Brandon Traugh took a handoff from Ryan Slater on a reverse and raced 40 yards to tie the game at 7-7. The teams traded blows in the second quarter. Slater rumbled 10 yards for a touchdown and a 14-7 lead. The Huskies countered with a 2-yard scoring run to tie the game. Slater put Southern back in front on a 3-yard plunge, and the Tigers led 21-14 at the break. Southern put their foot on the gas in the third quarter. Traugh scored on a 3-yard run. Bob Admire leveled the return man on the ensuing kickoff and forced a fumble that Ken Thomas recovered at the Bishop Carroll 32-yard line. Slater then pounded in from 5 yards out to push the Tiger lead to 35-14. Mike Wydra recovered a Husky fumble and set up Traugh's 42-yard touchdown run. The Tigers had scored three touchdowns in two and a half minutes. Bishop Carroll scored on a 20-yard pass, and Southern led 42-20 after three. Jon Adams piled in from one yard out to push the Tigers' lead to 49-20 in the fourth. Southern turned the game over to their magnificent defense. The unit controlled the Huskies for the remainder of the game. Doug Woodruff registered two sacks and Kale Roth had two interceptions. With Roth's picks, every starter in the secondary and the linebacker corps had an interception on the season. The defense recorded nine tackles for loss. With the snow continuing to fall and the time ticking off the clock, the Southern Columbia Tigers defeated Bishop Carroll 49-20 and won their second consecutive PIAA Class A Football Championship and third overall. The players, coaches, and fans celebrated another title in Chocolatetown. Several records fell in the Tigers' championship win. Southern rushed for 402 yards, which set the record for a PIAA Class A Championship Game. Brandon Traugh rushed for a PIAA Class

## 2003 SEASON

| Opponent | Location | W/L | Score |
|---|---|---|---|
| Loyalsock | Home | W | 36-17 |
| Bloomsburg | Away | W | 33-6 |
| Mount Carmel | Away | L | 28-34 (OT) |
| Lewisburg | Home | W | 53-7 |
| Warrior Run | Away | W | 55-0 |
| Hughesville | Home | W | 41-0 |
| South Williamsport | Home | W | 34-14 |
| Crestwood | Home | W | 55-14 |
| Central Columbia | Away | W | 42-0 |
| Danville | Away | W | 48-0 |
| **District IV Class A Semifinal Game** | | | |
| Bristol | Home | W | 38-14 |
| **District IV Class A Championship Game** | | | |
| Bloomsburg | Home | W | 29-8 |
| **PIAA Class A Quarterfinal Game** | | | |
| Steelton-Highspire | Neutral | W | 45-25 |
| **PIAA Class A Semifinal Game** | | | |
| Lackawanna Trail | Neutral | W | 42-8 |
| **PIAA Class A Championship Game** | | | |
| Bishop Carroll | Neutral | W | 49-20 |

COACHING STAFF: Jim Roth, Head Coach; Randall Campbell, Assistant Coach; Al Cihocki, Assistant Coach; Jason Crawford, Assistant Coach; Troy Heath, Assistant Coach; Andy Helwig, Assistant Coach; Mike Johnston, Assistant Coach; John Marks, Assistant Coach; Andy Mills, Assistant Coach; Pete Saylor, Assistant Coach; Rick Steele, Assistant Coach; Curt Stellfox, Assistant Coach; Don Traugh, Assistant Coach

ATHLETIC DIRECTOR: Terry Sharrow

ROSTER: Jon Adams, Bob Admire, Zach Allen, Kevin Beishline, Kyle Berns, Steve Breskiewicz, Jason Campbell, Nate Carl, Kyle Connaghan, Dan Crowl, Derek Crowl, Jeremy Evans, Josh Fidler, Dave Forney, Jeremy Fowler, Ian Fullmer, Alex Gehron, Ryan Hall, Andy Hassinger, Josh Hoagland, Henry Hynoski, Matt Koziol, Dan Kreisher, Dan Latorre, Tarik Leghlid, Dustin Lindemuth, Blaine Madara, Josh Marks, Victor Northern, Marcus Odorizzi, Kirk Peiffer, Adam Phillips, Corey Pilkus, Devin Raught, Kale Roth, Jeremy Sargent, Wes Servose, Ryan Slater, Ray Snarski, Eric Spotts, Brenton Surak, Brian Terry, Ken Thomas, Brandon Traugh, Ryan Weaver, Shane Wells, Kurt Wimble, Doug Woodruff, Jeff Woodruff, Jon Woodruff, Mike Wydra

A Championship Game record 165 yards. Wes Servose broke the Tigers' team record for return yardage. In addition to his record-setting 165 rushing yards, Traugh had three scoring runs. Adams ran for 104 yards and a touchdown. Slater rushed for 66 yards and three touchdowns.

The 2003 back-to-back state champion Southern Columbia Tigers finished the season with a 14-1 record. Coach Roth's team compiled some incredible individual statistics. Brandon Traugh rushed for 1,247 yards and 27 touchdowns. He would finish his career with the Tigers with 2,630 rushing yards and 50 touchdowns. Henry Hynoski ran for 814 yards and 12 scores. Jon Adams had 519 rushing yards and seven touchdowns. Ryan Slater added 420 yards on the ground and ten scores. Southern received touchdown runs from Dan Latorre (5), Derek Crowl (4), Ray Snarski (3), Kyle Connaghan (2), and one each from Victor Northern and Jeremy Sargent. Dan Latorre threw for 1,643 yards and 14 touchdowns. Ryan Hall had 499 receiving yards and four scores. Doug Woodruff added 365 receiving yards and two scores. Kale Roth registered 204 yards receiving and three touchdowns. Roth would continue his football career at the University of Pennsylvania. The Tigers got touchdown receptions from Brandon Traugh (3) and one each from Jon Adams and Henry Hynoski. Ryan Slater registered 112 tackles (67 solo). Bob Admire totaled 100 tackles (64 solo). Kasey McBride had 12 sacks. Matt Murdock recorded nine interceptions. Slater, Josh Hoagland, Dan Latorre, Kirk Pfeiffer, and Doug Woodruff were All-State selections.

**2004** In the summer of 2004, unthinkable tragedy struck the Tigers and the Southern Columbia community. Several members of the football team took part in a summer skills camp at Bloomsburg University. On July 28, 2004, after a morning session, members of the Southern football team went to nearby Big Fishing Creek in Mount Pleasant Township to go swimming. Junior Tarik Leghlid and freshman Colby Snyder entered the water and were caught in the current, and began to struggle to stay afloat. Junior Eric Barnes and senior Bob Admire jumped into the water to help, seeing their friends in trouble. Admire was able to reach Snyder and pull him ashore. He immediately began performing CPR and was able to resuscitate Snyder on the bank of the creek. The rest of their teammates started to panic as they lost sight of Leghlid and Barnes. They called for help, and several rescue units and local police officers soon arrived at the scene. A Pennsylvania State Police helicopter flew overhead and spotted the two boys in the water. The chopper landed, and police personnel tried to rescue Leghlid and Barnes, but, unfortunately, it was too late. Both boys were pronounced dead as a result of drowning. They were both just 16 years old. After receiving a telephone call with the shocking news, head coach Jim Roth made the decision to load the football team onto buses and met with them at Southern Columbia High School. In a sad and somber room, Coach Roth gave the devastating news to his team. The entire Southern Columbia community was deeply saddened and mourned the loss of two outstanding young men. Tarik Leghlid was an honor student and a member of the Tigers' wrestling team. Eric Barnes was a star pitcher on the Southern baseball team. Both were projected to be starters on the Tigers' defense. The team spent the rest of the summer grieving the loss of their friends and faced the difficult task of preparing to defend their back-to-back state championships. As the Tigers began their preseason workouts, Coach Roth sought input from captains Bob Admire, Dan Latorre, Kevin Beishline, and the rest of the team on ways to respectfully honor and pay tribute to their fallen teammates. The idea of taking the field with only nine players on their first defensive play of each game, leaving two positions empty where Leghlid and Barnes would have played, was proposed and received the overwhelming support of the team and the coaching staff. The Tigers would also wear patches on their jerseys with "55-17" to honor Tarik Leghlid and Eric Barnes.

The Tigers opened the 2004 season on the road against the Loyalsock Lancers. The Southern defense took the field for their first defensive play with only nine players as planned. Fittingly, it would be the defense that would score the first points of the season. Dan Crowl hit the Lancers' quarterback, causing a fumble that was picked up by Bob Admire, who returned it 6 yards for a touchdown. Tarik and Eric would have been so proud of their defensive mates. Derek Crowl and Henry Hynoski added scoring runs of one and 5 yards, and the Tigers took a 19-0 lead after one. Dan Latorre found Crowl for a 33-yard touchdown pass, and Hynoski capped the scoring with touchdown runs of 21 and 23 yards for a 40-0 lead at the half. The defense held the Loyalsock to -20 yards rushing and just 38 yards of total offense while pitching a shutout against the Lancers. The Tigers rushed for 381 yards. Jeremy Sargent ran for 98 yards. Hynoski had 81 rushing yards and three touchdowns. Crowl rushed for 30 yards and a score and had a touchdown reception. Latorre threw for 69 yards and a touchdown. The Tigers earned an emotional 40-0 opening-day victory.

Emotions continued to run high in the home opener against Bloomsburg. Prior to the game, the Southern Columbia community paid tribute to Tarik Leghlid and Eric Barnes. The school also honored the tenth anniversary of the Tigers' first state championship team in 1994. Again, with only nine players on the field for Southern's first defensive play, Zach Allen intercepted a Panthers' pass on the game's first play. It was another incredible moment in honor of the Tigers' fallen teammates. Dan Latorre fired a 10-yard touchdown pass to Josh Fidler to open the scoring. Later in the first, Latorre hit Derek Crowl on a 34-yard scoring throw to push the lead to 14-0 after the opening period. Latorre scrambled 85 yards for a touchdown, Zach Allen hauled in a Latorre pass for a 24-yard score, and Kyle Connaghan rumbled 22 yards for a touchdown as Southern led 34-0 at the break. Henry Hynoski and Corey Sober added scoring runs of 50 and 42 yards in the third, and the Tigers defeated Bloomsburg, 47-0. The defense had another stellar effort, holding the Panthers to 19 yards rushing and only 52 through the air while registering their second straight shutout. The Southern ground attack rumbled for 398 yards. Hynoski led the way with 110 yards and a touchdown. Crowl ran for 64 yards and had a touchdown reception. Sober rushed for 55 yards and a score. Connaghan added 31 yards on the ground and a touchdown. Latorre passed for 82 yards and three scores. He also had 100 yards rushing and a touchdown. Allen had 24 receiving yards and a scoring catch. Fidler hauled in 10 receiving yards and a touchdown. The Tigers won another emotional game with heavy hearts.

The Tigers hosted Mount Carmel, which would be a matchup of two state football superpowers. Southern was the top-ranked team in Class A, and the Red Tornadoes were the number one AA team. The game was delayed a day due to heavy rains. The teams traded blows like heavyweight fighters. Derek Crowl struck first for the Tigers in the first quarter on a 5-yard touchdown run. Mount Carmel tied the score with a 29-yard scoring run in the second. The teams were deadlocked at 7-7 at the intermission. Henry Hynoski put Southern back in front on an 8-yard run in the third. However, the Tornadoes pulled even with an 18-yard pass, and the contest was tied 14-14 heading into the final period. Dan Latorre scored on a 40-yard quarterback keeper with 9:44 left in the fourth. The Tigers left the matter to their magnificent defense. Southern held Mount Carmel in check down the stretch and earned a hard-fought 21-14 victory. Hynoski had 106 rushing yards and a touchdown. Crowl ran for 29 yards and a score. Latorre threw for 123 yards and had a rushing touchdown.

Southern traveled to Lewisburg for a week four game with the Green Dragons. Dan Latorre found Matt Koziol for a 25-yard touchdown pass and a 7-0 lead. Lewisburg responded with a scoring pass and cut the lead to 7-6 after one. The Tigers put the game out of reach in the second quarter. Latorre ran for an 11-yard touchdown, Koziol and Latorre hooked up again on a 12-yard scoring play, Kyle Connaghan scampered 9 yards for a touchdown, and Latorre scored again on a 49-yard keeper as Southern took a commanding 34-6 lead at halftime. Derek Crowl returned the second-half kickoff 97 yards for a score. Nich Gallinot added a 24-yard touchdown run, and the Tigers led 48-12 after three. Dan Crowl pounded in from 2 yards out, and Southern won the game 55-18 over the Green Dragons. The defense registered two interceptions and recovered two fumbles. Latorre passed for 123 yards and two touchdowns. He also ran for 100 yards and a score. Koziol had 37 receiving yards and two touchdown receptions. Gallinot rushed for 32 yards and a touchdown. The Tigers also got scoring runs from Connaghan and Dan Crowl.

The Tigers got off to a fast start in a home game against Warrior Run. Dan Latorre fired a 25-yard touchdown strike to Zach Allen, Henry Hynoski rumbled 6 yards for a score, Latorre added touchdown runs of 75 and 20 yards, and Southern led 28-0 after the opening quarter. Hynoski tacked on a 10-yard scoring jaunt, and the Tigers took a 34-6 lead into the half. After a Defenders' touchdown run early in the third, Allen and Latorre hooked up again on a 53-yard scoring bomb. Warrior Run scored again in the fourth, and Jeremy Sargent finished off the Defenders with an 80-yard touchdown burst for a 47-20 victory. Southern pounded out 413 yards on the ground. Latorre led the offense with 95 rushing yards and two touchdowns. He also threw for 144 yards and two scores. Sargent ran for 82 yards and a touchdown. Hynoski rushed for 60 yards and two scores. Allen had 95 receiving yards and two touchdowns.

Southern continued to roll on the road versus Hughesville. Kyle Connaghan rumbled 45 yards for a score, Dan Latorre hit Zach Allen for an 18-yard touchdown pass, and the Tigers took a 14-0 lead after one. Henry Hynoski scored from 7 yards out and pushed the lead to 20-0 at the break. Derek Crowl and Jeremy Sargent put away the Spartans with touchdown runs of 75 and 11 yards in the third to make the final score, 33-0. Crowl ran for 98 yards and a touchdown. Hynoski added 74 rushing yards and a score. Connaghan rushed for 47 yards and a touchdown. Sargent chipped in with 15 yards on the ground and a scoring run. Latorre passed for 123 yards and a touchdown. Allen had 26 receiving yards and a score.

The Tigers visited South Williamsport for a week seven contest. Bob Admire snuffed out the Mountaineers' first possession with a fumble recovery, Derek Crowl would plow in from 2 yards out, and Southern took a 6-0 first-quarter lead. Ray Snarski caught a 15-yard touchdown pass from Dan Latorre, and Crowl added a 5-yard scoring run to push the lead to 19-0. After a South Williamsport touchdown pass, Latorre hit Henry Hynoski for a 39-yard score, and the Tigers led 26-7 at the intermission. Latorre scrambled for a 44-yard touchdown in the third, and Southern earned a 32-13 win over the Mountaineers. Latorre threw for 210 yards and two scores. He added 78 rushing yards and a touchdown. Hynoski ran for 66 yards and had a touchdown reception. Crowl rushed for 29 yards and a score. Snarski had 29 yards rushing and a touchdown reception. The Southern defense held South Williamsport to 19 yards rushing.

Southern traveled to North Schuylkill in week eight. Dan Latorre hit Matt Koziol for touchdown passes of 7 and 47 yards, and Latorre raced 9 yards for another score, and the Tigers jumped to a 21-0 lead after one. Henry Hynoski added an 8-yard touchdown run in the second for a 27-0 halftime lead. Zach Allen returned an interception 40 yards for a pick six in the third, and Corey Sober scampered for a 46-yard score in the final period for a 40-0 victory over the Spartans. The Southern defense was utterly dominant. The Tigers did not allow a first down during the game. The Spartans had zero passing yards and only had 15 yards rushing. Hynoski ran for 79 yards and a touchdown. Sober gained 46 yards on the ground and had a scoring run. Latorre threw for 166 yards and two touchdowns and rushed for a score. Koziol had 54 receiving yards and a touchdown reception.

The Tigers returned home to face the Central Columbia Blue Jays. Central scored first on a 50-yard run, but Henry Hynoski responded with a 3-yard plunge to give the Tigers a 7-6 lead after the opening quarter. Dan Latorre threw a 30-yard touchdown strike to Matt Koziol, and Hynoski plowed in from one yard out for a 20-6 lead at the break. The Blue Jays scored on a 9-yard pass in the third, but Southern put the game away on Latorre's 10-yard run, Hynoski's 21-yard scamper, and Ray Snarski's one-yard plunge giving the Tigers a 40-13 victory. Hynoski ran for 107 yards and three touchdowns. Snarski rushed for 28 yards and a score. Latorre passed for 121 yards and a touchdown and ran for 95 yards and a score. Koziol had 30 yards receiving and a touchdown grab. With the win, Southern clinched another Central Susquehanna Conference Division II Championship.

Southern played the Danville Ironmen in the regular-season finale at Tiger Stadium. Henry Hynoski started the scoring with a one-yard run and a 7-0 Tiger lead. The Ironmen returned the ensuing kickoff 92 yards for a touchdown to tie the game at 7-7. Ray Snarski put the Tigers back in front with a 37-yard touchdown run, and Dan Latorre raced 17 yards to push the Southern lead to 21-7 at the end of the first quarter. In the second, Derek Crowl and Latorre scored on runs of 6 and 13 yards for a 35-7 Tiger advantage. Danville cut the lead to 35-14 with a 2-yard scoring run. Latorre hit Snarski for a 21-yard touchdown pass the give Southern a 42-14 lead at the intermission. Hynoski rumbled 52 yards for a score in the third, and Nich Gallinot capped the scoring with a one-yard touchdown run in the fourth. The Tigers defeated the Ironmen, 56-14. Hynoski rushed for 86 yards and two touchdowns. Snarski ran for 45 yards and a score and also had a touchdown reception. Crowl added 35 rushing yards and a score. Gallinot had 17 yards rushing and a touchdown. Latorre threw for 120 yards and a score and ran for 49 yards and two touchdowns. The defense controlled Danville with an interception and two fumble recoveries. The Tigers won their tenth game, marking their 18th consecutive season with ten or more wins.

The Tigers hosted Lourdes Regional in the District IV Class A Championship Game that was delayed a day due to torrential rains. Southern had no trouble handling the Red Raiders in their postseason opener. Derek Crowl scored on a 25-yard run, Dan Latorre connected with Crowl on a 60-yard touchdown bomb, Henry Hynoski returned an interception 9 yards for a pick six, and Ray Snarski bolted 31-yards for a score as Southern built a 27-0 first-quarter lead. Hynoski added a 19-yard touchdown scamper in the second, and the Tigers led 34-0 at the break. Southern salted the game away in the third on Crowl's 74-yard jaunt, Kyle Connaghan's 7-yard touchdown run, Snarski's 28-yards scamper, and Nich Gallinot's 5-yard touchdown run. The Tigers overwhelmed the Red Raiders, 61-0. Southern rushed for 375 yards. Crowl led the Tigers with 120 rushing yards and two touchdowns. He also had a scoring reception. Hynoski ran for 82 yards and a score. Connaghan rushed for 49 yards and a touchdown. Snarski had 38 rushing yards and a scoring run. Gallinot added six rushing yards and a touchdown. Latorre passed for 95 yards and a touchdown. The Tigers won their 13th straight District IV Class A Championship.

Southern entered the first round of the PIAA Class A Playoffs against Lackawanna Trail in Scranton. Dan Latorre scored in the first quarter on a 20-yard keeper for a 7-0 lead. Henry Hynoski rumbled for a 24-yard score, and Latorre scored his second touchdown of the game on an 8-yard run as the Tigers led 20-0 at the half. Derek Crowl scored on runs of 22 and one yard in the third to push the Southern lead to 34-0. The Lions sandwiched fourth-quarter scores around Nich Gallinot's 10-yard touchdown run, and Southern advanced with a 40-14 victory. The Tigers pounded out 425 yards on the ground. Hynoski rumbled for 218 rushing yards and a touchdown. Crowl ran for 32 yards and two scores. Gallinot added 24 rushing yards and a touchdown. Latorre threw for 143 yards and ran for two scores.

The top-ranked Tigers faced second-ranked Pius X in the PIAA Class A Quarterfinal Game in Selinsgrove that is considered an all-time high school football classic. Pius X scored on a 2-yard touchdown run early in the first to take a 7-0 lead. Kyle Connaghan tied the game at 7-7 on a 9-yard scoring run. The Royals reclaimed the lead with a one-yard touchdown plunge. Connaghan again answered with a 3-yard scoring burst, and the game was tied 14-14 after the first quarter. Henry Hynoski scored on runs of 3 and 91 yards in the second as Southern took a 27-14 lead. The Royals pulled within 27-21 on a 55-yard touchdown pass. Connaghan rumbled 38 yards for a score to push the lead to 35-21. Pius X scored on a 70-yard pass to cut the lead to 35-28. Connaghan scored again from one yard out, and Southern took a 41-28 lead into halftime. Dan Latorre opened the scoring in the third with a 2-yard keeper to push the Tigers' lead to 47-28. Hynoski rumbled 46 yards for a touchdown and a 55-28 advantage. The Royals scored on an 18-yard run to close the gap to 55-35. Hynoski ran for an 8-yard touchdown, and Southern took a 63-35 lead into the fourth quarter. Hynoski scored his fifth rushing touchdown of the game with a 2-yard run to up the Tigers' lead to 70-35. Pius X came back with a 2-yard scoring pass to make the score 70-41. Hynoski recovered his own fumble in the endzone to push the Southern lead to 76-41. The Royals capped the scoring in the shootout with a 33-yard touchdown pass. At the final gun, the Tigers had outscored Pius X 76-47 in their quarterfinal slugfest. When the final numbers were totaled, several national, state, and school records had fallen. Henry Hynoski rushed for a whopping 409 yards, setting PIAA playoff and Southern Columbia school records. The total broke the previous PIAA playoff mark of 315 set by Mount Carmel's Brett Veach in 2000 and eclipsed Southern Columbia's school record of 338 by Ricco Rosini in 1997. The Tigers rushed for a staggering 768 yards as a team, breaking the national high school record of 755 set by Indianapolis Warren Central in 2002. Southern Columbia had 803 total yards of offense. Pius X had 355 passing yards and 451 total yards of offense. The teams combined for an incredible 1,254 total yards of offense and 123 points, setting PIAA playoff records. The Tigers set a PIAA playoff mark with 76 points scored, which tied the school record for the most points scored in a game. Offensive lineman Josh Marks, Kevin Beishline, Dan Kreisher, Ian Fullmer, and Jake Stryjewski opened holes and paved the way for Southern's record-setting numbers. Hynoski rushed for 409 yards and five touchdowns. Connaghan ran for 175 yards and four scores. Latorre had 121 rushing yards and a touchdown. He also threw for 35 yards. Ray Snarski contributed 48 yards on the ground. Jason Campbell chipped in with 15 yards rushing.

For the second straight week, the Tigers played in Selinsgrove as they met the Camp Hill Lions in the PIAA Class A Semifinal Game. Ray Snarski scored on a 3-yard run, and Dan Latorre fired a 10-yard touchdown pass to Matt Koziol for a 14-0 lead in the first quarter. Camp Hill responded with a 20-yard touchdown run and a 40-yard field goal to trim the Southern lead to 14-10 at the half. Henry Hynoski plowed in from one yard out early in the third. The Lions countered with a 13-yard touchdown pass to make the score 21-17. Latorre found paydirt on a 10-yard keeper to push the Tigers' lead to 28-17. Defensive lineman Eric Spotts intercepted a Camp Hill pass and rumbled 42-yards for a score to make the score 35-17 after three. Camp Hill made it 35-24 on a 56-yard scoring pass. Latorre scampered 21-yards for a touchdown to put the game out of reach at 42-24. Camp Hill scored a late touchdown to make the final score 42-30. Southern rushed for 329 yards. Hynoski ran for 160 yards and a touchdown. Snarski added 10 rushing yards and a score. Latorre passed for 78 yards and a touchdown. He also rushed for 88 yards and two scores. Koziol had 25 receiving yards and a touchdown reception. The Tigers advanced to their seventh consecutive state championship game and their tenth title game overall.

The Southern Columbia Tigers and their fans had endured an emotional journey to reach the PIAA Class A Championship Game against the Rochester Rams at Hersheypark Stadium. The Tigers had great resolve to bring home a third straight championship in honor of their friends and teammates, Eric Barnes and Tarik Leghlid. Southern played with nine players on their first defensive play as they had done in every game throughout the season. Afterward, every player on the field and the sideline took a knee for several seconds of reflection. The Tigers then set out to finish what they had started. Dan Latorre scored on runs of 2 and 19 yards to open up a 14-0 lead in the first quarter. Latorre scored again from one yard out in the second, and Southern led 21-0 at halftime. In the third, Latorre scored his fourth touchdown of the afternoon on a 69-yard burst. Tigers fans will never forget legendary broadcaster Jim Doyle's call of Latorre's run. Ray Snarski capped off the scoring and the season with a 55-yard touchdown run. The Rams were never able to find any offensive success. With their fallen mates looking down on them, it was appropriate that the Tigers magnificent defense pitched one final shutout. The Southern Columbia Tigers defeated the Rochester Rams 35-0 to capture their third consecutive PIAA Class A Championship. They became the first Class A team to win three straight state championships and joined Berwick and Central Bucks West as the only teams in Pennsylvania high school football history to accomplish the feat. It was Southern's fourth state title overall, coming ten years to the day after their first championship in 1994. The Tigers extended their winning streak to 27 consecutive games. Southern rushed for 398 yards for the game. Latorre was the offensive star, rushing for 150 yards and four touchdowns. He threw for 34 yards. Henry Hynoski ran for 132 yards. Snarski had 71 rushing yards and a touchdown. The defense held Rochester to 70 rushing yards and 11 through the air. The unit had two fumble recoveries and three interceptions, two by Matt Koziol and one from Zach Allen. The Southern Columbia Tigers finished the 2004 season with a record of 15-0. In an emotional celebration after returning to Catawissa, Eric Barnes and Tarik Leghlid's families embraced each member of this magnificent team.

## 2004 SEASON

| Opponent | Location | W/L | Score |
|---|---|---|---|
| Loyalsock | Away | W | 40-0 |
| Bloomsburg | Home | W | 47-0 |
| Mount Carmel | Home | W | 21-14 |
| Lewisburg | Away | W | 55-18 |
| Warrior Run | Home | W | 47-20 |
| Hughesville | Away | W | 33-0 |
| South Williamsport | Away | W | 32-13 |
| North Schuylkill | Away | W | 40-0 |
| Central Columbia | Home | W | 40-13 |
| Danville | Home | W | 56-14 |
| **District IV Class A Championship Game** | | | |
| Lourdes Regional | Home | W | 61-0 |
| **District IV Class A Playoff Game** | | | |
| Lackawanna Trail | Neutral | W | 40-14 |
| **PIAA Class A Quarterfinal Game** | | | |
| Pius X | Neutral | W | 76-47 |
| **PIAA Class A Semifinal Game** | | | |
| Camp Hill | Neutral | W | 42-30 |
| **PIAA Class A Championship Game** | | | |
| Rochester | Neutral | W | 35-0 |

COACHING STAFF: Jim Roth, Head Coach; Randall Campbell, Assistant Coach; Al Cihocki, Assistant Coach; Troy Heath, Assistant Coach; Andy Helwig, Assistant Coach; Mike Johnston, Assistant Coach; John Marks, Assistant Coach; Andy Mills, Assistant Coach; Pete Saylor, Assistant Coach; Rick Steele, Assistant Coach; Curt Stellfox, Assistant Coach; Don Traugh, Assistant Coach

ATHLETIC DIRECTOR: Terry Sharrow

ROSTER: Dave Adams, Bob Admire, Tom Admire, Zach Allen, Kevin Beishline, Khyle Berns, Joel Bittner, Steve Breskiewicz, Jason Campbell, Nate Carl, Kyle Connaghan, Tyler Cox, Curtis Cranmer, Dan Crowl, Derek Crowl, Josh Fidler, Jeff Flemming, Dave Forney, Ian Fullmer, Nich Gallinot, Shaun Gooler, Reuben Guerra, Josh Gratti, Nick Hartnranft, Ted Heitzman, Henry Hynoski, Cody Jones, Justin Knoebel, Matt Koziol, Dan Kreisher, Daren Kremser, Dan Latorre, Josh Marks, Geoff Michalesko, Victor Northern, Marcus Odorizzi, Jeremy Oshman, Corey Pilkus, Devin Raught, Jeremy Sargent, Ray Snarski, Colby Snyder, Corey Sober, Eric Spotts, Sean Stout, Jake Stryjewski, Brenton Surak, Bryan Terry, Truman Webb, Shane Wells (In Memoriam) Eric Barnes and Tarik Leghlid

The Tigers had many outstanding performances in 2004. Henry Hynoski rushed for 1,826 yards and 22 touchdowns. Dan Latorre ran for 1,044 yards and 19 touchdowns. He also threw for 1,732 yards and 17 scores. Latorre became only the second Southern quarterback, joining Matt Kaskie, to have over 5,000 combined rushing and passing yards for their career. He was named the 2004 Small School Player of the Year. Derek Crowl had 600 yards rushing and ten touchdowns. Kyle Connaghan ran for 573 yards and eight scores. The Tigers also got touchdown runs from Ray Snarski (6), Nich Gallinot (4), Jeremy Sargent (2), Corey Sober (2), and Dan Crowl (1). Zach Allen had 548 receiving yards and four touchdowns. Matt Koziol had 291 yards receiving and six scores. Southern also had touchdown receptions from Derek Crowl (2), Josh Fidler (2), Ray Snarski (2), and Henry Hynoski (1). Bob Admire, who would continue his football career at the University of Maine, recorded 122 tackles (71 solo). Zach Allen and Kyle Connaghan each had five interceptions. Victor Northern registered 10.5 sacks. Admire, Hynoski, Latorre, Kevin Beishline, and Josh Marks were All-State selections.

Sadly, the 2004 Southern Columbia football team would endure several more tragic losses in the years to come. In 2007, Derek Crowl, a student at Bloomsburg University, passed away from injuries suffered in a fire in Massachusetts. He was just 19 years old. Geoff Michalesko died from injuries sustained in a motorcycle accident on July 31, 2010, at 23. Daren Kremser passed away at the age of 28 from injuries suffered in a car accident on December 23, 2015. Dan Crowl, the twin brother of Derek, died on May 8, 2018, at 28. The fallen players from this special team will never be forgotten.

**2005** The 2005 Tigers looked to win a fourth consecutive state championship. Coach Jim Roth would keep with the same winning formula; a bruising running game and a stout defense. Southern would enter the season with a new quarterback at the helm, and the team would need to rely on their strengths to give their new signal-caller time to develop. The Tigers opened the year with a home game agist Shamokin. It was the first time the teams had faced each other in 40 years. After a scoreless first quarter, Shamokin scored on a 20-yard run to open the scoring. Kyle Connaghan returned an interception 75 yards for a touchdown to put the Tigers in front 7-6 at the half. Henry Hynoski ran for a 6-yard touchdown, but Shamokin answered with a 57-yard scoring pass, and the game was tied at 13-13 after three. The Indians got a 32-yard field goal, and Ian Fullmer connected on a 22-yard boot, and the game was deadlocked at 16-16 at the end of regulation. Early in the overtime period, Shamokin connected on a 26-yard field goal to give the Indians a 19-16 overtime victory. The loss snapped the Tigers' 27-game winning streak. Hynoski ran for 145 yards and a touchdown in a losing effort. The defense played a solid game, with Nich Gallinot and Corey Sober registering sacks, Connaghan's interception for a pick six and Victor Northern recovered a fumble.

Southern looked to get back on a winning track in a road game at Bloomsburg. Henry Hynoski scored on runs of 5, 22, and 19 yards in the first, and the Tigers led 19-0. Kyle Connaghan scored from 46 yards out, and Hynoski scored his fourth touchdown of the game on a 10-yard run as Southern led 33-0 at the break. Dave Adams scored on a 10-yard run in the third, and the Panthers scored a late touchdown in the fourth to make the final, 39-6. Southern rushed for 316 yards. Hynoski rushed for 140 yards and four touchdowns. Connaghan ran for 62 yards and a score. Adams added 31 rushing yards and a touchdown. Defensively, Marcus Odorizzi and Bryan Terry had interceptions, and Khyle Berns and Victor Northern registered sacks. The win was historic for head coach Jim Roth, as it was the 250th career coaching victory.

The Tigers looked to move above .500 in an away game versus Mount Carmel. The Red Tornadoes scored first on an 8-yard run and led 7-0 after one. Henry Hynoski pulled the Tigers within a point on a one-yard dive, but Mount Carmel scored on a 33-yard pass play and took a 14-6 lead at halftime. Mount Carmel pushed the lead to 21-6 with a 65-yard touchdown pass in the third. Southern mounted a comeback in the fourth quarter. Nich Gallinot scored on an 8-yard scamper to cut the lead to 21-12. Kyle Connaghan scored from 8 yards out to pull the Tigers within 21-19. Tom Admire's interception set up Connaghan's 5-yard touchdown run, and Southern took their first lead of the game at 25-21. Hynoski sealed the Tigers' comeback victory with a 29-yard scoring run as Southern earned a thrilling 32-21 win over the Red Tornadoes. Southern rushed for 334 yards. Hynoski rumbled for 238 yards and two touchdowns. Connaghan ran for 44 yards and two scores. Gallinot rushed for 25 yards and a touchdown. Admire recorded two interceptions.

Southern traveled to Lewisburg to take on the Green Dragons. Kyle Connaghan and Nich Gallinot scored on runs of 8 and 74 yards, and the Tigers built a 14-0 first-quarter lead. Henry Hynoski pounded in from one yard out and rumbled for a 33-yard touchdown, and Connaghan raced 30-yards for a score, and Southern led 35-0 at the intermission. Ted Heitzman and Austin Carpenter added touchdown runs of 6 and 11 yards in the third. In the fourth, Andrew Wimble capped the scoring with a 21-yard jaunt, and the Tigers shutout Lewisburg, 55-0. When the Green Dragons began to lose players due to injuries,

Coach Jim Roth agreed to reduce the fourth quarter to eight minutes rather than the standard twelve. Connaghan ran for 130 yards and two touchdowns. Gallinot rushed for 74 yards and a score. Hynoski had 62 yards rushing and two touchdowns. Carpenter added 23 yards on the ground and a score. Wimble ran for 21 yards and a touchdown. Heitzman threw for 91 yards and had a rushing score. Wimble and Tom Admire each had interceptions.

Things went off the rails for the Tigers in a home game with Warrior Run. The Defenders scored on three touchdown passes in the first quarter. Kyle Connaghan ran for a 14-yard score to cut the lead to 21-7 after one, and Ted Heitzman scored on a one-yard keeper to close the gap to 21-14. Warrior Run got a fourth touchdown pass, and Southern trailed 28-14 at halftime. Nich Gallinot ran for a 26-yard touchdown in the third, but the Tigers could get no closer, and the Defenders defeated Southern, 28-21. Connaghan ran for 51 yards and a score. Gallinot had 46 yards rushing and a touchdown. Heitzman passed for 54 yards and ran for a score.

Southern hosted the Hughesville Spartans at Tiger Stadium. Hughesville scored in the first quarter on a one-yard run for a 7-0 lead. Henry Hynoski raced for a 10-yard touchdown, and a successful two-point conversion gave Southern an 8-6 halftime lead. After a scoreless third quarter, Hynoski put the Spartans away with touchdown runs of 31 and 24 yards in the fourth as the Tigers earned a 21-7 victory. Hynoski was a one-man wrecking crew for the offense, rushing for 170 yards and three touchdowns.

The Loyalsock Lancers visited Tiger Stadium in week seven. Ted Heitzman hit Kyle Connaghan for an 85-yard touchdown pass, but Loyalsock scored twice to take a 14-7 lead after the opening quarter. Henry Hynoski scored on a 14-yard burst, and the game was tied at 14-14 at the break. Southern's running game took over in the third quarter. Hynoski ran for touchdowns of 14 and 2 yards, Connaghan scored from 11-yards out, and the Tigers took control, 33-14. Connaghan opened the fourth with an 11-yard scoring run. The Lancers scored a late touchdown to bring the final score to 40-21. The Tigers had 426 yards on the ground. Hynoski led the way with 177 rushing yards and three touchdowns. Connaghan ran for 99 yards and two scores. He also had 117 receiving yards and a touchdown reception. Heitzman threw for 148 yards passing and a touchdown. Connaghan also starred on defense with an interception and a fumble recovery.

Southern played host to North Schuylkill at Tiger Stadium. They jumped to a fast start. Ted Heitzman spotted Colby Snyder for an 8-yard touchdown pass, Henry Hynoski ran for a 23-yard touchdown, and Kyle Connaghan raced

68 yards for a score as Southern built a 21-0 lead after the first. Hynoski added touchdown runs of 40 and one yard before the Spartans got on the board with a 73-yard pass, and the Tigers led 35-7 at the break. Heitzman scored on a 61-yard scamper in the third for a 42-7 lead. After a North Schuylkill 59-yard scoring pass in the fourth, Andrew Wimble returned the ensuing kickoff 70 yards for a touchdown. Southern defeated the Spartans by a score of 48-13. The Tigers ran for 384 yards. Hynoski rushed for 87 yards and three touchdowns. Connaghan ran for 85 yards and a score. Heitzman threw for 82 yards and a touchdown and also contributed a scoring run. Snyder had 20 yards receiving and a touchdown reception.

The Tigers traveled to Central Columbia for a matchup with the Blue Jays. Southern completely dominated the contest. Jeremy Sargent opened the scoring with a one-yard plunge in the first quarter. Henry Hynoski scored on runs of 5 and 19 yards, Dave Adams and Kyle Connaghan had rushing touchdowns of 5 and 6 yards, and the Tigers led 34-0 by halftime. Adams added a 14-yard touchdown burst in the third and Southern shutout Central Columbia, 41-0. The Tigers rumbled for 346 yards rushing. Hynoski ran for 107 yards and two scores. Connaghan rushed for 80 yards and a touchdown. Sargent had 54 yards rushing and a score. Adams contributed 39 yards on the ground and two touchdowns. The defense got fumble recoveries from Tyler Cox, Nick Hartranft, Corey Sober, and Andrew Wimble. Austin Carpenter and Marcus Odorizzi registered interceptions.

Southern wrapped up the regular season with a trip to Danville. After the Ironmen opened the scoring with a 30-yard pass, it was all Tigers the rest of the way. Kyle Connaghan and Ted Heitzman scored on runs of 2 and 5 years for a 14-7 Southern lead after the opening period. Henry Hynoski rumbled 58 yards for a touchdown, and Heitzman fired a 12-yard scoring pass to Tom Admire to push the Tigers' lead to 27-7 at the intermission. After a scoreless third, Connaghan and Austin Carpenter put the final nails in Danville's coffin with touchdown runs of 20 and 29 yards in the fourth to make the final 40-7. The Southern ground attack continued to roll with 391 rushing yards. Connaghan ran for 122 yards and two touchdowns. Hynoski totaled 113 yards on the ground and a scoring run. Carpenter added 26 rushing yards and a touchdown. Heitzman passed for 28 yards and a score and had a rushing touchdown. Admire had 28 receiving yards and a scoring catch. Victor Northern had an interception and Nich Gallinot recovered a Danville fumble.

The Tigers played Muncy in the District IV Class A Championship Game at Tiger Stadium. Southern struck quickly and made short work of the Indians.

Henry Hynoski caught a 25-yard touchdown pass from Ted Heitzman, Ian Fullmer booted a 27-yard field goal, Kyle Connaghan raced 27 yards for a score, and Hynoski scored his second touchdown of the first quarter on a 15-yard run as the Tigers built a 23-0 lead. In the second, Southern got scoring runs of 63 yards from Connaghan, 14 yards from Hynoski, 16 yards from Jeremy Sargent, and 3 yards from Nich Gallinot, and the rout was on. The Tigers led 50-0 at the break. Muncy scored a touchdown in the third, and Zeke Conrad ended the scoring with a 97-yard interception return for a score in the fourth. The final score was 56-7. Southern bludgeoned the Indians for 330 rushing yards. Connaghan ran for 106 yards and two touchdowns. Hynoski rushed for 85 yards and two scores and had a touchdown reception. Sargent had 28 rushing yards and a touchdown. Gallinot added 20 yards on the ground and a scoring run. Heitzman threw for 101 yards and a touchdown. The Tigers' defense got interceptions from Conrad, Ted Admire, and Marcus Odorizzi. Dave Adams and Curtis Cranmer recovered fumbles. Southern claimed their 14th consecutive District IV Championship.

Southern began the PIAA Class A Playoffs against Lackawanna Trail in Shamokin. Henry Hynoski rumbled for a 12-yard touchdown run for a 6-0 lead after one. After a Lions' field goal, Hynoski raced for a 47-yard touchdown, Ted Heitzman scored on a 6-yard keeper, and Tom Admire hauled in an 11-yard touchdown pass from Heitzman, and Southern led 26-3 at the half. The Lions scored on a 4-yard run, and Kyle Connaghan ripped off a 56-yard touchdown scamper to push the Tigers' lead to 33-9 after three. Lackawanna Trail got a touchdown pass in mop-up time as Southern defeated the Lions, 33-15. The Tigers' rushing attack had another 300-yard game, gaining 314 on the ground. Hynoski ran for 119 yards and two touchdowns. Connaghan rushed for 101 yards and a score. Heitzman threw for 99 yards and a score and added a touchdown run. Admire had 43 receiving yards and a touchdown catch.

The Tigers advanced to face Schuylkill Haven in the PIAA Class A Quarterfinal Game in Pottsville. Starting quarterback Ted Heitzman missed the game with an infection in his right leg, so Kyle Connaghan stepped in as the Southern signal-caller. After a scoreless first quarter, Henry Hynoski rumbled 47 yards for the opening touchdown. Hynoski then raced 95 yards to put the Tigers up 14-0. Ian Fullmer connected on a 37-yard field goal, and Southern took a 17-0 lead into the half. Connaghan scored on a 66-yard burst in the third quarter to push the lead to 24-0. Jeremy Sargent scored from one yard out before the Hurricanes got a late touchdown to make the final score 31-6. Southern, again, topped 300 yards rushing, rolling for 378 on the ground. Hynoski led the way with 205 yards rushing and two touchdowns. Connaghan ran for 107 yards and a score. Sargent scored a touchdown with three rushing yards. Ted Admire and Kyle Stavinski had interceptions for the Tigers' defense. Although he did not complete a pass, Connaghan filled in effectively for the injured Heitzman at quarterback.

Before their PIAA Class A Semifinal Game against Steelton-Highspire at Hersheypark Stadium, the Tigers learned that starting quarterback Ted Heitzman would miss his second straight game with an infection in his right leg. The team again called on Kyle Connaghan to step behind center and lead the offense. Steel High appeared to be off to a fast start with a 72-yard touchdown pass in the first quarter. However, that was all she wrote for the Rollers. Nich Gallinot pulled Southern even with a 15-yard scoring run. Henry Hynoski put the Tigers in front to stay with a 3-yard touchdown plunge. Southern led 14-7 at halftime. Hynoski put the game away in the third quarter with scoring runs of 20 and 2 yards, and the Tigers pulled ahead 28-7 after three. Connaghan and Andrew Wimble finished the scoring with touchdown runs of 2 and one yard in the fourth as Southern routed Steel High, 41-7. The Tigers' ground machine continued to roll with 411 rushing yards. Hynoski ran for 187 yards and three scores. Connaghan added 90 rushing yards at quarterback and had a touchdown run. Gallinot rushed for 43 years and a score. Wimble tacked on 31 rushing yards and a touchdown. Marcus Odorizzi had an interception, and Kyle Berns, Kyle Breech, and Victor Northern recovered Roller fumbles to lead an outstanding defensive effort.

The Tigers advanced to the PIAA Class A Championship Game against the Duquesne Dukes at Hersheypark Stadium. Southern was looking to become only the second team in Pennsylvania high school football history to win four consecutive state championships. Kyle Connaghan would be substituting for starting quarterback Ted Heitzman, who was recovering from a staph infection in his right leg for the third straight game. The game would be played in 30-mile per hour winds, and the Tigers would need to lean on their outstanding running game. Duquesne scored first on a 79-yard pass. Connaghan answered with an 18-yard quarterback keeper giving Southern a 7-6 first-quarter lead. Henry Hynoski rumbled 7 yards for a touchdown, and the Tigers led 14-6 after one. Hynoski plowed in from one yard out, but the Dukes scored twice on a 59-yard run and a 25-yard pass to pull within one, making the score 20-19 at the break. Hynoski took the game into his hands in the third quarter. He scored on runs of 3 and 34 yards to push the Southern lead to 34-19 after three. Ian Fullmer booted a 31-yard field goal, Nich Gallinot scored from 3 yards out, and Shane

Wells finished off the Dukes with a 20-yard touchdown run, and the Southern Columbia Tigers defeated Duquesne 50-19 to win their fourth straight PIAA Class A Championship. Southern joined Berwick as the only teams to ever win four straight Pennsylvania state football titles. The Tigers running attack amassed a staggering 509 rushing yards, tying the record for the most in a state final game. Henry Hynoski set a new PIAA Class A Championship Game record with 271 yards, breaking the previous record of 165 set by Southern's Brandon Traugh in 2003. Hynoski would also add four rushing touchdowns to

## 2005 SEASON

| Opponent | Location | W/L | Score |
|---|---|---|---|
| Shamokin | Away | L | 16-19 (Overtime) |
| Bloomsburg | Away | W | 39-6 |
| Mount Carmel | Away | W | 32-21 |
| Lewisburg | Home | W | 55-0 |
| Warrior Run | Away | L | 21-28 |
| Hughesville | Home | W | 21-7 |
| Loyalsock | Home | W | 40-21 |
| North Schuylkill | Home | W | 48-13 |
| Central Columbia | Away | W | 41-0 |
| Danville | Away | W | 40-7 |
| **District IV Class A Semifinal Game** | | | |
| Muncy | Home | W | 56-7 |
| **District IV Class A Championship Game** | | | |
| Lackawanna Trail | Away | W | 33-15 |
| **PIAA Class A Quarterfinal Game** | | | |
| Schuylkill Haven | Neutral | W | 31-6 |
| **PIAA Class A Semifinal Game** | | | |
| Steelton-Highspire | Neutral | W | 41-7 |
| **PIAA Class A Championship Game** | | | |
| Duquesne | Neutral | W | 50-19 |

COACHING STAFF: Jim Roth, Head Coach; Randall Campbell, Assistant Coach; Al Cihocki, Assistant Coach; Troy Heath, Assistant Coach; Andy Helwig, Assistant Coach; Mike Johnston, Assistant Coach; John Marks, Assistant Coach; Andy Mills, Assistant Coach; Pete Saylor, Assistant Coach; Rick Steele, Assistant Coach; Curt Stellfox, Assistant Coach; Dewey Townsend, Assistant Coach; Don Traugh, Assistant Coach

ATHLETIC DIRECTOR: Terry Sharrow

ROSTER: Aaron Adams, Dave Adams, Tom Admire, Brandon Bennett, Khyle Berns, Joel Bittner, Kyle Breech, Nathan Brophy, Jason Campbell, Nate Carl, Austin Carpenter, Tyler Clark, Kyle Connaghan, Zeke Conrad, Tyler Cox, Curtis Cranmer, Jeff Davis, Aaron Farnsworth, Jeff Flemming, Dave Forney, Ian Fullmer, Nich Gallinot, Shawn Gooler, Nick Hartnranft, Ted Heitzman, Henry Hynoski, Cody Jones, Mike Joseph, Justin Knoebel, Mike Lucas, Josh Marks, Matt Mindler, Michael Moyer, Colin Mychak, Victor Northern, Marcus Odorizzi, Jeremy Oshman, Joe Picarelli, Steve Rey, Jeremy Sargent, Colby Snyder, Corey Sober, Eric Spotts, Sean Stout, Kyle Stavinski, Jake Stryjewski, Bryan Terry, Truman Webb, Shane Wells, Tyler Wilson, Andrew Wimble (In Memoriam) Eric Barnes and Tarik Leghlid his record-setting yardage. Connaghan ran for 139 yards and a score. His play was invaluable during the team's playoff run, filling in effectively for injured quarterback Ted Heitzman. Gallinot had 80 rushing yards and a touchdown. Wells scored a rushing touchdown and had 6 yards on the ground. Jeremy Sargent (10) and Dave Adams (8) contributed to the record-setting yardage total. The defense put in an outstanding effort, with Connaghan, Victor Northern, and Eric Spotts intercepting Duquesne passes and Josh Marks registering four tackles for loss. With the victory, the senior class won a state championship in each of their varsity seasons. Coach Roth's Tigers finished the 2005 season with an overall record of 13-2.

The 2005 Tigers put up some impressive offensive numbers, especially in the running game. Henry Hynoski ran for 2,164 yards and 34 touchdowns. Kyle Connaghan rushed for 1,280 yards and 18 scores. Nich Gallinot added 459 rushing yards and six touchdowns. Southern also had touchdown runs from Ted Heitzman (5), Dave Adams (3), Jeremy Sargent (3), Austin Carpenter (2), and Andrew Wimble (2). Ted Heitzman threw for 776 yards and five touchdowns. The Tigers had touchdown receptions from Tom Admire (2) and one each from Kyle Connaghan, Henry Hynoski, and Colby Snyder. Gallinot registered 85 tackles (60 solo). Gallinot and Corey Sober recorded eight sacks. Marcus Odorizzi had five interceptions. Connaghan, Hynoski, Ian Fullmer, and Josh Marks were All-State selections.

**2006** The Southern Columbia Tigers entered the 2006 season attempting to accomplish something no other Pennsylvania football team had ever done; win five consecutive PIAA state championships. With the best running back in the state returning for his senior year, surrounded by a talented supporting cast, an experienced quarterback returning behind center, a dominant offensive line, and a sensational defensive unit, the Tigers looked poised to make history. The journey started with a rare Sunday night game in Shamokin. Henry Hynoski began his senior season in style, scoring the first points of the year on a 3-yard touchdown run. Southern led 7-0 after the first quarter. Hynoski scored again on a 17-yard run, but the Indians cut the lead with a 51-yard touchdown pass. The Tigers led 14-7 at the half. Hynoski rumbled 13 yards for a touchdown, and Dave Adams scored from 3 yards out to push the Southern lead to 28-7. Shamokin scored on a 12-yard pass, and the Tigers' lead was 28-13 after three. Hynoski scored his fourth touchdown of the game with a 14-yard jaunt early in the fourth. Shamokin returned a fumble 56 yards for a score and cut the lead to 28-21. However, Austin Carpenter and Steve Roth scored on runs of 34 and 31 yards, and the Tigers outlasted Shamokin for a 48-21 opening-night victory. Southern started the year with 435 rushing yards. Hynoski ran for 217 yards and four scores. Carpenter rushed for 59 yards and a touchdown. Roth added 45 rushing yards and a score. Adams chipped in with 22 yards on the ground and a rushing touchdown. The defense held Shamokin to -6 yards rushing.

The Tigers' first home game of the season was against the Bloomsburg Panthers. Henry Hynoski ran for a 32-yard touchdown to open the scoring. Bloomsburg answered with a 9-yard scoring pass, and Southern led 7-6 after one. Justin Knoebel came up with a great defensive play, recovering a Panther fumble in the endzone for a touchdown and a 14-6 lead. Tom Admire returned a punt 56 yards for a score, and Southern led 21-6. Ted Heitzman scored on a one-yard quarterback sneak, and the Tigers took a 28-6 lead into halftime. In the third, Hynoski raced 79 yards for a touchdown, and Heitzman scampered 30 yards for a score to push the lead to 41-6. Steve Roth capped the scoring in the fourth quarter with a 17-yard scoring run, and the Tigers earned a 47-6 victory over Bloomsburg. Southern rushed for 340 yards. Hynoski ran for 148 yards and two touchdowns. Roth rushed for 24 yards and a score. Heitzman had 76 rushing yards and a touchdown. The defense had an interception and two fumble recoveries.

Southern hosted Mount Carmel in week three. Henry Hynoski carried the load in the first quarter. He scored on runs of 6, 31, and 25 yards, and the Tigers built a 21-0 lead. In the second, Hynoski sandwiched touchdown runs of 17 and 31 yards around Ted Heitzman's 42-yard keeper to carry a 41-0 lead into the half. Nich Gallinot rumbled 55 yards for a score in the third, and Sam Springer finished off the Red Tornadoes with a one-yard touchdown plunge. Southern dominated Mount Carmel with a 54-0 shutout win. The Tigers' rushing attack continued to roll with 450 yards against the Red Tornadoes. Hynoski ran for 155 yards and five touchdowns. Gallinot rushed for 68 yards and a score. Springer added 24 rushing yards and a touchdown. Heitzman chipped in with 52 yards on the ground and a score. The defense got interceptions from Gallinot, Zeke Conrad and Colby Snyder, and Dave Adams and Tyler Cox recovered Mount Carmel fumbles.

The Tigers traveled to Lewisburg to take on the Green Dragons. Again, Southern got off to a quick start. Henry Hynoski got the Tigers on the board with a 12-yard touchdown run early in the first. Ted Heitzman fired a 7-yard scoring pass to Tom Admire and then hit Austin Carpenter for a 24-yard touchdown strike to give Southern a 21-0 lead after the opening period.

Lewisburg kicked an 18-yard field goal early in the second. Heitzman hooked up with Colby Snyder on a 23-yard touchdown pass to make the score 28-3. Dave Adams scored from 5 yards out for a 35-3 lead. The Dragons scored just before the half to make the score 24-10 at the intermission. Andrew Wimble scampered 11 yards for a score in the third, and Steve Roth capped the scoring with a 3-yard touchdown run in the fourth as the Tigers defeated Lewisburg, 47-10. Southern again topped the 300-yard rushing mark with 392. Hynoski ran for 92 yards and a touchdown. Roth rushed for 87 yards and a score. Wimble added 48 rushing yards and a touchdown. Adams had 41 yards on the ground and a rushing score. Heitzman threw for 117 yards and three touchdowns. Snyder had 35 receiving yards and a scoring grab. Admire had 29 yards receiving and a touchdown reception. Carpenter chipped in with a touchdown catch.

The Warrior Run Defenders visited Tiger Stadium in week five. Henry Hynoski pounded in from one yard out, Ted Heitzman found Auston Carpenter for a 38-yard touchdown pass, Hynoski scored on a 2-yard dive, and Heitzman and Carpenter hooked up again on a 30-yard scoring throw as the Tigers led 27-0 after one. Hynoski scored on runs of 16 and 7 yards in the second and Southern took a 41-0 lead at the break. Kyle Breech had touchdown runs of 10 and 5 yards in the third, and Daniel Schankweiler rumbled 7 yards for a score in the fourth. The Tigers shutout Warrior Run, 59-0. The defense held the Defenders to -11 yards rushing and just 43 through the air. The Tigers rushing machine pounded out 436 yards on the ground. Hynoski ran for 87 yards and four touchdowns. Breach added 32 yards rushing and two scores. Schankweiler had 31 rushing yards and a touchdown. Roth ran for 105 yards. Heitzman passed for 109 yards and two scores. Carpenter had two touchdown receptions.

Southern traveled to Hughesville for a matchup with the Spartans. Ted Heitzman hit Tom Admire for a 13-yard touchdown pass, Henry Hynoski rumbled 25 yards for a score, and the Tigers led 14-0 after the first. Hynoski raced 75 yards for a touchdown, and Dave Adams added a 15-yard scoring run for a 30-0 halftime lead. Adams scored again in the third on a 52-yard touchdown jaunt, and Andrew Wimble darted 85 yards for a score as Southern built a 42-0 lead after three. Hughesville scored a touchdown in the fourth to make the final score 42-7. The Tigers ran for 384 yards. Hynoski rushed for 142 yards and two scores. Wimble rushed for 89 yards and a touchdown. Adams had 78 rushing yards and two scoring runs. Heitzman threw for 66 yards and a touchdown. Admire had 42 receiving yards and a scoring catch.

The Tigers took on Loyalsock in a road contest. Henry Hynoski had first-quarter touchdown runs of 2 and 55 yards for a 14-0 Southern lead. Ted Heitzman scored on a 4-yard keeper and hit Colby Snyder for a 49-yard touchdown throw. The Lancers scored on a 12-yard run before Hynoski capped the scoring in the first half with a 9-yard scoring burst. The Tigers led 36-8 at the intermission. In the third, Andrew Wimble raced 29 yards for a score, and Steve Roth had touchdown runs of 13 and 47 yards as the Tigers easily handled Loyalsock, 56-8. Southern topped the 400-yard rushing mark with 420. Hynoski led the way with 154 yards on the ground and three touchdowns. Roth added 72 rushing yards and two scores. Wimble ran for 51 yards and a touchdown. Heitzman threw for 92 yards and a touchdown. He also had a scoring run. Snyder had 49 yards receiving and a touchdown reception.

The Clarion Bobcats traveled over three hours to face Southern at Tiger Stadium. The Tigers proved to be ungracious hosts as they completely dominated the contest. Henry Hynoski tumbled in from one yard out, and Andrew Wimble raced 52 yards for a touchdown as Southern took a 14-0 first-quarter lead. Hynoski had scoring runs of 11 and 7 yards and Dave Adams had a one-yard touchdown plunge, and the Tigers led 35-0 at halftime. Southern held Clarion scoreless in the second half, and the game ended with a 35-0 Tigers victory. Southern ran for 362 yards. Wimble had 121 rushing yards and a touchdown. Hynoski ran for 98 yards and three scores. Adams rushed for 76 yards and a touchdown.

Up next was a home game against the Central Columbia Blue Jays. Henry Hynoski put the Tigers on the board in the first with a 5-yard touchdown run. Hynoski rumbled 54 yards for a score, Andrew Wimble scored on runs of 48 and 39 yards, and Ted Heitzman fired a 5-yard touchdown strike to Colby Snyder, and the Tigers led 35-0 at the break. The Blue Jays added two second-half touchdowns to make the final 35-12. Wimble rushed for 94 yards and two scores. Hynoski ran for 93 yards and two touchdowns. Heitzman passed for 63 yards and a score. Snyder had 20 yards receiving and a touchdown. Austin Carpenter and Zeke Conrad each had an interception to lead a solid defensive effort.

The Tigers faced Danville at home in the regular-season finale. Dave Adams scored from 2 yards out, and Ted Heitzman hooked up with Tom Admire for a 24-yard touchdown pass as Southern built a 14-0 lead after the first period. Heitman hit Truman Webb on a 29-yard scoring pass, and Henry Hynoski rumbled 7 yards for a touchdown as the Tigers pushed the lead to 28-0 at the break. Heitzman threw his third touchdown pass of the game on a 67-yard bomb to Colby Snyder in the third, and the defense pitched another shutout as the Tigers routed the Ironmen, 35-0. Amazingly, the Tigers won all ten regular-season games by the mercy rule, marking the first time they had accomplished the feat in school history. The defense held Danville to just nine rushing yards and only 89 through the air. Hynoski ran for 150 yards and a touchdown. Heitzman threw for 142 yards and three scores. Snyder had 90 receiving yards and a touchdown reception. Webb added 29 receiving yards and a score. Admire had 24 yards receiving and a touchdown.

Southern hosted Bloomsburg in the District IV Class A Semifinal Game. Henry Hynoski, Dave Adams, and Austin Carpenter had touchdown runs of 41, 6, and 6 yards as the Tigers opened up a 20-0 first-quarter lead. Adams scored on runs of 2 and 4 yards, and Nich Gallinot scored from 8 yards out as Southern led 41-0 at the half. Gallinot raced 64 yards for a score in the third, and Bloomsburg scored two second-half touchdowns, and the Tigers defeated the Panthers, 48-12. Southern rushed for 437 yards, while the defense held Bloomsburg to just 5 yards on the ground. Hynoski ran for 114 yards and a touchdown. Andrew Wimble also rushed for 114 yards. Gallinot had 75 rushing yards and a touchdown. Carpenter ran for 65 yards and a score. Adams added 25 yards on the ground and three touchdowns.

The Tigers faced the Line Mountain Eagles in the District IV Class A Championship Game at Tiger Stadium. Line Mountain opened the scoring on a 3-yard run marking the first time all season that the Tigers had trailed in a game. Dave Adams put the Tigers in front with a 7-yard touchdown run, and Southern led 7-6 after one. Line Mountain retook the lead early in the second with a 6-yard scoring run. Henry Hynoski raced 74 yards for a touchdown to put the Tigers back on top, 14-12. Hynoski scored from 7 yards out, and Tom Admire hauled in a 23-yard touchdown pass from Ted Heitzman as Southern led 28-12 at halftime. Adams increased the lead to 35-12 with a 4-yard touchdown run early in the third. However, the Eagles cut the lead to 35-18 on a 9-yard scoring pass. In the fourth, Hynoski scored on a 4-yard dive for a 42-18 lead. Line Mountain got a 7-yard touchdown run and pulled within 42-25. Austin Carpenter put the game out of reach for the Eagles with a 21-yard scoring jaunt to push the lead to 49-25. Line Mountain scored a late touchdown to make the final score 49-31. It was a record-setting game for Henry Hynoski, who scored his 101st career touchdown, breaking the team record set by Jerry Marks. The Tigers rushed for a whopping 451 yards. Hynoski ran for 209 yards and three touchdowns. Adams rushed for 55 yards and two scores. Carpenter added 39 rushing yards and a touchdown. Heitzman threw for 45 yards and a touchdown. Admire had 45 receiving yards and a scoring reception. Southern clinched its 15th consecutive District IV Class A Championship.

The Tigers opened the PIAA Class A Playoffs against the Old Forge Blue Devils in Dunmore. Before the game, the Old Forge fans attempted to intimidate the Tigers, particularly Henry Hynoski. They placed a sign that read, "Henry Who?" near the field. As the Southern players entered the stadium, the Old Forge fans began chanting, "Over-Rated!" However, Hynoski quickly answered the Old Forge fans' question on the Tigers' first offensive play. He took the opening handoff and raced 52-yards for Southern's first touchdown of the day. The rout was on, and the Tigers showed the Blue Devils that the four-time defending state champions were far from overrated. Dave Adams added a 15-yard touchdown run, and Southern led 14-0 after one. Hynoski scored on a 27-yard run, Steve Roth pounded in from 3 yards out, and Ted Heitzman raced 59 yards for a touchdown as the Tigers took a 34-0 lead into the half. The Tigers put the final daggers in Old Forge in the third quarter. Hynoski rumbled for a 63-yard score, and Nich Gallinot capped the scoring with a 3-yard touchdown run. The defense completely dominated the Blue Devils and sent the Old Forge fans home with their tails between their legs with a convincing 48-0 shutout victory. After the game, Hynoski was presented with the crumpled-up banner as a souvenir of his outstanding performance. The "overrated" Tigers racked up 448 rushing yards. Hynoski ran for 214 yards and three touchdowns. Adams rushed for 41 yards and a score. Roth totaled 27 rushing yards and a touchdown. Gallinot added 17 yards on the ground and a scoring run. Heitzman also chipped in with a rushing touchdown. During the game, Hynoski moved past Ricco Rosini for second place on Southern Columbia's all-time career rushing list with 6,620 yards, trailing only Jerry Marks' 7,075 rushing yards.

Southern played Shenandoah Valley in the PIAA Class A Quarterfinal Game in Sunbury. Henry Hynoski scored from one yard out, and Andrew Wimble ran 19 yards to give the Tigers a 14-0 lead. The Blue Devils scored on a 29-yard pass to cut the lead in half. Hynoski pushed the lead to 21-7 at the end of the first quarter with a 45-yard touchdown run. Southern blew the game open in the second quarter. Hynoski ran for an 11-yard touchdown, Austin Carpenter scored from 3 yards out, and Ted Heitzman hit Hynoski for a 30-yard touchdown pass to push the lead to 42-7 at the intermission. Carpenter raced 30 yards for a score, and Southern led 49-7 after three. Nich Gallinot and Steve Roth scored on runs of 80 and 30 yards, and Shenandoah Valley added a late touchdown in the fourth to make the final, 61-15. The Tigers' ground game rolled for a staggering 519 yards. Hynoski ran for 207 yards and three touchdowns. He also had a scoring reception. Gallinot rushed for 80 yards and a touchdown. Carpenter had 69 rushing yards and two scores. Wimble added 69 yards on the ground and a touchdown. Roth contributed 38 yards rushing and a score. Heitzman passed for 79 yards and a touchdown. The defense controlled the Blue Devils with an interception and two fumble recoveries.

For the third straight week, the Tigers faced a Blue Devils team as they took on Bellwood Antis in the PIAA Class A Semifinal Game in Coal Township. Henry Hynoski opened the scoring with a one-yard touchdown dive. After the Blue Devils drove into field goal range, Nick Hartranft blocked the kick, which Zeke Conrad recovered, who returned it to the Tigers' 45-yard line. The play set up Hynsoki's 55-yard scoring run, and Southern took a 14-0 lead that stood until the half. Hynoski and Andrew Wimble scored on runs of 31 and one yard, and the Tigers pushed the lead to 28-0 after three. Dave Adams capped the day with a 3-yard touchdown plunge, and Southern earned a 35-0 shutout victory over Bellwood Antis. The Tigers rushed for 377 yards. Hynoski ran for 206 yards and three scores. Wimble rushed for 83 yards and a touchdown. Adams had 35 yards rushing and a scoring run. Southern Columbia advanced to their ninth straight PIAA Class A Championship Game and their 12th in the last 13 years.

The Southern Columbia Tigers were on the verge of history as they looked to win their fifth consecutive PIAA Class A Championship when they faced West Middlesex at Hersheypark Stadium. Entering the game, Henry Hynoski looked to become Southern Columbia's all-time leader in rushing yards. The Tigers and the Southern faithful seemed primed for a monumental afternoon. In the first quarter, Henry Hynoski got things started with a bang with a 52-yard touchdown run and a 7-0 lead. Ted Heitzman hit Colby Snyder with a 58-yard scoring bomb to push the lead to 14-0. The defense flexed its muscles when Cory Sober intercepted a Big Red pass and returned it 30 yards for a touchdown to give the Tigers a 21-0 advantage. Heitzman scored on a 14-yard keeper, and Southern led 28-0 after one. Heitzman connected with Hynoski for a 70-yard scoring pass early in the second to run the lead to 35-0. West Middlesex got on the board with a 9-yard touchdown pass to make the score 35-6. Nich Gallinot raced 57 yards for another Tigers' score, and Southern took a 42-6 halftime lead. Austin Carpenter joined the scoring parade with a 47-yard scoring jaunt in the third, and Hynoski scored the final touchdown of his illustrious high school career on a 9-yard run to push the score to 56-6 after three. The Big Reds scored one final touchdown in the fourth quarter, and the Southern Columbia Tigers won their fifth consecutive PIAA Class A Championship with a 56-14 rout of West Middlesex. Southern became the first program in Pennsylvania high school football history to win five straight state titles. The victory gave the Tigers their sixth state championship, joining Berwick with the most in Pennsylvania history. Henry Hynoski broke Jerry Marks' record for career rushing yards with 7,165. He finished the game with

## 2006 SEASON

| Opponent | Location | W/L | Score |
|----------|----------|-----|-------|
| Shamokin | Away | W | 48-21 |
| Bloomsburg | Home | W | 47-6 |
| Mount Carmel | Home | W | 54-0 |
| Lewisburg | Away | W | 47-10 |
| Warrior Run | Home | W | 59-0 |
| Hughesville | Away | W | 42-7 |
| Loyalsock | Away | W | 56-8 |
| Clarion | Home | W | 35-0 |
| Central Columbia | Home | W | 35-12 |
| Danville | Home | W | 35-0 |
| **District IV Class A Semifinal Game** | | | |
| Bloomsburg | Home | W | 48-12 |
| **District IV Class A Championship Game** | | | |
| Line Mountain | Home | W | 49-31 |
| **PIAA Class A Playoff Game** | | | |
| Old Forge | Neutral | W | 48-0 |
| **PIAA Class A Quarterfinal Game** | | | |
| Shenandoah Valley | Neutral | W | 61-15 |
| **PIAA Class A Semifinal Game** | | | |
| Bellwood Antis | Neutral | W | 35-0 |
| **PIAA Class A Championship Game** | | | |
| West Middlesex | Neutral | W | 56-14 |

COACHING STAFF: Jim Roth, Head Coach; Randall Campbell, Assistant Coach; Al Cihocki, Assistant Coach; Troy Heath, Assistant Coach; Andy Helwig, Assistant Coach; Mike Johnston, Assistant Coach; John Marks, Assistant Coach; Andy Mills, Assistant Coach; Roger Nunkester, Assistant Coach; Pete Saylor, Assistant Coach; Rick Steele, Assistant Coach; Curt Stellfox, Assistant Coach; Dewey Townsend, Assistant Coach; Don Traugh, Assistant Coach

ATHLETIC DIRECTOR: Terry Sharrow

ROSTER: Aaron Adams, Dave Adams, Tom Admire, Joel Bittner, Kyle Breech, Jeremy Campbell, Austin Carpenter, Tyler Clark, Lloyd Collier, Zeke Conrad, Tyler Cox, Curtis Cranmer, Jeff Davis, Tony Drain, Aaron Farnsworth, Dave Fegley, Tyler Fleishauer, Jeff Fleming, Chase Fraley, Nich Gallinot, Shaun Gooler, Nick Hartnranft, Ted Heitzman, Henry Hynoski, Andrew Jones, Cody Jones, Mike Joseph, Justin Knoebel, Austin Lonoconus, Josh Marks, Matt Miller, Mike Moyer, Curtis Nichols, Jeremy Oshman, Joe Picarelli, Matt Rooney, Brent Rosenbaum, Steve Roth, Joe Samuels, Dan Schankweiler, Ken Schetroma, B.J. Snyder, Colby Snyder, Corey Sober, Sam Springer, Kyle Stavinski, Sean Stout, Tyler Weaver, Truman Webb, Tyler Wilson, Andrew Wimble, Brad Witcoskie, Adam Wittenrich, Aaron Yoder

126 rushing yards and three touchdowns. Hynoski also had a scoring reception. Carpenter rushed for 82 yards and a touchdown. Gallinot ran for 57 yards and a score. The Tigers yet again topped the 300-yard rushing mark with 324. Heitzman threw for 172 yards and two scores. He also had a rushing touchdown. Snyder had 63 receiving yards and a touchdown. Southern Columbia ended the 2006 season with a 16-0 record.

The Tigers had several incredible achievements in 2006. Henry Hynoski rushed for 2,414 yards and 43 touchdowns. Andrew Wimble ran for 810 yards and 13 scores. Dave Adams had 601 yards and eight touchdowns. The Tigers also had touchdown runs from Steve Roth (7), Austin Carpenter (6), Nich Gallinot (6), Ted Heitzman (5), Kyle Breech (2), and one each from Dan Schankweiler and Sam Springer. Ted Heitzman passed for 1,208 yards and 15 touchdowns. Colby Snyder had 335 receiving yards and five touchdowns. Tom Admire had 302 yards receiving and four scoring receptions. Southern also had touchdown receptions from Austin Carpenter (3), Henry Hynoski (2), and Truman Webb (1). B.J. Snyder kicked 71 extra points. Gallinot had 74 tackles (45 solo). Corey Sober registered 8.5 sacks. Admire recorded seven interceptions. Admire, Hynoski, Cody Jones, Justin Knoebel, Josh Marks, and Tyler Wilson were All-State selections.

**2007** Henry Hynoski had arguably the greatest career in Southern Columbia football history up to that point. His list of accomplishments is staggering. He was the Tigers' all-time leader in rushing yardage with 7,165 (6th most in Pennsylvania high school football history) and scored 113 touchdowns. In twenty career playoff games (all victories), Hynoski rushed for 3,234 yards and 41 touchdowns. He was named the Associated Press Pennsylvania Class A Player of the Year in 2006, named Associated Press Class A First Team All-State as a junior and senior, a Wendy's High School Heisman State Finalist, selected to represent Pennsylvania in the Big 33 Football Classic, a two-time Central Susquehanna Conference Offensive Back of the Year, a letterman for Southern Columbia in baseball, basketball, and track and was named all-conference in baseball. In addition to being a stellar athlete, Hynoski was a distinguished honor student. He attended the University of Pittsburgh, where he played football for the Panthers. He redshirted his freshman year in 2007. As a redshirt freshman in 2008, Hynoski was a special teams player. Midway through his sophomore season in 2009, he was named the Panthers' starting fullback. In 2009, Hynoski rushed for 117 yards on 24 carries, averaging 4.5 yards per attempt. He scored one rushing touchdown. Hynoski also had 15 receptions for 109 yards. As a junior in 2010, Hynoski rushed for 33 yards and had 25 receptions for 174 yards and a touchdown. He chose to forego his senior season at Pitt and enter the NFL Draft. At Pittsburgh, Hynoski totaled 143 rushing yards and a touchdown. He also had 40 receptions for 283 yards and a touchdown. He was regarded as one of the top fullbacks in the 2011 NFL Draft but suffered a hamstring injury at the scouting combine and went undrafted. Hynoski signed as an undrafted free agent with the New York Giants. He made the team out of training camp and was named the Giants' starting fullback in his rookie season in 2011. He had 12 receptions for 83 yards during his rookie campaign. Hynoski's rookie season would wind up with a trip to Super Bowl XLVI, as the Giants faced the New England Patriots. In the Super Bowl, Hynoski had two receptions for 19 yards and had a key fumble recovery in the third quarter that helped the Giants maintain possession. The Giants would defeat the Patriots, and Hynoski earned a Super Bowl ring in his first season in the NFL. He scored his only NFL touchdown on December 30, 2012, against the Philadelphia Eagles. In 2012, Hynoski carried the ball five times for 20 yards and had 11 receptions for 50 yards and a touchdown. During the 2013 season, Hynoski had one reception for five yards. He totaled 13 rushing yards. Hynoski played with the New York Giants from 2011 to 2014, accumulating 33 rushing yards, and 24 receptions for 138 yards and a touchdown. He is currently an educator in the Shamokin School District and head football coach for the Indians.

Josh Marks was a three-time All-State selection for the Tigers. He was named the *Pennsylvania Football News* Class A Defensive Player of the Year in 2006. He registered nearly 250 tackles and 15 sacks in his career with Southern. He was the first athlete in school history to reach state competition in three sports. He won two medals at the PIAA State Wrestling Championships and qualified for the PIAA State Track and Field Championships in the discus as a senior. He committed to Penn State University as an offensive lineman and later transferred to the University of Pittsburgh.

Entering the 2007 season, Coach Jim Roth had to replace eight starters on the defensive side of the ball and the most dominant running back in school history. With the Tigers seeking a sixth straight state championship, they would need their veteran players to lead the way. Things got off to a great start with a 27-0 shutout of Shamokin at Tigers Stadium. Southern scored in each quarter with Andrew Wimble rushing for two touchdowns, Steve Roth running for a score, and Ted Heitzman connecting with Colby Snyder on a touchdown pass. Heitzman threw for 148 yards, and Snyder had 105 yards receiving.

Things did not go well in a road game versus Bloomsburg. The Panthers' defense smothered the Tigers and earned a 19-0 shutout victory. It was the first time that Bloomsburg defeated Southern in 23 years. The loss ended the Tigers' 27-game winning streak. Ted Heitzman threw for 132 yards for the game.

Southern's offense got back on track on a trip to Mount Carmel. Andrew Wimble rushed for two touchdowns, Kyle Breech had a scoring run, and B.J. Snyder connected on a field goal. Wimble rushed for 154 yards. Steve Roth returned an interception for a touchdown, one of three picks for the defense on the night. The Tigers defeated the Red Tornadoes, 34-14.

The Tigers would continue their winning ways at home against Lewisburg. Ted Heitzman and Colby Snyder connected twice for scoring passes, and Sam Springer and Andrew Wimble had a pair of touchdown runs as Southern downed the Green Dragons, 42-21. Heitzman threw for 235 yards, and Snyder had 189 yards receiving. Wimble rushed for 115 yards.

Five different players would contribute touchdown runs in a 33-6 win at Warrior Run. Ted Heitzman, Kyle Breech, Steve Roth, Austin Carpenter, and David Shoop would each score as the Southern rushing attack totaled 393 yards. Breech and Roth would combine for 172 yards on the ground. Carpenter would also register an interception in a solid defensive effort.

The Tigers returned home for a matchup with Hughesville. The kicking game and defense would provide the early scoring as B.J. Snyder kicked a field goal and Sam Springer returned an interception for a pick six. Andrew Wimble would rush for two touchdowns, Steve Roth ran for a score, and Ted Heitzman fired a touchdown pass to Colby Snyder as the Tigers rolled to a 38-14 win. Wimble, Roth, and would combine for 192 rushing yards.

Southern found themselves in a tight contest at home against Loyalsock. The Tigers trailed for much of the first half before Ted Heitzman found Colby Snyder for a scoring pass. Andrew Wimble had two touchdown runs in the second half as Southern outlasted the Lancers, 21-17. Roth rushed for 138 yards, and Wimble totaled 112 rushing yards.

Clarion traveled to Tigers Stadium in week eight. In a low-scoring affair, Steve Roth had two scoring runs, and Ted Heitzman added a rushing touchdown, and Southern defeated the Bobcats, 19-6. Roth ran for 104 yards for the game.

Ted Heitzman had a huge game at Central Columbia. He threw four touchdown passes, three to Colby Snyder and one to Aaron Farnsworth, as the Tigers rolled to a 42-18 victory. Heitzman passed for 173 yards, and Snyder had 112 yards receiving. Andrew Wimble had a touchdown run, and Tony Drain returned an interception for a pick six to round out the scoring. Wimble and Steve Roth combined for 115 rushing yards.

The Tigers finished the regular season on the road at Danville. Steve Roth scored four touchdowns on the ground, Austin Carpenter rushed for a score, and Ted Heitzman threw touchdown passes to Andrew Wimble and Colby Snyder as Southern downed the Ironmen, 47-34. Roth ran for 188 yards. Heitzman threw for 159 yards. Snyder had 115 yards receiving. The defense held Danville to -25 yards rushing.

Southern hosted Line Mountain in the District IV Class A Semifinal Game. In the second quarter, B.J. Snyder connected for a field goal, and the Tigers got a scoring run from Steve Roth and a touchdown pass from Ted Heitzman to Andrew Wimble in the fourth, but it wasn't enough as Line Mountain defeated Southern, 22-17. Roth and Wimble combined for 163 rushing yards for the game. It was the Tigers' first loss in District IV tournament play in 16 years. It would be the first time that Southern would not play for a state championship since 1997. It was an unexpected and disappointing end to the 2007 season. The Tigers would finish with a record of 9-2.

## 2007 SEASON

| Opponent | Location | W/L | Score |
|---|---|---|---|
| Shamokin | Home | W | 27-0 |
| Bloomsburg | Away | L | 0-19 |
| Mount Carmel | Away | W | 31-14 |
| Lewisburg | Home | W | 42-21 |
| Warrior Run | Away | W | 33-6 |
| Hughesville | Home | W | 38-14 |
| Loyalsock | Home | W | 21-17 |
| Clarion | Away | W | 19-6 |
| Central Columbia | Away | W | 42-18 |
| Danville | Away | W | 47-34 |
| **District IV Class A Semifinal Game** | | | |
| Line Mountain | Home | L | 17-22 |

COACHING STAFF: Jim Roth, Head Coach; Randall Campbell, Assistant Coach; Al Cihocki, Assistant Coach; Troy Heath, Assistant Coach; Andy Helwig, Assistant Coach; Mike Johnston, Assistant Coach; John Marks, Assistant Coach; Andy Mills, Assistant Coach; Roger Nunkester, Assistant Coach; Pete Saylor, Assistant Coach; Rick Steele, Assistant Coach; Curt Stellfox, Assistant Coach; Dewey Townsend, Assistant Coach; Brandon Traugh, Assistant Coach; Don Traugh, Assistant Coach

ATHLETIC DIRECTOR: Terry Sharrow

ROSTER: Aaron Adams, Joe Admire, Corey Bittner, Randon Boyer, Kyle Breech, Neil Breskiewicz, Aaron Brophy, Jeremy Campbell, Austin Carpenter, Zeke Conrad, Logan Crowl, Jeff Davis, Nick Diak, Tony Drain, Kyle Fabian, Tim Fabian, Aaron Farnsworth, Dave Fegley, Tyler Fleishauer, Evan Foust, Chase Fraley, Ben Halderman, Jared Hallick, Zach Hampton, Ted Heitzman, Adam Hower, Mike Joseph, Joe Klebon, Justin Knoebel, John Lamb, Matt Miller, Kevin Mostik, Mike Moyer, Kurt Myhre, Curtis Nichols, Colin Parsons, Joe Picarelli, Brent Rosenbaum, Steve Roth, Joe Samuels, Dan Schankweiler, Ken Schetroma, Billy Shoop, David Shoop, Justin Sivak, Ben Snarski, B.J. Snyder, Colby Snyder, Sam Springer, Kyle Stavinski, Ian Van Wieren, Tyler Weaver, Tyler Wilson, Andrew Wimble, Brad Witcoskie, Adam Wittenrich, Aaron Yoder

Andrew Wimble would rush for 842 yards and 11 touchdowns. Steve Roth ran for 809 yards and ten scores. The Tigers had touchdown runs from Austin Carpenter (2), Sam Springer (2), and one each from Kyle Breech, Ted Heitzman, and David Shoop. Ted Heitzman threw for 1,206 yards and 12 touchdowns. Colby Snyder had 772 receiving yards and nine touchdowns. The Tigers also had touchdown receptions from Andrew Wimble (2) and Aaron Farnsworth (1). B.J. Snyder kicked 71 extra points. Tony Drain registered 79 tackles (50 solo). Springer had 4.5 sacks. Snyder and Drain each recorded three interceptions. Snyder and Justin Knoebel were All-State selections.

2
0
0
8    The 2008 Southern Columbia Tigers entered the season in unfamiliar territory. For the first time in many years, there were questions about whether they were still the dominant team in District IV. Coach Roth's Tigers looked to re-establish their reputation as the top cat in the area. Things got off to a good start in the season opener against Shamokin at Tiger Stadium. Steve Roth rushed for 170 yards and three touchdowns. Sam Springer ran for 151 yards and a score. Austin Carpenter had 69 yards on the ground and a touchdown. Southern rushed for 401 yards as they defeated the Indians, 35-22.

The Tigers were locked up in a tight contest on the road against Montoursville. The defense got Southern on the board in the second quarter when they tackled the Warrior ballcarrier in the endzone for a safety. In the fourth, Jeremy Campbell found Joe Admire for a touchdown pass to pull the Tigers within 20-15. With less than five minutes left in the game, Ben Snarski recovered a Montoursville fumble to set up Steve Roth's go-ahead touchdown run. The Tigers registered a second safety when the Warriors' punter, kicking out of his own endzone, stepped on the end line as Southern won a thrilling 23-20 come-from-behind victory. Roth, Sam Springer, and Austin Carpenter combined for 226 rushing yards.

Southern traveled to Jersey Shore for a week three matchup with the Bulldogs. Sam Springer ran for two touchdowns, Steve Roth added a scoring run, Jeremy Campbell fired a touchdown pass to Matt Miller, and B.J. Snyder booted a field goal as the Tigers blew out the Bulldogs, 31-3. Springer rushed for 179 yards, and Campbell threw for 149 yards in the game.

The Tigers absolutely dominated the Loyalsock Lancers at Tiger Stadium. Southern got a pair of rushing touchdowns from both Steve Roth and Dan Schankweiler, and scoring runs from Sam Springer and Jeremy Campbell. Campbell also hit Joe Admire for a pair of touchdown passes, and Southern rolled to a 54-7 win. The Tigers rushed for 302 yards, including 111 on the ground by Roth. Campbell passed for 122 yards.

The offense continued to roll in a win at Warrior Run. Austin Carpenter scored three rushing touchdowns in the first quarter, and Steve Roth also scored in the opening period as the Tigers built a 28-0 lead. Roth scored again in the third, and the Tigers downed the Defenders, 35-6. Carpenter, Roth, and Sam Springer combined for 193 rushing yards.

The Tigers faced Bloomsburg in a home game at Tiger Stadium. Matt Miller recovered a fumble on Bloomsburg's second play to set up a touchdown run by Steve Roth. Roth would score two more times on the ground, Sam Springer would add a pair of touchdown runs, and Austin Carpenter and Dan Garvine would also find paydirt. Jeremy Campbell would hook up with Joe Admire on a touchdown pass, and the Tigers routed the Panthers 55-14. Springer rushed for 159 yards, Roth ran for 122 yards, and Carpenter added 90 yards on the ground as Southern battered the Panthers for 453 rushing yards.

The Tigers' hopes for an undefeated season came crashing down in a blow-out loss at Selinsgrove. Steve Roth provided the only points with a touchdown run, but the Seals absolutely dominated the game in a 47-7 win. Roth ran for 97 yards for the game.

Southern righted the ship in a road contest with Central Columbia. The Tigers got two touchdown runs from Sam Springer, Steve Roth, and Dan Schankweiler, and Austin Carpenter added another rushing score as Southern blew out the Blue Jays, 51-21. The Tigers rumbled for 370 yards on the ground. Roth led the way with 108 rushing yards. Jeremy Campbell threw for 109 yards. B.J. Snyder connected on a field goal for Southern.

For the second time in three weeks, Steve Roth provided the only points on a touchdown run as the Tigers lost a matchup at home against Mount Carmel. Roth's first-quarter score was the only offensive success as the Red Tornadoes kept Southern's vaunted running game in check the rest of the way. Roth, Sam Springer, and Austin Campbell combined for 190 rushing yards.

The Tigers closed out the regular season at home against Milton. Sam Springer scored three touchdowns, two on scoring runs and one on a touchdown pass from Jeremy Campbell. Austin Carpenter, David Shoop, and Dan Schankweiler also found the endzone on scoring runs as the Tigers closed out the Black Panthers, 42-0. Springer, Carpenter, and Schankweiler combined for 174 rushing yards.

Southern faced Bloomsburg in the District IV Class A Semifinal Game at Tiger Stadium. Dave Fegley had a key interception in the endzone to snuff out a Panther scoring threat in the first quarter, and the offense took over the game. Steve Roth had three scoring runs, Dan Schankweiler and David Shoop scored rushing touchdowns, and Jeremy Campbell hooked up with Austin Carpenter for a scoring pass as the Tigers advanced with a 41-0 shutout victory. Southern ran for 343 yards, including 154 by Roth and 102 by Schankweiler. Ben Snarski had a key fumble recovery for the Southern defense.

The Tigers hosted Line Mountain in the District IV Class A Championship Game. Steve Roth scored three times on the ground in the first half, B.J. Snyder kicked three field goals, and Joe Admire hauled in a scoring pass from Jeremy Campbell as the Tigers reclaimed the District IV Class A Championship 37-14. Southern bludgeoned the Eagles for 434 rushing yards. Roth had a huge game, running for 221 yards. Sam Springer also topped the century mark with 109 yards on the ground. Adam Wittenrich had a fumble recovery to contribute to the Tigers' terrific defensive effort.

## 2008 SEASON

| Opponent | Location | W/L | Score |
|---|---|---|---|
| Shamokin | Home | W | 35-22 |
| Montoursville | Away | W | 23-20 |
| Jersey Shore | Away | W | 31-3 |
| Loyalsock | Home | W | 54-7 |
| Warrior Run | Away | W | 35-6 |
| Bloomsburg | Home | W | 55-14 |
| Selinsgrove | Away | L | 7-47 |
| Central Columbia | Away | W | 51-21 |
| Mount Carmel | Home | L | 7-21 |
| Milton | Home | W | 42-0 |
| **District IV Class A Semifinal Game** | | | |
| Bloomsburg | Home | W | 41-0 |
| **District IV Class A Championship Game** | | | |
| Line Mountain | Home | W | 37-14 |
| **PIAA Class A Playoff Game** | | | |
| Riverside | Neutral | L | 7-25 |

COACHING STAFF: Jim Roth, Head Coach; Randall Campbell, Assistant Coach; Al Cihocki, Assistant Coach; Troy Heath, Assistant Coach; Andy Helwig, Assistant Coach; Mike Johnston, Assistant Coach; John Marks, Assistant Coach; Andy Mills, Assistant Coach; Roger Nunkester, Assistant Coach; Pete Saylor, Assistant Coach; Rick Steele, Assistant Coach; Curt Stellfox, Assistant Coach; Dewey Townsend, Assistant Coach; Brandon Traugh, Assistant Coach; Don Traugh, Assistant Coach

ATHLETIC DIRECTOR: Terry Sharrow

ROSTER: Cenan Abdul-al, Joe Admire, Tim Benner, Jeremy Berkheiser, Corey Bittner, Neil Breskiewicz, Aaron Brophy, Jeremy Campbell, Austin Carpenter, Austin Clark, Logan Crowl, Nick Diak, Tony Drain, Dave Fegley, Alex Fidler, Evan Foust, Chase Fraley, Dan Garvine, Ben Halderman, Colin Heitzman, Kurt Henrie, Matt Hoffman, Adam Hower, David Kistner, Joe Klebon, John Lamb, Logan Mensinger, Matt Miller, Jake Morton, Kurt Myhre, Blake Nevius, Curtis Nichols, Colin Parsons, Hayden Reed, Cody Rosenberger, Steve Roth, Joe Samuels, Dan Schankweiler, Ken Schetroma, Tom Schetroma, Justin Shaffer, Billy Shoop, David Shoop, Justin Sivak, Ben Snarski, B.J. Snyder, Ethan Snyder, Sam Springer, Jake Townsend, Ian Van Wieren, Tyler Weaver, Josh Wells, Brad Witcoskie, Adam Wittenrich, Aaron Yoder

Southern advanced to play the Riverside Vikings in a PIAA Class A Playoff Game in Archbald. It was a frustrating afternoon for the Tigers as they could only muster a third-quarter touchdown run from Sam Springer as Riverside put the clamps on the Southern running game. The Tigers' season would come to a disappointing end with a 25-7 loss to the Vikings. Springer would rush for 116 yards on the day, but Southern could not sustain much offensive success.

Although the Tigers were able to reclaim the District IV title and advance to the state playoffs, they were frustrated with a premature end to their season. Southern would end the 2008 season with a record of 10-3. Steve Roth rushed for 1,424 yards and 22 touchdowns. He would total 2,879 yards and 41 touchdowns in his career at Southern Columbia. Sam Springer ran for 1,112 yards and ten scores. Austin Carpenter had 653 rushing yards and seven touchdowns. Southern had touchdown runs from Dan Schankweiler (6), David Shoop (2), and one each from Jeremy Campbell and Dan Garvine. Jeremy Campbell threw for 915 yards and seven touchdowns. Joe Admire had 319 receiving yards and four touchdowns. The Tigers had touchdown receptions from Austin Carpenter, Matt Miller, and Sam Springer. B.J. Snyder kicked 62 extra points and five field goals. Aaron Yoder had 62 tackles (15 solo). Dave Fegley and Curtis Nichols each recorded three interceptions. Ken Schetroma registered 4.5 sacks. Yoder, Chase Fraley, and Steve Roth were All-State selections.

2 0 0 9 Southern would begin 2009 with a retooled backfield and a new starting quarterback. Coach Roth hoped for a balanced offensive attack to compliment his talented defense. The Tigers opened the season in Shamokin. Jake Morton scored twice on touchdown runs in the first quarter, Tyrell Thomas added a fourth-quarter scoring run, and the defense kept the Indians in check as Southern earned a 21-7 opening-day victory. Morton led the way with 140 rushing yards.

The Tigers' home opener with Montoursville was delayed a day due to heavy rains. Southern trailed for most of the game, managing only a Tyrell Thomas touchdown run in the first half. Thomas scored again in the third, and Jake Townsend hit Aaron Zigarski for a touchdown pass in the fourth, but the Warriors held on for a 28-20 win. Thomas and Jake Morton combined for 121 rushing yards. Townsend threw for 202 yards in the loss.

Jersey Shore visited Tigers Stadium in a week three matchup. Jake Morton had two touchdown runs, and Tyrell Thomas, Tim Benner, Tyler Levan, and Jamie Sloltterback found paydirt as Southern cruised to a 43-6 victory over the

Bulldogs The Tigers rumbled for 412 rushing yards and had 528 total yards of offense in the blowout win. Morton ran for 194 yards, and Benner, Thomas, and Levan combined for 160 more on the ground. Townsend passed for 116 yards. B.J. Snyder connected on a 37-yard field goal.

Southern's offense struggled in a road game against Loyalsock. The Tigers could only manage a touchdown pass from Jake Townsend to Billy Shoop in the fourth quarter as the Lancers' defense controlled the game. Southern suffered a 14-7 loss to Loyalsock. Jake Morton, Tyrell Thomas, and Tim Benner combined for 126 rushing yards. Townsend threw for 100 yards for the game.

The week five home game against Warrior Run was a historic night for Head Coach Jim Roth. The Tigers dominated the Defenders in a 42-6 rout. Southern got two rushing touchdowns from Jake Morton and Tim Benner, and Tyrell Thomas and David Shoop also had scoring runs. They combined for 199 rushing yards. Jim Roth earned his 300th career coaching victory, becoming only the eighth coach in Pennsylvania high school football history to reach that mark. After the game, Coach Roth thanked everyone in attendance for his historic milestone and reflected on his 26-year career. He told the crowd, "I never thought much of the number 100, 200 or this win. It still is about the players and all the hard work they've put in over the years to keep us on top. And you have to go right down to the parents, administration, and loyal staff who put the team in front of their own personal glory."

The Tigers found themselves in a nail-biter in the next week in Bloomsburg. Jake Morton had two rushing touchdowns, Tyrell Thomas had a scoring run, and B.J. Snyder connected on a field goal, but the Tigers dropped a 27-24 decision to the Panthers. Morton rushed for 104 yards, and Jake Townsend had 128 yards through the air in the tough loss.

Jake Townsend threw for three touchdowns, two to Jared Hallick and one to Tim Benner, and Corey Bittner recovered a fumble in the endzone for a score, but the Tigers suffered their second straight loss in a home game against Selinsgrove. The Seals pulled out a 35-28 victory, winning their first game at Tiger Stadium since 1977. Benner, Tyrell Thomas, and Jake Morton combined for 170 rushing yards in the game.

The Tigers turned things around in a home game against Central Columbia. Tyrell Thomas ran for three touchdowns, Jamie Slotterback had a scoring run, and Jake Townsend hit Billy Shoop for a touchdown pass, as Southern shut out the Blue Jays, 35-0. The defense limited Central to just five first downs for the game and had three interceptions. Southern rushed for 428 yards, including 174 from Thomas.

Jake Townsend threw touchdown passes to Jared Hallick and Billy Shoop, Jake Morton and Tyrell Thomas had scoring runs, and B.J. Snyder booted a field goal as the Tigers earned a much-needed 31-20 victory over Mount Carmel to keep their playoff hopes alive. Thomas rushed for 149 yards, and Townsend passed for 129 in the win.

Southern wrapped up the regular season with a trip to Milton. Tyrell Thomas had two touchdown runs, and Jake Morton rumbled for a score. Billy Shoop hauled in a scoring pass from Jake Townsend, and Alex Fidler returned a punt for a touchdown as the Tigers qualified for the District IV Playoffs with a 38-0 victory over the Black Panthers. The defense pitched a shutout and

## 2009 SEASON

| Opponent | Location | W/L | Score |
|---|---|---|---|
| Shamokin | Away | W | 21-7 |
| Montoursville | Home | L | 20-28 |
| Jersey Shore | Home | W | 43-6 |
| Loyalsock | Away | L | 7-14 |
| Warrior Run | Home | W | 42-6 |
| Bloomsburg | Away | L | 24-27 |
| Selinsgrove | Home | L | 28-35 |
| Central Columbia | Home | W | 35-0 |
| Mount Carmel | Away | W | 31-20 |
| Milton | Away | W | 38-0 |
| **District IV Class A Semifinal Game** | | | |
| Bloomsburg | Away | W | 28-6 |
| **District IV Class A Championship Game** | | | |
| Line Mountain | Away | W | 42-12 |
| **PIAA Class A Playoff Game** | | | |
| Northwest Area | Neutral | W | 60-7 |
| **PIAA Class A Quarterfinal Game** | | | |
| Tri-Valley | Neutral | L | 32-35 |

COACHING STAFF: Jim Roth, Head Coach; Randall Campbell, Assistant Coach; Al Cihocki, Assistant Coach; Troy Heath, Assistant Coach; Andy Helwig, Assistant Coach; Mike Johnston, Assistant Coach; John Marks, Assistant Coach; Andy Mills, Assistant Coach; Roger Nunkester, Assistant Coach; Pete Saylor, Assistant Coach; Rick Steele, Assistant Coach; Dewey Townsend, Assistant Coach; Brandon Traugh, Assistant Coach; Don Traugh, Assistant Coach

ATHLETIC DIRECTOR: Terry Sharrow

ROSTER: Cenan Abdul-al, Jake Becker, Tim Benner, Jeremy Berkheiser, Corey Bittner, Randon Boyer, Neil Breskiewicz, Logan Crowl, Keith Day, Nick Diak, Dylan Eck, Brad Fegley, Alex Fidler Cameron Flore, Bryan Gedman, Joe Grosch, Jared Hallick, Colin Heitzman, Kurt Henrie, Matt Hoffman, David Jeremiah, Joe Klebon, John Lamb, Tyler Levan, Mike Marraquin, Matt Moore, Jake Morton, Kurt Myhre, Blake Nevius, Colin Parsons, Hayden Reed, Bill Reigle, Cody Rosenberger, Casey Savitski, Tom Schetroma, Billy Shoop, David Shoop, Jamie Slotterback, Ben Snarski, B.J. Snyder, Ethan Snyder, Tyrell Thomas, Tyler Torres, Jake Townsend, Ian Van Wieren, Brad Witcoskie, Tanar Yacko, Colton Yeick, Aaron Zigarski registered two safeties. Southern ran for 411 yards. Morton rushed for 154 yards, and Thomas added 116 on the ground.

The Tigers traveled to Bloomsburg for the District IV Class A Semifinal Game. Jake Townsend threw for 144 yards and two touchdowns to Tim Benner and Jake Becker, and Jake Morton ran for 132 yards and two scores as Southern avenged their week six loss to the Panthers with a 28-6 victory.

Southern faced the Line Mountain Eagles on the road in the District IV Class A Championship Game. Jake Townsend hit David Shoop and Cody Rosenberger for touchdown passes. Jake Morton and Tyrell Thomas had rushing scores as the Tigers won their second consecutive District IV title with a convincing 42-12 win. Morton ran for 130 yards, and Townsend had 130 through the air.

The Tigers opened the PIAA Playoffs against Northwest Area in Shamokin. Jake Morton ran for four touchdowns, and Tyler Levan had three scoring runs as Southern overwhelmed the Rangers, 60-7. Jake Townsend had a touchdown pass to Billy Shoop and added a scoring run in the victory. Southern ran for 341 yards. Morton, Leva, Tyrell Thomas, and Tim Benner combined for 215 rushing yards. The defense held Northwest Area to -18 passing yards.

Southern advanced to play Tri-Valley in the PIAA Class A Quarterfinal Game at Schuylkill Haven. Jake Townsend fired three touchdown passes, two to Tim Benner and one to Jake Morton, Morton had a scoring run, and B.J. Snyder connected for a field goal, but the Tigers dropped a hard-fought game to the Bulldogs, 35-32. Morton rushed for 190 yards, and Townsend threw for 146 in the disappointing loss.

After starting 3-4, Southern turned their season around to win the District IV Championship and advanced to the PIAA quarterfinals. It was a truly impressive reversal of fortune, and the Tigers showed real resilience in making the state playoffs. Jake Morton rushed for 1,509 yards and 20 touchdowns. Tyrell Thomas ran for 942 yards and 13 scores. Southern had touchdown runs from Tyler Levan (4), Tim Benner (3), and one each from David Shoop and Jamie Slotterback. Jake Townsend threw for 1,473 yards and 17 touchdowns. The Tigers had touchdown receptions from Billy Shoop (5), Tim Benner (4), Jared Hallick (3), and one each from Jake Becker, Jake Morton, Cody Rosenberger, David Shoop, and Aaron Zigarski. B.J. Snyder kicked 51 extra points and four field goals. Ethan Snyder registered 82 tackles (20 solo). Alex Fidler and Tom Schetroma each had 3.5 sacks. Shoop and Jared Hallick each recorded three interceptions. Morton and Brad Witcoskie were All-State selections. The 2009 Southern Columbia Tigers finished with a record of 9-5.

Mike Daveler in action in 1973. (Jim Eveland/*The Daily Item*)

Gary Shaw looks for running room in 1979. (Charles Moyer/*The Daily Item*)

Dave Longer (30) battles for an interception in 1981. (Fred Williams/ *The Daily Item*)

Bob Haney (31) and Buddy Hartman (68) close in on the ballcarrier in 1982 action.
(Fred Williams/*The Daily Item*)

Tom Reich fires a pass in 1983. (Fred Williams/ *The Daily Item*)

Jay Drumheller on the sideline in 1983. (Christopher A. Record/ *The Daily Item*)

Dewey Townsend intercepts a pass in the 1983 Eastern Conference playoffs.
(Christopher A. Record/ *The Daily Item*)

Jay Drumheller's touchdown clinches the 1983 Eastern Conference Class C Championship. (Christopher A. Record/*The Daily Item*)

On October 31, 1986, Jerry Marks became the all-time leading rusher in Pennsylvania high school football history. (Charlie Moyer/*The Daily Item*)

Defensive Coordinator Andy Mills rallying the troops in a 1988 game. (Margie Chambers/ *The Daily Item*)

Kenyon Brenish make an over the shoulder catch in 1988 action. (Margie Chambers/ The Daily Item)

Ed Levan looks for running room in the 1988 Eastern Conference Class III
Championship Game. (Margie Chambers/ *The Daily Item*)

Marc Freeman closes in on a sack as the defense dominates in the Tigers' 1988 Eastern
Conference Class III Championship victory. (Margie Chambers/ *The Daily Item*)

Nate Roadarmel looks for daylight as Jeremy Hoagland clears the way in a 1994 game. (Charlie Moyer/*The Daily Item*)

Scott Bloom finds daylight in a 1996 game. (Butch Comegys/*The Daily Item*)

Ken Ruckle and Marc Osevala combine for a sack in 1997. (Joe Hermitt/ *The Daily Item)*

Brian Shroyer picks off a pass in a 1997 game. (Joe Hermitt/*The Daily Item*)

Ricco Rosini races for a touchdown in the 1997 PIAA State Playoffs. (Butch Comegys/*The Daily Item*)

Matt Kaskie scrambles for yardage in 2000 game action. (Kate Collins/ *The Daily Item*)

Kasey McBride and Blaine Madara take down the quarterback in 2002. (Melanie Krneta/*The Daily Item*)

Coach Jim Roth celebrates with his players after the Tigers' PIAA Class A
Championship in 2002. (Jacob Kepler/*The Daily Item*)

Henry Hynoski finds running room in the 2003 PIAA Playoffs. (Ron Schmick/*The Daily Item*)

Southern celebrates their second straight PIAA Class A Championship in 2003.
(Jacob Kapler/*The Daily Item*)

Dan Latorre picks up yardage in 2004. (Jacob Kapler/*The Daily Item*)

Ray Snarski eludes a tackle in the 2004 PIAA Playoffs. (Kate Collins/*The Daily Item*)

The Tigers celebrate their third consecutive PIAA Class A Championship in 2004.
(Kate Collins/*The Daily Item*)

Ted Heitzman turns up field in 2005. (Jacob Kapler/*The Daily Item*)

Henry Hynoski finds a hole in the 2005 PIAA Playoffs. (Jacob Kapler/*The Daily Item*)

Southern celebrates their fourth straight PIAA Class A Championship in 2005. (Jacob Kapler/*The Daily Item*)

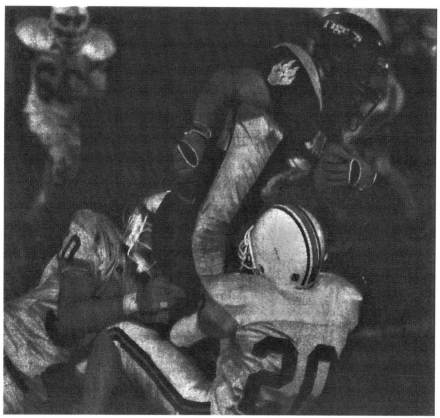

Austin Carpenter runs over tacklers in a 2006 game. (Robert Inglis/*The Daily Item*)

Henry Hynoski looks for yardage in the 2006 PIAA Playoffs. (Seth Hoover/*The Daily Item*)

The Southern Columbia Tigers celebrates their record fifth consecutive PIAA Class A Championship in 2006. (Seth Hoover/*The Daily Item*)

Tyrell Thomas on the move in 2010. (Liz Rohde/*The Daily Item*)

Brad Fegley fires downfield in 2011. (Liz Rohde/*The Daily Item*)

Matt Moore jumps over tacklers in 2011 action. (Matt Smith/*The Daily Item*)

Adam Feudale breaks a tackle in 2012. (Liz Rohde/*The Daily Item*)

Robert Delbo makes a tackle in 2012. (Amanda August/*The Daily Item*)

Blake Marks gains yardage in 2013 game action. (Robert Inglis/ *The Daily Item*)

Nick Becker rolls out on a keeper in 2015. (Justin Engle/*The Daily Item*)

Matt Bell, Austin Knepp, Nick Freeman and Joshua Yoder celebrate a sack in 2015 action. (Amanda August/ *The Daily Item*)

Southern Columbia students at a pep rally prior to the 2015 PIAA Class AA Championship Game. (Justin Engle/ *The Daily Item*)

The Tigers celebrate their seventh PIAA State Football Championship in 2015. (Justin Engle/*The Daily Item*)

Head Coach Jim Roth celebrates with his team at a postgame ceremony renaming the field at Tiger Stadium in his honor in 2016. (Barbara Krohn/ *The Daily Item*)

Head Coach Jim Roth celebrates his 400th career victory with his grandson in 2017. (Justin Engle/ *The Daily Item*)

Stone Hollenbach runs for yardage in 2017. (Brett R, Crossley/*The Daily Item*)

Lear Quinton closes in for a sack in the 2017 PIAA Playoffs. (Justin Engle/*The Daily Item*

Southern celebrates their eighth PIAA State Football Championship in 2017. (Robert Inglis/ *The Daily Item*)

Southern Columbia fans cheer on the Tigers at the 2017 PIAA Class AA Championship Game. (Robert Inglis/ *The Daily Item*)

Cal Haladay with a big hit in 2018. (Justin Engle/*The Daily Item*)

The Tigers celebrate their ninth PIAA State Football Championship in 2018. (Robert Inglis/*The Daily Item*)

Gaige Garcia finds a hole in 2019. (Robert Inglis/*The Daily Item*)

Julian Fleming makes the catch in 2019 action. (Robert Inglis/*The Daily Item*)

Southern Columbia celebrates their tenth PIAA State Football Championship in 2019. (Robert Inglis/*The Daily Item*)

Gaige Garcia and Julian Fleming give Head Coach Jim Roth a well-deserved shower after winning the 2019 PIAA Class AA Championship. (Justin Engle/*The Daily Item*)

Gavin Garcia on a breakaway in 2020. (Robert Inglis/ *The Daily Item*)

Nick Zeigler carries the flag honoring Keegan Shultz onto the field in 2020. (Robert Inglis/ *The Daily Item*)

The Tigers celebrate their eleventh PIAA State Football Championship in 2020. (Robert Inglis/*The Daily Item*)

Head Coach Jim Roth celebrates with his team after winning their eleventh PIAA State Football Championship. The victory also gave Coach Roth his 456th win, giving him the most career coaching victories in Pennsylvania high school football history. (Robert Inglis/*The Daily Item*)

# THE 2010s
## (A DECADE OF DOMINANCE)

In 2010, the Tigers looked to build upon their remarkable turnaround in the second half of the 2009 season. Southern opened the year on the road against Line Mountain. After falling behind 20-0 in the first quarter, the Tigers came roaring back with 49 unanswered points to take down the Eagles. Tyrell Thomas and Jake Morton scored a pair of rushing touchdowns, and Aaron Zigarski, Jake Townsend, and Jamie Slotterback had scoring runs. Thomas rushed for 104 yards, and Morton, Slotterback, and Zigarski combined for 100 more in the opening night victory.

The Tigers dominated their week two matchup at Montoursville. The defense held the Warriors to just six first downs in the game and -7 yards rushing. Jake Townsend fired three touchdown passes to Jake Morton, Aaron Zigarski, and Tyrell Thomas. Morton, Thomas, and Tyler Levan had scoring runs and combined for 140 rushing yards as Southern defeated Montoursville, 42-6. Townsend passed for 226 yards in the win.

The offense continued to roll in the Tigers' home opener against Shamokin. Jake Townsend threw for three touchdowns to Tyrell Thomas (2) and Jake Becker. Thomas and Jake Morton each had a scoring run, and Keith Day recovered a fumble and returned it 5 yards for a touchdown as Southern downed the Indians, 42-13. Thomas, Morton, Bo Kiesling, and Aaron Zigarski combined for 162 rushing tards. Townsend threw for 170 yards in a winning effort.

In a road game with the Central Columbia, the Southern defense grounded the Blue Jays in a 37-0 shutout win. Central was limited to just 14 yards of total offense for the game. Tyrell Thomas rushed for two touchdowns and had a scoring reception from Jake Townsend, and Jake Morton and Aaron Zigarski rumbled for scoring runs and combined for 139 rushing yards. Colton Yeick connected for a field goal in the victory.

Lewisburg visited Tiger Stadium in week five. Tyrell Thomas ran for two touchdowns, and Jake Morton added another scoring run, but the Tigers dropped a close decision, 28-21. Thomas rushed for 100 yards in the tough loss.

Southern racked up 588 total yards of offense in a home victory over Bloomsburg, including 394 on the ground. Jake Morton scored three rushing touchdowns, and Tyrell Thomas and Tyler Levan also had scoring runs. Jake Townsend hooked up with Cody Rosenberger for a touchdown pass in Southern's 41-14 victory. Townsend threw for 194 yards, and Thomas had 145 rushing yards for the Tigers.

The Tigers had touchdown runs from Jake Morton and Tyrell Thomas, and Tim Benner caught a scoring pass from Jake Townsend, but Southern lost a tough game at Danville, 28-18. The Ironmen took the lead in the first half, and the Tigers weren't able to recover from the early deficit. Townsend passed for 116 yards in the loss.

Jake Townsend threw for three touchdowns, two to Tim Benner and one to Tyrell Thomas, as the Tigers won a road shootout with the Loyalsock Lancers. The Southern ground game rumbled for 364 yards and got two scoring runs from Thomas and Jake Morton and one from Aaron Zigarski in the Southern's 56-42 win. Townsend passed for 164 yards, and Thomas had 134 on the ground.

The Tigers found themselves in another close battle with rival Mount Carmel at Tiger Stadium in week nine. Jake Morton and Tyrell Thomas scored on first-half touchdown runs, and Colton Yeick's third-quarter field goal was the difference in Southern's 17-14 victory over the Red Tornadoes. Thomas and Morton combined for 189 rushing yards in the hard-fought win.

Southern hosted Selinsgrove in the season finale. Jake Morton ran for 126 yards and two touchdowns, and Tyrell Thomas rushed for 126 yards and a score as the Tigers blew out the Seals, 48-7. Tim Benner, Tyler Levan, and Casey Savitski added scoring runs, and Jake Townsend threw a touchdown pass to Thomas to round out the scoring. Southern rushed for 329 yards in the contest.

The Tigers faced Canton in the District IV Class A Semifinal Game at Tiger Stadium. Southern rushed for 469 yards and scored ten touchdowns in a wild 68-52 victory. Tyler Levan and Tim Benner each scored three touchdowns to lead the Tigers. Southern had rushing touchdowns from Leven (3), Benner (3), and one each from Jake Morton and Tyrell Thomas. Jake Townsend fired scoring passes to Benner and Keith Day. Thomas rushed for 148 yards, Levan ran for 136 yards, and Townsend passed for 121 yards.

Southern advanced to the District IV Class Championship Game at home against Line Mountain. Jake Morton ran for two scores, and Tyrell Thomas and Jamie Slotterback had touchdown runs as the Tigers defeated the Eagles, 48-13. Southern rushed for 388 yards in the game. Jake Townsend passed for two touchdowns to Thomas and Keith Day. Morton had a huge day, rushing for 196 yards. Tim Benner also topped the century mark with 102 yards on the ground.

The Tigers traveled to Peckville to take on the Riverside Vikings for a PIAA Class A Playoff Game. The trip turned into a nightmare for the Tigers as the Vikings completely dominated the contest. Southern's formidable rushing attack

## 2010 SEASON

| Opponent | Location | W/L | Score |
|----------|----------|-----|-------|
| Line Mountain | Away | W | 49-20 |
| Montoursville | Away | W | 42-6 |
| Shamokin | Home | W | 42-13 |
| Central Columbia | Away | W | 37-0 |
| Lewisburg | Home | L | 21-28 |
| Bloomsburg | Home | W | 41-14 |
| Danville | Away | L | 18-28 |
| Loyalsock | Away | W | 56-42 |
| Mount Carmel | Home | W | 17-14 |
| Selinsgrove | Home | W | 48-7 |
| **District IV Class A Semifinal Game** | | | |
| Canton | Home | W | 68-52 |
| **District IV Class A Championship Game** | | | |
| Line Mountain | Home | W | 48-13 |
| **PIAA Class A Playoff Game** | | | |
| Riverside | Neutral | L | 0-36 |

COACHING STAFF: Jim Roth, Head Coach; Randall Campbell, Assistant Coach; Alex Carawan, Assistant Coach; Al Cihocki, Assistant Coach; Troy Heath, Assistant Coach; Andy Helwig, Assistant Coach; Mike Johnston, Assistant Coach; John Marks, Assistant Coach; Andy Mills, Assistant Coach; Roger Nunkester, Assistant Coach; Pete Saylor, Assistant Coach; Rick Steele, Assistant Coach; Assistant Coach; Dewey Townsend, Assistant Coach; Brandon Traugh, Assistant Coach; Don Traugh, Assistant Coach

ATHLETIC DIRECTOR: Jim Roth

ROSTER: Cernan Abdul-al, Jake Becker, Tim Benner, Ryan Cherwinski, Tony Chiavaroli, Aaron Crawford, Keith Day, Dylan Eck, Brad Fegley, Alex Fidler, Cameron Flore, Vinny Forti, Bryan Gedman, Ryan Gooler, Joe Grosch, Kurt Henrie, Matt Hoffman, David Jeremiah, Jesse Keefer, Bo Kiessling, Joe Kleman, Matt Klock, Tyler Levan, Matt Lupold, Matt Moore, Jake Morton, Blake Nevius, Diego Otero, Bryce Parry, Hayden Reed, Bill Reigle, Cody Rosenberger, Casey Savitski, Tom Schetroma, Zach Schreffler, Jamie Slotterback, Ethan Snyder, Dylan Stimer, Paul Thomas, Tyrell Thomas, Jake Townsend, Josh Tripp, William Wertman, Chris Woods, Colton Yeick, Austin Zelinski, Aaron Zigarski was held to -6 yards for the game. Riverside brought the Tigers' season to an end with a dominant 36-0 victory.

Southern saw many outstanding individual performances during the 2010 season. Tyrell Thomas rushed for 1,123 yards and 15 touchdowns. Jake Morton ran for 992 yards and 18 scores. Morton would end his career at Southern Columbia with 2,620 yards and 39 touchdowns. The Tigers had touchdown runs from Tyler Levan (6), Tim Benner (4), Aaron Zigarski (2), Jamie Slotterback (2), and one each from Casey Savitski and Jake Townsend. Jake Townsend passed for 1,670 yards and 17 touchdowns. Southern had touchdown receptions from Tyrell Thomas (7), Tim Benner (4), Keith Day (2), and one each from Jake Becker, Jake Morton, Cody Rosenberger, and Aaron Zigarski. Alex Fidler registered 100 tackles (38 solo) and 9.5 sacks. Day recorded five interceptions. Tyrell Thomas earned All-State honors. The Tigers would end the season with a record of 10-3.

**2011** The 2011 season got off to an ominous start before a down was played. Coach Jim Roth learned that the squad's leading rusher from 2010, Tyrell Thomas, was lost for the year with a knee injury. That meant the Tigers would be starting an all-rookie backfield, including a new quarterback in 2011. The young Tigers would have to learn under fire if Southern hoped to continue their success. The Tigers opened the season with a home game versus Line Mountain. The Southern defense started the year with a bang when Tyler Levan recovered an Eagle fumble on the third play to put the Tigers offense in scoring range. Casey Savitski scored from 5 yards out for Southern's first points of the year. Brad Fegley scrambled for a 22-yard touchdown before Line Mountain got on the board with a scoring run as the Tigers led 14-7 after one. Matt Moore scampered 18 yards for a touchdown in the second, and the Eagles scored on a 63-yard run before the half as Southern took a 21-13 lead into the break. Moore rumbled 55 yards for a touchdown, and Savitski scored on a 5-yard plunge after a Line Mountain touchdown run, and the Tigers led 35-18 after three. The Eagles cut the lead to 35-25 on a 43-yard run in the fourth, but Savitski scored his third touchdown of the game to put the Eagles away, 42-25. Southern rushed for 419 yards. Moore ran for 137 yards and two scores. Savitski rushed for 95 yards and three touchdowns. Levan chipped in with 131 yards on the ground. Fegley also scored a rushing touchdown.

Southern's home game against Montoursville was postponed for two days due to bad weather. However, the wait did little to slow the Tigers' offense.

Tyler Levan got Southern on the board early in the first quarter with a 6-yard touchdown run. Keith Day intercepted a Montoursville pass and returned it to the Warriors' 2-yard line. Casey Savitski plowed into the endzone for a 14-0 lead after one. Montoursville cut the lead in half in the second on a 32-yard pass play, but Levan scored on a 7-yard run to give Southern a 21-7 lead at halftime. In the third, Brad Fegley hit Keith Day for a 35-yard touchdown pass to push the lead to 28-7. Dylan Eck returned an interception to the Warriors' 5-yard line to set up Matt Lupold's 3-yard scoring run. Adam Feudale capped the scoring with a 19-yard touchdown burst as the Tigers defeated Montoursville, 42-7. Fegley threw for 175 yards and a touchdown. Day had 88 receiving yards and a scoring catch. Levan ran for 35 yards and two touchdowns. Feudale rushed for 31 yards and a score. Savitski had 12 yards on the ground and a scoring run.

The Tigers traveled to Shamokin for their first road contest of the season. Matt Moore had touchdown runs of 31 and 37 yards, and Tyler Levan raced 80 yards for a score as Southern built an 18-0 first-quarter lead. Shamokin cut the lead to 18-7 on a 65-yard run, but Casey Savitski answered with a 13-yard scoring jaunt, and the Tigers led 25-7 after the opening period. The Indians scored on a 2-yard pass in the second, and Levan rumbled 6 yards for a touchdown as Southern took a 33-14 lead into the intermission. Levan and Cody Pavlick scored on runs of one and 20 yards to push the Southern lead to 46-14 after three. Shamokin scored a late touchdown in the fourth quarter to make the final score 46-21. Levan led the way with 115 rushing yards and three touchdowns. Moore added 78 yards on the ground and a scoring run. Savitski ran for 39 yards and a touchdown. Pavlick had 20 rushing yards and a score.

Southern hosted the Central Columbia Blue Jays in week four. The defense scored the first points of the night as Nate Hunter returned an interception 38 yards for a touchdown. Casey Savitski scored on runs of 31 and 39 yards, and Brad Fegley fired a 31-yard touchdown pass to Matt Moore, and the Tigers led 26-0 after one. Tyler Levan had touchdown runs of 5 and 67 yards in the second to finish the scoring as Southern earned a 40-0 shutout victory over the Blue Jays. Levan ran for 95 yards and two scores. Savitski rushed for 75 yards and two touchdowns. Fegley threw for 80 yards and a touchdown to Moore.

A road contest against Lewisburg would prove to be one of the classic games in Heartland Conference history. Lewisburg took an early lead with a 48-yard touchdown run. Tyler Levan scored the equalizer with a 5-yard scoring burst. The Green Dragons scored on a 21-yard run to give Lewisburg a 13-7 lead after one. Levan plowed in from one yard out early in the second to give Southern a 14-13 lead. Lewisburg jumped back on top with a 15-yard touchdown run as the Green Dragons led 20-14 at the break. In the third, Levan put the Tigers back in front with a 2-yard scoring plunge. However, Lewisburg scored on a 99-yard touchdown pass to take a 28-21 lead into the fourth quarter. The Green Dragons maintained the lead until late in the final period. Levan scored from one yard out with 50 seconds remaining in the game to pull Southern within 28-27. Coach Roth called a timeout and asked his team if they wanted to kick the extra point to tie the game or go for the win with a two-point conversion. The Tigers unanimously chose to go for the victory and lined up for the conversion. Levan took the handoff, followed his blockers on a perfectly executed dive, and piled into the endzone for a 29-28 Southern lead. However, the game was far from over. With less than 50 seconds remaining in regulation, Lewisburg took over and drove the ball deep into Southern territory. With seconds remaining in the game, the Green Dragons had the ball first and goal from the Tigers' 8-yard line. After a timeout, Lewisburg sent their placekicker onto the field to try a game-winning field goal. The snap was down, the kick was strong. However, it drifted to the left, and Southern had escaped with a thrilling 29-28 victory. Levan ran for 163 yards and four touchdowns and scored the winning conversion. Many have called this the greatest high school or college game ever played at Bucknell University's Christy Mathewson Stadium.

Up next was a visit to Bloomsburg to take on the Panthers. Tyler Levan and Casey Savitski scored from one yard out to give the Tigers a 14-7 first-quarter lead. Bloomsburg tied the game early in the second before Southern erupted for 27 unanswered points before the half. Brad Fegley hit Matt Moore for a 40-yard touchdown pass, Moore raced 50 yards for a score, Levan pounded in from the one, and Fegley found Keith Day on a 21-yard scoring pass. The Tigers took a 41-14 lead into the break. In the third, Moore scored again on a 10-yard run, Savitski rumbled for a 4-yard touchdown, Mitch Stanziale scored on a 15-yard scamper, and Taylor Young capped the scoring with a 3-yard touchdown run. Southern defeated Bloomsburg going away, 67-27. The Tigers rushed 442 yards. Moore led the way with 117 yards rushing and two touchdowns. He also had a touchdown reception. Levan ran for 92 yards and two scores. Stanziale had 23 yards on the ground and a scoring run. Young rushed for 7 yards and a score. Fegley threw for 120 yards and two touchdowns. Keith Day had 33 yards receiving and a scoring catch. The defense registered four interceptions against the Panthers.

The Tigers hosted the Danville Ironmen in week seven. After a scoreless first, Matt Moore got Southern on the board with a 10-yard run early in the second. After Danville tied the score, Tyler Levan and Moore followed with 67 and 66 yards touchdown runs. The Ironmen narrowed the gap with a scoring run and a field goal, and the Tigers led 21-17 at the intermission. Southern put the game away in the third. Brad Fegley fired a 28-yard touchdown pass to Moore and scored on a 40-yard quarterback keeper to up the lead to 35-17. Levan tacked on a 57-yard touchdown run in the fourth to make the final score 41-17. Southern rushed for 366 yards. Levan ran for 176 yards and two scores. Moore had 77 rushing yards and two touchdowns, and a scoring reception. Fegley passed for 77 yards and a touchdown and added a scoring run.

Former Southern running back Henry Hynoski addressed the team before their home game against Loyalsock. In a pre-game ceremony, the Tigers retired Hynoski's number 27. Hynoski inspired the team in a 41-0 shutout of the Lancers. Brad Fegley threw touchdown passes to Keith Day (27 yards), Tyler Levan (68 yards), and Casey Savitski (23 yards), and Matt Moore scored on a 7-yard run as the Tigers opened up a 28-0 lead after one. In the second, Levan added an 11-yard touchdown run to push the lead to 35-0 at halftime. Adam Feudale capped the scoring with a 2-yard scoring plunge in the final quarter. In shutting out the Lancers, the defense held Loyalsock to 96 total yards. Moore ran for 70 yards and a touchdown. Levan rushed for 21 yards and a score and had a touchdown reception. Feudale had 29 yards rushing and a touchdown. Fegley threw for 136 yards and fired three touchdown passes. Day had 56 yards receiving and a touchdown, and Savitski had a scoring catch.

A week nine trip to Mount Carmel dashed the Tigers' hopes for an undefeated regular season in a game that went down to the wire. The Red Tornadoes returned the opening kickoff for a touchdown, and Southern trailed 7-0 after one. Tyler Levan and Casey Savitski scored on runs of 13 and 6 yards in the second to give the Tigers a 14-7 lead at the half. The teams played a scoreless third quarter. In the fourth, Brad Fegley hit Keith Day on a 21-yard touchdown pass to push the lead to 21-7. Mount Carmel scored on a 60-yard run to cut the lead to 21-14. Late in regulation, the Red Tornadoes drove inside the Tigers' 10-yard line. Mount Carmel scored on a 7-yard touchdown pass with 36.9 seconds remaining in the game. Rather than kick the extra point to tie the game, Mount Carmel chose to go for the win. They threw for a two-point conversion to win the game, 22-21. It was a devastating loss for the Tigers. Levan ran for 106 yards and a touchdown. Savitski rushed for 32 yards and a score. Fegley passed for 156 yards and a touchdown. Day had 48 receiving yards and a touchdown reception.

The Tigers rebounded with a shutout victory over host Selinsgrove in the regular-season finale. After a scoreless opening quarter, Tyler Levan rumbled 98 yards for Southern's first score. Adam Feudale added a 2-yard touchdown run, and the Tigers led 13-0 at the break. Casey Savitski had touchdown runs of 41 and 10 yards, and Levan scored on an 8-yard scamper to push the lead to 35-0 after three. Cody Pavlick punched it in from one yard out to cap the scoring in the fourth to give Southern a 42-0 victory over the Seals. The Tigers ran for 420 yards. Levan rushed for 185 yards and two touchdowns. Savitski ran for 65 yards and two scores. Feudale had 36 yards rushing and a touchdown. Pavlick contributed 13 yards on the ground and a scoring run. Fegley threw for 145 yards. The Southern defense held the Seals to 34 yards rushing.

Southern hosted the Sayre Redskins in the District IV Class A Semifinal Game at Tiger Stadium. Matt Moore scored from one yard out to open the scoring. Jake Becker returned a Sayre fumble 30 yards for a touchdown and a 14-0 lead. Moore rumbled 21 yards for a touchdown, Tyler Levan ran 31 yards for a score, and Southern led 28-0 after the opening period. Brad Fegley found Casey Savitski for a 43-yard touchdown pass, and Levan and Adam Feudale scored on runs of 14 and 6 yards to push the lead to 49-0 at the half. Feudale finished off Sayre with a 34-yard touchdown run in the fourth, and the Tigers earned a lopsided 55-7 victory. Levan ran for 69 yards and two scores. Moore rushed for 53 yards and two touchdowns. Feudale had 52 rushing yards and a pair of touchdowns. Fegley threw for 103 yards and a touchdown pass to Savitski.

Line Mountain visited Tiger Stadium for the District IV Class A Championship Game. Brad Fegley and Casey Savitski scored first-quarter touchdowns on runs of one and 7 yards, and Southern led 14-6 after one. Tyler Levan scored on a 6-yard burst, and Fegley fired an 11-yard touchdown pass to Keith Day in the second for a 28-6 halftime lead. In the third, Fegley hit Jake Becker for a 38-yard scoring pass as the Tigers defeated Line Mountain, 35-14. Southern rushed for 346 yards. Levan had 160 yards rushing and a touchdown. Savitski rushed for 40 yards and a score. Fegley threw for 130 yards and two touchdowns and added a scoring run. Day had 48 yards receiving and a touchdown. Becker hauled in 38 receiving yards and a scoring catch.

Southern opened the PIAA Class A Playoffs versus Old Forge at Coal Township. Dylan Swank connected on a 25-yard field goal to give the Tigers a 3-0 lead after the opening quarter. Tyler Levan and Matt Moore scored on runs of 52 and 22 yards in the second. However, the Blue Devils scored three touchdowns to take a 21-17 lead at the break. Levan and Moore scored again on runs of 22 and 68 yards to give the Tigers a 31-27 third-quarter lead. In the final period, Moore put the game away on touchdown runs of 19 and 82 yards as the Tigers outlasted Old Forge, 45-34. Southern ground out 466 rushing yards. Moore rumbled for 259 yards and four touchdowns. Levan ran for 211 yards and two scores.

The Tigers faced Pius X in the PIAA Class A Quarterfinal Game in Nazareth. Pius X scored twice, and Brad Fegley fired a 16-yard touchdown pass to Keith Day as the Royals led 13-7 after one. Pius X scored again early in the second to push their lead to 19-7. Fegley pounded in from 2 yards out and scored on a one-yard sneak, and Tyler Levan scored on a 2-yard run. The Royals got a touchdown pass, and the Tigers took a 29-25 at the half. Fegley scored his third rushing touchdown on a 13-yard scamper in the third quarter. Southern finally put the game away in the fourth. Matt Moore had touchdown runs of 31 and 7 yards, and Levan raced 76 yards for a score as Southern advanced with a hard-fought 55-25 win over the Royals. The Tigers rushed for 430 yards. Levan ran for 189 yards and two touchdowns. Moore rushed for 133 yards and a pair of scores. Fegley ran for 94 yards and three touchdowns. He passed for 126 yards and a score. Day had 72 receiving yards and a touchdown.

Southern faced off against Penns Manor in the PIAA Class A Semifinal Game in Mill Hall. The Tigers got off to a quick start when Tyler Levan scored on touchdown runs of 64 and 2 yards to take a 14-0 lead in the first quarter. Matt Moore and Adam Feudale scored on runs of 3 and 21 yards as Southern built a 28-6 lead by halftime. A Comets' snap out of the endzone on a punt gave the Tigers a safety, and Moore finished on Penns Manor with a one-yard touchdown plunge as Southern advanced to the state title game with a convincing 37-6 victory. Levan ran for 91 yards and two touchdowns. Feudale rushed for 50 yards and a score. Moore ran for 39 yards and two touchdowns, and he had 104 receiving yards. Brad Fegley had 137 yards through the air.

Southern advanced to the PIAA Class A Championship Game against the Clairton Bears at Hersheypark Stadium. Clairton scored on an 88-yard pass play in the first quarter for an 8-0 lead. The Tigers cut the lead to 8-6 on a 5-yard touchdown run from Tyler Levan. The Bears pushed the lead to 14-6 with a 65-yard scoring pass. Matt Moore scored from 3 yards out to pull Southern within 14-12. Clairton scored on a one-yard run before the half and took a 21-12 lead at the intermission. Moore closed the gap to 21-19 with a 5-yard touchdown pass from Brad Fegley. However, Clairton put the game out of reach for the Tigers with two touchdown runs in the fourth quarter, and the Bears won their third straight PIAA Class A Championship with a 35-19 win. Moore ran for 136 yards and a touchdown. Levan rushed for 70 yards and a score. Fegley threw for 74 yards and a touchdown to Moore.

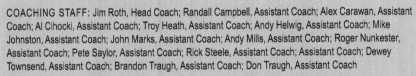

## 2011 SEASON

| Opponent | Location | W/L | Score |
|---|---|---|---|
| Line Mountain | Home | W | 42-25 |
| Montoursville | Home | W | 42-7 |
| Shamokin | Away | W | 46-21 |
| Central Columbia | Home | W | 40-0 |
| Lewisburg | Away | W | 29-28 |
| Bloomsburg | Away | W | 67-27 |
| Danville | Home | W | 41-17 |
| Loyalsock | Home | W | 41-0 |
| Mount Carmel | Away | L | 21-22 |
| Selinsgrove | Away | W | 42-0 |
| **District IV Class A Semifinal Game** | | | |
| Sayre | Home | W | 55-7 |
| **District IV Class A Championship Game** | | | |
| Line Mountain | Home | W | 35-14 |
| **PIAA Class A Playoff Game** | | | |
| Old Forge | Neutral | W | 45-34 |
| **PIAA Class A Quarterfinal Game** | | | |
| Pius X | Neutral | W | 55-25 |
| **PIAA Class A Semifinal Game** | | | |
| Penns Manor | Neutral | W | 37-6 |
| **PIAA Class A Championship Game** | | | |
| Clairton | Neutral | L | 19-35 |

COACHING STAFF: Jim Roth, Head Coach; Randall Campbell, Assistant Coach; Alex Carawan, Assistant Coach; Al Cihocki, Assistant Coach; Troy Heath, Assistant Coach; Andy Helwig, Assistant Coach; Mike Johnston, Assistant Coach; John Marks, Assistant Coach; Andy Mills, Assistant Coach; Roger Nunkester, Assistant Coach; Pete Saylor, Assistant Coach; Rick Steele, Assistant Coach; Assistant Coach; Dewey Townsend, Assistant Coach; Brandon Traugh, Assistant Coach; Don Traugh, Assistant Coach

ATHLETIC DIRECTOR: Jim Roth

ROSTER: Jake Becker, Ryan Cherwinski, Tony Chiavaroli, Brandon Cox, Aaron Crawford, Keith Day, Robert Delbo, Trent Donlan, Collyn Drake, Dylan Eck, Brad Fegley, Ken Fegley, Adam Feudale, Cameron Flore, Angelo Forti, Bryan Gedman, Ryan Gooler, Joe Grosch, Nate Hunter, David Jeremiah, Bo Kiessling, Joe Kleman, Matt Klok, Tyler Levan, Matt Lupold, Matt Moore, Don Orr, Bryce Parry, Cody Pavlik, Luke Rarig, Bill Reigle, Logan Reynolds, Casey Savitski, Tom Schetroma, Jamie Slotterback, Garett Sosnoski, John Stanishefski, Mitch Stanziale, Dylan Stimer, Dylan Swank, Paul Thomas, Tyrell Thomas, Jake Townsend, Josh Tripp, William Wertman, Chris Woods, Taylor Young, Aaron Zigarski

The disappointment of the championship game loss did not diminish the sensational effort by the Tigers. Tyler Levan rushed for 1,889 yards and 28 touchdowns. Matt Moore ran for 1,332 yards and 19 scores. Casey Savitski added 535 rushing yards and 11 scoring runs. Southern had touchdown runs from Brad Fegley (6), Adam Feudale (6), and one each from Cody Pavlick, Mitch Stanziale, and Taylor Young. Brad Fegley threw for 1,731 yards and 14 touchdowns. Fegley became the only quarterback in Pennsylvania high school history to play an entire 16-game season, reaching the state championship game and not throw an interception the entire year. Keith Day had 685 receiving yards and six touchdown receptions. The Tigers had scoring receptions from Matt Moore (4) and one each from Jake Becker, Tyler Levan, and Casey Savitski. Dylan Swank kicked 55 extra points and one field goal. Moore had 91 tackles (31 solo). Day registered nine interceptions. Dylan Eck recorded six sacks. Day, Moore, and Tom Schetroma were All-state selections. Southern finished 2011 with a record of 15-1.

2
0
1
2
The 2012 Southern Columbia Tigers looked to repeat the success that the team achieved in 2011. Coach Roth would again have a new quarterback under center, and Southern looked to their always-dangerous ground game to provide stability. The Tigers opened the season on the road against Pius X. Southern was dominant on both sides of the line of scrimmage as they rolled to a 61-0 shutout over the Royals. Taylor Young fired his first touchdown pass of the season, a 64-yard strike to Bryce Parry, and Southern led 6-0 after one. Matt Lupold scored on a 6-yard run, Adam Feudale rumbled 14 yards for a touchdown, and Lupold ran for a 6-yard score as the Tigers led 27-0 at halftime. The special teams put on a show in the third quarter. Feudale returned the second-half kickoff 75-yards for a touchdown, and Joe Kleman returned a punt 50 yards for a score to push the Tigers' lead to 41-0. Brad Noll scored on a 10-yard burst, and Blake Marks scored on runs of 28 and 55 yards to cap the scoring in the fourth. Feudale ran for 77 yards and a touchdown. Lupold rushed 26 yards and a score. Noll had 17 yards on the ground and a rushing touchdown. Young threw for 86 yards and a score. Parry had 72 receiving yards and a touchdown reception.

The home opener was against the Montgomery Red Raiders. Southern wasted little time in blowing the game open. Adam Feudale raced 55 yards for a touchdown, Taylor Young hit Joe Kleman for a 20-yard scoring pass, Mitch Stanziale sacked the Red Raiders' quarterback in the endzone for a safety, Young connected with Nate Hunter on a 26-yard touchdown pass, Kleman and Hunter hooked up again on a 20-yard scoring strike, Feudale rumbled 7 yards for a touchdown, and Matt Lupold scampered 27 yards for a score as the Tigers led 43-0 after the first twelve minutes. Brad Noll added a 5-yard touchdown run before the half and pushed the Southern lead to 49-0 at the break. Blake Marks put an end to the scoring in the fourth quarter with a one-yard plunge to make the final score 55-0. While the Tigers rumbled for 410 yards rushing, the Southern defense held Montgomery to -13 yards on the ground. Noll led the rushing attack with 104 yards and a score. Marks ran for 97 yards and a touchdown. Feudale added 73 yards and two scores. Lupold rushed for 58 yards and a touchdown. Young passed for 99 yards and three touchdowns. Kleman had 73 receiving yards and two scores. Hunter contributed with 26 yards receiving and a touchdown reception.

Southern hosted Mount Carmel in week three. Matt Lupold piled in from 2 yards out in the first, and Adam Feudale scored on a one-yard plunge in the second, but the Tigers trailed 19-14 at the intermission. Taylor Young hit Bryce Parry for a 25-yard touchdown pass, and Nate Hunter scored on an 11-yard scamper as Southern took the lead 28-25 after three. The Tigers salted the game away in the final period. Young raced 38 yards on a quarterback keeper, and Feudale scored on runs of 54 and 15 yards as Southern defeated the Red Tornadoes, 49-33. The Tigers rushed for 397 yards. Feudale ran for 126 yards and three touchdowns. Lupold rushed for 89 yards and a score. Hunter added 78 yards rushing and a scoring run. Young threw for 71 yards and a touchdown and added a rushing score. Parry had 29 receiving yards and a touchdown reception.

The Tigers made the trek to South Williamsport to tangle with Mountaineers. Nate Hunter opened the scoring with a 28-yard touchdown run in the first quarter. Matt Lupold scored on a 6-yard run, Luke Rarig returned an interception 45 yards for a score, Adam Feudale raced 63-yards for a touchdown, and Taylor Young fired a 53-yard scoring pass to Bryce Parry as Southern built a 35-7 halftime lead. Hunter rumbled 9 yards for a score, and the Mountaineers scored two late touchdowns to make the final 42-21. The Tigers' rushing machine continued to roll with 340 yards on the ground. Feudale ran for 106 yards and a touchdown. Lupold rushed for 86 yards and a score. Hunter added 66 yards and two rushing touchdowns. Young passed for 107 yards and a touchdown. Parry had 53 yards receiving and a scoring reception.

The winning ways continued in a week five home game with Muncy. The Tigers bolted to an early lead and made quick work of the Indians. Taylor Young ran 24 yards for a score, Young hit Jake Becker for a 49-yard touchdown pass, Matt Lupold rumbled for a 16-yard touchdown, Nate Hunter raced 78 yards for a score, and Adam Feudale streaked 53 yards for a touchdown, and the Tigers led 35-0 after one. Hunter added a 48-yard touchdown run in the second to push the lead to 41-0 at the break. Ross Crowl ran for a 70-yard score in the fourth, and the Tigers defeated Muncy, 47-7. Southern ran for 424 yards. Hunter rumbled for 132 yards and two touchdowns. Feudale and Crowl each ran for 78 yards and a score. Lupold added 32 yards and a scoring run.

Young threw for 62 yards and a score and added a rushing touchdown. Becker registered 49 receiving yards and a touchdown reception.

Southern traveled to Selinsgrove for a matchup with the Seals. Adam Feudale and Nate Hunter had touchdown runs of 2 and 11 yards to give the Tigers a 14-7 lead after the opening stanza. Feudale ran for a 5-yard score, Taylor Young connected with Hunter on a 10-yard touchdown pass, Bryce Parry caught a 31-yard scoring strike from Young, and Southern took a 36-21 lead into the half. Young found Luke Rarig for a 21-yard touchdown throw in the third to push the lead to 43-21. Feudale put the final nail in the coffin with a 22-yard scoring scamper to make the final score 50-21. Feudale rushed for 116 yards and three touchdowns. Hunter ran for 31 yards and a score. He also had a touchdown reception. Young passed for 158 yards and three scores. Parry had 66 receiving yards and a touchdown. Rarig hauled in 21 yards receiving and a scoring catch.

The Tigers faced the Bloomsburg Panthers in a road tussle in week seven. Southern took a 2-0 lead when a Bloomsburg snap on a punt sailed out of the endzone for a safety. Matt Lupold ran for a 2-yard score, and the Tigers led 9-7 after the opening quarter. Blake Marks pounded in from 2 yards out to up the lead to 16-7 at the half. In the third, Joe Kleman's interception set up Taylor Young's 4-yard keeper to give Southern a 23-7 lead after three. Another Panther snap out of the endzone on a punt gave the Tigers another safety and a 25-7 lead. Adam Feudale scored on a 6-yard run to give Southern a 32-20 victory over Bloomsburg. Feudale rushed for 141 yards and a touchdown. Lupold ran for 28 yards and a score. Marks added 3 yards and a scoring run. Young threw for 80 yards and had a rushing touchdown.

The Shamokin Indians visited Tiger Stadium for a week eight contest. Southern quickly jumped on Shamokin in the first quarter. Taylor Young hit Bryce Parry for a 26-yard touchdown pass, Dylan Swank connected on a 38-yard field goal, and Garett Sosnoski returned an interception 14 yards for a pick six, and the Tigers led 18-0 after one. Adam Feudale and Matt Lupold scored on runs of 7 and 2 yards as Southern built a 32-0 lead at the intermission. Blake Marks pounded in from one yard out in the third, and Jacob Potter raced 19-yards for a fourth-quarter touchdown, as the Tigers easily defeated Shamokin, 45-6. Marks rushed for 53 yards and a touchdown. Lupoid and Feudale each ran for 28 yards and a score. Potter added 23 yards on the ground and a touchdown. Young passed for 114 years and a score. Parry had 44 receiving yards and a touchdown reception.

A home game against rival Central Columbia would be a special night for head coach Jim Roth. However, a victory would not come easy. The Blue

Jays scored the only touchdown of the first half and led 7-0 at halftime. Matt Lupold scored from one yard out, and a two-point conversion gave the Tigers the lead 8-7 in the third. Adam Feudale scored on a 2-yard run in the fourth, and the defense made the lead stand with a blocked punt by Mitch Stanziale and a fumble recovery by Tony Chiavaroli. Southern defeated the Blue Jays, 15-7. Feudale rushed for 123 yards and a touchdown. Lupold added 18 yards and a rushing score. Jim Roth reached a milestone by coaching in his 400th career game.

The regular-season finale was a road contest at Warrior Run. Coach Roth decided to rest many of his starters to prepare for the postseason. However, the young Tiger reserves had no problems handling the Defenders. Dylan Swank got things started with a 27-yard field goal. Backup quarterback Nick Becker then threw for three touchdowns to Jake Becker (16 yards), Bryce Parry (67 yards), and Matt Lupold (42 yards) as Southern took a 24-0 lead after one. Adam Feudale scampered 15 yards for a score, and the Tigers led 30-0 at the half. Blake Marks scored on a 5-yard burst in the third, and then the special teams flexed their muscles. After a Defenders' touchdown, Joe Kleman returned the ensuing kickoff 82 yards for a touchdown. Brad Noll then returned a punt 32 yards for a score. Warrior Run scored two late touchdowns in mop-up time, and the Tigers defeated the Defenders, 50-19. Feudale rushed for 95 yards and a touchdown. Marks ran for 30 yards and a score. In his first career start, Becker threw for 152 yards and three scores. Parry had 67 yards receiving and a touchdown. Becker added 16 receiving yards and a scoring reception.

The Tigers entered the postseason hosting Line Mountain in the District IV Class A Semifinal Game. The contest would turn into a barnburner, with the Eagles taking a 14-0 halftime lead. Adam Feudale finally broke through for the Tigers with a one-yard dive in the third, but Line Mountain also scored, and the Southern trailed 21-7 entering the fourth quarter. The Tigers mounted an epic comeback with Feudale finding paydirt again from 5 yards out to cut the lead to 21-14. Blake Marks rumbled for a 35-yard touchdown to tie the game at 21-21. With 3:18 left in regulation, Taylor Young fired a 44-yard touchdown pass to Feudale to give Southern its first lead at 28-21. However, the Eagles mounted a late drive, advancing to the Tigers' 35-yard line before Matt Klock intercepted a pass to preserve Southern's first-round victory. Marks rushed for 64 yards and a score. Feudale ran for 61 yards and two scores and had the game-winning touchdown reception. Young threw for 93 yards and a score.

## 2012 SEASON

| Opponent | Location | W/L | Score |
|---|---|---|---|
| Pius X | Away | W | 61-0 |
| Montgomery | Home | W | 55-0 |
| Mount Carmel | Home | W | 49-33 |
| South Williamsport | Away | W | 42-21 |
| Muncy | Home | W | 47-7 |
| Selinsgrove | Away | W | 50-21 |
| Bloomsburg | Away | W | 32-20 |
| Shamokin | Home | W | 45-6 |
| Central Columbia | Home | W | 15-7 |
| Warrior Run | Away | W | 50-19 |
| **District IV Class A Semifinal Game** | | | |
| Line Mountain | Home | W | 28-21 |
| **District IV Class A Championship Game** | | | |
| South Williamsport | Home | W | 47-12 |
| **PIAA Class A Playoff Game** | | | |
| Dunmore | Neutral | L | 29-35 |

COACHING STAFF: Jim Roth, Head Coach; Randall Campbell, Assistant Coach; Alex Carawan, Assistant Coach; Al Cihocki, Assistant Coach; Troy Heath, Assistant Coach; Andy Helwig, Assistant Coach; Mike Johnston, Assistant Coach; John Marks, Assistant Coach; Andy Mills, Assistant Coach; Roger Nunkester, Assistant Coach; Nate Roadarmel, Assistant Coach; Pete Saylor, Assistant Coach; Rick Steele, Assistant Coach; Assistant Coach; Dewey Townsend, Assistant Coach; Brandon Traugh, Assistant Coach; Don Traugh, Assistant Coach

ATHLETIC DIRECTOR: Jim Roth

ROSTER: Jake Becker, Nick Becker, Matt Bell, Grayson Belles, Jared Brezinski, Ryan Cherwinski, Tony Chiavaroli, Aaron Crawford, Ross Crowl, Gabe Delbo, Robert Delbo, Trent Donlan, Collyn Drake, Matt Fabian, Ken Fegley, Adam Feudale, Angelo Forti, Vinny Forti, Nick Freeman, Ryan Gooler, Nate Hunter, Matt Jeremiah, Joe Kleman, Matt Klock, Aaron Kroh, Matt Lupold, Blake Marks, Billy Marzeski, Adam Mommo, Brad Noll, Cody Pavlick, Bryce Parry, Jacob Potter, Luke Rarig, Logan Reynolds, Brandon Richendrfer, Jacob Ryan, Garett Sosnoski, John Stanishefski, Mitch Stanziale, Dylan Swank, Paul Thomas, Steve Toczylousky, Josh Tripp, Jason Vought, Charles Wertman, William Wertman, Auston Wilcox, Joshua Yoder, Taylor Young

The South Williamsport Mountaineers traveled to Tiger Stadium for the District IV Class A Championship Game. Taylor Young raced 31 yards on a quarterback keeper, and the game was tied 6-6 after the opening. Southern put the game away in the second quarter. Adam Feudale scored on a 13-yard run, Young connected with Matt Lupold on a 50-yard touchdown pass, Young pounded in from 2 yards out, and Feudale raced 25 yards for a touchdown as the Tigers took a commanding 35-6 lead at the break. Marks added a 4-yard touchdown run in the third, and Matt Jeremiah capped the scoring with a 19-yard run in the fourth. The Tigers downed the Mountaineers, 47-12. Southern rushed for 309 yards. Feudale ran for 65 yards and two touchdowns. Marks rushed for 48 yards and a score. Jeremiah added 23 yards and a scoring run. Young rushed for two touchdowns, threw a scoring pass to Lupold, and passed for 114 yards. The Tigers celebrated their 21st District Championship.

Southern faced Dunmore in the opening round of the PIAA Class Play-offs in Peckville. Trailing 6-0 in the second quarter, Taylor Young rumbled 13 yards for the go-ahead touchdown, and the Tigers led 7-6 at the half. Southern was outscored 22-7 in the third, with Young scoring on a 14-yard quarterback keeper. Southern trailed 28-14, heading into the final period. Matt Lupold and Adam Feudale scored on runs of 8 and 5 yards, but the Bucks also had a fourth-quarter touchdown, and Dunmore advanced with a 35-29 victory. Feudale ran for 96 yards and a touchdown. Lupold had 17 yards on the ground and a score. Young rushed for two touchdowns and threw for 60 yards in the disappointing loss.

On the season, Adam Feudale rushed for 1,183 yards and 20 touchdowns. Matt Lupold ran for 612 yards and ten scores. The Tigers had touchdown runs from Nate Hunter (6), Blake Marks (5), Taylor Young (5), Brad Noll (2), and one each from Ross Crowl, Matt Jeremiah, and Jacob Potter. Taylor Young passed for 1,091 yards and 13 touchdowns. Nick Becker threw for 152 yards and three scores. Bryce Parry had 441 receiving yards and six touchdowns. Southern had scoring receptions from Jake Becker (2), Nate Hunter (2), Joe Kleman (2), Matt Lupold (2), and one each from Adam Feudale and Luke Rarig. Dylan Swank kicked 53 extra points and two field goals. Cody Pavlick recorded 122 tackles (28 solo). Tony Chiavaroli had 3.5 sacks. Kleman and Rarig each registered three interceptions. Pavlick and Ryan Cherwinski were All-State selections. The Tigers finished 2012 with a record of 12-1.

2013   The Tigers began 2013 with a new starting quarterback for the third straight year. In his only start in 2012, Nick Becker showed the potential that had Southern fans having championship aspirations in the coming years. The Tigers hosted Pius X in the home opener. After a scoreless first quarter, Adam Feudale and Nick Becker had touchdown runs of 8 and one yard, and Luke Rarig returned a punt 78 yards for a score as Southern built a 20-0 halftime lead. Becker hit Nate Hunter on a 54-yard touchdown pass, and Hunter raced 25 yards for a score, but the Royals scored three touchdowns of their own to cut the Southern lead to 34-21 after three. Feudale rumbled for a 13-yard touchdown, Brad Noll punched it in from 2 yards out, and Matt Jeremiah had a 5-yard scoring run to put away the pesky Royals, 55-28. Southern rushed for 411 yards. Feudale ran for 126 yards and two touchdowns. Hunter rushed for 60 yards and a score and had a touchdown reception. Jeremiah chipped in with 19 yards on the ground and a touchdown. Noll ran for 7 yards and a scoring run. Becker threw for 41 yards and a touchdown and also had a rushing score.

Southern traveled for a week two road game versus Montgomery. The Tigers jumped on the Red Raiders in the first quarter. Blake Marks ran for a 9-yard touchdown, Adam Feudale scored on a 2-yard dive, Nick Becker found Nate Hunter for a 12-yard touchdown pass, and Becker fired an 11-yard scoring strike to Luke Rarig for a 26-0 lead. Hunter banged in from 8 yards out, and Marks raced 49 yards for a score as Southern led 40-0 at the break. In the third, Billy Marzeski scored on a 5-yard burst, Brad Noll rumbled 95 yards for a touchdown, and Steve Toczylousky returned an interception 57 yards for a pick six and the Tigers pounded Montgomery, 55-6. Southern ran for 358 yards. Noll rushed for 147 yards and a touchdown. Marks added 77 rushing yards and a scoring run. Feudale rushed for 29 yards and a touchdown. Marzeski chipped in with 9 yards and a score. Hunter had 8 yards rushing and a touchdown, and a scoring catch. Becker passed for 158 yards and two touchdowns. Rarig had 11 receiving yards and a touchdown reception.

The Tigers paid a visit to Mount Carmel for a road matchup with the Red Tornadoes. Ken Fegley's blocked punt set up Adam Feudale's one-yard touchdown dive to open the scoring. Luke Rarig intercepted a Mount Carmel pass, leading to a scoring throw from Nick Becker to Nate Hunter for a 13-0 lead. Hunter ran for a 9-yard touchdown, and Feudale scampered for a 13-yard score, and the Tigers led 25-0 after one. Feudale added a 26-yard touchdown run in the second, and Southern led 33-7 at the break. Becker hit Rarig for a 14-yard scoring pass, and Billy Marzeski rumbled 43 yards for a touchdown in the third as the Tigers defeated Mount Carmel, 45-7. Southern rushed for 317 yards. Feudale ran for 136 yards and three touchdowns. Marzeski rushed for 43 yards and a score. Hunter added 37 yards on the ground and a touchdown run and had a scoring reception. Becker threw for 139 yards and two scores. Rarig had 64 yards receiving and a touchdown catch. The Tigers' defense held the Red Tornadoes to -7 yards rushing for the game.

The South Williamsport Mountaineers visited Tiger Stadium for a week four matchup. In the first quarter, Garett Sosnoski's sack and fumble recovery set up Nick Becker's 23-yard touchdown pass to Luke Rarig, and Southern led 7-0 after one. Nate Hunter pounded in from one-yard out, Blake Marks caught a 9-yard scoring pass from Becker, Rarig and Becker hooked up again for a 9-yard touchdown pass, and Adam Feudale raced 50 yards for a score, and the Tigers built a 34-0 lead at the half. Feudale ran for a 7-yard touchdown in the third, and Marks scampered for a 12-yard score as Southern downed the Mountaineers, 48-14. Feudale ran for 122 yards and two touchdowns. Hunter rushed for 60 yards and a score. Marks added 58 yards and a scoring run. He also had a touchdown reception. Becker passed for 108 yards and three scores. Rarig had 54 yards receiving and two touchdown receptions.

The Tigers visited Muncy for a road game with the Indians. Nick Becker fired a 6-yard touchdown strike to Luke Rarig for a quick 7-0 lead. Chase Tillett blocked a Muncy punt that was recovered by Ken Fegley and set up Blake Marks' 6-yard scoring run to push the lead to 13-0. Matt Lupold punched it in from 3 yards out, and Southern led 20-0 after the opening period. Becker connected with Marks for a 9-yard touchdown pass, Nate Hunter piled in from 3 yards out, and Lupold scored on a 5-yard dive as the Tigers led 41-0 at the break. Adam Feudale raced 68 yards for a touchdown in the third, Billy Marzeski scored on a 9-yard burst, and Southern defeated the Indians, 55-13. The Tigers rushed for 306 yards. Feudale ran for 168 yards and a score. Marks rushed for 50 yards and a touchdown and added a scoring catch. Lupold had 13 yards rushing and two touchdowns. Marzeski added 15 yards on the ground and had a scoring run. Becker threw for 123 yards and two touchdowns. Rarig had 23 receiving yards and a scoring catch.

The Selinsgrove Seals visited Tiger Stadium in week six. Nick Becker hit Blake Marks for a 35-yard touchdown pass, Marks scored from 3 yards out, Becker hooked up with Marks on a 43-yard scoring pass, and Becker fired a 34-yard scoring strike to Zach Tillett as Southern took a 33-0 lead after one. Becker and Tillett connected again on a 50-yard touchdown pass, and Nate Hunter plowed in from one yard out to push the Tigers' lead to 47-0 at the half. Billy Marzeski capped the Tigers' scoring with a 12-yard third-quarter touchdown run, and Southern easily handled the Seals, 55-14. The Tigers rushed for 402 yards and had 621 yards of total offense. Feudale ran for 178 yards and a touchdown. Marks ran for 60 yards and a score. He also had two touchdown receptions. Marzeski added 30 rushing yards and a score. Hunter chipped in with five rushing yards and a touchdown run. Becker passed for 219 yards and four touchdowns. Tillett had 84 receiving yards and two scoring catches.

The Tigers faced Bloomsburg in a home game with the Panthers. Nate Hunter and Adam Feudale had first-quarter touchdown runs of 4 and 21 yards as Southern jumped to a 14-0 lead. Luke Rarig booted a 34-yard field goal, and Feudale raced 34 yards for a score as the Tigers took a 24-0 lead into the half. Blake Marks plowed in from 2 yards out, and Feudale scored his third touchdown of the game on a 34-yard run to increase the lead to 38-0 after three. Billy Marzeski scored on a 2-yard run, and Brad Noll finished off the Panthers with a 58-yard jaunt as Southern defeated Bloomsburg, 50-13. The Tigers rushed for 401 yards. Feudale ran for 145 yards and three scores. Hunter had 88 yards rushing and a touchdown. Noll added 66 yards on the ground and a score. Marks rushed for 42 yards and a touchdown. Marzeski ran for 34 yards and had a scoring run.

Southern visited Shamokin for a matchup with Indians. Nick Becker hit Zach Tillett on a 33-yard scoring pass for a 7-0 first-quarter lead. Matt Lupold scored on runs of 10 and 2 yards, Becker fired a 9-yard touchdown pass to Cody Pavlick, Nate Hunter rumbled for an 8-yard score, and the Tigers led 35-0 at the half. Blake Marks and Brad Noll had touchdown runs of 10 and 8 yards in the third. Noll capped the scoring with a 5-yard scoring burst in the fourth, and Southern shutout the Indians, 56-0. The defense held Shamokin to zero passing yards and just 69 total yards of offense. Noll led the rushing attack with 62 yards and two touchdowns. Lupold ran for 59 yards and had two scoring runs. Hunter rushed for 28 yards and a touchdown. Marks added 18 yards on the ground and a score. Becker threw for 148 yards and two touchdowns. Tillett had 33 receiving yards and a touchdown reception. Pavlick contributed 9 yards receiving and a scoring catch.

The Tigers faced Central Columbia in the final road game of the season. Matt Lupold ran for a 7-yard touchdown, and Adam Feudale had scoring runs of one and 3 yards as Southern built a 21-6 lead after one. In the second, the defense recorded a safety, Luke Rarig returned a punt 46 yards for a touchdown, Nick Becker found Blake Marks for a 25-yard scoring pass, and the Tigers led 37-6 at the intermission. Lupold plowed in from one yard out in the third, and the Tigers handled the Blue Jays, 44-12. Feudale rushed for 55 yards and a touchdown. Lupold ran for 42 yards and a score. Becker passed for 136 yards and had a scoring throw to Marks.

The Warrior Run Defenders visited Tiger Stadium in the regular-season finale. Adam Feudale got things started with a bang, returning the opening kickoff 85 yards for a touchdown. Luke Rarig took an interception back 61 yards for a pick six, Ken Fegley returned a blocked punt 8 yards for a score, Nate Hunter pounded in from one yard out, and Southern led 26-0 after the opening quarter. Nick Becker hit Rarig for an 82-yard touchdown pass, Matt Lupold scored on a 4-yard run, and Feudale raced 69 yards for a touchdown as the Tigers took a 47-0 lead into halftime. The Defenders scored two late touchdowns to make the final score 47-13. Feudale ran for 117 yards and two scores. Hunter rushed for 33 yards and a touchdown. Lupold had 11 rushing yards and had a scoring run. Becker threw for 129 yards and a touchdown. Rarig had 111 yards receiving and a touchdown reception. The defense controlled Warrior Run with four interceptions.

The Tigers faced Bloomsburg in the District IV Class A Semifinal Game at Tiger Stadium. Adam Feudale got things started with a one-yard scoring dive in the first for a 7-0 lead. Nate Hunter and Feudale had touchdown runs of 4 and 40 yards, and Southern led 21-7 at the break. Feudale scored on runs of 10 and 14 yards in the third to push the lead to 35-14. Feudale and Matt Jeremiah had touchdown runs of 25 and 4 yards in the fourth, and the Tigers advanced with a 49-14 victory. Southern rushed for 404 yards. Feudale led the way with 180 yards and five touchdowns. Hunter added 73 yards on the ground and a scoring run. Jeremiah ran for 13 yards and a touchdown.

Southern hosted South Williamsport in the District IV Class A Championship Game. Cody Pavlick recovered a Mountaineer fumble to set up Adam Feudale's 5-yard touchdown run for a 7-0 Tiger lead. Nick Becker threw a 35-yard pass to Luke Rarig, and Southern led 14-0 after one. Matt Lupold (31 yards), Nate Hunter (5 yards), and Blake Marks (10 yards) each had second-quarter touchdown runs, and the Tigers took a 35-7 lead into the half. Becker and Rarig hooked up again on a 27-yard touchdown pass, and Feudale rumbled 43 yards for a score as Southern defeated South Williamsport, 49-14. The Tigers had 401 rushing yards. Feudale ran for 219 yards and two touchdowns. Lupold rushed for 80 yards and a score. Hunter had 28 yards on the ground and had a scoring run. Marks had 28 rushing yards and a touchdown. Becker threw for 119 yards and two scores. Rarig had 96 receiving yards and two touchdown receptions. With the victory, the Tigers claimed their 22nd District IV Class A Championship.

The Tigers faced Old Forge in Coal Township in the first round of the PIAA Class A Playoffs. Nate Hunter and Adam Feudale scored first-quarter touchdowns on runs of 4 and 9 yards, and Southern jumped to a 14-0 lead. Unfortunately, after the promising start, the Tigers struggled to find sustained offensive success. The Blue Devils scored 19 unanswered points and advanced with a 19-14 victory. Southern's undefeated regular season and district championship ended with an opening-round loss in the PIAA playoffs for the second straight year. Feudale rushed for 107 yards and a touchdown. Hunter ran for 34 yards and a score.

During the 2013 season, Adam Feudale rushed for 1,625 yards and 25 touchdowns. Blake Marks ran for 533 yards and eight scores. Nate Hunter had 512 rushing yards and 11 touchdowns. Matt Lupold had 482 yards on the ground, and eight scoring runs. Southern had touchdown runs from Billy Marzeski (5), Brad Noll (4), Matt Jeremiah (2), and Nick Becker (1). Nick Becker passed for 1,547 yards and 20 touchdowns. Luke Rarig had 668 receiving yards and eight scores. The Tigers had touchdown receptions from Blake Marks (5), Nate Hunter (3), Zach Tillett (3), and Cody Pavlick (1). Rarig kicked 53 extra points and one field goal. Pavlick recorded 139 tackles (40 solo). Robert Delbo totaled 115 tackles (31 solo). Mitch Stanziale registered eight sacks. Rarig had

## 2013 SEASON

| Opponent | Location | W/L | Score |
|---|---|---|---|
| Pius X | Home | W | 55-28 |
| Montgomery | Away | W | 58-6 |
| Mount Carmel | Away | W | 45-7 |
| South Williamsport | Home | W | 48-14 |
| Muncy | Away | W | 55-13 |
| Selinsgrove | Home | W | 54-14 |
| Bloomsburg | Home | W | 50-13 |
| Shamokin | Away | W | 56-0 |
| Central Columbia | Away | W | 44-12 |
| Warrior Run | Home | W | 47-13 |
| **District IV Class A Semifinal Game** | | | |
| Bloomsburg | Home | W | 49-14 |
| **District IV Class A Championship Game** | | | |
| South Williamsport | Home | W | 47-21 |
| **PIAA Class A Playoff Game** | | | |
| Old Forge | Neutral | L | 14-19 |

COACHING STAFF: Jim Roth, Head Coach; Jason Campbell, Assistant Coach; Randall Campbell, Assistant Coach; Alex Carawan, Assistant Coach; Al Cihocki, Assistant Coach; Tom Donlan, Assistant Coach; Troy Heath, Assistant Coach; Andy Helwig, Assistant Coach; Mike Johnston, Assistant Coach; John Marks, Assistant Coach; Andy Mills, Assistant Coach; Roger Nunkester, Assistant Coach; Nate Roadarmel, Assistant Coach; Pete Saylor, Assistant Coach; Rick Steele, Assistant Coach; Assistant Coach; Dewey Townsend, Assistant Coach; Brandon Traugh, Assistant Coach; Don Traugh, Assistant Coach

ATHLETIC DIRECTOR: Jim Roth

ROSTER: Sami Abdul, Nick Becker, Matt Bell, Grayson Belles, Andrew Bendas, Jared Brezinski, Brandon Cox, Aaron Crawford, Mitchell Croal, Ross Crowl, Elias Deitrick, Gabe Delbo, Robert Delbo, Trent Donlan, Collyn Drake, Matt Fabian, Ken Fegley, Adam Feudale, Angelo Forti, Nick Freeman, Chris Grosch, Dylan Herr, Dale Houser, Nate Hunter, Dean Ivey, Tom Ivey, Patrick Jarvelin, Matt Jeremiah, Mike Klebon, Dylan Kranzel, Aaron Kroh, Matt Lupold, Blake Marks, Billy Marzeski, Adam Mommo, Kyle Mostic, Brad Noll, Cody Pavlick, Mason Peters, Jacob Potter, Luke Rarig, Logan Reynolds, Brandon Richendrfer, Jacob Ryan, Garett Sosnoski, Matt Srednicki, John Stanishefski, Mitch Stanziale, Virgil Sudol, Chase Tillett, Zach Tillett, Steve Toczylousky, Jared Torres, Josh Tripp, Alex Valencik, Jason Vought, Charles Wertman, Austin Wilcox, Josh Yoder five interceptions. Pavlick, Rarig, and Josh Tripp were All-State selections. Southern finished 2013 with an overall record of 12-1.

**2**
**0**
**1**
**4**

In 2014 the Southern Columbia Tigers moved up in classification and would play their first season in AA. Coach Roth prepared his team to face larger schools in postseason competition. The Tigers opened the season on the road against Mifflinburg. Nick Becker found Luke Rarig for a 12-yard touchdown pass for the first points of the year and a 7-0 lead. Matt Jeremiah scored from one yard out, and Southern led 14-0 after one. Hunter Thomas and Becker scored on runs of one and 7 yards, and the Tigers took a 26-0 lead into the break. Jeremiah and Brad Noll had touchdown runs of 24 and 2 yards in the third quarter as Southern defeated the Wildcats, 40-14. The Tigers rushed for 328 yards. Jeremiah ran for 97 yards and two touchdowns. Thomas rushed for 82 yards and a score. Noll had 61 rushing yards and a touchdown. Becker threw for 79 yards and a touchdown and added a scoring run. Rarig had 12 yards receiving and a touchdown reception.

Southern faced Bloomsburg in the home opener. Matt Jeremiah raced 17 yards for a touchdown, and Southern led 7-0 after the opening period. Blake Marks rumbled 58 yards for a score, Nick Becker hit Steve Toczylousky on a 28-yard touchdown pass, and Marks scored from 3 yards out to push the lead to 28-0 at the break. Jeremiah ran 54 yards for a score, Brad Noll raced 49 yards for a touchdown, and Southern led 41-0 after three. Sami Abdul capped the scoring with a 12-yard touchdown run in the fourth, and the Tigers shutout Bloomsburg, 47-0. Southern ran for 362 yards for the game. Jeremiah ran for 80 yards and two scores. Marks, who returned wearing a flak jacket to protect a bruised kidney, rushed for 76 yards and two touchdowns. Noll had 71 yards rushing and a scoring run. Abdul chipped in with 12 rushing yards and a touchdown. Becker passed for 123 yards and a score. Toczylousky had 28 receiving yards and a touchdown reception. The victory proved costly as receiver Luke Rarig was lost for the season with a knee injury.

The Tigers continued to roll in a home game against Shamokin. Blake Marks scored on an 8-yard burst, and Southern led 7-6 after one. Marks and Matt Jeremiah scored on runs of 3 and 11 yards, and Steve Toczylousky returned a punt 69 yards for a touchdown as the Tigers took a 25-7 lead into halftime. Jeremiah (3 yards), Marks (10 yards), and Jacob Potter (10 yards) each had touchdown runs in the third to push the lead to 46-7. Potter capped the scoring with an 18-yard scamper in the fourth, and Southern defeated the Indians, 52-14. The Tigers ran for 324 yards. Hunter Thomas topped the century mark with 113 yards rushing. Marks rushed for 52 yards and three touchdowns. Jeremiah ran for 51 yards and two scores. Potter had 45 rushing yards and two touchdowns.

Southern traveled to Danville for a week four battle with the Ironmen. Hunter Thomas scored on a one-yard dive, and the Tigers led 6-0 after the opening period. Nick Becker fired a 26-yard touchdown pass to Hunter, Matt Jeremiah rumbled 20 yards for a score, and Becker snuck in from one yard out to give the Tigers a 25-0 halftime lead. Becker hit Blake Marks for a 49-yard touchdown, Thomas raced 60 yards for a score, and Southern led 39-0 after three. Billy Marzeski finished off the Ironmen with an 88-yard scoring burst in the fourth and Southern shutout Danville, 46-0. The Tigers pounded out 347 yards on the ground. Thomas ran for 92 yards and two scores. He also had a touchdown reception. Jeremiah had 89 rushing yards, Marzeski rushed for 88, and they each had a scoring run. Becker threw for 144 yards and two scores and also ran for a touchdown. Marks had a scoring reception.

Central Columbia hosted the Tigers in week five. Matt Jeremiah ran 5 yards for a score, and Blake Marks raced 52 yards for a touchdown as Southern led 14-7 after one. Marks and Hunter Thomas scored on runs of 9 and 6 yards, and Nick Becker found Steve Toczylousky on a 17-yard touchdown pass, and the Tigers built a 35-7 halftime lead. Marks scored on a 3-yard run in the third as the Tigers downed the Blue Jays, 42-21. Southern rushed for 307 yards. Marks ran for 105 yards and three touchdowns. Jeremiah rushed for 61 yards and a score. Thomas had 45 rushing yards and a scoring run. Becker passed for 107 yards and a score. Toczylousky had 29 receiving yards and a touchdown reception.

Southern continued their winning ways in a road game versus Mount Carmel. Hunter Thomas and Matt Jeremiah scored on runs of 55 and one yard, and Nick Becker hit Mike Klebon for a 65-yard touchdown pass, and the Tigers opened up a 21-0 first-quarter lead. Becker scored on touchdown runs of 5 and 7 yards, and Marks scored from 5 yards out as Southern led 42-0 at the break. Jeremiah and Billy Marzeski scored on runs of 27 and 33 yards in the third, and the Tigers beat the Red Tornadoes, 55-13. Southern rumbled for 325 yards on the ground. Thomas ran for 82 yards and a score. Jeremiah rushed for 61 yards and two touchdowns. Marzeski added 59 yards on the ground and a scoring run. Marks ran for 40 yards and a score. Becker threw for 109 yards and a touchdown. Klebon had 65 receiving yards and a touchdown reception.

The Tigers played their fourth straight road game versus Warrior Run. Blake Marks recovered a fumble and returned it 16-yards for the opening score.

Hunter Thomas raced 45 yards for a touchdown, and Southern led 14-0 after one. Matt Jeremiah and Thomas scored on runs of 8 and 9 yards, and Marks hauled in a touchdown pass from Nick Becker as the Tigers built a 35-0 lead at the half. Jeremiah rumbled 30 yards for a touchdown, and Mike Klebon returned an interception 28 yards for a score to push the lead to 50-0 after three. Billy Marzeski capped the scoring in the fourth with a 7-yard touchdown run as Southern shutout the Defenders, 57-0. Jeremiah rushed for 110 yards and two scores. Thomas ran for 60 yards and two touchdowns. Marzeski added 49 rushing yards and a scoring run. Becker passed for 120 yards and threw a touchdown pass to Marks.

Southern returned home for a week eight matchup with Lewisburg. Matt Jeremiah ran for a 10-yard touchdown in the first, and the game was tied 7-7 at halftime. Jeremiah and Hunter Thomas scored on runs of 8 and 2 yards as the Tigers took a 21-7 lead after three. Becker scored on an 11-yard jaunt, and Tyler Keiser connected on a 34-yard field goal as Southern downed the Green Dragons, 31-14. The Tigers rushed for 434 yards. Jeremiah ran for 123 yards and two touchdowns. Thomas had 108 rushing yards and a scoring run. Becker threw for 43 yards and had a rushing touchdown.

The Central Columbia Blue Jays visited Tiger Stadium in a week nine contest. Brad Noll opened the scoring with a 13-yard touchdown run, and Steve Toczylousky returned a punt 75 yards for a score as Southern opened up a 14-0 first-quarter lead. Billy Barnes returned a blocked punt 5 yards for a touchdown, Blake Marks scored from 2 yards out, Nick Becker found Mike Klebon for a 20-yard touchdown pass, and Barnes picked off a Blue Jay pass and returned it 43 yards for a pick six as the Tigers jumped to a 42-0 lead at the break. Jarred Torres pounded in from the one in the third and Billy Marzeski raced 45 yards for a score in the fourth, and Southern pounded Central Columbia, 55-13. Marzeski rushed for 56 yards and a touchdown. Torres ran for 55 yards and a score. Noll had 16 yards rushing and a scoring run. Blake Marks contributed a touchdown run. Becker threw for 118 yards and a touchdown. Klebon had 83 receiving yards and a scoring catch.

Southern took on Selinsgrove in the regular-season finale at Tiger Stadium. Matt Jeremiah scored on a 6-yard run, but Southern trailed the Seals 14-7 after one. Nick Becker hit Jeremiah on a 16-yard touchdown pass to pull the Tigers even at the half. Jeremiah put Southern back in front 21-14 with a one-yard plunge in the third. Selinsgrove tied the game with a touchdown early in the fourth. Jeremiah scored his fourth touchdown of the game with a 44-yard run late in the final period to give the Tigers a 28-21 lead. The Seals mounted one last drive, but Billy Barnes preserved the Southern victory with an interception with 21 seconds left in the game. Jeremiah rushed for 167 yards and three touchdowns, and he had a scoring reception. Becker passed for 105 yards and a touchdown.

The Tigers hosted Hughesville in the District IV Class AA Quarterfinal Game. Steve Toczylousky scored on a 4-yard run, and Southern led 7-6 after the first period. Toczylousky rumbled 28 yards for a touchdown, and Nick Becker hit Brad Noll on a 7-yard scoring pass to push the lead to 21-6 at the intermission. Toczylousky scored on a 5-yard dive in the third. Billy Marzeski finished off the Spartans in the fourth with a 51-yard touchdown run as the Tigers advanced with a 35-13 victory. Southern rumbled for 459 yards on the ground. Matt Jeremiah ran for 171 yards. Toczylousky totaled 138 rushing yards and

## 2014 SEASON

| Opponent | Location | W/L | Score |
|----------|----------|-----|-------|
| Mifflinburg | Away | W | 40-14 |
| Bloomsburg | Home | W | 47-0 |
| Shamokin | Home | W | 52-14 |
| Danville | Away | W | 48-0 |
| Central Columbia | Away | W | 42-21 |
| Mount Carmel | Away | W | 55-13 |
| Warrior Run | Away | W | 57-0 |
| Lewisburg | Home | W | 31-14 |
| Central Mountain | Home | W | 55-13 |
| Selinsgrove | Home | W | 28-21 |
| **District IV Class AA Semifinal Game** | | | |
| Hughesville | Home | W | 35-13 |
| **District IV Class AA Championship Game** | | | |
| Montoursville | Home | L | 14-25 |

COACHING STAFF: Jim Roth, Head Coach; Jason Campbell, Assistant Coach; Randall Campbell, Assistant Coach; Alex Carawan, Assistant Coach; Al Cihocki, Assistant Coach; Tom Donlan, Assistant Coach; Troy Heath, Assistant Coach; Andy Helwig, Assistant Coach; Mike Johnston, Assistant Coach; Curt Jones, Assistant Coach; John Marks, Assistant Coach; Andy Mills, Assistant Coach; Roger Nunkester, Assistant Coach; Nate Roadarmel, Assistant Coach; Pete Saylor, Assistant Coach; Rick Steele, Assistant Coach; Assistant Coach; Dewey Townsend, Assistant Coach; Brandon Traugh, Assistant Coach; Don Traugh, Assistant Coach

ATHLETIC DIRECTOR: Jim Roth

ROSTER: Sami Abdul, Jacob Bainbridge, Billy Barnes, Nick Becker, Andrew Bell, Matt Bell, Grayson Belles, Tyler Bendas, Logan Bittner, Jared Brezinski, Colby Carl, William Clark, Michael Conner, Jeffrey Cox, Mitchell Croal, Ross Crowl, Blake Day, Justin Derk, Elias Deitrick, Gabe Delbo, Justin Derk, Trent Donlan, Matt Fabian, Nicholas Fetterman, Nick Freeman, Anthony Girardi, Chris Grosch, Garrett Henry, Dylan Herr, Dale Houser, Dean Ivey, Tommy Ivey, Matt Jeremiah, Nathan Kehoe, Tyler Keiser, Mike Klebon, Dylan Kranzel, Aaron Kroh, Blake Marks, Billy Marzeski, Adam Mommo, Kyle Mostic, Brad Noll. Jacob Potter, Luke Rarig, Brandon Richendrfer, Jacob Ryan, Matt Sredniski, Virgil Sudol, Hunter Thomas, Chase Tillett, Steve Toczylousky, Jared Torres, Jason Vought, Charles Wertman, Austin Wilcox, Joshua Yoder, Cameron Young three touchdowns. Marzeski rushed for 73 yards and a score. Becker threw for 47 yards and a touchdown to Noll.

Southern faced Montoursville in the District IV Class AA Semifinal game at Tiger Stadium. After a scoreless first quarter, Nick Becker snuck in from one yard out, but the Tigers trailed 13-7 at the half. Becker found Mike Klebon for a 6-yard touchdown pass in the fourth, but the Warriors scored 13 second-half points to eliminate the Tigers, 25-14. Becker threw for 175 yards and a touchdown to Klebon, and he had a scoring run.

In 2014, Matt Jeremiah ran for 1,096 yards and 17 touchdowns. Hunter Thomas rushed for 685 yards and eight scores. The Tigers had touchdowns runs from Blake Marks (10), Billy Marzeski (5), Nick Becker (4), Brad Noll (3), Steve Toczylousky (3), Jacob Potter (2), Jared Torres (2), and Sami Abdul (1). Nick Becker passed for 1,289 yards and 11 touchdowns. Southern had touchdown receptions from Mike Klebon (3), Blake Marks (2), Steve Toczylousky (2), and one each from Matt Jeremiah, Brad Noll, Luke Rarig, and Hunter Thomas. Tyler Keiser kicked 56 extra points and one field goal. Billy Barnes recorded 105 tackles (48 solo) and six sacks. Barnes and Steve Toczylousky each registered four interceptions. Barnes and Trent Donlan were All-State selections. The 2014 Tigers finished the season with an 11-1 record.

**2015** The disappointing ending to the 2014 season motivated the Tigers as they prepared for the 2015 campaign. With their ever-present ground attack and an experienced quarterback under center, Southern looked to make a deep postseason run and return to glory. The Tigers opened the year with a home game against Mifflinburg. Early in the first, Steve Toczylousky sacked the Wildcats' quarterback, causing a fumble that was picked up by Chase Tillett and returned 36 yards for the opening touchdown. Jarred Torres scored from 5 yards out before a Mifflinburg 5-yard touchdown pass, and Southern led 13-7 after one. The Wildcats scored on a 70-yard run and took the lead 14-13 early in the second. Hunter Thomas immediately put the Tigers back in front when he returned the ensuing kickoff 92 yards for a touchdown for a 19-14 Southern lead. Tyler Keiser drilled a 34-yard field goal, and the Tigers took a 22-14 lead into halftime. Southern took control of the game in the third quarter. Torres pounded in from 3 yards out, Thomas raced 42 yards for a score, and Blake Marks rumbled 38 yards for a touchdown as the Tigers opened up a 43-14 lead after three. After a Mifflinburg touchdown run early in the fourth, Nic Fetterman salted the game away with a 3-yard scoring bolt to make the final score 49-21. Southern rushed for 372 yards. Marks led the way with 109 rushing yards and a score. Thomas ran for 77 yards and a touchdown. Torres had 33 yards rushing and two scoring runs. Fetterman chipped in with 9 yards on the ground and a touchdown. Southern would face their first adversity of the year as starting quarterback Nick Becker was taken from the field by ambulance with an injury to his left shoulder.

The Tigers traveled to Bloomsburg for a matchup with the Panthers. Blake Marks opened the scoring with a 73-yard jaunt. Backup quarterback Drew Michaels hit Hunter Thomas for a 58-yard touchdown, and Southern jumped to a 14-0 lead. However, the Panthers cut the lead in half with a 5-yard scoring run. Michaels found Steve Toczylousky on an 18-yard touchdown pass to make it 21-7. Bloomsburg scored on a 39-yard touchdown pass late in the quarter, and the Tigers led 21-13 after one. Thomas scored on runs of 7 and 77 yards to push the lead to 35-13 in the second. Michaels and Toczylousky hooked up again for a 13-yard touchdown pass, and Southern led 42-13 at the break. Thomas returned an interception 39 yards for a score in the third, and Billy Marzeski scampered 9 yards for a touchdown to put the game out of reach at 56-13. The Panthers scored a late touchdown to make the final score 56-19. Southern rushed for 373 yards. Marks ran for 113 yards and a score. Thomas rushed for 112 yards and two touchdowns and had a scoring reception. Marzeski added 10 yards on the ground and a touchdown. Michaels was impressive in his first start, passing for 141 yards and three touchdowns. Toczylousky had 63 receiving yards and two scoring catches.

Nick Becker returned from a separated shoulder after a one-game absence on the road at Shamokin. Jared Torres ran for a 19-yard touchdown early in the opening quarter. Becker got back in the saddle with an 18-yard scoring strike to Hunter Thomas. Austin Knepp picked off an Indian pass and returned it 13 yards for a touchdown. Becker hit Cameron Young for a 17-yard scoring pass, and Southern led 28-0 after one. Shamokin got on the board with a 53-yard run early in the second quarter. Becker hooked up with Thomas again on a 51-yard touchdown pass, and Thomas raced 46-yards for a score to push the lead to 42-7 at the half. Shamokin scored on a 12-yard run in the third and an 81-yard pass play to start the fourth quarter. Thomas Manley rumbled 11 yards for a touchdown, and the Indians capped the scoring with a 22-yard pass. The Tigers defeated Shamokin 49-27. Thomas ran for 67 yards and a score and had two touchdown receptions. Manley rushed for 48 yards and a score. Torres had 44 rushing yards and a scoring run. Becker threw for 151 yards and three touchdowns in his return. Young had 69 receiving yards and a touchdown reception. The Tigers' defense intercepted four Indian passes.

Southern played host to the Danville Ironmen in week four. Blake Marks raced 57 yards to open the scoring. Nick Becker connected with Hunter Thomas for a 14-yard touchdown pass. On the play, Becker became the Tigers' all-time leader in career touchdown passes. Southern led 14-0 after the opening period. The teams played a scoreless second quarter. Thomas scored from 9 yards out early in the third. Danville trimmed the lead to 21-7 with a 9-yard scoring pass. Becker hit Steve Toczylousky for a 47-yard touchdown to up the Tigers' lead to 28-7. Thomas scored his third touchdown of the game on a 4-yard run, and Southern took a 35-7 lead into the fourth. Nic Fetterman ran for a 5-yard touchdown, and the Ironmen capped the scoring with a 3-yard run as the Tigers put the Ironmen away, 42-14. Marks rushed for 99 yards and a score. Thomas ran for 48 yards and two touchdowns and had a scoring catch. Fetterman added 10 rushing yards and a touchdown run. Becker passed for 171 yards and two scores. Toczylousky had 72 yards receiving and a touchdown.

The offense continued to roll in a home game with Central Columbia. Blake Marks plowed in from 5 yards out, Hunter Thomas raced 70 yards for a touchdown, and Nick Becker fired a 5-yard scoring strike to Garrett Henry. The Tigers led 21-0 after one. Nic Fetterman ran 6 yards for a score, Thomas rumbled 35 yards for a touchdown, and Jared Torres capped the scoring with a 43-yard jaunt and Southern shutout the Blue Jays, 40-0. The Tigers rushed for 369 yards. Thomas ran for 127 yards and two scores. Torres rushed for 102 yards and a touchdown. Marks had 60 rushing yards and a scoring run. Fetterman added 17 yards on the ground and a touchdown. Becker threw for 128 yards and a score. Henry had a touchdown reception.

Up next for the Tigers was a home game with Mount Carmel. Nick Becker and Steve Toczylousky hooked up for a 68-yard scoring bomb, and Southern jumped out to a 7-0 lead after the first stanza. The Tigers took control of the game in the second quarter. Blake Marks rumbled 12 yards for a score, Jared Torres scored from 7 yards out, and Marks had touchdown runs of one and 17 yards as Southern took a commanding 35-0 lead into the intermission. Hunter Thomas finished the scoring with an 18-yard jaunt in the third, and the Tigers shutout the Red Tornadoes, 42-0. The defense held Mount Carmel to 84 total yards of offense. Torres ran for 68 yards and a touchdown. Marks rushed for 54 yards and three scores. Thomas added 43 rushing yards and a touchdown. Becker threw for 115 yards and a score. Toczylousky hauled in 68 receiving yards and a touchdown reception.

The Warrior Run Defenders visited Tiger Stadium for a week seven contest. Nick Becker and Steve Toczylousky sandwiched touchdown passes of 13 and

78 yards around Blake Marks' 12-yard scoring run for a 21-0 first-quarter lead. Toczylousky and Becker hooked up for a third time on a 29-yard touchdown pass, and Becker hit Cameron Young for a 36-yard scoring strike to push the lead to 35-0 in the second. Hunter Thomas raced 68 yards for a score, and Jared Torres scored from 7 yards out for a 49-0 halftime advantage. In the third, Cole Potter ran 3 yards for a touchdown, and the Defenders scored late in the fourth quarter to make the final 56-7. Thomas ran for 93 yards and a touchdown. Marks had 57 yards and a scoring run. Torres rushed for 35 yards and a touchdown. Potter added 14 rushing yards and a score. Becker passed for 192 yards and four touchdowns. Toczylousky had 120 receiving yards and three scoring receptions.

Tigers traveled to Lewisburg for a road game with the Green Dragons. Blake Marks pounded in from 2 yards out to get Southern on the board. Lewisburg tied the game at 7-7 with a 68-yard pass. Jared Torres put the Tigers back in front with a 48-yard scoring burst. Nick Becker found Hunter Thomas for a 39-yard touchdown pass, and Southern led 21-7 after one. The Green Dragons kicked a 35-yard field goal early in the second. Thomas returned the ensuing kickoff 85 yards for a touchdown to push the lead to 28-10. Marks scored on runs of 3 and 5 yards, and Becker fired a 10-yard touchdown strike to Steve Toczylousky for a 49-10 lead at the break. Lewisburg scored twice in mop-up time, and the Tigers earned a 49-24 victory. Torres ran for 65 yards and a touchdown. Marks rushed for 33 yards and three scores. Becker threw for 110 yards and two touchdowns. Thomas hauled in a scoring catch. Toczylousky had 14 yards receiving and a touchdown reception. The Southern defense held Lewisburg to -43 yards rushing for the game.

Southern made the trek to Central Mountain for a game against the Wildcats. Hunter Thomas scored the only touchdown of the first quarter with a 9-yard run. Nick Becker and Steve Toczylousky hooked up for scoring passes of 57 and 8 yards to up the lead to 21-0 in the second. The Wildcats scored on a 90-yard kickoff return, and Southern led 21-7 at the break. In the third, Toczylousky returned an interception 82 yards for a pick six. Blake Marks and Thomas scored on runs of 10 and 12 yards for a 42-7 Tiger lead. Jacob Potter (10 yards), A.J. Goodlunas (5 yards), and Jeff Cox (12 yards) each had touchdown runs in the fourth as the Tigers routed Central Mountain, 62-7. Southern rushed for 334 yards. Marks ran for 95 yards and a score. Thomas rushed for 87 yards and two touchdowns. Cox had 21 yards rushing and a scoring run. Potter added 17 rushing yards and a touchdown. Goodlunas had 16 yards on the ground and a score. Becker passed for 157 yards and two touchdowns.

Toczylousky had 79 receiving yards and two scores. The Tigers' defense held Central Mountain to -9 yards rushing.

The undefeated Selinsgrove Seals hosted the Tigers in the regular-season finale. Both teams entered the highly anticipated matchup with perfect 9-0 records. Nick Becker threw a 5-yard scoring strike to Blake Marks to open the scoring in the first. Selinsgrove tied the game at 7-7 early in the second quarter with a 36-yard pass. Nick Becker called his own number and scored on a 7-yard keeper to put the Tigers back in front. However, the Seals rumbled 53 yards for the tying score. Marks scored from 4 yards out to give Southern a 21-14 lead at halftime. The game became a defensive battle in the second half. The Tigers registered three interceptions, two by Cameron Young, and Southern made the lead stand and defeated Selinsgrove, 21-14. Marks rushed for 62 yards and had a scoring run. Becker threw for 68 yards and a scoring pass to Marks. He also had a touchdown run.

Southern faced off against Troy in the District IV Class AA Quarterfinal Game at Tiger Stadium. Hunter Thomas raced 33 yards for the opening score, and the Tigers led 7-0 after one. Jared Torres ran 13 yards for a touchdown early in the second. Thomas pushed the lead to 21-0 with a one-yard plunge. Nick Becker hit Steve Toczylousky for a 29-yard touchdown pass, and Torres scored from 2 yards out to extend the Tigers' lead to 35-0 at the intermission. Troy scored on an 84-yard run, Thomas rumbled 55 yards for a touchdown, and Southern led 42-7 after three. The Trojans scored twice in the fourth quarter to make the final score 42-22. The Tigers rushed for 345 yards. Thomas ran for 134 yards and three scores. Torres had 97 rushing yards and two touchdowns. Becker threw for 103 yards and had a scoring pass. Toczylousky had 83 receiving yards and a touchdown reception.

The Tigers hosted Hughesville in the District IV Class AA Semifinal Game. The Spartans scored first on a 19-yard run, but Southern quickly recovered. Billy Marzeski returned the ensuing kickoff 72 yards to tie the game at 7-7. Hunter Thomas put the Tigers in front with an 81-yard scoring burst. Thomas scored again on a 5-yard run to give Southern a 21-7 lead after one. Nick Becker found Steve Toczylousky for a 26-yard touchdown pass. On the play, Toczylousky set the team record for touchdown receptions in a season with 12, breaking the previous mark set by Andy Helwig in 1995. Becker then connected with Cameron Young for a 13-yard scoring strike. Jared Torres closed out the first-half scoring with a 20-yard jaunt, and Southern led 42-7 at the break. Hughesville opened the second half with a 96-yard touchdown pass. Blake Marks and Thomas answered with scoring runs of 63 and 46 yards to push the lead to 56-14 after three. The Spartans scored a fourth-quarter touchdown to bring the final score to 56-20. The Tigers rushed for a whopping 505 yards. Thomas ran for 163 yards and three scores. Torres rushed for 117 yards and a touchdown. Marks had 84 rushing yards and a scoring run. Becker threw for 78 yards and two scores. Toczylousky had 35 receiving yards and a touchdown. Young hauled in 25 yards receiving and a scoring catch.

Southern faced Montoursville in a showdown for the District IV Class AA Championship Game at Tiger Stadium. The Tigers jumped to a 14-0 first-quarter lead on touchdown runs of 8 and 17 yards by Jared Torres and Hunter Thomas. Early in the second, the Warriors cut the lead in half on a 7-yard run. Thomas pushed the lead to 21-7 with an 80-yard touchdown burst. Montoursville returned the ensuing kickoff 90 yards for a score to make it 21-13. Nick Becker snuck in from one yard out to give the Tigers a 29-13 lead. The Warriors scored twice on runs of one and 20 yards, and the game was tied 29-29 at halftime. In the third, Cameron Young intercepted a pass and returned it 33 yards for a score. Montoursville answered back with an 8-yard touchdown run. Torres ran for an 8-yard touchdown only to see the Warriors score from one yard out, and the game was stalemated at 43-43. Thomas opened the fourth quarter with a 15-yard touchdown run. Montoursville again answered the bell and tied the game at 50-50 with a 2-yard scoring dive. Southern took possession with 8:36 left in regulation. The Tigers put together a scoring drive capped off by Thomas' 2-yard touchdown plunge to take a 56-50 lead. The Warriors mounted one final drive and moved the ball to their own 48-yard line. With 90 seconds left and Montoursville facing a 4th and 8, Austin Knepp and Matt Bell broke through and sacked the Warriors' quarterback to preserve the Tigers' victory. Southern rushed for 470 yards. Thomas ran for 243 yards and three scores. Torres added 119 rushing yards and two touchdowns. Becker had two scoring runs. The Tigers won their first Class AA District Championship.

The Tigers advanced to the PIAA Class AA Quarterfinal Game against Berks Catholic in Shillington. Nick Becker scored on a 6-yard keeper for a 7-0 lead after one. Blake Marks pounded in from 2 yards out to push the lead to 13-0 in the second. The Saints scored on a 4-yard run before the half to cut the Tigers' lead to 13-7. Jared Torres opened the third quarter with a 7-yard touchdown scamper. Berks Catholic recovered a Southern fumble in the end-zone for a touchdown and then scored on a 4-yard pass to tie the game at 21-21 after three. Becker rumbled 18 yards for a score to take a 28-21 lead. Hunter Thomas finally iced the game with a 74-yard touchdown run, and the Tigers outlasted the Saints, 34-21. Thomas ran for 145 yards and a touchdown. He also had 118 receiving yards. Torres rushed for 35 yards and a score. Marks had 31 rushing yards and a scoring run. Becker threw for 220 yards and had two rushing touchdowns.

Southern moved on to face West Catholic in the PIAA Class AA Semifinal Game in Slatington. The game got off to an ominous start as the Burrs returned the opening kickoff 84 yards for a touchdown, and West Catholic took a 7-0 lead after one. The Tigers answered back early in the second when Nick Becker hit Blake Marks for a 19-yard touchdown pass to tie the game at 7-7. The Burrs reclaimed the lead with a 21-yard scoring pass. Becker plowed in from 3 yards out, and Southern led 14-13 at the break. West Catholic went back in front with a 32-yard touchdown pass for a 19-14 lead after three. Becker scored on a 5-yard keeper in the fourth to put Southern back on top 20-19. Marks pushed the lead to 27-19 with a 12-yard jaunt. Becker sealed the win with a 12-yard keeper, and Southern defeated West Catholic, 34-19. The Tigers rushed for 420 yards. Thomas ran for 113 yards. Marks had 94 yards rushing and a touchdown. Becker threw for 91 yards and a touchdown pass to Marks. He also ran for three scores.

The Tigers advanced to their first PIAA Class AA Championship Game. They reached their first state final game since 2011. Southern would face Aliquippa at Hersheypark Stadium. The Quips opened the scoring with a one-yard plunge for a 6-0 lead. Jared Torres got Southern on the board with a 3-yard touchdown run and put the Tigers in front 7-6. Nick Becker scored on a 15-yard keeper early in the second quarter. Billy Mazerski returned an interception 38 yards for a touchdown to push the lead to 21-6. Aliquippa closed the gap to 21-14 with a 44-yard pass. Becker raced 30 yards for a touchdown, and the Tigers led 28-14 at halftime. Torres plowed in from one yard out to up the lead to 35-14 after three. Hunter Thomas finished off the Quips with touchdown runs of one and 10 yards in the fourth quarter, and the Southern Columbia Tigers won the 2015 PIAA Class AA Championship with a 49-14 victory. The Tigers became the first team to win seven PIAA State Football Championships. It was Southern first title since 2006 and their first since moving up in classification to AA. The Tigers finished with a 16-0 record, joining the 1994, 2004, and 2006 teams as undefeated state champions. Tyler Keiser set a Class AA Championship Game record with seven extra points. The Southern defense set a PIAA Championship Game record by registering seven turnovers. The Tigers had three interceptions (two by Billy Marzeski) and four fumble recoveries. Thomas ran for 59 yards and two scores. Torres rushed for 50 yards and two touchdowns. Becker threw for 82 yards and had two scoring runs.

The 2015 State Champion Southern Columbia Tigers had several outstanding performances. Hunter Thomas rushed for 1,623 yards and 24 touchdowns. Blake Marks ran for 1,080 yards and 16 scores. Jared Torres had 998 rushing yards and 15 scoring runs. Southern had touchdown runs from Nick Becker (10), Nic Fetterman (3), and one each from Jeff Cox, A.J. Goodlunas, Thomas

## 2015 SEASON

| Opponent | Location | W/L | Score |
|----------|----------|-----|-------|
| Mifflinburg | Home | W | 49-21 |
| Bloomsburg | Away | W | 56-19 |
| Shamokin | Away | W | 49-27 |
| Danville | Home | W | 42-14 |
| Central Columbia | Home | W | 40-0 |
| Mount Carmel | Home | W | 42-0 |
| Warrior Run | Home | W | 56-7 |
| Lewisburg | Away | W | 49-24 |
| Central Mountain | Away | W | 62-7 |
| Selinsgrove | Away | W | 21-14 |
| **District IV Class AA Semifinal Game** | | | |
| Troy | Home | W | 42-22 |
| **District IV Class AA Championship Game** | | | |
| Hughesville | Home | W | 56-20 |
| **PIAA Class AA Playoff Game** | | | |
| Montoursville | Home | W | 56-50 |
| **PIAA Class AA Quarterfinal Game** | | | |
| Berks Catholic | Neutral | W | 34-21 |
| **PIAA Class AA Semifinal Game** | | | |
| West Catholic | Neutral | W | 34-19 |
| **PIAA Class AA Championship Game** | | | |
| Aliquippa | Neutral | W | 49-14 |

COACHING STAFF: Jim Roth Head Coach; Jason Campbell, Assistant Coach; Randall Campbell, Assistant Coach; Alex Carawan, Assistant Coach; Al Cihocki, Assistant Coach; Tom Donlan, Assistant Coach; Troy Heath, Assistant Coach; Andy Helwig, Assistant Coach; Mike Johnston, Assistant Coach; Curt Jones, Assistant Coach; John Marks, Assistant Coach; Andy Mills, Assistant Coach; Roger Nunkester, Assistant Coach; Nate Roadarmel, Assistant Coach; Pete Saylor, Assistant Coach; Rick Steele, Assistant Coach; Assistant Coach; Brandon Traugh, Assistant Coach; Don Traugh, Assistant Coach

ATHLETIC DIRECTOR: Jim Roth

ROSTER: Sami Abdul, Jeff Achy, Nick Becker, Duncan Bedford, Andrew Bell, Matt Bell, Tyler Bendas, Logan Bittner, Colby Carl, Jeffrey Cox, Mitchell Croal, Ross Crowl, Sydney Damgaard, Blake Day, Elias Deitrick, Gabe Delbo, Justin Derk, Troy Donlan, Nic Fetterman, Nick Freeman, Connor Fulmer, Anthony Girardi, A.J. Goodlunas, Cavern Gosciminski, Chris Grosch, Andrew Haupt, Tristan Heim, Cole Helwig, Garrett Henry, Dylan Herr, Dale Houser, Dean Ivey, Tommy Ivey, Nathan Kehoe, Tyler Keiser, Austin Knepp, Dylan Kranzel, Aaron Kroh, Thomas Manley, Blake Marks, Billy Marzeski, Drew Michaels, Cole Potter, Jacob Potter, Anthony Scicchitano, Oak Six, Matt Srednicki, Virgil Sudol, Hunter Thomas, Chase Tillett, Steve Toczylousky, Jared Torres, Joshua Yoder, Cameron Young

Manley, Billy Marzeski, Cole Potter, and Jacob Potter. Nick Becker threw for 1,756 yards and 20 touchdowns. One of the unsung heroes for the Tigers was Drew Michaels. His steady play during Becker's injury kept Southern's perfect season on track. Michaels passed for 215 yards and three touchdowns. Steve Tczylousky had 754 receiving yards and 12 touchdowns. The Tigers had scoring receptions from Hunter Thomas (5), Cameron Young (3), Blake Marks (2), and Garrett Henry (1). Tyler Keiser kicked 91 extra points and one field goal. Andrew Bell had 128 tackles (32 solo). Austin Knepp totaled 127 tackles (35 solo). Chase Tillett registered eight sacks. Cameron Young recorded eight interceptions. The 2015 Southern Columbia finished with a 16-0 record.

**2015**  Coming off a state championship, Coach Roth's Tigers were confident of another run at the title, even with a new quarterback taking the reins of the offense. Southern opened the season at home versus Shamokin. The defense put up the first points as Cal Haladay returned an interception 25 yards for a touchdown. However, the Indians scored on a 4-yard run, and the game was tied 7-7 after the first. Gaige Garcia rumbled 11 yards for a 13-7 lead. Shamokin took a 14-13 halftime lead with a one-yard scoring dive. Hunter Thomas put the Tigers back in front with a 22-yard burst early in the third. Stone Hollenbach fired a 36-yard touchdown pass to Julian Fleming to make the score 27-13. Fleming then returned a punt 57 yards for a score to make it 33-13. Hollenbach found Cameron Young for a 21-yard touchdown strike, and the Tigers led 40-13 after three. The Indians pulled within 40-20 early in the fourth. Thomas finished off Shamokin with a 15-yard scoring burst, and Southern earned a 47-20 opening-night victory. Garcia ran for 97 yards and a touchdown. Thomas rushed for 90 yards and two scores. Hollenbach threw for 94 yards and a touchdown. Fleming had 36 yards receiving and a touchdown reception. Young contributed 21 receiving yards and a scoring catch.

The Bloomsburg Panthers paid a visit to Tiger Stadium in week two. Hunter Thomas got things going with a 49-yard touchdown jaunt and a 7-0 lead. Bloomsburg scored on an 89-yard pass play to pull within 7-6. Nic Fetterman pounded in from one yard out, and Southern led 14-6 after one. Gaige Garcia scored on a 4-yard dive, and Stone Hollenbach hit Julian Fleming for a 28-yard touchdown pass to push the Tigers' to 28-6. The Panthers returned a kickoff 95 yards for a score to trim the lead to 28-14. Hollenbach scored on a 28-yard keeper, and Garcia ran for touchdowns of 6 and 64 yards for a 49-14 halftime lead. Fleming returned the second-half kickoff 94 yards for a touchdown to up the Southern lead to 56-14. Bloomsburg got a 2-yard scoring run to make it

56-21. Fetterman rumbled 35 yards for a touchdown for a 63-21 margin after three. Southern got a fourth-quarter safety when the Panthers snapped the ball out of the endzone on a punt, and the Tigers defeated Bloomsburg, 65-21. Southern rushed for 367 yards. Garcia ran for 148 yards and three scores. Fetterman added 62 rushing yards and two touchdowns. Thomas rushed for 58 yards and a scoring run. Hollenbach threw for 149 yards and a touchdown. He also had a rushing score. Fleming had 95 receiving yards and a touchdown reception.

Southern traveled to Mount Carmel for the first road contest of the season. Hunter Thomas ran for a 54-yard touchdown and a 7-0 lead. Mount Carmel tied the game with a 4-yard scoring run. Gaige Garcia put the Tigers back in front on a 67-yard romp, and Southern led 14-7 after one. The Red Tornadoes answered with a one-yard touchdown dive and tied the game at 14-14. Mount Carmel took the lead on a 43-yard pass play, but Thomas pulled the Tigers even on a 54-yard touchdown burst. The game was deadlocked at 28-28 at the half. Southern took over the game in the third quarter. Thomas rumbled 31 yards for a score, Garcia raced 74 yards for a touchdown, Stone Hollenbach found Julian Fleming for an 87-yard scoring bomb, and Nic Fetterman ran 27 yards for a touchdown as the Tigers built a 56-28 lead after three. Fetterman scored from 7 yards out, and the Red Tornadoes capped the scoring with a late 19-yard touchdown run. Southern earned a 63-34 victory over Mount Carmel. The Tigers rushed for a staggering 508 yards. Garcia ran for 198 yards and three scores. Thomas tacked on 179 yards rushing and three touchdowns. Fetterman added 77 yards on the ground and two scoring runs. Hollenbach passed for 136 yards and a score. Fleming had 119 receiving yards and a touchdown reception.

Next was a road game versus Hughesville. Gaige Garcia pounded in from 5 yards out, and Stone Hollenbach fired a 65-yard touchdown pass to Hunter Thomas as Southern built a 14-0 first-quarter lead. Garcia rumbled 13 yards for a score, and Hollenbach connected with Julian Fleming on a 27-yard touchdown pass for a 28-0 lead at the break. Cameron Young hauled in a 6-yard touchdown throw from Hollenbach to push the lead to 35-0. The Spartans scored three late touchdowns to bring the final to 35-19. Garcia rushed for 74 yards and two touchdowns. Thomas ran for 44 yards and had a scoring catch. Hollenbach threw for 240 yards and three scores. Young had 47 yards receiving and a touchdown reception. Fleming added 27 receiving yards and a scoring catch.

The Tigers returned home for a matchup with Lewisburg. Gaige Garcia opened the scoring in the first with a one-yard dive and a 7-0 lead. Garcia scored again from one yard out, Thomas Manley had a 3-yard touchdown run, and Cameron Young returned an interception 52 yards for a pick six as Southern comfortably led 28-0 at halftime. Stone Hollenbach hit Young for a 12-yard touchdown pass to cap the scoring. The Tigers shutout the Green Dragons, 35-0. Garcia ran for 80 yards and two scores. Hollenbach passed for 102 yards and a touchdown. Young had 50 yards receiving and a scoring catch. In a postgame ceremony, the playing field at Tiger Stadium was named "Jim Roth Field" in honor of the legendary coach's incredible career at Southern Columbia.

Southern dominated Milton in a week six road game. Gaige Garcia scored on runs of 10 and 39 yards, and Nic Fetterman rumbled for an 18-yard touchdown as the Tigers led 21-0 after one. Garcia pounded in from one yard out, Thomas Manley scored on a 7-yard run, and Garcia raced 83 yards for a touchdown for a 42-0 halftime lead. Ty Roadarmel finished off the Black Panthers with a 2-yard scoring dive in the third and a 9-yard touchdown scamper in the fourth, and the Tigers shutout Milton, 56-0. Southern rushed for 460 yards. Garcia rumbled for 200 yards and four touchdowns. Manley ran for 68 yards and a score. Roadarmel rushed for 63 yards and two touchdowns. Fetterman had 33 rushing yards and a scoring run.

Up next was an away game with Montoursville. Hunter Thomas ran for a 25-yard touchdown, and Cameron Young returned an interception 42 yards for a score and a 14-0 lead. The Warriors scored on a one-yard run to cut the lead in half. However, Julian Fleming returned the ensuing kickoff 95 yards for a touchdown, and Southern took a 21-7 lead at the half. In the third, Fleming returned an interception 87 yards for a pick six to push the lead to 28-7. Montoursville scored on a 55-yard touchdown pass to pull within 28-14 early in the fourth. Stone Hollenbach hit Thomas with a 55-yard scoring pass to put the Tigers up 35-14. The Warriors got a 5-yard touchdown run to pull within 35-21. Garcia finally put away the pesky Warriors with a 42-yard scoring jaunt, and Southern defeated Montoursville, 42-21. Garcia rushed for 111 yards and a score. Thomas ran for 87 yards and a touchdown. Hollenbach threw for 116 yards and a scoring pass to Thomas.

The Tigers continued to roll on the road against Danville. Hunter Thomas rumbled 40 yards for a score, and Stone Hollenbach found Julian Fleming for a 75-yard touchdown pass as Southern built a 14-0 lead after one. The Ironmen trimmed the lead to 14-7 with a 72-yard scoring run to start the second quarter. Gaige Garcia scampered 21 yards for a touchdown, and Fleming and Hollenbach hooked up again for a 9-yard scoring pass to push the lead to 27-7 at the break. Garcia raced 72 yards for a touchdown in the third, and Southern got fourth-quarter scoring runs of one and 5 yards from Thomas and Ty Roadarmel to make the final 47-7. The Tigers ran for 355 yards for the game. Garcia rushed for 128 yards and two scores. Thomas ran for 126 yards and two touchdowns. Roadarmel had 27 rushing yards and a scoring run. Hollenbach threw for 155 yards and two touchdowns. Fleming had 119 receiving yards and two scoring receptions.

Southern entertained Central Columbia in a home game at Jim Roth Field at Tiger Stadium. The Tigers jumped on Central in the first quarter. Hunter Thomas piled in from one yard out, Tyler Bendas blocked a punt out of the endzone for a safety, Stone Hollenbach fired an 11-yard touchdown pass to Garrett Henry, and Gaige Garcia pounded in from a yard out as Southern pulled out to a 21-0 lead. Hollenbach and Henry hooked up again on an 18-yard touchdown pass, and Thomas raced 70 and 11 yards for scores to put the Tigers in front 42-0 at the half. Jeff Cox ran for a 2-yard touchdown in the third, and the Blue Jays avoided a shutout with a touchdown in the fourth to make the final score 49-6. Southern rushed for 382 yards. Thomas ran for 126 yards and three scores. Garcia had 69 rushing yards and a touchdown run. Cox rushed for 42 yards and a score. Hollenbach passed for 128 yards and two touchdowns. Henry had 38 yards receiving and two scoring receptions.

The Tigers played host to the Selinsgrove Seals to close out the regular season. The teams played a scoreless first quarter. Hunter Thomas had scoring runs of 4 and one yard, and Nic Fetterman rumbled 14 yards for a touchdown as Southern built a 21-0 lead in the second. The Seals scored on a one-yard dive to cut the lead to 21-7. Elijah Hoffman nailed a 30-yard field goal to put the Tigers up 24-7 at the intermission. Gaige Garcia scored on an 8-yard burst to push the lead to 31-7 early in the third. Selinsgrove responded with a 24-yard touchdown pass and a 56-yard run to pull within 31-21. Garcia scored on runs of 56 and 20 yards to put Southern up 45-21. Again, the Seals fought back with touchdown runs of 18 and 69 yards to cut the Southern lead to 45-35, heading into the final period. Thomas finally salted the game away with a 25-yard touchdown run in the fourth to give the Tigers a 52-35 victory. Southern rumbled for 469 yards on the ground. Garcia led the way with 216 rushing yards and three scores. Thomas ran for 158 yards and three touchdowns. Fetterman had 70 yards rushing and a scoring run. The victory was the Tigers' 50th consecutive regular-season win.

Southern played Towanda in the District IV Class AA Quarterfinal Game at Tiger Stadium. Julian Fleming hauled in a 23-yard touchdown pass from Stone Hollenbach to open the scoring. Towanda got on the board with a 47-yard run to tie the game at 7-7. Hollenbach fired three touchdowns to Gaige Garcia (20 yards), Cameron Young (34 yards), and Fleming (57 yards) as the Tigers built a 28-7 lead after one. Garcia scored on runs of 10 and 56 yards, and Hunter Thomas ran for a 5-yard touchdown to put Southern up 42-7 in the second. The Black Knights cut the lead to 42-14 with a 72-yard run. Garcia scored on a one-yard plunge, and the Tigers led 56-14 at the half. Towanda had a 17-yard touchdown run in the third to make the score 56-20. Nic Fetterman joined the scoring parade with a 7-yard touchdown run early in the fourth. Towanda scored on a 61-yard pass, Andrew Haupt returned an interception 41 yards for a pick six, and the Black Knights closed the scoring with a 41-yard touchdown run to make the final score 69-34. Southern had a whopping 582 yards of total offense, including 413 on the ground. Garcia ran for 178 yards and three scores. He also had a touchdown reception. Thomas rushed for 133 yards and a touchdown. Fetterman had 39 rushing yards and a scoring run. Hollenbach threw for 158 yards and four scores. Fleming had 89 receiving yards and two touchdown receptions. Young pulled in 49 yards receiving and a scoring catch.

The Tigers hosted Line Mountain in the District IV Class AA Semifinal Game. Stone Hollenbach hit Julian Fleming for a 48-yard touchdown pass, Hunter Thomas rumbled 14 yards for a score, and Southern led 14-0 after the opening quarter. Thomas ran for touchdowns of 21 and 45 yards in the second, and Fleming and Hollenbach hooked up again for a 38-yard scoring pass to put the Tigers up 35-0 at halftime. Thomas raced 74 yards for a third-quarter touchdown, and Gaige Garcia scored on an 80-yard bolt to finish off the Eagles, 49-0. The defense pitched a shutout and had three interceptions and a fumble recovery. Southern rushed for 318 yards. Thomas ran for 172 yards and four scores. Garcia rushed for 108 yards and a touchdown. Hollenbach passed for 145 yards and two touchdowns. Fleming had 94 receiving yards and two scoring catches.

Southern played South Williamsport in the District IV Class AA Championship Game at Jim Roth Field at Tiger Stadium. Stone Hollenbach found Julian Fleming for a 38-yard touchdown pass, and Gaige Garcia rumbled 37 yards for a score to open a 14-0 lead after one. Hollenbach threw touchdown passes of 55 and 25 yards to Hunter Thomas and Fleming, and Garcia scored from 8 yards as Southern pushed the lead to 35-0 at the break. Garcia ran for a 50-yard touchdown to open the third quarter. The Mountaineers got on the board with a 4-yard run. Nic Fetterman went 18-yards for a touchdown run, and the Tigers took a commanding 49-7 lead into the final period. South Williamsport scored two late touchdowns, and the Tigers won their second straight District IV Class AA Championship, 49-21. Garcia rushed for 128 yards and three touchdowns.

Fetterman ran for 58 yards and a score. Hollenbach threw for 127 yards and three scores. Fleming had 63 receiving yards and two touchdown receptions. Thomas chipped in with a scoring catch.

The Tigers advanced to the PIAA Class AA Quarterfinal Game against Schuylkill Haven in Coal Township. Hunter Thomas got Southern off to a quick start by returning the opening kickoff 92 yards for a touchdown. The Hurricanes answered with a 25-yard field goal to cut the lead to 7-3. Stone Hollenbach hit Julian Fleming for a 65-yard touchdown bomb to make the score 14-3 after one. After a scoreless second, Schuylkill Haven was awarded a safety after a Tigers' holding penalty in the endzone to make the score 14-5. Teagan Wilk finished off the Hurricanes with a 55-yard interception return for a touchdown, and Southern advanced with a 20-5 victory. Hollenbach threw for 89 yards and a score, and Fleming had 69 yards receiving and a touchdown reception. Gaige Garcia ran for 72 yards and broke Jerry Marks' freshman record for rushing yards in a season set in 1984.

Southern traveled to Wingate to take on Ligonier Valley in the PIAA Class AA Semifinal Game. Gaige Garcia scored from 8 yards out to put the Tigers up 7-0 after one. Elijah Hoffman connected on a 25-yard field goal to push the lead to 10-0. The Rams cut the lead to 10-7 with a 50-yard run. Southern answered right back when Garcia rumbled 4-yards for a score and Hunter Thomas raced 33 yards for a touchdown. The Tigers took a 24-7 lead into the break. Ligonier Valley closed the gap with a 57-yard scoring pass early in the third. Hunter Thomas countered with an 8-yard touchdown burst, but the Rams came back with a one-yard scoring run, and Southern held a 31-21 advantage after three. The Rams closed to within 31-27 with a 5-yard scoring run in the fourth. The Tigers' defense tightened and controlled Ligonier Valley the rest of the way, and Southern held on for a 31-27 victory. The Tigers rushed for 358 yards. Thomas ran for 181 yards and two touchdowns. Garcia rushed for 108 yards and two scores. Southern advanced to their second straight PIAA Class AA Championship Game and their 15th state title game overall. The victory gave the Tigers their 31st consecutive win. However, Gaige Garcia appeared to injure his foot, and his status for the championship game was unknown.

The Tigers faced Steel Valley in the PIAA Class AA Championship Game at Hersheypark Stadium. Gaige Garcia would miss the game with a broken ankle. The Ironmen scored first on a 26-yard pass. Southern answered when Stone Hollenbach hit Cameron Young for a 24-yard touchdown pass to tie the game at 7-7. However, Steel Valley struck again with a 53-yard scoring run and a 14-7 lead after one. The Ironmen scored on runs of 5 and 15 yards in the second to take a 29-7 lead at the half. The Tigers were not able to find any offensive success against the formidable Rams' defense. Steel valley scored three times in the second half, and the Rams won the state championship, 49-7. The defeat snapped Southern's 31-game winning streak. Hollenbach threw for 150 yards and a touchdown. Young had 83 receiving yards and a scoring reception.

## 2016 SEASON

| Opponent | Location | W/L | Score |
|---|---|---|---|
| Shamokin | Home | W | 47-20 |
| Bloomsburg | Home | W | 65-21 |
| Mount Carmel | Away | W | 63-34 |
| Hughesville | Away | W | 35-19 |
| Lewisburg | Home | W | 35-0 |
| Milton | Away | W | 56-0 |
| Montoursville | Away | W | 42-21 |
| Danville | Away | W | 47-7 |
| Central Columbia | Home | W | 49-6 |
| Selinsgrove | Home | W | 52-35 |
| **District IV Class AA Semifinal Game** | | | |
| Towanda | Home | W | 69-34 |
| **District IV Class AA Championship Game** | | | |
| Line Mountain | Home | W | 49-0 |
| **PIAA Class AA Playoff Game** | | | |
| South Williamsport | Home | W | 49-21 |
| **PIAA Class AA Quarterfinal Game** | | | |
| Schuylkill Haven | Neutral | W | 20-5 |
| **PIAA Class AA Semifinal Game** | | | |
| Ligonier Valley | Neutral | W | 31-27 |
| **PIAA Class AA Championship Game** | | | |
| Steel Valley | Neutral | L | 7-49 |

COACHING STAFF: Jim Roth, Head Coach; Jason Campbell, Assistant Coach; Randall Campbell, Assistant Coach; Alex Carawan, Assistant Coach; Al Cihocki, Assistant Coach; Tom Donlan, Assistant Coach; Troy Heath, Assistant Coach; Andy Helwig, Assistant Coach; Mike Johnston, Assistant Coach; Curt Jones, Assistant Coach; John Marks, Assistant Coach; Andy Mills, Assistant Coach; Roger Nunkester, Assistant Coach; Nate Roadarmel, Assistant Coach; Pete Saylor, Assistant Coach; Rick Steele, Assistant Coach; Assistant Coach; Brandon Traugh, Assistant Coach; Don Traugh, Assistant Coach

ATHLETIC DIRECTOR: Jim Roth

ROSTER: Jeffrey Achy, Andrew Bell, Tyler Bendas, Brett Brassington, Tyler Brophy, Jeffrey Cox, Kurt Crowl, Nate Crowl, Sydney Damgaard, Blake Day, Calvin Deitrick, Justin Derk, Josh Deska, Troy Donlan, Nic Fetterman, Julian Fleming, Connor Fulmer, Gaige Garcia, Jacob Gessner, A.J. Goodlunas, Cavern Gosciminiski, Eric Grosch, Cal Haladay, Cam Haladay, Andrew Haupt, Tristan Heim, Cole Helwig, Garrett Henry, Elijah Hoffman, Stone Hollenbach, Matt Irons, Johnny Knisely, Thomas Manley, Drew Michaels, Shane Miller, Cole Potter, Payton Pursel, Lear Quinton, Ty Roadarmel, Cole Schankweiler, Anthony Scicchitano, Alex Showver, Oak Six, Jake Snyder, John Stabinski, Max Tillett, Hunter Thomas, Ross Wertman, Teagan Wilk, Robert Williams, Cameron Young, Preston Zachman

For the season, Gaige Garcia rushed for 1,915 yards and 31 touchdowns. Hunter Thomas ran for 1,559 yards and 22 scores. Southern had touchdown runs from Ty Roadarmel (3) and one each from Jeff Cox, Stone Hollenbach, and Thomas Manley. Stone Hollenbach passed for 2,162 yards and 24 touchdowns. Julian Fleming had 940 receiving yards and 13 touchdown receptions. Cameron Young had 513 yards receiving and five scoring receptions. The Tigers had touchdown receptions from Hunter Thomas (3), Garrett Henry (2), and Gaige Garcia. Cal Haladay recorded 151 tackles. Teagan Wilk totaled 115 tackles. Cameron Young had eight interceptions. Manley and Tyler Bendas registered five sacks. Fleming, Garcia, Haladay, Young, Andrew Bell, and Hunter Thomas were All-State selections. Southern finished the 2016 season with a 15-1 record.

**2 0 1 7** The 2017 Southern Columbia looked to build off the success of the previous two seasons and reach the top of the mountain once again. The Tigers started the year on the road against Shamokin. Stone Hollenbach accounted for three first-quarter touchdowns, hitting Julian Fleming for an 11-yard score, running 34-yards on a quarterback keeper, and connecting with Fleming again on a 25-yard scoring strike. Southern led 21-0 after one. Gaige Garcia found the endzone on a 32-yard scamper, Thomas Manley scored from 3 yards out, and Fleming hauled in a 61-yard scoring bomb from Hollenbach as the Tigers took a commanding 42-0 lead at halftime. Manley tacked on a 15-yard touchdown burst in the third. Shamokin avoided a shutout with a late touchdown in the fourth, and Tristan Heim capped the scoring with a 44-yard scoring run as Southern easily handled the Indians, 55-7. The Tigers rolled with 368 rushing yards. Garcia ran for 146 yards and a touchdown. Heim had 92 rushing yards and a score. Manley had 55 rushing yards and two scoring runs. Hollenbach threw for 144 yards and three touchdowns and ran for a score. Fleming had 111 receiving yards and three touchdown receptions.

Southern traveled to Bloomsburg for a matchup with the Panthers. Gaige Garcia raced 30 yards for a touchdown, Jeff Cox plowed in from 2 yards out, and Stone Hollenbach found Julian Fleming for a 47-yard scoring pass, and the Tigers built a 21-0 lead after the opening quarter. Hollenbach snuck in from the one, connected with Fleming again on a 12-yard touchdown throw, and Southern led 35-0 at the break. Garcia rumbled 53 yards for a score in the third, and Tristan Heim finished off the Panthers in the fourth with a 5-yard touchdown run as the Tigers shutout Bloomsburg, 49-0. Garcia rushed for 126 yards and two scores. Cox ran for 51 yards and a touchdown. Heim had 20 yards rushing and a scoring run. Hollenbach passed for 115 yards and two touchdowns. Fleming had 100 yards receiving, and two scoring catches.

The Tigers faced Mount Carmel in the home opener. Elijah Hoffman kicked field goals of 37 and 29 yards for a 6-0 first-quarter lead. Stone Hollenbach fired a 53-yard touchdown pass to Julian Fleming to push the lead to 12-0 at the intermission. Hoffman booted a 29-yard field goal for a 15-0 advantage after three. Mount Carmel pulled within 15-7 with a one-yard touchdown run early in the fourth. Max Tillett sacked the Red Tornadoes' quarterback, causing a fumble that was recovered in the endzone by Connor Fulmer for a touchdown. Gaige Garcia put the final nail in Mount Carmel's coffin with a 58-yard scoring burst, and Southern took down the Red Tornadoes, 29-7. Garcia ran for 72 yards and a touchdown. Hollenbach threw for 219 yards and a score. Fleming had 81 receiving yards and a touchdown reception.

It was a historic night as Southern hosted the Hughesville Spartans at Jim Roth Field at Tiger Stadium. Julian Fleming hauled in a 23-yard touchdown pass from Stone Hollenbach, and Gaige Garcia scored on runs of 50 and 59 yards, and the rout was on. The Tigers led 21-0 after one. Hollenbach and Fleming teamed up again on a 23-yard touchdown pass early in the second. The Southern defense tackled a Spartan ball carrier in the endzone for a safety, and Thomas Manley rumbled 19 yards for a score as the Tigers built a 37-0 halftime lead. Manley scored again in the third on a 34-yard touchdown jaunt, and Nate Crowl tacked on two scoring runs of 10 and 40 yards in the fourth as Southern shutout Hughesville, 57-0. With the victory, Jim Roth became the fourth coach in Pennsylvania high school football history and just the 19th coach in the country to reach 400 wins. The Tigers' players wore t-shirts stating, "Some Have A Story, We Have A Legacy" in honor of their legendary coach's accomplishment. Southern rushed for 430 yards in the game. Garcia ran for 134 yards and two scores. Crowl had 81 yards on the ground and two touchdowns. Manley rushed for 61 yards and a scoring run. Hollenbach passed for 109 yards and two touchdowns. Fleming had 87 receiving yards and two scoring receptions.

The Southern racked up 558 total yards of offense, including 337 on the ground in a road game against Lewisburg. Stone Hollenbach fired two touchdown passes to Julian Fleming (53 yards) and Gaige Garcia (24 yards), and Garcia raced 71 yards for a score as the Tigers opened up a 21-0 lead after one. In the second, Hollenbach and Garcia hooked up again on a 17-yard touchdown pass, and Southern led 28-0 at the break. Fleming hauled in a 52-yard scoring strike from Hollenbach, and Garcia punched it in from one yard out to up the

Southern lead to 42-0 in the third. Lewisburg got on the board with a 69-yard touchdown pass before Ty Roadarmel scored on a 3-yard dive for a 49-7 lead heading into the fourth quarter. The Green Dragons scored on a 26-yard to make it 49-14. Tristan Heim added an 8-yard touchdown burst. Lewisburg returned the ensuing kickoff 92 yards to cap the scoring, and Southern defeated the Green Dragons, 56-21. Garcia rushed for 105 yards and two touchdowns. He also added two scoring catches. Roadarmel ran for 77 yards and a touchdown. Heim had 16 yards on the ground and a scoring run. Hollenbach threw for 221 yards and four scores. Fleming posted 145 receiving yards and two touchdown receptions.

The Tigers took on Milton in a week six home game. Gaige Garcia had touchdown runs of 10 and 65 yards to open up a 14-0 lead. Milton scored on a 61-yard pass play to cut the lead to 14-7. Garcia returned the ensuing kickoff 78 yards for a touchdown, and Stone Hollenbach hit Julian Fleming with a 30-yard scoring throw to make it 28-7. The Black Panthers connected on a 67-yard touchdown pass before Jeff Cox rumbled 40 yards for a score to give the Tigers a 35-14 advantage after one. Cal Haladay returned an interception 42 yards for a pick six, Fleming and Hollenbach hooked up again on a 41-yard touchdown pass, and Garcia raced 74 yards for a touchdown to push the lead to 56-14. Milton got a 77-yard scoring pass, and Cox capped off a wild first half for a 63-21 Southern lead at the break. The teams played a scoreless third quarter. Payton Pursel plowed in from 2 yards out, Milton scored on a 36-yard run, Nate Crowl rumbled 61-yards for a touchdown, and the Tigers outslugged the Black Panthers, 75-28. Southern put up a whopping 548 total yards of offense, with 409 on the ground. Garcia ran for 115 yards and three scores. Crowl rushed for 97 yards and a touchdown. Cox added 76 rushing yards and two scoring runs. Heim had 47 yards on the ground and a touchdown. Pursel chipped in with 6 rushing yards and a score. Hollenbach passed for 139 yards and two scores. Fleming had 109 receiving yards and two touchdown receptions.

Southern hosted Montoursville at Tiger Stadium. Stone Hollenbach fired scoring strikes of 20 and 32 yards to Julian Fleming, and Gaige Garcia ran for a 6-yard touchdown as the Tigers led 21-0 after the opening quarter. Garcia scored on runs of 9 and 16 yards, and Fleming pulled in a 32-yard touchdown pass from Hollenbach to push the lead to 42-0 at halftime. The Warriors avoided a shutout with a late touchdown in the fourth quarter, and Southern routed Montoursville, 42-7. Garcia ran for 89 yards and three touchdowns. Hollenbach threw for 170 yards and three scores. Fleming had 110 yards receiving and three touchdown receptions.

The Danville Ironmen paid a visit to Tiger Stadium in week eight. Leading up to the game, Danville students had posted on social media that the Ironmen would shut down Julian Fleming. Their prediction proved to be false. Danville got on the board first with a 33-yard field goal. Fleming then quieted the Danville faithful with a 60-yard touchdown reception from Stone Hollenbach. Elijah Hoffman booted a 24-yard field goal to put the Tigers up 10-3 after one. Hoffman added a 35-yard field goal, and Hollenbach hit Preston Zachman for a 39-yard touchdown pass to push the lead to 20-3 at the half. Gaige Garcia raced 60 yards for a score, and Fleming returned a punt 62 yards for a touchdown for a 34-3 Southern lead after three. Ty Roadarmel rumbled 54 yards for a touchdown, and the Ironmen ended the scoring in the fourth with a one-yard run as the Tigers downed Danville, 41-10. Garcia rushed for 105 yards and a touchdown. Roadarmel had 61 rushing yards and a score. Hollenbach threw for 194 yards and two touchdowns. Danville failed to shutdown Fleming as he had 111 receiving yards and a scoring reception, and had a touchdown on an interception.

The Tigers traveled to Central Columbia for a road contest with the Blue Jays. Gaige Garcia got things started for Southern as he ran for touchdowns of 4 and 8 yards as the Tigers led 14-0 after the opening stanza. Stone Hollenbach connected with Garcia and Julian Fleming on scoring passes of 21 and 38 yards and a 28-0 halftime lead. Garcia ran for a 5-yard score, and Tristan Heim had an 8-yard touchdown burst in the third, and Southern blew out the Blue Jays, 42-0. Garcia ran for 77 yards and three scores. On the night, he became only the second player in school history to rush for 1,000 yards in both his freshman and sophomore seasons. He also had a touchdown reception. Heim rushed for 15 yards and a scoring run. Hollenbach passed for 157 yards and two touchdowns. Fleming added 111 receiving yards and a touchdown reception. With the victory, Southern won their 60th consecutive regular-season game.

Southern played Selinsgrove on the road to finish out the regular season. Gaige Garcia scored from one yard out, and Elijah Hoffman connected on a 30-yard field goal to put the Tigers in front 10-0 after the first. Garcia plowed in from 2 yards out, and Stone Hollenbach scored on a one-yard keeper to push the lead to 24-0. However, the Seals came storming back. They scored on passes of 86 and 63 yards to pull within 24-14. After a 32-yard field goal by Hoffman, Selinsgrove returned the ensuing kickoff 96 yards for a touchdown and cut the Southern lead to 27-21 at the intermission. The teams played a scoreless third quarter. In the fourth, Hollenbach snuck in from the one, and Garcia rumbled 22 yards for a touchdown to make it 42-21. The Seals scored on a 12-yard pass play before Cal Haladay finished off Selinsgrove with a 97-yard interception return for a touchdown. The Tigers outlasted the Seals, 49-28. Garcia ran for 168 yards and three touchdowns. Hollenbach threw for 250 yards. Fleming had 152 receiving yards.

The Tigers opened the postseason in the District IV Class AA Quarterfinal Game at Jim Roth Field at Tiger Stadium versus North Penn-Mansfield. Tristan Heim started the scoring with a one-yard touchdown plunge and a 7-0 lead. The Panthers made it 7-6 with a 9-yard scoring pass. Stone Hollenbach threw a 14-yard touchdown pass to Anthony Scicchitano, and Gaige Garcia rumbled for a 5-yard scoring run pushing the Southern lead to 21-6. North Penn had a 78-yard touchdown pass to cut the lead to 21-12 after one. Early in the second, Hollenbach found Preston Zachman for a 34-yard touchdown pass, but the Panthers answered with a 48-yard score through the air. Scicchitano returned an interception 5 yards for a pick six, and Garcia piled in from one yard out as Southern took a 42-20 lead into the half. Heim scored on a 9-yard touchdown burst, and Garcia bolted 26-yards for a score for a 56-21 lead after three. Ty Roadarmel plowed in from 4 yards out, and North Penn got a touchdown late in the fourth as the Tigers defeated the Panthers, 63-26. Southern rushed for 327 yards. Garcia ran for 187 yards and three scores. Roadarmel rushed for 59 yards and a touchdown. Heim had 32 yards rushing and two scoring runs. Hollenbach passed for 147 yards and two scores. Zachman had 82 yards receiving and a touchdown reception. Scicchitano pulled in 14 yards receiving and a scoring catch.

Southern hosted Central Columbia in the District IV Class AA Semifinal Game. Gaige Garcia raced 39 yards for a touchdown and caught a 39-yard scoring pass from Stone Hollenbach to open a 14-0 lead. Hollenbach scored on a 15-yard keeper, and Garcia rumbled 32 yards for a touchdown as the Tigers led 28-0 after the opening quarter. Garcia ran 4 yards for a score before the Blue Jays got on the board with a one-yard touchdown plunge to make the score 35-7. Elijah Hoffman tacked on a 24-yard field goal, and Southern led 38-7 at the break. Tristan Heim bolted 6 yards for a touchdown, and Jeff Cox scored from one yard out the push the lead to 52-7 after three. Payton Pursel picked off a Central pass and returned it 52 yards for a touchdown, and the Blue Jays capped the scoring with a late touchdown pass in the fourth as the Tigers pounded Central Columbia, 59-14. Garcia had 139 rushing yards and two touchdowns. He also had a scoring reception. Cox ran for 59 yards and a touchdown. Heim added 29 rushing yards and a scoring run. Hollenbach threw for 173 yards and two touchdowns.

The final home game of the season was the District IV Class AA Championship Game versus Mount Carmel. Elijah Hoffman put the Tigers in front 3-0 with a 21-yard field goal. Mount Carmel scored on a 13-yard run, and the Red Tornadoes led 7-3 after one. Hoffman booted a 41-yard field goal, and Gaige Garcia rumbled 28 yards for a touchdown as the Tigers took a 14-7 lead at the half. Garcia ran 36 yards for a score and caught a 49-yard touchdown pass from Stone Hollenbach to push the lead to 28-7 after three. Tristan Heim scored from one yard out, and Garcia plowed in for a 3-yard touchdown run for a 42-7 lead. The Red Tornadoes scored on a 70-yard run, and Nate Crowl capped the scoring with a 42-yard jaunt, and the Tigers won their 25th District IV Championship with a 49-14 victory. Southern rushed for 383 yards and had 515 yards of total offense. Garcia led the way with 248 yards and three scores. He also had a touchdown reception. Heim ran for 61 yards and a score. Crowl rushed for 47 yards and a touchdown. Hollenbach threw for 132 yards and a score. The defense registered three sacks, four tackles for loss, three interceptions (two by Julian Fleming and one by Preston Zachman), and a fumble recovery.

Southern played Neumann-Goretti in the PIAA Quarterfinal Game in Lehighton. Gaige Garcia got the PIAA Playoffs started with a bang as he returned the opening kickoff 83 yards for a touchdown. Stone Hollenbach snuck in from one yard out, and the Tigers led 14-0 after the first quarter. Hollenbach connected with Julian Fleming with a 53-yard touchdown pass, and Elijah Hoffman connected on a 32-yard field goal to put Southern up 24-0 at the break. Neumann-Goretti scored twice in the third quarter to pull within 24-12. Garcia scored on runs of 8 and 4 yards, and Brett Szuler returned an interception 56 yards for a touchdown as the Tigers advanced with a 45-12 win over the Saints. Garcia ran for 101 yards and two touchdowns. Hollenbach passed for 109 yards and a score. Fleming had 80 receiving yards and a touchdown reception.

The Tigers faced Dunmore in the PIAA Class AA Semifinal game in Danville. Dunmore scored first on a 15-yard touchdown pass. Stone Hollenbach put Southern in front 7-6 with a 20-yard scamper. The Bucks answered and retook the lead with a 16-yard run. Gaige Garcia scored from 8 yards out, and Hollenbach hit Julian Fleming with a 29-yard scoring strike, and Southern led 21-13 after one. Jeff Cox rumbled 22 yards for a touchdown and Garcia raced 39 yards for a score, and the Tigers took a 35-13 lead into the half. In the third, Garcia put the game away with scoring jaunts of 73 and 60 yards for a 49-13 lead. Ty Roadarmel scored from 5 yards out, and Dunmore got a touchdown late in the fourth to make the final score 56-19. Southern rushed for 405 yards.

Garcia ran for 239 yards and four touchdowns. Roadarmel rushed for 82 yards and a score. Cox had 63 rushing yards and a scoring run. Hollenbach threw for 125 yards and a touchdown, and had a rushing score. Fleming had 103 receiving yards and a touchdown reception. The Tigers advanced to their third straight PIAA Class AA Championship Game and their 16th title game overall.

Southern again met the Wilmington Greyhounds in the PIAA Class AA Championship Game at Hersheypark Stadium. Wilmington got off to a quick start and appeared to be on their way to a touchdown on their first drive with a long run. However, Julian Fleming ran down the ball carrier and forced a fumble that Brett Szuler recovered. From there, the Tigers began to roll. Stone Hollenbach fired an 11-yard touchdown strike to Fleming, and Elijah Hoffman booted a 29-yard field goal as Southern took a 10-0 first-quarter lead. Hollenbach hit Preston Zachman with a 7-yard scoring pass and connected with Gaige Garcia on a 15-yard touchdown throw to push the Tigers' lead to 24-0 at the intermission. In the third, Garcia ran for a 57-yard touchdown, Hoffman kicked a 21-yard field goal, Jeff Cox scored from one yard out, and Southern had a commanding 41-0 lead after three. Cox tacked on a 4-yard touchdown run in the fourth, and the Southern Columbia Tigers won the 2017 PIAA Class AA Championship with a 48-0 shutout of Wilmington. Southern earned their eighth PIAA State Football Championship. The Tigers' run through the PIAA Playoffs was most impressive as they defeated three undefeated teams on their way to the championship, outscoring them 149-31. Southern completed their fifth undefeated season. Garcia ran for 158 yards and a touchdown. He also had a scoring reception. Cox rushed for 45 yards and two scores. Hollenbach threw for 144 yards and three touchdowns. Fleming had 73 receiving yards and a touchdown reception. Zachman added 9 receiving yards and a scoring catch.

The 2017 State Champion Tigers had many sensational performances. Gaige Garcia rushed for 2,209 yards and 36 touchdowns. Jeff Cox ran for 601 yards and seven scores. Tristan Heim had 503 rushing yards and eight scoring runs. Southern had touchdown runs from Nate Crowl (4), Thomas Manley (4), Ty Roadarmel (4), Stone Hollenbach (2), and Payton Prsel (1). Stone Hollenbach passed for 2,548 yards and 30 touchdowns. Julian Fleming had 1,484 receiving yards and 20 touchdown receptions. Preston Zachman had 374 yards receiving and three scoring receptions. The Tigers had touchdown receptions from Gaige Garcia (6) and Anthony Scicchitano (1). Elijah Hoffman kicked 102 extra points and 13 field goals. Cal Haladay registered 109 tackles. Max Tillett totaled 106 tackles. Fleming recorded four interceptions. Haladay and

## 2017 SEASON

| Opponent | Location | W/L | Score |
|---|---|---|---|
| Shamokin | Away | W | 55-7 |
| Bloomsburg | Away | W | 49-0 |
| Mount Carmel | Home | W | 29-7 |
| Hughesville | Home | W | 57-0 |
| Lewisburg | Away | W | 56-21 |
| Milton | Home | W | 75-28 |
| Montoursville | Home | W | 42-7 |
| Danville | Home | W | 41-10 |
| Central Columbia | Away | W | 42-0 |
| Selinsgrove | Away | W | 49-28 |
| **District IV Class AA Quarterfinal Game** | | | |
| North Penn-Mansfield | Home | W | 63-26 |
| **District IV Class AA Semifinal Game** | | | |
| Central Columbia | Home | W | 59-14 |
| **District IV Class AA Championship Game** | | | |
| Mount Carmel | Home | W | 49-14 |
| **PIAA Class AA Quarterfinal Game** | | | |
| Neumann-Goretti | Neutral | W | 45-12 |
| **PIAA Class AA Semifinal Game** | | | |
| Dunmore | Neutral | W | 56-19 |
| **PIAA Class AA Championship Game** | | | |
| Wilmington | Neutral | W | 48-0 |

COACHING STAFF: Jim Roth, Head Coach; Jason Campbell; Assistant Coach; Randall Campbell, Assistant Coach; Alex Carawan, Assistant Coach; Al Cihocki, Assistant Coach; Tom Donlan, Assistant Coach; Troy Heath, Assistant Coach; Andy Helwig, Assistant Coach; Mike Johnston, Assistant Coach; Curt Jones, Assistant Coach; Mike Kemmerer, Assistant Coach; John Marks, Assistant Coach; Andy Mills, Assistant Coach; Roger Nunkester, Assistant Coach; Chad. Romig, Assistant Coach; Pete Saylor, Assistant Coach; Rick Steele, Assistant Coach; Brandon Traugh, Assistant Coach; Don Traugh, Assistant Coach

ATHLETIC DIRECTOR: Jim Roth

ROSTER: Jeffrey Achy, Andrew Bell, Tyler Bendas, Tyler Brophy, Jeffrey Cox, Kurt Crowl, Nate Crowl, Jake Davis, Blake Day, Calvin Deitrick, Josh Deska, Troy Donlan, Collin Doraski, Julian Fleming, Conner Fulmer, Gaige Garcia, Jacob Gessner, A.J. Goodlunas, Cavern Gosciminiski, Eric Grosch, Cal Haladay, Cam Haladay, Andrew Haupt, Tristan Heim, Cole Helwig, Jacob Herr, Elijah Hoffman, Stone Hollenbach, Matt Irons, Nate Kearney, Wade Kerstetter, Johnny Knisely, Cade Linn, Shane Miller, Owyne Pursel, Payton Pursel, Lear Quinton, Andrew Rarig, Ty Roadarmel, Cole Schankweiler, Anthony Scicchitano, Alex Showver, Oak Six, Jake Snyder, John Stabinski, Brett Szuler, Max Tillett, Ross Wertman, Kaiden Whitenight, Robert Williams, Preston Zachman, Ron Zsido

Tyler Bendas each had eight sacks. Bendas, Fleming, Garcia, Haladay, Hoffman, Hollenbach, and Andrew Bell were All-State selections. Fleming was named the Associated Press Player of the Year. Jim Roth received the Associated Press Coach of the Year. Andy Mills became the first coordinator to achieve 400 victories. Southern finished 2017 with a record of 16-0.

2
0
1
8
The Southern Columbia Tigers entered the 2018 season supremely confident in the possibility of repeating as state champions. Coming off a dominant year with nearly all of their offensive weapons returning, the Tigers looked to continue their winning ways. Southern opened the season at home against Bloomsburg. Gaige Garcia scored on a 9-yard touchdown run for the first points of the year. Julian Fleming returned an interception 21 yards for a pick six and Stone Hollenbach hit Preston Zachman with a 36-yard scoring pass as the Tigers built a 21-0 lead after one. Hollenbach found Gaige Garcia for a 21-yard touchdown to make it 28-0 early in the second. Bloomsburg got on the board with a 70-yard scoring pass. Gavin Garcia scored from one yard out to give Southern a 35-6 halftime lead. Gaige Garcia rumbled 12 yards for a score in the third and a 42-6 lead. Braden Heim and Brandon Gedman scored on runs of 6 and 19 yards in the fourth, and the Tigers defeated the Panthers, 56-6. Southern rushed for 318 yards and two scores. Gaige Garcia ran for 150 yards and two touchdowns. He also added a scoring catch. Gedman rushed for 59 yards and a touchdown. Gavin Garcia added 34 rushing yards and a score. Heim had 26 yards on the ground and a scoring run. Hollenbach threw for 173 yards and two scores. Zachman had 45 yards receiving and a touchdown reception. Fleming had 107 receiving yards.

The Tigers traveled to Mount Carmel for a matchup with the Red Tornadoes. The teams played a scoreless first quarter. In the second, Gavin Garcia ran for a 24-yard touchdown and Stone Hollenbach hit Julian Fleming with scoring passes of 16 and 3 yards, and Southern took a 20-0 lead at halftime. In the third, Gaige Garcia caught a 19-yard touchdown pass from Hollenbach for a 27-0 lead. Mount Carmel got on the board with a 4-yard scoring run. Gaige Garcia pounded in from 2 yards out, and Fleming and Hollenbach hooked up again on a 66-yard touchdown pass, and the Tigers handled Mount Carmel, 41-7. Southern ran for 301 yards for the game. Gaige Garcia rushed for 54 yards and a score. He also had a touchdown reception. Gavin Garcia ran for 32 yards and a scoring run. Hollenbach passed for 301 yards and four touchdowns. Fleming had 113 receiving yards and three scoring receptions.

Southern dominated on both sides of the ball in a home game against Selinsgrove. Stone Hollenbach found Julian Fleming for a 7-yard touchdown pass, and Gavin Garcia scored on runs of 37 and 26 yards as the Tigers built a 20-0 lead in the first. Gaige Garcia raced 34 yards for a touchdown, Preston Zachman returned an interception 22 yards for a score, Gavin Garcia rumbled 53 yards for a touchdown, and Ty Roadarnel capped the scoring with a 5-yard scoring burst as Southern shutout the Seals, 48-0. The defense had five sacks in the first half, eleven tackles for loss, and Zachman's interception for a pick six. Southern rushed for 344 yards. Gaige Garcia ran for 123 yards and a touchdown. Gavin Garcia rushed for 95 yards and two scores and had a touchdown reception. Roadarmel had 33 rushing yards and a scoring run. Hollenbach threw for 90 yards and two touchdowns. Fleming had 64 receiving yards and a scoring catch.

Henry Hynoski returned to Tiger Stadium as the head coach of the Shamokin Indians for a week four contest. Gavin Garcia scored from 2 yards out, and Stone Hollenbach hit Julian Fleming for touchdown passes of 71 and 66 yards as Southern took a 20-0 lead after one. Hollenbach connected with Gaige Garcia on a 36-yard scoring pass, and Gavin and Gaige Garcia had touchdown runs of 12 and 86 yards as the Tigers had a 41-0 advantage at the break. Gaige Garcia capped the scoring when he returned the second-half kickoff 85 yards for a touchdown as Southern dominated Shamokin, 48-0. Gaige Garcia ran for 104 yards and a touchdown. He also had a scoring catch. Gavin Garcia rushed for 33 yards and two scores. Hollenbach threw for 173 yards and three touchdowns. Fleming had 137 receiving yards and two scoring receptions. The Tigers' defense held the Indians to zero passing yards and only 31 yards on the ground.

Southern traveled to Central Columbia to tangle with the rival Blue Jays. Preston Zachman substituted at quarterback for an injured Stone Hollenbach. Central scored first on a 24-yard touchdown run and took a 6-0 lead. The Tigers responded when Gaige Garcia scored from 4 yards out to give Southern a 7-6 lead. The Blue Jays retook the lead early in the second with a one-yard scoring run. Zachman scampered 45 yards on a keeper and then hit Julian Fleming for a 17-yard touchdown throw to put Southern back in front 20-13. However, Central tied the game with a 35-yard scoring pass, and the score was deadlocked at 20-20 at the half. Southern took control of the game in the third. Gaige Garcia plowed in from 3 yards out, Gavin Garcia raced 42 yards for a score, Ty Roadarmel ran for a 5-yard touchdown, and Gaige Garcia scored on a 3-yard dive to make it 47-20. The Blue Jays got a touchdown on a 34-yard run, and Gavin Garcia finished the scoring in the fourth with a 17-yard touchdown burst as Southern outslugged Central, 54-27. The Tigers rushed for 340 yards. Gaige Garcia had 137 yards rushing and three touchdowns. Gavin Garcia ran for 90 yards and two scores. Roadarmel rushed for 16 yards and a scoring run. Zachman threw for 142 yards and a touchdown. He also had a rushing score. Fleming hauled in 132 receiving yards and a touchdown reception.

The Tigers faced South Williamsport in a week six road game. The Mountaineers scored on a 70-yard touchdown pass for a 6-0 lead. Gaige Garcia scored on runs of 5 and 8 yards and caught a 6-yard touchdown pass from Preston Zachman. Gavin Garcia added a 30-yard scoring burst, and the Tigers led 27-6 after the opening quarter. Zachman found Julian Fleming for a 15-yard touchdown pass, and Gaige Garcia rumbled 10 yards for a score as Southern built a 40-6 lead at the break. In the third, the Garcia brothers had touchdown runs, Gaige with a 46-yard jaunt and Gavin on a 15-yard burst, and the Tigers led 54-6 heading into the final period. South Williamsport scored two late touchdowns to make the final score 54-21. Gaige Garcia rushed for 109 yards and four scores. He also added a touchdown reception. Gavin Garcia ran for 91 yards and two scores. Zachman threw for 156 yards and two touchdowns. Fleming had 134 receiving yards and a scoring catch.

Southern hosted Jersey Shore at Jim Roth Field at Tiger Stadium. Gavin Garcia ran for a 6-yard touchdown, Gaige Garcia scored from 4 yards out and Preston Zachman hit Julian Fleming for an 18-yard touchdown pass, and the Tigers had a 20-0 lead after the first. Zachman connected with Gavin Garcia on a 54-yard touchdown pass, Gaige Garcia rumbled 35 yards for a score, and Southern led 34-0 at the intermission. Gaige Garcia scored on runs of 54 and 25 yards to push the lead to 48-0 after three. The Bulldogs avoided being shutout with a 12-yard touchdown run early in the fourth. Gavin Garcia and Braden Heim capped the scoring with runs of 64 and 4 yards to bring the final score to 62-7. Southern rushed for 439 yards and had 581 yards of total offense. Gaige Garcia ran for 213 yards and four scores. Gavin Garcia rushed for 104 yards and two touchdowns and had a receiving score. Heim had 27 rushing yards and a scoring run. Zachman passed for 123 yards and two touchdowns. Fleming had 69 receiving yards and a touchdown reception.

The Tigers took on the Shikellamy Braves in a week eight road contest. Southern put the game away early with 34 first-quarter points. Gaige Garcia ran for a 10-yard touchdown, Preston Zachman found Julian Fleming for an 11-yard scoring pass, Gavin Garcia scored from 4 yards out, Cade Linn returned an interception 16 yards for a pick six, and Zachman and Fleming teamed up again for a 25-yard touchdown pass. In the second, Gavin Garcia raced 48 yards for a score, Gaige Garcia ran 29 yards for a touchdown, and Ty Roadarmel rumbled 16 yards for a score as the Tigers led 55-0 at halftime. Shikellamy got in the endzone on a 33-yard touchdown run in the third. Braden Heim and Brandon Gedman scored fourth-quarter touchdowns, and Southern overwhelmed the Braves, 69-7. The Tigers rushed for 372 yards. Gavin Garcia ran for 133 yards and two scores. Gaige Garcia rushed for 115 yards and two touchdowns. Gedman and Heim each had 39 rushing yards and scoring runs. Roadarmel tacked on 16 rushing yards and a touchdown. Zachman threw for 71 yards and two scores. Fleming had 58 receiving yards and two touchdown receptions.

Hughesville traveled to Tigers Stadium for the final regular-season home game. Gavin Garcia ran 28 yards for a touchdown, Preston Zachman hit Julian Fleming with a 59-yard scoring pass, Gavin Garcia rumbled 53 yards for a score, and Gaige Garcia raced 65 yards for a touchdown as Southern jumped to a 28-0 lead after one. Gaige Garcia scored on a 12-yard run, Gavin Garcia went 29 yards for a touchdown, Ty Roadarmel ran 64 yards for a score, and Gaige Garcia scored on a 30-yard burst to push the lead to 55-0 at the half. Braden Heim pounded in from 3 yards out for a 62-0 lead after three. The Spartans scored on an 18-yard run and Heim finished the scoring with a 13-yard touchdown jaunt as the Tigers manhandled Hughesville, 69-8. Southern pounded out 449 yards on the ground and totaled 552 yards of total offense. Gaige Garcia ran for 137 yards and three scores. Gavin Garcia rushed for 114 yards and three touchdowns. Roadarmel had 80 rushing yards and a scoring run. Heim added 50 yards on the ground and two touchdowns. Zachman passed for 103 yards and a score. Fleming had 103 receiving yards and a touchdown reception. The victory gave Southern their 70th consecutive regular-season win and the Heartland Athletic Conference Division III Championship.

Stone Hollenbach returned at quarterback after a six-week absence due to a wrist injury in the regular-season finale at Danville. The Ironmen scored first with an 11-yard run and took a 7-0 lead early in the first. Hollenbach connected with Julian Fleming for a 63-yard touchdown pass, Fleming returned an interception 31 yards for a pick six, and Gaige Garcia scored from one yard out to put Southern in front 21-7 after one. The teams played a scoreless second quarter. Hollenbach and Fleming hooked up again for a 48-yard scoring pass, Gavin Garcia pounded in from one yard out, and Gaige Garcia rumbled for a 6-yard touchdown to push the lead to 42-7 after three. Braden Heim finished off Danville with a 4-yard touchdown run in the fourth as the Tigers earned a 49-7 blowout victory. Gaige Garcia ran for 114 yards and two touchdowns. Heim rushed for 20 yards and a score. Gavin Garcia added 9 rushing yards and a scoring run. Hollenbach passed for 212 yards and two touchdowns. Fleming had 162 yards receiving and two scoring grabs.

Southern began the postseason in the District IV Class AA Quarterfinal Game at Tiger Stadium against Line Mountain. Stone Hollenbach hit Gaige Garcia with a 36-yard scoring strike, Ty Roadarmel ran for a 16-yard touchdown, Gaige Garcia rumbled 12 yards for a score, and Gavin Garcia added a rushing touchdown as the Tigers opened up a 27-0 first-quarter lead. Gaige

Garcia raced 19 yards for a score, Roadarmel scored from 8 yards out, Gaige Garcia pounded in from the one, and Preston Zachman returned a fumble 24 yards for a touchdown as Southern closed out the Eagles, 55-0. The defense limited Line Mountain to 6 total yards of offense. The unit registered two fumble recoveries and had interceptions from Cade Linn, Wade Kerstetter, Logan Potter, and Ian Yoder. Roadarmel ran for 82 yards and a touchdown. Gaige Garcia added 74 rushing yards and three scores. He also had a touchdown reception. Gavin Garcia rushed for 49 yards and two scores. Hollenbach threw for 90 yards and a touchdown.

Troy came to Tiger Stadium for the District IV Class AA Semifinal Game. Stone Hollenbach threw touchdown passes of 29 and 18 yards to Julian Fleming and Gaige Garcia, and Garcia scored from 2 yards out to put Southern up 20-0 after one. Hollenbach hit Fleming again for a 9-yard touchdown strike, Ty Roadarmel rumbled 42 yards for a score, Garcia raced 63 yards for a touchdown, and Fleming returned an interception 32 yards for a pick six to push the lead to 48-0 at the intermission. In the third, Fleming returned his second interception 35 yards for a touchdown to up the lead to 55-0. Braden Heim and Jayden McCormick scored on runs of 3 and 5 yards, and Troy added two fourth-quarter touchdowns to make the final score 69-16. Southern rushed for 315 yards. Garcia ran for 109 yards and two touchdowns. He also added a scoring reception. Roadarmel rushed for 52 yards and a touchdown. Heim totaled 42 yards on the ground and a rushing touchdown. McCormick chipped in with 34 rushing yards and a scoring run. Hollenbach threw for 123 yards and three scores. Fleming had 105 receiving yards and two touchdown receptions.

The Tigers hosted Mount Carmel in the District IV Class AA Championship Game. Stone Hollenbach passed for touchdowns of 28 and 10 yards to Julian Fleming and Preston Zachman to give Southern a 13-0 lead after one. In the second, Mount Carmel scored on a 45-yard pass to cut the lead to 13-8 at the half. Gaige Garcia returned the second-half kickoff 89 yards for a score and Fleming and Hollenbach hooked up again for a 17-yard touchdown pass, and the Tigers took a 25-8 advantage into the final period. Garcia scored on runs of 12 and 3 yards, and the Red Tornadoes closed the scoring with a late touchdown to make the final score 39-14. Garcia ran for 126 yards and two touchdowns. Hollenbach passed for 119 yards and three scores. Fleming had 54 receiving yards and two touchdown receptions. Zachman hauled in 28 yards receiving and a scoring catch. The Tigers won their 26th District IV Championship.

Southern advanced to the PIAA Class AA Quarterfinal Game against York Catholic in Coal Township. Stone Hollenbach found Julian Fleming for a

49-yard touchdown pass and a 7-0 lead. York Catholic tied the game at 7-7 with a 14-yard pass. Hollenbach and Fleming teamed up again on a 12-yard scoring pass, and Gaige Garcia ran for a 3-yard touchdown to give Southern a 22-7 lead after the opening stanza. Gavin Garcia rumbled 21 yards for a score, Hollenbach found Preston Zachman for a 72-yard touchdown bomb, and Gavin Garcia scored from 3 yards out to push the lead 42-7 lead at the break. Gaige Garcia piled in from the 2 and raced 92 yards for a touchdown to make it 56-7. The Fighting Irish scored on a touchdown run late in the third and capped the scoring with a 5-yard scoring run in the fourth as the Tigers defeated York Catholic, 56-23. Southern rushed for 373 yards and totaled a staggering 622 yards of total offense. Gaige Garcia ran for 186 yards and three touchdowns. Gavin Garcia added 106 rushing yards and two scores. Hollenbach passed for 249 yards and three touchdowns. Fleming had 147 receiving yards and two scoring receptions. Zachman had 102 yards receiving and a touchdown catch.

The Tigers took on West Catholic in the PIAA Class AA Semifinal Game in Slatington. Gaige Garcia had touchdown runs of 67 and 10 yards and Preston Zachman caught a scoring pass from Stone Hollenbach, and Southern opened up a 21-0 first-quarter lead. Hollenbach fired a 12-yard touchdown strike to Julian Fleming to push the lead to 28-0 at halftime. Ty Roadarmel raced 51 yards for a score, and Hollenbach and Fleming hooked up again for a 25-yard touchdown pass to make it 42-0. The Burrs capped the scoring late in the third, and the Tigers moved on with a 42-6 win over West Catholic. The defense held the Burrs to -7 yards rushing. Gaige Garcia rushed for 174 yards and two scores. Roadarmel ran for 74 yards and a touchdown. Hollenbach threw for 70 yards and three scores. Fleming had 51 receiving yards and two touchdowns. Zachman hauled in 13 yards receiving and a scoring reception. The Tigers advanced to their fourth consecutive PIAA Class AA Championship Game.

Southern once again faced Wilmington in the PIAA Class AA Championship Game at Hersheypark Stadium. The teams played a scoreless first quarter. Wilmington opened the scoring with a 3-yard run early in the second. Gaige Garcia tied the game with a 5-yard touchdown run. The Greyhounds retook the lead on a 13-yard scoring pass. Gaige Garcia answered with a 32-yard touchdown reception from Stone Hollenbach, and the game was tied at 14-14 at the half. The Garcia brothers took over the game in the second half. Gaige ran for a 26-yard touchdown and caught a 32-yard scoring pass from Hollenbach for a 28-14 lead after three. Gavin sandwiched scoring runs of 38 and 33 yards around Gaige's 18-yard touchdown bolt, and the Southern Columbia Tigers won the 2018 PIAA Class AA Championship, 49-14. The victory gave

Southern back-to-back titles and their ninth overall state championship. Gaige Garcia ran for 117 yards and three scores. He also had two touchdown receptions. Gavin Garcia rushed for 98 yards and two scores. Hollenbach passed for 166 yards and two touchdowns. Shane Miller led a solid defensive effort with two interceptions.

## 2018 SEASON

| Opponent | Location | W/L | Score |
|---|---|---|---|
| Bloomsburg | Home | W | 56-6 |
| Mount Carmel | Away | W | 41-7 |
| Selinsgrove | Home | W | 48-0 |
| Shamokin | Home | W | 48-0 |
| Central Columbia | Away | W | 54-27 |
| South Williamsport | Away | W | 54-20 |
| Jersey Shore | Home | W | 62-7 |
| Shikellamy | Away | W | 69-7 |
| Hughesville | Home | W | 69-8 |
| Danville | Away | W | 49-7 |
| **District IV Class AA Semifinal Game** | | | |
| Line Mountain | Home | W | 55-0 |
| **District IV Class AA Championship Game** | | | |
| Troy | Home | W | 69-16 |
| **PIAA Class AA Playoff Game** | | | |
| Mount Carmel | Home | W | 39-14 |
| **PIAA Class AA Quarterfinal Game** | | | |
| York Catholic | Neutral | W | 56-23 |
| **PIAA Class AA Semifinal Game** | | | |
| West Catholic | Neutral | W | 42-6 |
| **PIAA Class AA Championship Game** | | | |
| Wilmington | Neutral | W | 49-14 |

COACHING STAFF: Jim Roth, Head Coach; Jason Campbell; Assistant Coach; Randall Campbell, Assistant Coach; Alex Carawan, Assistant Coach; Al Cihocki, Assistant Coach; Tom Donlan, Assistant Coach; Troy Heath, Assistant Coach; Andy Helwig, Assistant Coach; Mike Johnston, Assistant Coach; Curt Jones, Assistant Coach; Mike Kemmerer, Assistant Coach; John Marks, Assistant Coach; Andy Mills, Assistant Coach; Roger Nunkester, Assistant Coach; Chad. Romig, Assistant Coach; Pete Saylor, Assistant Coach; Rick Steele, Assistant Coach; Brandon Traugh, Assistant Coach; Don Traugh, Assistant Coach

ATHLETIC DIRECTOR: Jim Roth

ROSTER: Matt Carl, Kurt Crowl, Nate Crowl, Jake Davis, Troy Donlan, Collin Doraski, Ethan Dunkleberger, Julian Fleming, Jordan Fosse, Gaige Garcia, Gavin Garcia, Brandon Gedman, Jacob Gessner, Cal Haladay, Cam Haladay, Braden Heim, Jacob Herr, Stone Hollenbach, Matt Irons, Nate Kearney, Wade Kerstetter, Johnny Knisely, Cade Linn, Jayden McCormick, Shane Miller, Nick Minor, Seth Pletcher, Logan Potter, Jaxson Purnell, Owyne Pursel, Payton Pursel, Lear Quinton, Andrew Rarig, Jacob Reynolds, Ty Roadarmel, Cole Schankweiler, Colin Sharrow, Keegan Shultz, Oak Six, John Stabinski, Dyer Stine, Max Tillett, Tyler Waltman, Derek Wertman, Ross Wertman, Robert Williams, Timothy Witcoskie, Ian Yoder, Preston Zachman, Nick Zeigler, Ron Zsido

The 2018 Tigers had many great individual and team performances. Gaige Garcia rushed for 2,042 yards and 38 touchdowns. Gavin Garcia ran for 1,152 yards and 24 scores. Ty Roadarmel had 569 rushing yards and eight scoring runs. Southern had touchdown runs by Branden Heim (7) and one each from Brandon Gedman, Jayden McCormick, and Preston Zachman. Stone Hollenbach passed for 1,766 yards and 28 touchdowns. Preston Zachman filled in wonderfully at quarterback during Hollenbach's injury. He threw for 595 yards and eight touchdowns. Julian Fleming had 1,512 receiving yards and 22 touchdown receptions. Preston Zachman had 374 yards receiving and four scoring receptions. The Tigers had touchdown receptions from Gaige Garcia (8) and Gavin Garcia (2). Ethan Dunkleberger kicked 105 extra points. Southern scored 860 points on the season, breaking Jeanette's Class AA record set in 2007. Cal Haladay registered 131 tackles. Max Tillett totaled 124 tackles. Fleming and Shane Miller each had four interceptions. Tillett recorded 6.5 sacks. Fleming, Gaige Garcia, Haladay, Hollenbach, Tillett, Lear Quinton, Cole Schankweiler and Oak Six were All-State selections. Jim Roth was named Mr. PA Football Coach of the Year. The Southern Columbia Tigers were named the 2018 *High School Football America (USA Today)* Small School National Champions. Southern finished 2018 with a record of 16-0.

2
0
1
9
The Tigers football team and the entire Southern Columbia community mourned the loss of Keegan Shultz, who tragically took his life on March 5, 2019. Shultz was 17 years old, a sophomore who was a straight-A honor student and a lineman on offense and defense for the Tigers. Popular with his teammates and friends, the loss of Shultz was a tremendous blow for the Southern Columbia football program. The team would play with heavy hearts for seasons to come.

As the team was coping with the loss of Keegan Shultz, tragedy struck the Southern Columbia Community again on July 7, 2019, when Assistant Coach Don Traugh suddenly passed away at the age of 68. He had been a member of the coaching staff for 18 years. The loss of Coach Traugh was not only felt by the Southern football team but was an extremely sad blow to the Catawissa area, where he was a member of the town council, a Boy Scout leader, chief of the fire department, and an assistant minister at his church.

Southern Columbia entered the 2019 season with very lofty goals. The back-to-back PIAA Class AA Champions were riding a 32-game winning streak and had won 71 consecutive regular-season games. The Tigers were the defending *High School Football America (USA Today)* Small School National

Champions. With one of the most talented and decorated groups of seniors in recent memory, Southern was primed for a truly magical season.

The Tigers opened the year with one of the most anticipated matchups on the national high school football scene. Southern traveled to Columbia, South Carolina, to take on the heralded Hammond School Skyhawks, back-to-back South Carolina Independent School Association Class 3A Champions, and winners of 25 consecutive games. The Skyhawks featured University of South Carolina recruits defensive end Jordan Burch and defensive lineman Boogie Huntley, University of Georgia recruit quarterback Jackson Muschamp and 6'7" 280-pound lineman Braceland Dregenhart. The game was broadcast to a national television audience on ESPN2. Several hundred fans made the 10-hour trek to cheer on the Tigers in one of the most important games in the program's history. Fans began arriving at Edens Stadium at 8:00 am for the 2:00 pm kickoff. When Southern took the field, they received a rousing ovation from the Tiger faithful. Hammond opened the game with a first down, but the Southern defense batted down a third-down pass to force a punt. Southern Columbia moved the ball 64 yards, with quarterback Preston Zachman scoring on a 38-yard keeper with 7:20 left in the first quarter. An errant snap on the extra point attempt forced holder Tim Witcoskie to retrieve the ball, and he ran to the corner of the endzone for a two-point conversion to make the score 8-0. On Hammond's second drive, Cade Linn intercepted a Skyhawk pass at the Hammond 36-yard line. However, Southern's drive stalled. The Tigers immediately got the ball back when Max Tillett forced a fumble that Jake Davis recovered at the Skyhawk 10-yard line. With twelve seconds left in the opening quarter, Gaige Garcia scored on a 5-yard run for a 15-0 lead. Davis stopped a screen pass on a fourth and seven, and the Tigers went on a quick 60-yard drive culminating in Garcia's second touchdown on a 31-yard burst with 3:14 left in the half. The lead increased to 29-0 at halftime when Ian Huntington batted a pass in the air and ran it back 39 yards for a score. The Skyhawks tried to make a game of it in the third quarter. They intercepted a Southern pass at the Tiger 26 but gained only two yards in four plays and turned the ball over on downs. The Tigers put the game out of reach, and into the mercy rule, on a 10-play, 66-yard drive lasting 5:49 in the third quarter capped off by Ty Roadarmel's 25-yard touchdown run. When the final gun sounded, the Tigers had a convincing 36-0 win over a talented Hammond Skyhawk team on national television. Southern's offense ground out 255 yards rushing. Gaige Garcia had 78 yards and scored two touchdowns. Preston Zachman chipped in another 61 yards and a score. Ty Roadarmel scored a touchdown and had 50 yards rushing.

Gavin Garcia contributed another 66 yards on the ground. The Tiger defense had a sensational game. Southern held Hammond to 59 total yards of offense. Jake Davis had two interceptions and a fumble recovery. Ian Yoder and Cade Linn each had an interception, and Ian Huntington scored with a pick six. The Tigers and their fans returned to Catawissa with a satisfying and historic victory on the national stage. The Hammond School would win a third straight South Carolina Independent School Association Class 3A Championship.

A week two matchup with Mount Caramel was expected to be a potentially competitive contest. It turned into the Garcia Brothers' Show, as senior Gaige and sophomore Gavin combined for 180 rushing yards and six touchdowns in a 48-0 romp over the Red Tornadoes. Gaige Garcia opened the scoring with a 2-yard touchdown early in the first quarter. Julian Fleming returned a Mount Carmel punt 50 yards to set up Gavin Garcia's first score of the night from 4 yards out. The Tigers' defense forced seven Mount Carmel punts in the first half. Gavin Garcia scored again on a 7-yard run to make the score 20-0 with 11:28 left in the second. The younger Garcia scored touchdowns on his next two carries on runs of 38 and 35 yards to push the score to 34-0 at halftime. Gaige Garcia scored on a 30-yard touchdown run in the third, and Nick Zeigler ended the scoring in the fourth quarter with a 57-yard interception for a pick six as the Tigers shut out Mount Carmel 48-0. Southern rushed for 291 yards as a team, with Gaige Garcia compiling 94 yards and two touchdowns and Gavin Garcia pounding out 86 yards and four scores.

The Tigers' week three trip to Selinsgrove would prove to be an unforgettable evening for running back Gaige Garcia. When Garcia scored on a one-yard run early in the opening period, he tied South Williamsport's Dominick Bragalone for the most career touchdowns in Pennsylvania high school football history with 129. With 2:34 left in the first quarter, Gaige Garcia set a new Pennsylvania state record with his 130th career touchdown on a 3-yard scoring run. The game was briefly stopped to acknowledge Garcia's remarkable accomplishment, and three gold balloons with "1-3-0" appeared on the Tigers' sideline. The record-setting night spurred Southern on to a 76-0 blowout of the Seals. The offense rolled with 379 rushing yards and 475 overall. Gaige Garcia rushed for 64 yards and two touchdowns, and brother Gavin totaled 99 yards and added a scoring run. Ty Roadarmel and Wes Barnes added a pair of rushing touchdowns, and Brandon Heim chipped in with another 67 rushing yards. Heim also recovered a Seals' fumble in the endzone to contribute to the scoring. Julian Fleming had 95 receiving yards and a touchdown reception. He also returned a blocked kick for an 83-yard score. Kicker Ethan Haupt converted ten extra points. The defense held Selinsgrove to negative rushing and passing yards, totaling -32 for the game. Jake Davis led the way with two interceptions. The win tied the state record for the most consecutive regular-season victories.

Another week, another record for the Tigers. Southern Columbia's 62-0 win at Shamokin was their 75th consecutive regular-season victory, breaking the Pennsylvania high school football record set by Strath Haven in 2004. The Tigers' last regular-season defeat was against Mount Carmel in 2011 when the senior class was in fourth grade. Their 75th win was never in doubt. Gaige Garcia scored on a 54-yard run on the second play of the game. Julian Fleming scored the next three touchdowns on receptions of 50, 9, and 46 yards from Preston Zachman. Garcia scored again on a 20-yard run to make the score 35-0 before the end of the first quarter. Gavin Garcia sandwiched touchdown runs of 23 and 54 yards around Gaige's 38 yarder to push the score to 55-0 at the half. Trevor Yorks capped the scoring with an 11-yard run in the fourth quarter. Southern pounded out 395 yards on the ground. The Garcia brothers combined for 263 yards and five touchdowns. Ty Roadarmel and Brandon Heim contributed 50 and 40 additional rushing yards. Julian Fleming had 105 receiving yards and three touchdowns from Preston Zachman. The defense held Shamokin to 117 total yards with an interception and fumble recovery.

Next on the schedule was a home game versus Central Columbia. The Tigers got off to a quick start when nine seconds into the game, Preston Zachman hit Julian Fleming for a 69-yard touchdown for a 7-0 lead. Gaige Garcia then scored first-quarter touchdowns on runs of 7, 23, and one yard, and the game was already out of reach for the Blue Jays. The Tigers scored on every possession in the first half as Gavin Garcia had a pair of touchdown runs of 17 and 48 yards, and Zachman hooked up with Ty Roadarmel on a 17-yard scoring pass, pushing the lead to 48-0 at halftime. Nate Crowl and Matt Masala scored third-quarter touchdowns to cap the scoring in a 62-0 win. The Tigers racked up 637 yards of offense, with 380 on the ground. Gavin Garcia had 102 yards and two touchdowns, Gaige Garcia put up 80 yards and three scores, Ty Roadarmel picked up 79 yards and rushing and receiving touchdowns, and Matt Masala contributed 50 yards and a score. Preston Zachman completed 8 of 11 passes for 257 yards and two touchdowns. Julian Fleming had 165 yards receiving and a touchdown. The Tiger defense held Central Columbia to two first downs and 27 total yards of offense for the game with an interception and two fumble recoveries.

In a week six matchup at Tiger Stadium, more state records fell in a 76-6 mauling of South Williamsport. Southern scored on the second play of the game when Preston Zachman spotted Julian Fleming in the back of the endzone for a 29-yard touchdown. The Tigers scored on the first play of their second drive when Zachman and Fleming hooked up again for a 49-yard touchdown. Julian Fleming set new Pennsylvania high school football records for career receiving yards and touchdowns on that play. The previous record for receiving yards had been 4,457 by Brian Lemelle of Bishop McDevitt, and the career touchdown mark of 61 was held by Ligonier Valley's Aaron Tutino. It was also a big night for Gaige Garcia. After scoring runs of 42 and 19 yards in the opening period, Garcia scored his 121st career rushing touchdown on a 70-yard run to break the previous record held by Lamont Wade of Clairton. Ty Roadarmel and Gavin Garcia added a pair of touchdowns, and Braden Heim chipped in with another scoring run. For the second time on the season, Ethan Haupt connected for ten extra points. The offense rushed for 409 yards, averaging a remarkable 24 yards per carry. Gaige Garcia carried the ball six times for 235 yards and three touchdowns. Gavin Garcia had 98 rushing yards and two touchdowns, and Ty Roadarmel had 40 yards on the ground and two scores. Julian Fleming scored touchdowns on his two catches for 77 yards. Although the defense gave up their first points of the season, they recovered two fumbles and held the Mountaineers to 71 passing yards.

In week seven, Southern Columbia traveled to Jersey Shore and continued their pattern of fast starts, scoring on five of their first six possessions in a 56-14 rout of the Bulldogs. Southern ran only twelve plays on their first five scoring drives. The Tigers built a 35-0 first-quarter lead on a 52-yard keeper by Preston Zachman, a 43-yard run by Gavin Garcia, a Gaige Garcia 78-yard burst, and Gaige Garcia's 48-yard reception. Ty Roadarmel scored on a 46-yard run, Julian Fleming caught a 58-yard scoring pass from Zachman, and Gavin Garcia scored from 6 yards out. Southern led 56-6 at halftime. The Tigers ran for 401 yards and threw for another 174. Gaige Garcia led the way with 125 yards, with Gavin Garcia chipping in with 96 and Roadarmel adding 54. The defense had two interceptions in the game.

The week eight contest between Southern Columbia and Wyoming Area was billed as a clash of Pennsylvania football superpowers. The Tigers were the top-ranked Class AA team in the state, and Wyoming Area was ranked fourth in Class AAA. However, just a week before their anticipated matchup, it looked as though it would not happen. On the original schedule, Southern Columbia was to play Shikellamy, who was 1-5 and had lost 14 of their last 16 games in week eight. Wyoming Area was scheduled to play Holy Redeemer, who had lost 15 games in a row and had only scored three touchdowns all season. Jim Roth reached out to Wyoming Area Athletic Director Joe Pizano about a possible change to the schedule to play a more competitive game and set up a potential state power matchup. Both teams agreed to the change, as did Shikellamy and Holy Redeemer, and the schools received approval from their respective districts. Wyoming Area School District met with local businesses and law enforcement regarding the increased traffic and parking needs due to the expected crowd size. They made arrangements to have shuttle buses take fans to and from Soboski Stadium. However, the Pennsylvania Heartland Athletic Conference claimed they were not notified of the schedule change and threatened to impose sanctions against Southern Columbia if they played the game against Wyoming Area. The PHAC claimed that their bylaws prohibited a school from dropping a conference opponent to play a game against a non-conference team, even though they had approved the Tigers dropping Bloomsburg from their schedule to play the Hammond School in South Carolina to start the 2019 season. Because of the threat of sanctions against Southern Columbia, the four schools decided to drop the proposed changes and resume with their originally scheduled games, much to the disappointment of high school football fans across the state. However, a last-minute petition to the PHAC by Shikellamy, who requested to play Holy Redeemer during week eight of the season, was approved, meaning the game between Southern Columbia and Wyoming Area was back on. An overflow crowd packed Anthony "Jack" Soboski Stadium to watch the powerhouse matchup. A hard-hitting first quarter ended in a scoreless tie. However, the Garcia brothers took over the game in the second stanza. Gaige Garcia opened the scoring with a 4-yard touchdown run. Gavin Garcia followed with a 13-yard scoring burst. Gaige would give the Tigers a 21-0 halftime lead when he caught a screen pass to the left, eluded a tackler, cut across the field, avoided other tackles, and raced down the right sideline for a spectacular 49-yard touchdown. After the half, Gaige and Gavin Garcia scored on runs of 17 and 2 yards. Preston Zachman closed the scoring with a 53-yard interception for a touchdown. The defense put in another stellar effort. They had five sacks and held the Warriors to 4 rushing yards and 100 yards of total offense. In the end, the Tigers turned the highly anticipated contest into a lopsided 42-0 blowout. Making the victory more impressive was the fact that this would prove to be the only loss during the 2019 season for Wyoming Area, who would win the PIAA Class AAA Football Championship.

The Tigers' traveled to Montoursville for the final road game of the regular season. The Warriors were undefeated and came into the game averaging more than 47 points per game. However, on this night, they were playing the best team in the state. The Tigers held Montoursville to negative yardage in the first half, led by Max Tillet's two sacks in the opening 24 minutes. The offense quickly crushed any hopes for a Warriors victory in the first quarter. Julian Fleming caught a wide receiver screen for a 15-yard touchdown halfway through the first. Preston Zachman scored on a 21-yard run with 3:11 left in the opening quarter. Zachman hit Fleming for a 42-yard touchdown to make it 21-0 before the end of the first quarter. On an 11-play, 61 yard drive that took up over five minutes of the second quarter, Gaige Garcia tacked on a four-yard touchdown run for a 28-0 halftime lead. Gavin Garcia put the game into the mercy rule in the third quarter with an 83-yard touchdown run to cap the scoring. Southern knocked the Warriors from the ranks of the unbeaten with a solid 35-0 shutout victory. The defense held the high-scoring Montoursville offense to 34 rushing yards and just 48 through the air. Gavin Garcia ran for 123 yards and a touchdown, while Gaige Garcia totaled 116 yards and a score. Preston Zachman went 8 for 10 for 135 passing yards and two touchdowns. Julian Fleming hauled in seven passes for 127 yards and two scores.

The final regular-season game at Tiger Stadium celebrated the present with a nod to the past. Before the game, members of the 1994 team that won the Tigers' first-ever state championship presented a plaque to the current seniors proclaiming the Class of 2020 as the greatest in school history. On senior night, the Tigers finished perhaps the greatest regular season in Pennsylvania high school football history in grand fashion with a 49-6 victory over Danville. Southern racked up 373 yards of offense in the first half. Gaige Garcia opened the scoring with a 66-yard run early in the first. Julian Fleming made it 14-0 on a 15-yard touchdown catch from Preston Zachman. Gavin Garcia tacked on another score on a one-yard run for a 21-0 first-quarter lead. Fleming and Zachman hooked up for another score with a 19-yard touchdown in the second quarter. Fleming became the first receiver in Pennsylvania high school history to reach 5,00 career receiving yards on this drive. Southern led 28-6 at the half. In the third quarter, Gaige and Gavin Garcia had 9-yard scoring runs, and Branden Heim iced the game with a 10-yard touchdown run in the final quarter. The Tigers posted 575 yards of total offense, with 386 on the ground and 189 through the air. Gaige Garcia had 143 yards and two touchdowns, and Gavin Garcia chipped in with 125 yards and two scores. Preston Zachman went 8 for 12 for 189 passing yards and two scores. Julian Fleming had seven receptions for 150 yards and two touchdowns. The Tigers' defense held the Ironmen to 99 total yards. Southern Columbia extended their state-record regular-season winning streak to 81 games. The 2019 Tigers became the second team in school history to win all ten games during the season by the mercy rule. Southern ended the season in dominant fashion and seemed primed for a deep postseason run in search of their third consecutive PIAA championship.

Southern opened the postseason with a District IV Quarterfinal Game against the Towanda Blue Knights at Tiger Stadium. The Tigers picked up right where they left off the regular season, scoring touchdowns on eight of their first nine offensive plays, racking up over 500 yards of offense in the first half as they cruised to a 75-0 first-round victory. Preston Zachman hit Julian Fleming, playing in front of Ohio State coach Ryan Day, for a 64-yard touchdown on the game's first play. After a 37-yard touchdown run by Gaige Garcia, Fleming and Zachman hooked up again on a 44-yard scoring pass. Gavin Garcia then scored on runs of 72 and 35 yards, and Gaige tacked on a 74-yard touchdown to give the Tigers a 42-0 lead at the end of the first quarter. Gaige Garcia added a 93-yard touchdown run, and Ty Roadarmel scored from 14 yards out to push the score to 56-0 at halftime. Wes Barnes, Matt Masala, and Trevor Yorks added second-half scoring runs to end the offensive onslaught. The Tigers had 537 rushing yards and 645 overall. Gaige Garcia had three carries for 178 yards and two touchdowns. Gavin Garcia carried three times for 143 yards and three scores. Barnes had 64 yards and a touchdown, Roadarmel picked up 62 yards and a touchdown, Matt Masala chipped in with 58 rushing yards and a score, and Yorks added another rushing touchdown. Fleming had two receptions for 108 yards and two scores. Southern's defense held Towanda to one first down for the game. The Black Knights gained only 5 rushing yards on 32 carries and were held to 16 passing yards. The Tigers opened the 2019 postseason in dominant fashion.

The District IV Class AA Semifinal game was played at Tiger Stadium against Penn-Mansfield. The Tigers scored on their first five possessions, and the defense posted another shutout in a 42-0 win over the Panthers. Julian Fleming scored on a 10-yard touchdown reception from Preston Zachman, Gaige Garcia had a 45-yard touchdown run, Fleming caught a 19-yard touchdown pass from Zachman, and Gavin Garcia scored on a 26-yard touchdown run to give Southern a 28-0 first-quarter lead. Gaige Garcia had an 89-yard scoring run, and Gavin returned an interception 42 yards for a touchdown to close the scoring in the second quarter and for the game. The Tigers rushed for 354 yards. Gaige Garcia had four rushes for 154 yards and two scores. Gavin Garcia gained 89 yards and scored a touchdown. Wes Barnes contributed 68 yards rushing. Julian Fleming caught four balls for 63 yards and two scores.

The defense limited the Panthers to 26 rushing yards on 24 carries and had two interceptions and a fumble recovery.

Southern hosted Mount Carmel at Tiger Stadium for the District IV Class AA Championship Game. The Red Tornadoes surprised the Tigers with an on-side kick on the opening kickoff, recovering the ball on the Southern 48-yard line. However, after a one-yard run, Lear Quinton recorded sacks on consecutive plays to force a Mount Carmel punt. In what had become a pattern in the opening quarter in the postseason, Gaige and Gavin Garcia, Julian Fleming, and Preston Zachman put the game out of reach of the Red Tornadoes. Gavin Garcia opened the scoring with a 46-yard run. On the first play of Mount Carmel's second series, Cade Linn recovered a fumble. On the next play, Zachman hit Fleming for a 23-yard touchdown pass. The Tigers had two scores in a matter of twenty seconds. Gaige Garcia had a 22-yard touchdown run, and Fleming caught a 4-yard touchdown pass from Zachman for a 28-0 first-quarter lead. On Mount Carmel's next drive, Jake Davis picked off a pass at the Red Tornado's 30-yard line to set up Wade Kerstetter's 3-yard touchdown reception from Zachman in the second quarter. Gaige Garcia would then score on runs of 48 and 60 yards to cap the scoring and push the lead to 49-0 at halftime. Two unfortunate and ugly incidents marred the game. Mount Carmel's Shane Weidner was injured on the sideline on a kickoff in the first half. The game was delayed for approximately 35 minutes while medical staff tended to Weidner, and he was transported by ambulance to a local hospital. A near-brawl occurred in the third quarter resulting in two Mount Carmel players being ejected from the game. The defense pitched a third consecutive postseason shutout, holding Mount Carmel to 3 yards of total offense in the first half. Gaige Garcia rushed for 170 yards and three touchdowns. Gavin Garcia added 89 rushing yards and a score. Preston Zachman had three touchdown passes, two to Julian Fleming and one to Wade Kerstetter. The Tigers clinched their 27th District IV Championship in 29 years. Southern entered the PIAA Playoffs as the overwhelming favorite to bring home another state championship.

The Tigers opened the PIAA Class AA Playoffs with a Quarterfinal Game versus the Upper Dauphin Trojans in Selinsgrove. Upper Dauphin got off to a promising start, returning the opening kickoff to midfield. However, Southern forced a three and out, and the Trojans had to punt. On the ensuing drive, Preston Zachman scored on a 22-yard quarterback keeper to give the Tigers a 7-0 lead. On their second offensive series, Upper Dauphin used a quick huddle to confuse the Tigers' defense during a 12-play drive, however, Cade Linn recovered a Trojan fumble to end the threat. Zachman scored his second rushing touchdown on a 54-yard run to make it 14-0 at the end of the first quarter. The Southern defense buckled down and held the Trojans to one first down in their next five possessions. Gavin Garcia scored on a 6-yard run, followed by Julian Fleming's 16-yard touchdown catch. Ty Roadarmel pushed the score to 42-0 with a 2-yard touchdown plunge. Upper Dauphin scored the first points against the Tigers defense in the postseason with a touchdown just before the half. Southern led 42-7 at the break. Gavin Garcia scored on a 20-yard run early in the third. Upper Dauphin scored a second touchdown only to have Wes Barnes return the ensuing kickoff 92 yards for a score. The Tigers had a 56-14 lead after three quarters. The Trojans scored a third touchdown and converted a two-point conversion in the fourth quarter. Barnes ended the scoring with his second touchdown of the game on a 7-yard run. Southern earned a 63-22 opening-round victory. The Tigers had 383 yards rushing and 133 through the air. Zachman ran the ball three times for 120 yards and two touchdowns. He added 113 passing yards and a scoring throw. Gaige Garcia ran for 95 yards and a touchdown. Gavin Garcia had 91 yards on the ground and a score. Barnes and Roadarmel each added rushing touchdowns. Fleming had 80 receiving yards and a score.

Up next for the Tigers was a PIAA Class AA Semifinal matchup with the Richland Rams in Selinsgrove. Richland's high-powered passing attack looked to challenge the vaunted Tiger defense. After Gaige Garcia's 2-yard run early in the first, the Rams stunned the Tigers with a 62-yard touchdown pass to make it 7-7. It was the first time Southern had been in a tie game all season. Richland recovered an onside kick on the ensuing kickoff, and the Tigers appeared to have a fight on their hands. However, Preston Zachman and Jake Davis stopped a third-down tight end screen, and the Rams were forced to punt. Then the Southern offense showed Richland who was the boss. Zachman ended the Tigers' second drive with a 4-yard touchdown run. Gavin Garcia then scored on a 28-yard pass from Zachman to make the score 21-7 at the end of the first quarter. Early in the second, Gaige Garcia took a handoff from his brother on a reverse and raced 59 yards for a touchdown. Gavin Garcia scored on a 4-yard run, Julian Fleming caught a 52-yard touchdown from Zachman, and Gaige Garcia capped the Tigers' scoring with a 39-yard touchdown run to push the lead to 49-7 at halftime. Richland scored 20 points in mop-up time in the fourth quarter, making the final score 49-27. Southern rushed for 309 yards and had 455 total yards of offense. Gaige Garcia had 153 yards rushing and three touchdowns. Gavin Garcia totaled 123 yards on the ground and had a rushing and receiving touchdown. Preston Zachman threw for 146 yards and had two touchdown passes and a scoring run. Julian Fleming hauled in six passes for 118 yards and a touchdown. The Tigers' defense controlled Richland with three interceptions and a fumble recovery. Southern advanced to their 18th PIAA Championship Game.

The Tigers were looking to cap off their magical 2019 season and faced the Avonworth Antelopes in the PIAA Class AA Championship Game at Hersheypark Stadium. However, the game got off to an ominous start. Avonworth marched down the field on their first drive and stunned the Tigers with a 43-yard touchdown pass. It was the first time Southern had trailed in a game during the 2019 season. Gavin Garcia returned the ensuing kickoff for an apparent 76-yard touchdown only to have the run called back on a penalty. Undaunted, the Tigers drove 86 yards on eleven plays capped off by Julian Fleming's 12-yard touchdown reception from Preston Zachman. Avonworth's early touchdown unleashed the beast in the Tigers' defense. On Avonworth's next possession, Max Tillett recovered an Antelope fumble setting up Gaige Garcia's 8-yard touchdown run on the next play, and the rout was on. Gaige Garcia caught a 32-yard scoring pass from Zachman. Then the Tigers' defense flexed its muscles. Incredibly, Avonworth would throw interceptions on their next four offensive drives, three of which were returned for Southern touchdowns. Cal Haladay returned the first 39 yards for a score, Jake Davis returned the next one 42 yards for a pick six, and Cade Linn took the third back 46 yards for a touchdown. Davis, who would have three interceptions in the game, picked off the fourth consecutive pass to set up Ty Roadarmel's 8-yard screen pass for a score. Fleming would conclude the first-half scoring on a 63-yard touchdown reception from Zachman. The Tigers took a 55-7 lead into the break. Roadarmel had a 42-yard touchdown run, and Gavin Garcia scored from 11 yards out in the third quarter. Matt Masala ended the scoring onslaught with a 46-yad fumble return for a touchdown in the fourth. After giving up the touchdown on Avonworth's opening drive, the Tigers scored 74 unanswered points, winning their tenth PIAA State Football Championship 74-7. Southern set PIAA records the most points scored in a championship game and the largest margin of victory. As the players celebrated on the sidelines and the Tiger faithful cheered in the stands, Coach Jim Roth received a well-deserved Gatorade shower. The Tigers had entered the game needing to score 41 points to break Jeanette's 2007 record of 860 points scored in a Pennsylvania high school season. The record was broken by halftime as Southern Columbia scored 894 points in 2019. The Tigers rushed for 260 yards, threw for 177, totaling 437 for the game. Zachman went 7-11 for 177 yards and four touchdowns. Gavin Garcia rushed for 96 yards and a touchdown. Roadarmel had 59 yards rushing and a score and added a touchdown reception. Gaige Garcia tallied 58 yards on the ground and had a rushing and receiving touchdown. Julian Fleming had four catches for 120 yards and two scores. The Tigers defense had one of the most dominating performances in school history. They held Avonworth to 32 rushing yards on 24 attempts. Southern forced nine turnovers with six interceptions and three fumble recoveries. The Tigers got defensive touchdowns from Haladay, Davis, Linn, and Masala. Haladay had nine tackles, an interception, and a pass defended. Max Tillett recorded seven tackles, a pass defended, and a fumble recovery. Linn had six tackles and an interception. Zachman chipped in defensively with an interception. Contributing to the Tigers' defensive effort were Tim Witcoskie, Cole Schankweiler, Wade Kerstetter, Ian Yoder, Tyler Waltman, Nate Kearney, Branden Heim, Ty Roadarmel, Nate Crowl, Jake Rose, Wes Barnes, Carson Savitski, Connor Gallagher, Gabe Leffler, Chris Treshock and Gavin Garcia who all registered tackles.

Are the 2019 Southern Columbia Tigers the greatest Pennsylvania high school football team of all time? That argument can certainly be made. In addition to winning their third consecutive PIAA State Championship, the Tigers were named *High School Football America* Small School National Champions for the second year in a row. Southern extended their winning streak to 48 consecutive games and 81 regular-season contests. They outscored their opponents 894-82, with the average score of their games being 55.9-5.1. Southern rushed for 5,687 yards for the season, averaging 355.4 yards per game. They averaged 476.3 yards of total offense a game. Placekicker Ethan Haupt scored 118 points (a PIAA record) for the season, outscoring every team the Tigers played just by kicking extra points. The Tigers won all 16 games in the 2019 season by the mercy rule, including ten shutout victories. The Southern defense had 25 interceptions, 19 fumble recoveries, and recorded 39 sacks. Cade Linn registered 85 tackles. Jake Davis had nine interceptions. Dyer Stine recorded 6.5 sacks.

Julian Fleming had 72 receptions for 1,539 yards and 23 touchdowns. He was named the National High School Coaches Association Player of the Year, Maxpreps USA Football Player of the Year, Gatorade Football Pennsylvania Player of the Year, Under Armour All-American Captain, *USA Today* First Team All-American, Mr. Pennsylvania Football Player of the Year, *Pennsylvania Football News* Coach's Select All-State Player of the Year, Sportswriters All-State Player of the Year, Super 16 Dream Team Overall Player of the Year, All-Eastern Pennsylvania Football Player of the Year, Pennsylvania Heartland Athletic Conference First Team All-Star, *Daily Item Newspaper* Player of the

Year, *Press Enterprise* Player of the Year and *News Item* Co-Player of the Year. Gaige Garcia had 126 carries for 1,960 yards, averaging 15.6 yards per carry, and scored 32 touchdowns. Garcia was named to the Maxpreps USA Football Second Team, *Pennsylvania Football News* Coach's Select First Team All-State, Sportswriters All-State Selection, Super 16 Dream Team Offensive Player of the Year, All-Eastern Pennsylvania Football First Team, Pennsylvania Heartland Athletic Conference First Team All-Star, *Daily Item Newspaper* First Team, *Press Enterprise* First Team, and *New Item* First Team. Gavin Garcia rushed for 1,700 yards on 103 carries, averaging 16.5 yards per carry, and scored 28 touchdowns. He was a Sportswriters All-State Selection, All-Eastern Pennsylvania Football First Team, Pennsylvania Heartland Athletic Conference First Team, *Daily Item Newspaper* First Team, *Press Enterprise* First Team, and *News Item* First Team. Preston Zachman was 92-144 for 1,933 yards passing and 30 touchdowns. Zachman was *Pennsylvania Football News* Coach's Select First Team All-State, Sportswriters All-State Selection, All-Eastern Pennsylvania Football First Team, Pennsylvania Heartland Athletic Conference First Team All-Star, *Daily Item Newspaper* First Team, *Press Enterprise* First Team, and *News Item* First Team. Cal Haladay registered 83 tackles and was named Maxpreps USA Football Second Team, *Pennsylvania Football News* Coach's Select First Team All-State, Sportswriters All-State Selection, Super 16 Dream Team Defensive Player of the Year, All-Eastern Pennsylvania Football First Team, Pennsylvania Heartland Conference First Team All-Star, *Daily Item Newspaper* First Team, *Press Enterprise* Linebacker of the Year and *News Item* First Team. Cade Linn recorded 85 tackles and was a *Pennsylvania Football News* Coach's Select First Team All-State, All-Eastern Pennsylvania Football Honorable Mention, Pennsylvania Heartland Athletic Conference First Team All-Star, *Daily Item Newspaper* Second Team, *Press Enterprise* First Team, and *News Item* First Team. Max Tillett registered 78 tackles and was named *Pennsylvania Football News* Coach's Select First Team All-State, Sportswriters All-State Selection, East/West All-Star, All-Eastern Pennsylvania Football First Team, Pennsylvania Heartland Conference First Team All-Star, *Daily Item Newspaper* First Team, *Press Enterprise* First Team, and *News Item* First Team. Jake Davis intercepted nine passes and was *Pennsylvania Football News* Coach's Select First Team All-State, All-Eastern Pennsylvania Football Honorable Mention, Pennsylvania Heartland Athletic Conference Second Team All-Star, *Daily Item Newspaper* Second Team, *Press Enterprise* Defensive Back of the Year, and *News Item* First Team. Dyer Stine led the Tigers with 6.5 sacks and was named a Pennsylvania Heartland Athletic Conference Second Team All-Star, *Daily Item Newspaper* Second Team, and *Press Enterprise*

Second Team. Lear Quinton and Cole Schankweiler were named *Pennsylvania Football News* Coach's Select First Team All-State, and Ethan Haupt was Second Team All-State. Lear Quinton and Cole Schankweiler were Sportswriters All-State Selections. Cole Schankweiler was an East/West All-Star. Lear Quinton, Cole Schankweiler, and Ethan Haupt were All-Eastern Pennsylvania Football

## 2019 SEASON

| Opponent | Location | W/L | Score |
|---|---|---|---|
| Hammond (South Carolina) | Away | W | 36-0 |
| Mount Carmel | Home | W | 48-0 |
| Selinsgrove | Away | W | 76-0 |
| Shamokin | Away | W | 62-0 |
| Central Columbia | Home | W | 62-0 |
| South Williamsport | Home | W | 76-6 |
| Jersey Shore | Away | W | 56-14 |
| Wyoming Area | Away | W | 42-0 |
| Montoursville | Away | W | 35-0 |
| Danville | Home | W | 49-6 |
| **District IV Class AA Quarterfinal Game** | | | |
| Towanda | Home | W | 75-0 |
| **District IV Class Semifinal Game** | | | |
| North Penn-Mansfield | Home | W | 42-0 |
| **District IV Class AA Championship Game** | | | |
| Mount Carmel | Home | W | 49-0 |
| **PIAA Class AA Quarterfinal Game** | | | |
| Upper Dauphin | Neutral | W | 63-22 |
| **PIAA Class AA Semifinal Game** | | | |
| Richland | Neutral | W | 49-27 |
| **PIAA Class AA Championship Game** | | | |
| Avonworth | Neutral | W | 74-7 |

COACHING STAFF: Jim Roth, Head Coach; Jason Campbell; Assistant Coach; Randall Campbell, Assistant Coach; Alex Carawan, Assistant Coach; Al Cihocki, Assistant Coach; Ted Deljanovan. Assistant Coach; Troy Heath, Assistant Coach; Andy Helwig, Assistant Coach; Mike Johnston, Assistant Coach; Curt Jones, Assistant Coach; John Marks, Assistant Coach; Andy Mills, Assistant Coach; Roger Nunkester, Assistant Coach; Chad. Romig, Assistant Coach; Pete Saylor, Assistant Coach; Sean Smith, Assistant Coach; Rick Steele, Assistant Coach; Wes Tillett, Assistant Coach; Brandon Traugh, Assistant Coach

ATHLETIC DIRECTOR: Jim Roth

ROSTER: Wes Barnes, Kole Biscoe, Matt Carl, Nate Crowl, Jake Davis, Collin Doraski, Julian Fleming, Jordan Fosse, Connor Gallagher, Gaige Garcia, Gavin Garcia, Brandon Gedman, Cal Haladay, Cam Haladay, Ethan Haupt, Braden Heim, Ashton Helwig, Jacob Herr, Ian Huntington, Nate Kearney, Wade Kerstetter, Liam Klebon, Gabe Leffler, Cade Linn, Matt Masala, Jayden McCormick, Logan Potter, Jaxson Purnell, Owyne Pursel, Joe Quinton, Lear Quinton, Andrew Rarig, Austin Reeder, Jacob Reynolds, Ty Roadarmel, Jake Rose, Carson Savitski, Cole Schankweiler, Nate Seroskie, Colin Sharrow, Greyson Shaud, Dyer Stine, Max Tillett, Chris Treshock, Tyler Waltman, Derek Wertman, Tim Witcoskie, Michael Yancoskie, Ian Yoder, Trevor Yorks, Preston Zachman, Nick Zeigler, Michael Zsido, Ron Zsido (In Memoriam) Keegan Shultz

First Team, and Jacob Herr and Ian Huntington were Honorable Mention. Lear Quinton, Jacob Herr, Ian Huntington, Cole Schankweiler, and Ethan Haupt were First Team Pennsylvania Heartland Athletic Conference All-Stars, and Cam Haladay, Derek Wertman, Wade Kerstetter, and Nate Crowl were named Second Team All-Stars. Lear Quinton, Ethan Haupt, Jacob Herr, and Cole Schankweiler were *Daily Item Newspaper* First Team selections, and Nate Crowl, Cam Haladay, Ian Huntington, Wade Kerstetter, and Derek Wertman were Honorable Mention. Jacob Herr, Ethan Haupt, Ian Huntington, and Cole Schankweiler were named *Press Enterprise* First Team selections, and Nate Crowl, Cam Haladay, and Ty Roadarmel were Second Team picks. Lear Quinton was a *News Item* First Team selection. Head Coach Jim Roth was named *Pennsylvania Football News* Coach's Select All-State Coach of the Year, All-Eastern Pennsylvania Football Coach of the Year, and *Press Enterprise* Coach of the Year.

The 2019 Southern Columbia Tigers were undoubtedly the greatest football team in school history. This historical season certainly places the Tigers in the conversation as one of the best high school football teams Pennsylvania has ever seen and puts them among the great programs on the national level.

———

Julian Fleming ended his career at Southern Columbia as the all-time leader in receiving yards (5,481) and touchdown receptions (78) in Pennsylvania high school history. A member of three state championship teams, Fleming played in the ESPN Under Armour All-American Game. He was the top-ranked wide receiver recruit in the country by most national scouting organizations. Fleming committed to attend Ohio State University. In addition to football, Fleming starred in basketball and track, winning a state championship in the PIAA Class AA 100-meter dash.

Gaige Garcia finished his career at Southern Columbia as the record holder for career touchdowns (159) and rushing touchdowns (138) in Pennsylvania high school history. He rushed for 8,232 yards and gained 10,429 all-purpose yards in his career. Garcia was a member of three state championship teams. He also starred in wrestling for the Tigers, winning two PIAA Class AA championships. Garcia enrolled at the University of Michigan as a member of both the football and wrestling teams and later transferred to Lehigh University.

Cal Haladay is the all-time leader in tackles in Southern Columbia history. A member of three state championship teams, Haladay was the top-rated inside linebacker recruit in Pennsylvania by ESPN and Rivals.com and one of the top overall prospects in the state. ESPN ranked him as one of the top inside linebacker recruits in the country. Haladay committed to attend Michigan State University.

Preston Zachman was a sensational linebacker during his career at Southern Columbia. His play at outside linebacker attracted the attention of college scouts. Zachman was rated as a top-twenty recruit in Pennsylvania by numerous national scouting organizations. He committed to attend the University of Wisconsin.

Max Tillett continued his football career at the University of New Hampshire, and Lear Quinton committed to wrestle for Brown University.

**2020** Head Coach Jim Roth entered the 2020 season twelve wins shy of breaking George Curry's record for the most career coaching victories in Pennsylvania high school football history and the Tigers seeking a fourth straight PIAA state championship. However, beginning in the spring, Southern faced perhaps the most challenging foe they had ever encountered; COVID-19. With schools across Pennsylvania and the nation closing for in-person learning in March, starting a new school year and even having a fall football season seemed very much in doubt. For much of the summer, there was little information or guidelines from the Commonwealth or the PIAA regarding the prospects of playing the upcoming season. The uncertainty surrounding the 2020 season only added to the anxiety and despair brought on by the pandemic. However, August brought a glimmer of hope after a very trying summer. The PIAA Board of Directors met on August 21, 2020, and voted to permit the start of the high school fall sports season. High school football teams were required to have five days of heat acclimation, followed by another five days of full practice before scheduling any scrimmage games. After completing the required training period, Southern played a scrimmage game against Berwick on September 5, 2020. After a four-week delay, the Tigers were ready to begin the defense of their titles under never-before-seen circumstances.

Before the season, seniors Nick Zeigler and Wade Kerstetter approached Coach Jim Roth with ideas to honor their fallen friend and teammate, Keegan Shultz. They proposed carrying a flag onto the field for each game, placing tribute stickers on the team's helmets, and wearing t-shirts honoring Shultz under their uniforms. Roth fully supported the players' wishes and gave his approval. Zeigler got the blessing of Shultz's family and ordered the flag. It was emblazoned with a football helmet with Shultz's number 70 surrounded by a ring of roses. The bottom of the flag featured the powerful statement, "Stop And Think, Your Story Isn't Over." The flagpole was painted in teal and purple, the national colors for suicide prevention. Zeigler would carry the flag onto the field, and he and Kerstetter would meet in the endzone for a moment of silence before each game. The 2020 season was dedicated to Keegan Shultz.

The Tigers opened the season at home versus Bloomsburg on September 18, 2020. The offseason distractions had little effect on Southern as they overwhelmed the Panthers, 41-0. Jake Davis scored the first points of the season on a 17-yard touchdown pass from Liam Klebon early in the first quarter. Gavin Garcia scored on a 25-yard run and a 74-yard punt return to make it 21-0 after one. Davis then hooked up with Greyson Shaud on a 36-yard touchdown pass, and Garcia ran for a 64-yard score to push the lead to 35-0 at halftime. Braeden Wisloski capped the scoring with a 46-yard touchdown run in the third quarter. Garcia led the Tigers' rushing attack, which racked up 330 yards on the ground, and Southern had 395 yards of total offense. Garcia scored twice and rushed for 149 yards on nine carries. He also scored on a 75-yard punt return. Wisloski contributed 82 yards on seven carries and had a touchdown run. Davis had two receptions for 53 yards and scored two touchdowns. Quarterbacks Liam Klebon and Greyson Shaud each had two completions and threw for a score. The Tigers' defense held Bloomsburg to -11 rushing yards and 96 total yards of offense. Jake Rose led the way with two interceptions. The victory gave Coach Jim Roth win number 445, breaking the tie with Jack Henzes of Dunmore for second place in Pennsylvania high school football history.

Southern next traveled for a week two matchup with Warrior Run. The Tigers started the game with a bang as Braeden Wisloski returned the opening kickoff 81 yards for a touchdown. That was all the scoring Southern would need to win the game, but it was only the beginning of the onslaught, as the Tigers mauled the Defenders, 67-0. The Tigers dominated on both sides of the ball. Wade Kerstetter had a 42-yard fumble recovery for a touchdown, and Gavin Garcia scored on runs of 9 and 12 yards for a 28-0 lead after a quarter. Garcia ran for a 75-yard touchdown, Jake Davis picked off a Defender pass for a 44-yard score, Braeden Heim tacked on a one-yard touchdown plunge, and Southern led 49-0 at the break. Connor Gallagher, Matt Masala, and Trevor Yorks had scoring runs in the fourth to cap the scoring. The Tigers ran for 313 yards on the ground and had 339 yards of total offense. Garcia had 133 yards on only five carries and scored three touchdowns. Yorks had 68 yards rushing and a score. Masala rushed for 48 yards and a touchdown. Heim chipped in with 27 yards and a rushing touchdown. Gallagher contributed an 8-yard scoring run.

The defense held Warrior Run to 13 rushing yards and 27 total yards of offense. The Defenders completed just one pass on the night.

Starting with Southern's week three game against Loyalsock, COVID-19 began to wreak havoc on the local 2020 football schedule. The home game was moved to Thursday night due to scheduling issues. The changes did nothing to slow the Tigers' offense. Gavin Garcia opened the scoring with a 38-yard scoring reception from Liam Klebon. Braeden Wisloski followed with rushing touchdowns of 8 and 4 yards, and Garcia scored again on a 42-yard scamper to give the Tigers a 28-0 lead in the opening quarter. Wisloski scored early in the second on a 2-yard plunge. The special teams then scored a safety when they tackled the Loyalsock punter in the endzone. Garcia closed the scoring in the first half with a 78-yard run. With touchdown runs in the third and early in the fourth quarter, Loyalsock cut the lead to 44-14. Wes Barnes closed out Lancers with a 71-yard scoring run. The Tigers earned a 50-20 victory over the Lancers. Garcia ran for 195 yards and two touchdowns and had a scoring catch. Barnes contributed 109 rushing yards and a touchdown. Wisloski rushed for 20 yards and three scores. The Tigers' offense racked up 405 yards of total offense, including 357 rushing yards, averaging 10.8 yards per carry. Nick Zeigler led the defensive effort with an interception, and Southern recovered two fumbles. The scheduling roller coaster continued the next week as the Tigers were awarded a forfeit win over Mount Carmel.

The season continued with a road game against Hughesville. The Spartans proved to be no match for Southern's high-powered offense. The Tigers scored touchdowns on six of their first eleven offensive plays, and Southern ran away from Hughesville, 56-7. Gavin Garcia scored on a 71-yard run early in the opening quarter. Wes Barnes followed with a 45-yard touchdown run. Hughesville then snapped the ball over the punter's head and out of the endzone for a safety. Jake Davis hauled in a 37-yard pass from Liam Klebon, Garcia scored on a 53-yard run, Braeden Wisloski tacked on a 60-yard scamper, and Southern led 36-0 after one. Wisloski and Garcia scored on runs of 21 and 54 yards for a 50-0 Tiger lead at the break. Hughesville got on the board with a 10-yard run early in the fourth. Matt Masala capped the scoring with a 16-yard run. Garcia, again, led the ground attack, racking up 186 yards on just four carries, scoring three touchdowns. Garcia averaged a whopping 46.5 yards per carry for the game. Barnes ran for 96 yards and a touchdown. Wisloski rushed for 60 yards and a score. He also had a touchdown reception. Masala added 19 yards on the ground and a touchdown. Klebon had 63 yards passing and threw for two scores. Davis had 42 yards receiving and a touchdown grab. The team rushed for 425 yards, averaging 16.3 yards per carry.

In the regular-season home finale, Southern easily defeated Lewisburg, 42-7. The team continued their bruising ground attack, rushing for 338 yards. The Tigers got first-half touchdowns from Gavin Garcia on a one-yard plunge, Braeden Wisloski's 2-yard run, Nick Zeiger's 31-yard interception return, and a Wisloski one-yard dive to take a 28-0 lead. Garcia scored from 5 yards out early in the third. The defense scored again when Jake Davis recovered a fumble in the endzone, and Southern led 42-0 going into the fourth quarter. Lewisburg scored a late touchdown to end the game. Garcia ran for 181 yards and two touchdowns. Wisloski rushed for 52 yards and two scores. The defense held the Green Dragons to 167 total yards with two interceptions and two fumble recoveries. It was a historic win for Coach Jim Roth, as he became only the second coach in Pennsylvania high school football history to reach 450 victories.

The Tigers wrapped up the 2020 regular season with a convincing road victory over Central Columbia, 52-3. Gavin Garcia got the scoring started early, returning the opening kickoff 71-yards for a touchdown. He scored again on a 26-yard touchdown run. The Blue Jays' fumbled the ball out of the endzone for a safety. The special teams got in on the scoring by blocking a punt out of the Blue Jays' endzone for the second safety of the first quarter. Braeden Wisloski ran for a 57-yard score to start the second quarter. Central Columbia converted a 31-yard field goal. Garcia ran for a 45-yard touchdown, and the Tigers led 32-3 at the intermission. Wes Barnes and Ian Yoder joined the scoring parade with touchdown runs of 16 and 12 yards in the third. Tyler Arnold capped the scoring with a 3-yard touchdown run in the final period. Garcia punctuated his fantastic season with 158 yards and two touchdowns. Barnes rushed for 113 yards and a score. Wisloski contributed 77 rushing yards and a scoring run. Yoder and Arnold each pitched in with scoring runs. The Tigers' defense put in a tremendous effort. They scored a safety, recovered two fumbles, and intercepted two passes. Southern held the Blue Jays to 88 total yards of offense. Southern Columbia completed their ninth consecutive undefeated regular season, won their 55th game in a row, and earned their 88th straight regular-season victory.

The Tigers began their postseason run with a home District IV Class AA Semifinal Game against Line Mountain. Southern racked up 401 total yards of offense, including 301 on the ground, and the defense recorded two interceptions and recovered two fumbles as the Tigers cruised to a 49-7 victory. Liam

Klebon hit Jake Rose with a 45-yard scoring pass, Gavin Garcia ran for touchdowns of 27 and 12 yards, and Braeden Wisloski rumbled 32 yards for a score to put the game out of reach in the first quarter. Garcia scored on a 56-yard run to push the Southern lead to 35-0 at halftime. In the third, offensive lineman Jaxson Purcell recovered a fumble in the Line Mountain endzone to make it 42-0. Ian Yoder ended the Tigers' scoring with a 23-yard touchdown run in the fourth. The Tigers held Line Mountain to zero rushing yards and just 133 total yards of offense for the game. The Southern offense continued to roll behind Garcia's 134 rushing yards and three touchdowns. Barnes ran for 78 yards on the ground. Wisloski chipped in with 51 yards and a scoring run. Yoder ran for 20 yards and a touchdown. Klebon passed for 100 yards and a touchdown. Rose had 51 receiving yards and a scoring grab.

Up next was South Williamsport in the District IV Class AA Championship Game at Tiger Stadium. The Mountaineers proved no match for the Tigers' high-powered running attack, and Southern rolled to another mercy-rule victory, 49-14. The Tigers' rushing machine cranked out 435 yards. Gavin Garcia opened the scoring with a 40-yard touchdown run. Wes Barnes scored on a 55-yard touchdown scamper. Garcia followed with a 4-yard scoring run. Southern led 21-0 after one. Garcia scored on a run of 26 yards early in the second quarter. Derek Berlitz blocked a South Williamsport punt to set up Braeden Wisloski's one-yard scoring dive, and Garcia tacked on a 76-yard touchdown run to give the Tigers a 42-0 halftime lead. Barnes made it 49-0 on a one-yard scoring plunge in the third, and South Williamsport got two touchdowns in mop-up time to close the game. Garcia rushed for 171 yards and four touchdowns. Barnes ran for 122 yards and two scores. Wisloski chipped in with 17 yards rushing and a touchdown. Wade Kerstetter recovered a fumble, and the defense had two interceptions. The Tigers clinched their record 28th District IV Title.

The Tigers traveled to Mansion Park in Altoona to open the PIAA Class AA Playoffs in a quarterfinal game against Richland. It appeared that Southern would roll to an easy victory early on, but the Rams were determined to make a game of their state playoff opener. Wes Barnes scored on touchdown runs of 9 and 40 yards and caught a 64-yard scoring pass from Liam Klebon to give the Tigers a 20-0 first-quarter lead. Braeden Wisloski had a one-yard touchdown run in the second, but Richland scored three times to make the score 27-22 at halftime. Early in the third, Gavin Garcia scored two touchdowns in less than a minute. He scored on a one-yard run, and on the first play of Richland's next possession, Garcia returned an interception 20 yards for a touchdown. Jake

Davis then intercepted a Richland pass to set up Wisloski's 33-yard scoring run. Southern led 49-22 after three. Garcia added a 78-yard touchdown jaunt in the fourth as the Tigers advanced with a 57-30 victory. Southern rushed for 368 yards. Garcia ran for 197 yards and two touchdowns. Barnes rushed for 119 yards and two scores and caught a touchdown pass. Wisloski had 33 rushing yards and two scoring runs. Klebon threw for 87 yards and a touchdown.

The Tigers' PIAA Class AA Semifinal Game against the Bishop McDevitt Royal Lancers was played in Selinsgrove. For the first time in the 2020 season, Southern found themselves trailing in a game. The Tigers saw Bishop McDevitt take a 6-0 lead with a touchdown on their first offensive series. However, Gavin Garcia scored on a 58-yard touchdown run on the first play of Southern's second possession to go up 7-6, and the Tigers took a lead that they would never relinquish. The Tigers' next touchdown was set up by a spectacular one-handed 33-yard reception by Jake Rose. Two plays later, Braeden Wisloski scored on a two-yard run, and the rout was on. Garcia rumbled 34 yards for a touchdown to give the Tigers a 21-6 halftime lead. Garcia sandwiched scoring runs of 34 and 4 yards around Wisloski's 47-yard touchdown reception from Liam Klebon in the third for a 42-6 lead. Bishop McDevitt scored a late touchdown to make the final score 42-14. Southern's defense held the Royal Lancers to -6 rushing yards. They capitalized on several Bishop McDevitt miscues resulting in two Tiger interceptions and a fumble recovery. Jake Davis' interception was the 17th of his career, tying him with Cameron Young for the most in Tiger history. Garcia bludgeoned the Royal Lancers for 205 yards on 12 carries, giving him his first career 200-yard rushing game. He scored four touchdowns. Wisloski added 47 rushing yards and a touchdown and had a scoring reception. Wes Barnes added 79 yards on the ground. Liam Klebon threw for 84 yards and a touchdown. The Tigers advanced to their 19th PIAA State Championship Game. They recorded their 30th consecutive mercy-rule victory and extended their winning streak to 59 games. The Tigers' victory was the 455th for head coach Jim Roth, tying him with the legendary George Curry for the most in Pennsylvania high school football history. The seniors hoisted Roth onto their shoulders, and the booster club presented him with a crystal award to commemorate his monumental achievement.

As the Tigers took the field at Hersheypark Stadium for the 2020 PIAA Class AA Championship Game against Wilmington, they carried the flag honoring Keegan Shultz, just as they had before every game during the season. More than a state championship was on the line for the Tigers. Jim Roth was on the brink of becoming the all-time winningest coach in Pennsylvania high school history.

The senior class was looking to complete an undefeated high school football career. The Tigers, perhaps unknowingly, were giving the Southern Columbia community and the Central Pennsylvania region a sense of hope, pride, and meaning at a time when we all needed something to cheer for. The Wilmington Greyhounds were to final hurdle in an unforgettable 2020 season. Gavin Garcia opened the scoring in the first quarter with a one-yard touchdown run. Wilmington put together two first downs on their opening drive before Jake Rose stopped the Greyhounds' momentum with a third-down sack to force a punt. Garcia would make the score 14-0 on a 65-yard screen pass. Wilmington cut the lead to 14-7 early in the second quarter. Pinned deep in their own territory, on a second and long play from the Tigers' 11-yard line, Garcia broke a run 89 yards for another touchdown, increasing the Southern lead to 21-7 at halftime. On their first possession of the second half, the Greyhounds went on a lengthy drive, lasting more than seven minutes, scoring a touchdown to make the score 21-14. The Wilmington defense held the Tigers to third and long on their own 26 when Garcia broke the Greyhounds' backs. He cut down the left sideline with one man to beat. The defender attempted to push Garcia out of bounds at the Wilmington 14-yard line, but he maintained his balance, tight-roped the sideline, and dove into the endzone for a spectacular 74-yard touchdown, increasing the lead to 28-14. The Tigers' defense would keep the Wilmington offense in check the rest of the game. In the fourth quarter, Jake Rose deflected a pass at the Southern 24-yard line to turn the ball over on downs. Liam Klebon would then connect with Jake Davis on a perfectly thrown 79-yard touchdown pass. Wes Barnes, who sprained his ankle in the first quarter, would cap off the afternoon with a 2-yard touchdown run with 3:49 left to play. On the Tigers' final offensive play, the team took the field with only ten players in tribute to Keegan Shultz, who would have been a senior this season. After taking a knee, the game ball was given to the Shultz family in an emotional and heartfelt gesture from the team. When the final gun sounded, The Southern Columbia Tigers had won their eleventh PIAA State Football Championship. Jim Roth had won his 456th game, giving him the record for the most career coaching victories in Pennsylvania high school football history. He received another customary Gatorade shower, and he gave an emotional post-game speech to his magnificent team. The Tigers won their 60th consecutive game. Southern's senior players completed an undefeated high school football career, never losing a game in their four years of varsity play, going 60-0. Garcia finished the game with a career-high 217 yards on just 13 carries and scored three touchdowns. He also added three receptions for 98 yards and a score. Barnes scored a rushing touchdown, and Braeden Wisloski chipped in with 53 rushing yards. Klebon threw for 177 yards and two touchdowns. Ever steady Isaac Carter converted six extra points. The team rumbled for 288 rushing yards and had 465 yards of total offense. The Tigers' defense allowed only one completed pass for 17 yards. The Tigers finished an unprecedented season in remarkable fashion. The Southern Columbia Tigers were named the 2020 Maxpreps Small-School National Champions. Southern finished 2020 with a record of 12-0

The 2020 state champion Tigers had many outstanding individual performances. Gavin Garcia ran for 1,921 yards and 30 touchdowns. Wes Barnes rushed for 785 yards and nine scores. Braeden Wisloski had 515 rushing yards and 13 scoring runs. The Tigers had rushing touchdowns from Matt Masala (2), Ian Yoder (2), and one each from Tyler Arnold, Connor Gallagher, Braden Heim, and Trevor Yorks. Liam Klebon passed for 681 yards and nine touchdowns. Greyson Shaud threw for 58 yards and a score. Southern had touchdown receptions from Jake Davis (4), Gavin Garcia (2), Braeden Wisloski (2), and one each from Wes Barnes and Jake Rose. Isaac Carter connected on 64 extra points. Garrett Garcia registered 105 tackles. Jake Davis had five interceptions. Derek Berlitz recorded 13 sacks. Gavin Garcia was a First Team All-State selection by Maxpreps, named to the Maxpreps Small-School Football, All-American Second Team, the Associated Press All-State Player of the Year, Pennsylvania Football News Coach's Select Player of the Year, Pennsylvania Heartland Athletic Conference First Team selection, All-Easternpennsylvaniafootball.com Player of the Year, Mr. Pennsylvania Football Final Five Finalist, *Daily Item Newspaper* First Team selection, *Press Enterprise* Player of the Year, and *News Item* Player of the Year. Jim Roth was named the 2020 Maxpreps Small-School National Football Coach of the Year, Pennsylvania Scholastic Football Coaches Association Coach of the Year, Pennsylvania Football News Coach's Select All-State Coach of the Year, Pennsylvania Heartland Athletic Conference Coach of the Year, All-Easternpennsylvaniafootball.com Coach of the Year, and *Press Enterprise* Coach of the Year. Derek Berlitz, Jake Davis , and Wade Kerstetter were Associated Press All-State selections. Derek Berlitz, Jake Davis, Garrett Garcia, Braden Heim, and Wade Kerstetter were named to the Pennsylvania Football News Coach's Select All-State First Team, and Braeden Wisloski was a Second Team selection. Wes Barnes, Derek Berlitz, Jake Davis, Garrett Garcia, Braden Heim, Wade Kerstetter, Logan Potter, Jaxson Purnell, Colin Sharrow, Derek Wertman, Ian Yoder, and Nick Zeigler earned Pennsylvania Heartland Athletic Conference First Team All-Star honors, and Brandon Gedman was a Second Team All-Star. Derek Berlitz, Jake Davis, Braden Heim, and Wade

Kerstetter were members of the All-Easternpennsylvaniafootball.com First Team, Garrett Garcia was named to the Second Team, and Wes Barnes, Derek Wertman, and Braeden Wisloski earned Honorable Mention honors. Braden Heim and Wade Kerstetter were named East/West All-Stars. Wes Barnes, Derek Berlitz, Jake Davis, Chris Treshock, and Derek Wertman received *Daily Item Newspaper* First Team honors. Jaxson Purnell and Nick Zeigler were named to the *Daily Item Newspaper* Second Team. Brandon Gedman, Braden Heim, Braeden Wisloski, and Ian Yoder earned *Daily Item Newspaper* Honorable Mention honors. Derek Wertman was named *Press Enterprise* Offensive Lineman

## 2020 SEASON

| Opponent | Location | W/L | Score |
|---|---|---|---|
| Bloomsburg | Home | W | 41-0 |
| Warrior Run | Away | W | 67-0 |
| Loyalsock | Home | W | 50-20 |
| Mount Carmel | Away | W | Forfeit |
| Hughesville | Away | W | 56-7 |
| Lewisburg | Home | W | 42-7 |
| Central Columbia | Away | W | 52-3 |
| **District IV Class AA Semifinal Game** | | | |
| Line Mountain | Home | W | 49-7 |
| **District IV Class AA Championship Game** | | | |
| South Williamsport | Home | W | 49-14 |
| **PIAA Class AA Quarterfinal Game** | | | |
| Richland | Neutral | W | 57-30 |
| **PIAA Class AA Semifinal Game** | | | |
| Bishop McDevitt | Neutral | W | 42-14 |
| **PIAA Class AA Championship Game** | | | |
| Wilmington | Neutral | W | 42-14 |

COACHING STAFF: Jim Roth, Head Coach; Jason Campbell; Assistant Coach; Randall Campbell, Assistant Coach; Alex Carawan, Assistant Coach; Al Cihocki, Assistant Coach; Ted Deljanovan, Assistant Coach; Trent Donlan, Assistant Coach; Troy Heath, Assistant Coach; Andy Helwig, Assistant Coach; Mike Johnston, Assistant Coach; Curt Jones, Assistant Coach; John Marks, Assistant Coach; Andy Mills, Assistant Coach; Chad. Romig, Assistant Coach; Sean Smith, Assistant Coach; Rick Steele, Assistant Coach; Wes Tillett, Assistant Coach; Brandon Traugh, Assistant Coach

ATHLETIC DIRECTOR: Jim Roth

ROSTER: Tyler Arnold, Aiden Barcavage, Wes Barnes, Derek Berlitz, Matt Carl, Isaac Carter, Austin Dabrowski, Jake Davis, Nevan Diehl, Jordan Fosse, Logan Fosse, Connor Gallagher, Garrett Garcia, Gavin Garcia, Brandon Gedman, Brandon Heim, Ashton Helwig, Ezra Herb, Brett Horton, Quincy Johnston, Ryan Kerstetter, Wade Kerstetter, Liam Klebon, Gabe Leffler, Matt Masala, Jayden McCormick, Logan Potter, Jaxson Purnell, Joseph Quinton, Austin Reeder, Jacob Reynolds, Jake Rose, Carson Savitski, Nate Seroskie, Carson Shadle, Colin Sharrow, Logan Sharrow, Greyson Shaud, Jake Toczylousky, Chris Treshock, Tyler Waltnman, Derek Wertman, Braeden Wisloski, Tim Witcoskie, Ian Yoder, Michael Yancoskie, Trevor Yorks, Nick Zeigler, Michael Zsido (In Memoriam) Keegan Shultz of the Year. Jake Davis earned the *Press Enterprise* Defensive Back of the Year. Wes Barnes, Derek Berlitz, Garrett Garcia, Wade Kerstetter, Jaxson Purnell, and Nick Zeigler were named to the *Press Enterprise* First Team. Isaac Carter, Liam Klebon, Chris Treshock, Carson Savitski, Braeden Wisloski, and Ian Yoder earned *Press Enterprise* Second Team honors. Wes Barnes, Derek Berlitz, Jake Davis, Garrett Garcia, Wade Kerstetter, Carson Savitski, Derek Wertman, and Nick Zeigler were named to the *News Item* First Team. Brandon Gedman and Braeden Wisloski earned *News Item* Honorable Mention honors.

If you were to say that Jim Roth is the greatest coach in Pennsylvania football history, you probably wouldn't get much of an argument, except maybe from the man himself. Coach Roth is quick to dodge praise and always credits his players, coaching staff, volunteers, and parents for the program's success. That is true. He has certainly surrounded himself with highly skilled and talented athletes and a devoted and loyal coaching staff. However, all extraordinary and worthwhile endeavors need a great leader, and the numbers don't lie. Eleven state championships, nineteen finals appearances, countless district and conference titles, 456 wins, three national championships, a trophy case full of national, state, and local awards, and never a losing season in his 37 years as the Tigers' head coach. Based on his accomplishments on the field, Jim Roth is a coaching legend. But it's more than that. Coach Roth has touched the lives of so many of his players in ways that go far beyond the gridiron. He has instilled pride, work ethic, compassion, and spirit that his players have carried with them long after their playing days. So many have gone on to great success in their personal and professional lives and have become tremendous assets to their communities. Coach Roth has led his teams into battle on the playing field, comforted and consoled them in times of great tragedy, anguished with them in defeat, and celebrated their incredible accomplishments. His decades of service in education and as athletic director with Southern Columbia have positively impacted many others beyond the football team. When asked about his legacy, Coach Roth said, "I don't like the term 'legacy.' The only thing that matters is doing things the right way. If I have done things to the best of my ability, I can live with that." Jim Roth has certainly accomplished that. His place as not only the greatest football coach in Pennsylvania high school history but a pillar in the Southern Columbia community is secure.

The Southern Columbia Tigers are the most successful high school football team in Pennsylvania history. They have achieved a level of success and longevity that has never been seen before. Through a tireless work ethic, meticulous preparation, continuity throughout the program, and an emphasis on strength, speed, and agility, it is likely that the Tigers will continue their dominance for years to come. However, Southern has never sacrificed ethics, academics, and sportsmanship for the sake of victory. Southern Columbia has not only produced championship teams and supremely talented athletes, but they have also shaped and molded their players into great men of character. We should all strive to follow Southern's example. Long may the Tigers roar.

# REFERENCES

Bluehens.com (University of Delaware Athletics)

Bucknellbison.com (Bucknell University Athletics)

Buhuskies.com (Bloomsburg University Athletics)

Citizensvoice.com (*Citizens Voice* newspaper, Wilkes-Barre, Pennsylvania)

Dailyitem.com (*Daily Item* newspaper, Sunbury, Pennsylvania)

Doyle, Jim (2015) *The Best Seat in the House: My 48 Years in Local Sports Broadcasting.* iUniverse

Easternpafootball.com

Espn.com

Golhu.com (Lock Haven University Athletics)

Gopsusports.com (Penn State University Athletics)

Highschoolfootballamerica.com

Inquirer.com (*Philadelphia Inquirer* newspaper, Philadelphia, Pennsylvania)

Interview with Rob Deeter

Interview with Jim Doyle

Interview with Dave Fegley

Interview with Gaige Garcia

Interview with Jim Roth

Interview with Terry Sharrow

Interview with Curt Stellfox

Interview with Andy Ulicny

Interview with Jon Vastine

Kochfuneralhome.com

Lehighsports.com (Lehigh University Athletics)

Lehighvalleylive.com

Maxpreps.com

Mcall.com (*Morning Call* newspaper, Allentown, Pennsylvania)

Mgoblue.com (University of Michigan Athletics)

Msuspartans.com (Michigan State University Athletics)

Mydallaspost.com

Ohiostatebuckeyes.com (Ohio State University Athletics)

Pafootballnews.com

Pennathletics.com (University of Pennsylvania Athletics)

Pennlive.com

Phacathletics.com (Pennsylvania Heartland Athletic Conference)

Piaa.org

Pittsburghpanthers.com (University of Pittsburgh Athletics)

Playbook Article for October 14, 2005, by Jim Doyle

Playbook Article for September 15, 2006, by Jim Doyle

Post-gazette.com (*Pittsburgh Post-Gazette* newspaper, Pittsburgh, Pennsylvania)

Pro-football-reference.com

Publicschoolview.com

Newspapers.com

Nfl.com

Rivals.com

Scasd.us (Southern Columbia School District)

Scatigerfootball.com (Southern Columbia Football)

Secv8.com

Sikids.com (*Sports Illustrated For Kids* magazine)

*Southern Columbia Football Record Book 1963-1991* (Andy Ulicny)

*Southern Columbia Football Statistical Book* (Editions 1993-2019)

Sungazette.com (*Williamsport Sun-Gazette* newspaper, Williamsport, Pennsylvania)

Unhwilcats.com University of New Hampshire Athletics)

Uwbadgers.com (University of Wisconsin Athletics)

Wlu.edu (Washington and Lee University)

Yorkdispatch.com (*York Dispatch* newspaper, York, Pennsylvania)

# ABOUT THE AUTHOR

MERRILL SHAFFER is an avid football fan with a passion for the history of the game. He is a diehard supporter of the Pittsburgh Steelers and the Southern Columbia Tigers. His previous book, *A Super Steelers Journey: The 23-Year Quest To Honor Pittsburgh's Dynasty Legends*, chronicled the team's Super Bowl Championship players in the 1970s. He was also a contributing author to *After The Pandemic: Visions Of Life Post COVID-19*. Merrill has been featured on *Good Day PA*, WTAE (Pittsburgh), *A Piece of the Game*, *The Sunbury Press Books Show*, *Pittsburgh Tribune-Review*, *Sports Collectors Daily*, and *Press Enterprise*.

Merrill earned an A.A. in Business Management from Harrisburg Area Community College and a B.S. in Criminal Justice from Pennsylvania State University. He has spent the past 19 years serving in law enforcement and lives with his wife and daughter in central Pennsylvania. He regularly attends professional, college, and high school football games each fall, and spent two years researching the 59-year history of the Southern Columbia Football Program.

Made in the USA
Middletown, DE
06 September 2023

38043838R00165